CASEBOOK FOR

A SPIRITUAL STRATEGY

IN

COUNSELING

AND

PSYCHOTHERAPY

EDITED BY

P. SCOTT RICHARDS

AND

ALLEN E. BERGIN

AMERICAN PSYCHOLOGICAL ASSOCIATION

Washington, DC

SECOND PRINTING, DECEMBER 2005

Published by
American Psychological Association
750 First Street, NE
Washington, DC 20002
www.apa.org

To order
APA Order Department
P.O. Box 92984
Washington, DC 20090-2984
Tel: (800) 374-2721; Direct: (202) 336-5510
Fax: (202) 336-5502; TDD/TTY: (202) 336-6123
Online: www.apa.org/books/
E-mail: order@apa.org

In the U.K., Europe, Africa, and the Middle East, copies may be ordered from
American Psychological Association
3 Henrietta Street
Covent Garden, London
WC2E 8LU England

Typeset in Goudy by Stephen McDougal, Mechanicsville, MD

Printer: Edwards Brothers, Inc., Ann Arbor, MI
Cover Designer: Minker Design, Bethesda, MD
Technical/Production Editors: Jen Zale and Tiffany Klaff

The opinions and statements published are the responsibility of the authors, and such opinions and statements do not necessarily represent the policies of the American Psychological Association.

Library of Congress Cataloging-in-Publication Data

Casebook for a spiritual strategy in counseling and psychotherapy / edited by P. Scott Richards and Allen E. Bergin.—1st ed.
    p. cm.
Includes bibliographical references and indexes.
    ISBN 1-59147-056-0
    1. Psychotherapy—Religious aspects—Case studies. 2. Mental health counseling—Religious aspects—Case studies. I. Richards, P. Scott. II. Bergin, Allen E., 1934–.

RC489.S676C37 2003   2003014054
616.89—dc21

British Library Cataloguing-in-Publication Data
A CIP record is available from the British Library.

Printed in the United States of America
First Edition

Dedicated to the late David B. Larson
and his wife Susan,
courageous leaders in the integration of spirituality and health.

CONTENTS

CONTRIBUTORS

Allen E. Bergin, PhD, Emeritus, Department of Psychology, Brigham Young University, Provo, UT

Michael E. Berrett, PhD, Center for Change, Provo, UT

Donelda A. Cook, PhD, Counseling Center, Loyola College, Baltimore, MD

Richard Dobbins, PhD, EMERGE Ministries, Akron, OH

Randy K. Hardman, PhD, Center for Change, Provo, UT

Zari Hedayat-Diba, PhD, private practice; Adjunct Faculty, Antioch University; Core Faculty, Infant Mental Health Interdisciplinary Training Institute, Los Angeles, CA

W. Brad Johnson, PhD, Department of Leadership, Ethics, and Law, United States Naval Academy, Annapolis, MD

Mark J. Krejci, PhD, Psychology Department, Concordia College, Moorhead, MN

Robert J. Lovinger, PhD, ABPP, Professional Psychology Program, Walden University, Minneapolis, MN

Sophie L. Lovinger, PhD, ABPP, Professional Psychology Program, Walden University, Minneapolis, MN

Lisa Miller, PhD, Clinical Psychology Program, Teachers College, Columbia University, New York

L. Jay Mitchell, LLD, Alldredge Academy, Davis, WV

Stevan Lars Nielsen, PhD, Brigham Young University, Provo, UT

Aaron Rabinowitz, PhD, Department of Psychology, Bar-Ilan University, Ramat Gan, Israel

Carole A. Rayburn, PhD, private practice, Silver Spring, MD

P. Scott Richards, PhD, Department of Counseling Psychology, Brigham Young University, Provo, UT

Edward P. Shafranske, PhD, ABPP, Graduate School of Education and Psychology, Pepperdine University, Irvine, CA

Brent D. Slife, PhD, Department of Psychology, Brigham Young University, Provo, UT

Len Sperry, MD, PhD, Department of Psychiatry and Behavioral Medicine, Medical College of Wisconsin, Milwaukee, WI; Department of Counseling, Florida Atlantic University, Boca Raton

William West, PhD, Faculty of Education, University of Manchester, Manchester, England

Matthew Whoolery, MS, Department of Social Science and Education, College of Southern Idaho, Twin Falls, ID

PREFACE

Not long after the publication of our book about psychotherapy and religious diversity,[1] our editors at the American Psychological Association (APA) Books Department encouraged us to begin planning for the second edition of our first APA book, *A Spiritual Strategy for Counseling and Psychotherapy*.[2] As we contemplated this possibility, we decided that a third book was needed to further assist practitioners—an applied book of spiritual strategy case studies.

In *A Spiritual Strategy for Counseling and Psychotherapy*, we described a theoretical framework and applied approach for implementing theistic spiritual perspectives into mainstream psychology and psychotherapy. The *Handbook of Psychotherapy and Religious Diversity* provided many additional religious–cultural and clinical insights that can assist mainstream professionals in working effectively with clients from a diversity of spiritual traditions.

This new volume, *Casebook for a Spiritual Strategy in Counseling and Psychotherapy*, provides in-depth, applied insight into the diversity of ways that theistic spiritual perspectives and interventions can positively influence the processes and outcomes of psychological treatment. We believe that this casebook will be especially helpful to practitioners and graduate students in the mental health professions. As we have read the fascinating case reports in this book, our own understandings about how spiritual perspectives can enhance clinical practice have broadened and deepened. We feel confident that you will have a similar experience.

---

[1]Richards, P. S., & Bergin, A. E. (Eds.). (2000). *Handbook of psychotherapy and religious diversity*. Washington, DC: American Psychological Association.
[2]Richards, P. S., & Bergin, A. E. (1997). *A spiritual strategy for counseling and psychotherapy*. Washington, DC: American Psychological Association.

ACKNOWLEDGMENTS

We are grateful to Susan Reynolds, our acquisitions editor at the American Psychological Association (APA). From the beginning, she recognized that a book of case studies illustrating the application of theistic perspectives in counseling and psychotherapy would be a valuable contribution to the literature. Her support and advice in the formative stages of the book were crucial.

We are grateful to Vanessa Downing and Tiffany Klaff, our editors at APA, and to the rest of the APA Books development and production staff. Their feedback and suggestions for refining the book manuscript were invaluable. We express our appreciation to two anonymous reviewers who offered wise feedback and helpful encouragement.

We are grateful to the authors of the case reports for their courage in publicly sharing their theistic treatment approaches. We regard them as our colleagues and friends. We respect their work and appreciate the time they gave in writing up their cases. We also appreciate the patience they demonstrated as they responded to our suggestions for refining their case reports and to our many requests for information and paperwork.

We express gratitude to several other professional colleagues, including Melissa Allen, Ronald D. Bingham, Lane Fischer, Richard A. Heaps, Aaron P. Jackson, Steven A. Smith, Timothy B. Smith, and James R. Young. Their encouragement and friendship over the years have been a source of inspiration and enjoyment.

We are grateful to several talented undergraduate psychology students at Brigham Young University: Jeremy Bartz, Adam Froerer, Kari O'Grady, and Coral Richards. Their insightful feedback about the book chapters and enthusiasm for the topic were extremely helpful.

Finally, we express our profound gratitude to our wives, Marcia Richards and Marian Bergin. Their love, support, and sacrifice on our behalf have made all the difference in the world.

I

INTRODUCTION

1

A THEISTIC SPIRITUAL STRATEGY FOR PSYCHOTHERAPY

P. SCOTT RICHARDS AND ALLEN E. BERGIN

The alienation that existed between psychology and religion during most of the 20th century has ended. Hundreds of articles on religion and mental health and spirituality and psychotherapy have been published in professional journals. Numerous presentations have been given at professional conferences. Many mainstream publishers have published books on these topics. All of the major mental health organizations now explicitly recognize that religion is one type of diversity that professionals are obligated to respect. Clearly, a more spiritually open *zeitgeist* or "spirit of the times" is upon us (Richards & Bergin, 1997).

The rise of a spiritual *zeitgeist* has opened the door to the development and integration of spiritual perspectives and interventions into mainstream psychological practice (Collins, 1977; Larson & Larson, 1994; Miller, 1999; Peck, 1978; Richards & Bergin, 1997, 2000; Shafranske, 1996). During the past decade, numerous spiritual psychotherapy approaches have been proposed, including those conceptually grounded in Buddhist, Hindu, Christian, Jewish, and Muslim spiritual thought (Collins, 1988; Epstein, 1995; Hedayat-Diba, 2000; Rabinowitz, 2001; Rubin, 1996; Sharma, 2000; Spero, 1985). Spiritual approaches based on Jungian, transpersonal, cognitive, and humanistic psychologies have also been proposed (Elkins, 1995; Helminiak, 1996; Nielsen, Johnson, & Ellis, 2001; Vaughan, Wittine, & Walsh, 1996). Several writers have also described multicultural psychotherapy approaches that are not grounded in a particular spiritual tradition or psychological theory, but that advocate respect for religious and spiritual diversity (Faiver, Ingersoll, O'Brien, & McNally, 2001; Griffith & Griffith, 2002; Kelly, 1995; Lovinger, 1984; Sperry, 2001; Swinton, 2001; West, 2000).

We regard the development of a variety of spiritual psychotherapy approaches as a positive trend in the mental health professions. The diversity of religious and spiritual beliefs and practices in the world is astonishing (Keller, 2000; Richards & Bergin, 2000). It seems obvious that a variety of spiritual approaches to psychotherapy will be needed to respond to this diversity. We hope that creative and competent theorists and practitioners from diverse spiritual traditions will continue the effort to develop and evaluate new and more effective spiritual psychotherapy approaches.

Although we think there is value in diversity, we have devoted our efforts during the past 25 years to the development of a specific theistic spiritual strategy for mainstream psychology and psychotherapy (Bergin, 1980a, 1983, 1985, 1988, 1991; Richards & Bergin, 1997). Given the fact that in North America and Europe more than 80% of the population professes belief in one of the theistic world religions (Barrett & Johnson, 1998), we think such an approach is a vital ingredient in the multicultural spectrum (Bergin, 1980a; Richards & Bergin, 2000). Although we do not endorse all of the teachings and practices advocated by the theistic world religions, there is nevertheless much therapeutic potential in these traditions for individuals and groups in need (Benson, 1996; Richards & Bergin, 1997), and we hope to tap their healing resources.

As we have developed and shared our theistic spiritual strategy over the years, we have had the opportunity to visit and correspond with mental health professionals from many different religious and theoretical backgrounds who have incorporated theistic perspectives into their professional work. These experiences have helped us appreciate more fully the implications of such perspectives for psychotherapy. A major purpose of the present book, *Casebook for a Spiritual Strategy in Counseling and Psychotherapy*, is to demonstrate the diverse and creative ways that theistic perspectives can influence clinical theory and practice. Consider the following preview of some of the cases.[1]

Case 1: Laura

Laura, a 16-year-old Caucasian woman, had no religious affiliation. Laura's birth mother and father were drug addicts, and neither was currently involved in Laura's life. Laura's grandparents had custody of her. Prior to her current treatment, Laura had been admitted to an inpatient

---

[1]In accordance with guidelines of the American Psychological Association, all cases in this book have been disguised by changing clients' names and other identifying details.

psychiatric ward for a number of problems, including running away, heavy drug use, and misdemeanor convictions for shoplifting and truancy. She had also been diagnosed with attention-deficit/hyperactivity disorder (ADHD; with secondary depression) and placed on Prozac, but her problem behaviors continued. An educational consultant for the psychiatric hospital with expertise in the special needs of youth had referred Laura to Alldredge Academy, a residential adolescent treatment program located in the mountains of West Virginia. Alldredge Community is based on a nonnaturalistic, ecumenical theistic treatment philosophy that among other things teaches adolescents spiritual values and helps them learn to listen to the "Source" (the Alldredge term for God or Spirit).

Case 2: Paul

Paul, a 52-year-old Caucasian man, was a Southern Baptist of moderate devoutness. Paul was experiencing much concern about why his family and friends had not accepted his most recent extramarital lover of 3 years, Fritzi. Paul was still married to Cathy, 51, his wife of 34 years, although he lived with Fritzi. Paul and Fritzi were experiencing conflict when Paul started therapy because Paul had become impotent, perhaps due to some heart medications he was taking. Fritzi had begun insulting Paul at every opportunity and criticizing his sexual prowess and appearance. Despite his extramarital relationship with Fritzi and many other extramarital affairs, Paul considered himself to be a religious and spiritual person, attended church services on a fairly regular basis, and professed his belief in God and Jesus Christ. Paul presented for individual therapy with Dr. Carole Rayburn, a Seventh-day Adventist woman, whose therapeutic approach is heavily influenced by a theistic, God and Christ-centered worldview.

Case 3: Grace

Grace, a 39-year-old, single African American woman, was affiliated with an African American Baptist church. Grace had a master's degree in school counseling and was employed in a high school as the head of the counseling department. Grace was also a recently licensed minister in her church. Grace was experiencing considerable stress trying to meet the demands of her life, including full-time employment, church ministry, and seminary. Grace had little time for herself because she was putting forth as much effort and energy in her part-time unpaid church ministry as in her full-time employment, because of her passion for ministry and her need for approval from her pastor. Grace also had unresolved issues because she had not yet married or had children. Grace sought therapy from Dr. Donelda Cook after participating in a weekend Scripture-based meditative prayer retreat conducted by Dr. Cook. Multicultural psychology and an ecumenical, theistic spiritual perspective inform Dr. Cook's therapeutic approach.

Case 4: Renee

Renee, a 16-year-old African American young woman, was a Christian with no current denominational affiliation. Renee was 5 months pregnant. Renee was experiencing severe depression and met diagnostic criteria according to the *Diagnostic and Statistical Manual of Mental Disorders* (4th ed.; *DSM–IV*; American Psychiatric Association, 1994) for major depressive disorder. Renee's depression stemmed from issues of abandonment and loss. Her mother had died within the past year, leaving her without a family or home. Renee's biological father would not allow her to live with him and his new wife, and he refused to speak to Renee because of her pregnancy. Renee's boyfriend, the father of her baby, had turned against Renee and disowned the baby when Renee refused to have an abortion. Renee was referred for group psychotherapy in a public high school in New York City. Dr. Lisa Miller, a Caucasian Jewish woman whose therapeutic orientation is influenced by a theistic spiritual perspective of pathology, resilience, and renewal, led the group.

In addition to illustrating the diverse ways that theistic perspectives can influence clinical practice, another major purpose of the *Casebook for a Spiritual Strategy in Counseling and Psychotherapy*, is to help mental health professionals more fully understand how to effectively implement theistic perspectives and interventions in their work. There is still much to be learned about implementing spiritual interventions in psychotherapy, and we think the case studies described in this book offer many valuable insights for clinicians.

A final purpose of this book is to help mental health professionals who would like to more fully incorporate theistic perspectives into their theoretical framework and therapy approach gain additional insight into how they might do so. Most mental health professionals are trained in secular psychotherapy traditions, and we suspect that they, like us, may find it easier to think and practice consistent with their secular training. Incorporating theistic perspectives into one's therapeutic orientation in a philosophically and theoretically sound manner is not necessarily easy. We hope that the *Casebook for a Spiritual Strategy in Counseling and Psychotherapy* helps mental health professionals more fully succeed at this challenging task.

The following is a brief summary of our theistic spiritual strategy for psychotherapy. We hope that this information will help you more fully understand and appreciate the case studies presented in the book. We also hope it helps make clear that our strategy provides a broad framework that psychotherapists of diverse theistic backgrounds and orientations can use to conceptualize, guide, and evaluate their work. We conclude this chapter by briefly describing the plan of the book.

A THEISTIC SPIRITUAL STRATEGY

In *A Spiritual Strategy for Counseling and Psychotherapy* (Richards & Bergin, 1997), we described an approach to psychotherapy that comprises two separate but related parts. First, it contains a new *psychotherapy orienta-*

tion—an orientation we have decided to call *Theistic Psychotherapy*. This orientation includes a theoretical framework for psychotherapy as well as a variety of spiritual therapeutic interventions. No other mainstream psychotherapy tradition has adequately incorporated theistic spiritual perspectives and practices into its approach, and so our orientation fills a void in the field (Bergin, 1980a, 1988). Although our orientation is stated broadly so as to make it suitable for therapists and clients from a variety of theistic religious traditions, including many branches within Judaism, Islam, and Christianity, it does not incorporate Eastern, transpersonal, or humanistic spiritual perspectives. Without prejudice, we have left the task of developing spiritual therapies based on these perspectives to those who are more familiar with and committed to them.

Second, our spiritual strategy describes an applied process for implementing spiritual perspectives in psychotherapy in an ethically appropriate and culturally sensitive manner. We offer process guidelines and recommendations concerning (a) multicultural spiritual sensitivity, (b) establishing a spiritually open and safe therapeutic relationship, (c) setting spiritual goals in psychotherapy, (d) conducting religious and spiritual assessments, (e) attending to ethical concerns in spiritual psychotherapy, and (f) implementing spiritual interventions appropriately in therapy.

As we have explained in more detail elsewhere (Richards & Bergin, 1997), our spiritual strategy is integrative in that we advocate that spiritual interventions should be combined in a treatment-tailoring fashion with a variety of standard mainstream techniques, including psychodynamic, behavioral, humanistic, cognitive, and systemic ones. The strategy is empirical in that it is grounded in current research about psychotherapy and spirituality, and will continue to submit its claims to empirical scrutiny. The strategy is ecumenical in that it can be applied sensitively to people from diverse theistic religious traditions. Finally, our strategy is denominational in that it leaves room for psychotherapists to tailor treatment to the fine nuances of specific religious denominations. In our view, these four characteristics are essential for any viable spiritual approach to psychotherapy. We now summarize both our theoretical orientation and the process for implementing it.

Conceptual Framework for Theistic Psychotherapy

Theological and Philosophical Foundations

The core assumptions of our theistic psychotherapy orientation are that "God exists, . . . human beings are the creations of God, and . . . there are unseen spiritual processes by which the link between God and humanity is maintained" (Bergin, 1980a, p. 99). These core assumptions are grounded firmly in the worldview of the five major theistic world religions: Judaism, Christianity, Islam, Sikhism, and Zoroastrianism (Smart, 1994).

Although there is great diversity between and within these five world religions in terms of specific beliefs and practices, at a more general level they share a common global worldview. According to the theistic worldview, God exists, human beings are the creations of God, there is a divine purpose to life, human beings can communicate with God through prayer and other spiritual practices, God has revealed moral truths to guide human behavior, and the human spirit or soul continues to exist after mortal death (Richards & Bergin, 1997).

Table 1.1 briefly compares the theistic spiritual worldview with the modernistic naturalistic-atheistic worldview on which all other mainstream theories of psychotherapy are grounded. It can be seen that the metaphysical assumptions of these two worldviews are almost diametrically opposed across all six dimensions in this table, including how they view deity, human nature, purpose of life, spirituality, morality, and death. The naturalistic-atheistic view excludes all reference to God and transcendent spiritual realities and assumes that the universe, life, and human nature can all be explained completely through natural forces and processes such as the Big Bang theory, the theory of evolution, and related perspectives. The theistic view focusing on God as creator and redeemer, therefore, provides a dramatically different position (Bergin, 1980a, 1980b).

To more fully understand the conceptual foundations of our theistic orientation, one may find it helpful to examine some additional underlying philosophical assumptions of our view and contrast them further with the assumptions of the modernistic, naturalistic-atheistic worldview. Table 1.2 reveals that the philosophical assumptions underlying our orientation starkly conflict with the deterministic, reductionistic, mechanistic, relativistic, and hedonistic assumptions adopted by scientists and behavioral scientists in the late 19th and early 20th centuries. We prefer theistically based alternatives such as agency, holism, contextuality, altruism, theistic realism, and epistemological pluralism (Richards & Bergin, 1997). It is interesting that contemporary postmodern views in science and the philosophy of science are now more compatible with these theistic perspectives than was the case in previous decades (Griffin, 2000, 2001; Jones, 1994; Richards & Bergin, 1997; Slife, 2003; Slife, Hope, & Nebeker, 1999).

There are several reasons why we ground our therapeutic orientation in the theistic worldview and reject the modernistic naturalistic-atheistic worldview. First, we believe in God and in spiritual realities. We are convinced that the naturalistic-atheistic worldview does not adequately account for the complexities and mysteries of life and of the universe (Barbour, 1990, 1997; Eccles & Robinson, 1984; Griffin, 2000). We agree with many other scientists and philosophers who have argued that spiritual perspectives are needed to enrich scientific understandings of human beings and of the origins and operations of the universe (Barbour, 1997; Griffin, 2000; Jones, 1994; Schroeder, 2001; Templeton & Herrmann, 1994).

TABLE 1.1
Comparison of the Theistic Spiritual Worldview With the Modernistic, Naturalistic-Atheistic Worldview

Worldview	View of deity	View of human nature	Purpose of life	View of spirituality	View of morality	View of life after death
Western (Monotheistic)	There is a God, a Supreme Being, who created the universe, the earth, and human beings. God is eternal, omnipotent, and all-knowing. God loves and assists human beings.	Human beings are creations of God. Human beings have an eternal soul or spirit. Human beings have free will and the capacity to choose good over evil and to obey God's commandments.	There is a transcendent, divine purpose to life. Human beings are here upon the earth to learn to be obedient to God's will, to choose good over evil, and to prepare to live in a joyful and peaceful afterlife.	Human beings can communicate with God through prayer and meditation. They grow spiritually as they obey God's will, worship him, and love and serve their fellow human beings.	God has revealed laws and commandments to guide human behavior. Obedience to God's laws promotes spiritual growth, harmonious social relations, personal happiness, and prepares human beings for rewards in the afterlife.	The spirit or soul of human beings continues to exist after mortal death. There is an afterlife of peace and joy for those who live righteously in mortal life. The wicked are punished or suffer for their sins in the afterlife.
Naturalistic-Atheistic	There is no God or Supreme Being, nor are there any supernatural gods or transcendent forces of any kind. The	Human beings are the end product of millions of years of evolutionary processes as theorized by Charles Darwin	There is no transcendent purpose or meaning in life. The only purpose or meaning in life is that which	Spirituality is just another world for naturalistic phenomena (i.e., psychological, physiological and cognitive	There are no moral absolutes or universals. Societies and groups may construct moral and ethical	There is no life after death. When human beings die, they cease to exist.

continues

TABLE 1.1 (Continued)

Worldview	View of deity	View of human nature	Purpose of life	View of spirituality	View of morality	View of life after death
	universe was produced and is maintained by natural forces, processes, and laws (e.g., the Big Bang, organic evolution).	and evolutionary scientists. Life originated upon this earth through natural processes; there was no God or transcendent force involved in the creation of life. Human beings do not have an immortal spirit or soul. Human consciousness can be completely accounted for with biological and physiological explanations. Human beings may or may not have free will depending on the particular naturalistic theory.	human beings construct or invent for themselves. Pursuing truth and knowledge and contributing to the betterment and welfare of humanity is seen as a meaningful purpose for science.	processes). There are no transcendent spiritual realities. Human beings cannot communicate with a God because there is no God to communicate with.	guidelines to help regulate social functioning and protect the welfare of individuals, but such moral and ethical guidelines are relativistic and may only be suitable for that particular society or group.	

Note. From *A Spiritual Strategy for Counseling and Psychotherapy* (pp. 72–73), by P. S. Richards & A. E. Bergin, 1997, Washington, DC: American Psychological Association. Copyright 1997 by the American Psychological Association. Adapted with permission of the authors and publisher.

TABLE 1.2
Conflicting Philosophical Assumptions of Naturalistic-Atheistic Science and Theistic Psychotherapy

Naturalistic-atheistic science and psychology	Theistic psychotherapy
Determinism: Human behavior is completely caused by forces outside of human control.	**Free will:** Human beings have agency and the capacity to choose and regulate their behavior, although biological and environmental influences may set some limits.
Universalism: Natural laws, including laws of human behavior, are context free; they apply across time, space, and persons. A phenomenon is not real if it is not generalizable and repeatable.	**Contextuality:** While there are natural laws that may be context free, there may also be some that are context bound; that is, they apply in some contexts but not others. There are real phenomena that are contextual, invisible, and private. They are not empirically observable, generalizable or repeatable (e.g., transcendent spiritual experiences).
Reductionism/atomism: All of human behavior can be reduced or divided into smaller parts or units.	**Holism:** Humans are more than the sum of their parts. They cannot be adequately understood by reducing or dividing them into smaller units.
Materialism/mechanism: Human beings are like a machine; composed of material or biological parts working together.	**Transcendent spirit/soul:** Humans are composed of a spirit or soul and physical body; they cannot be reduced simply to physiology or biology.
Ethical relativism: There are no universal or absolute moral or ethical principles. Values are culture-bound. What is right and good varies across social and individual situations.	**Universals/absolutes:** There are universal moral and ethical principles that regulate healthy psychological and spiritual development. Some values are more healthy and moral than others.
Ethical hedonism: Human beings always seek rewards (pleasure) and avoid punishments (pain). This is the basic valuing process built into human behavior.	**Altruism:** Human beings often forego their own rewards (pleasure) for the welfare of others. Responsibility, self-sacrifice, suffering, love, and altruistic service are valued above personal gratification.
Classical realism/positivism: The universe is real and can be accurately perceived and understood by human beings. Science provides the only valid knowledge. Scientific theories can be proven true on the basis of empirical evidence.	**Theistic realism:** God is the ultimate creative and controlling force in the universe and the ultimate reality. God and the universe can only be partially and imperfectly understood by human beings. Scientific methods can approximate some aspects of reality but must be transcended by spiritual ways of knowing in many realms.

continues

TABLE 1.2 *(Continued)*

Naturalistic-atheistic science and psychology	Theistic psychotherapy
Empiricism: Sensory experience provides human beings with the only reliable source of knowledge. Nothing is true or real save that which is observable through our sensory experience or measuring instruments.	**Epistemological pluralism:** Human beings can learn truth in a variety of ways, including authority, reason, sensory experience, and intuition/inspiration. Inspiration from God is a valid source of knowledge and truth.

Note. From *A Spiritual Strategy for Counseling and Psychotherapy* (pp. 30–31), by P. S. Richards & A. E. Bergin, 1997, Washington, DC: American Psychological Association. Copyright 1997 by the American Psychological Association. Adapted with permission of the authors and publisher.

Second, we think the modernistic naturalistic-atheistic worldview is philosophically and empirically problematic, for scientists in general, and behavioral scientists and mental health practitioners in particular (Bergin, 1980b; Griffin, 2000, 2001; Richards & Bergin, 1997; Slife, 2003; Slife et al., 1999). If mental health professionals accept the naturalistic-atheistic worldview, to be logically consistent, they are then compelled to accept several other problematic viewpoints commonly linked to the modern scientific worldview, including sensationism, mechanism, materialism, determinism, and reductionism (Griffin, 2000; Slife, 2003; Slife et al., 1999). The implications of this worldview were clearly stated by William Provine (1988), a historian of science:

> Modern science directly implies that the world is organized strictly in accordance with deterministic principles or chance. . . . There are no purposive principles whatsoever in nature. There are no gods and no designing forces that are rationally detectable. . . . Second, modern science directly implies that there are no inherent moral or ethical laws. . . . Third, human beings are marvelously complex machines. The individual human becomes an ethical person by means of only two mechanisms: deterministic heredity interacting with deterministic environmental influences. That is all there is.
>
> Fourth, we must conclude that when we die, we die and that is the end of us. There is no hope of life everlasting. . . . [F]ree will, as traditionally conceived, the freedom to make uncoerced and unpredictable choices among alternative possible courses of action, simply does not exist. . . . [T]he evolutionary process cannot produce a being that is truly free to make choices. . . . The universe cares nothing for us. . . . Humans are as nothing even in the evolutionary process on earth. . . . There is no ultimate meaning for humans. (pp. 64–66, 70)

Philosopher David Griffin (2000) has argued that the modernistic, naturalistic-atheistic worldview not only provides an impoverished view of human nature but also is inconsistent with the empirical evidence and with what he calls "hard-core common sense beliefs" or, in other words, beliefs that are "inevitably presupposed in practice" by both laypersons and scientists (p. 99). We agree with these critiques of the naturalistic-atheistic worldview. We think the theistic worldview provides a more adequate foundation on which to construct theories of human nature, personality, and therapeutic change.

Third, we reject the modernistic naturalistic-atheistic worldview as a foundation for our approach to psychotherapy because it fails to provide a culturally and spiritually sensitive framework for the large numbers of people in North America who believe in God and who are religiously committed. Bergin (1980a) argued that mainstream psychological theories and treatment approaches based on naturalistic assumptions "are not sufficient to cover the spectrum of values pertinent to human beings and the frameworks within which they function. Noticeably absent are theistically based values" (p. 98). He further wrote:

> Other alternatives are thus needed. Just as psychotherapy has been enhanced by the adoption of multiple techniques, so also in the values realm our frameworks can be improved by the use of additional perspectives.
>
> The alternative I wish to put forward is a spiritual one. It might be called theistic realism. I propose to show that this alternative is necessary for ethical and effective help among religious people, who constitute 30% to 90% of the U. S. population. . . . I also argue that the values on which this alternative is based are important ingredients in reforming and rejuvenating our society. (p. 99)

Theistic View of Personality

A concept of fundamental importance for the theistic, spiritual view of human personality is that of the eternal spiritual identity of human beings. Consistent with the teachings of most of the theistic world religions, we theorized that human beings are composed of both a mortal body and an eternal spirit, soul, or energy source that continues to exist beyond the death of the mortal body. This eternal spirit or soul is of divine creation and worth and constitutes the lasting or eternal identity of the individual. The spirit or soul "interacts with other aspects of the person to produce what is normally referred to as personality and behavior" (Richards & Bergin, 1997, p. 98).

Our theoretical views about human nature, personality, and therapeutic change are summarized in Table 1.3. Human development and personality is influenced by a variety of systems and processes (e.g., biological, cognitive, social, psychological), but the core essence of identity and personality is spiritual. People who believe in their eternal spiritual identity, follow the influence of God's spirit, and live in harmony with universal moral principles are more likely to develop in a healthy manner socially and psychologically. Spiritually mature people have the capacity to enjoy loving, affirming relationships with others, have a clear sense of identity and values, and their external behavior is in harmony with their value system (Bergin, 1980a;

TABLE 1.3
Theoretical Foundations of Theistic Psychotherapy

View of human nature	View of healthy functioning	View of psychopathology	View of therapeutic change
People have free will or agency, though both environmental and biological factors can limit agency. Agency gets expanded or restricted by the choices we make. Human beings are multisystemic organisms (i.e., biological, social, cognitive, psychological, and spiritual). Human beings have a spirit or soul which is eternal in nature. Spiritual processes exist which allow human beings to communicate with a Supreme Being. Human beings have great potential for growth and can realize their potential by seeking for spiritual awareness and growth. Human beings can also follow a path of deterioration by neglecting their spiritual growth and choosing evil.	Biological, social, psychological, and spiritual factors all influence personality development. People who believe in the influence of God's spirit, and live in harmony with universal moral principles are more likely to develop in a healthy manner socially and psychologically. Spiritually healthy people have the capacity to enjoy loving, affirming relationships with others, have a clear sense of identity and values, and their external behavior is in harmony with their value system. They also feel a sense of closeness and harmony with God and experience a sense of strength, meaning, and fulfillment from their spiritual beliefs.	Psychological disturbance and symptoms can be caused by a variety of influences, including physiological (e.g., neurotransmitter depletions), familial (e.g., abuse, marital conflict), social (e.g., prolonged work related stress), cognitive (e.g., irrational thinking), and spiritual (e.g., moral transgressions) problems. People who neglect their spiritual growth and well-being, or who consistently choose to ignore the Spirit of Truth and do evil, are more likely to suffer poor mental health and disturbed, unfulfilling interpersonal relationships.	Therapeutic change and healing can be facilitated through a variety of means, including physiological (e.g., medications), familial (e.g., improving communication), social (e.g., preventative education), cognitive (e.g., modifying irrational beliefs), and spiritual (e.g., prayer, repentance, meditation). At its core, healing and change is a spiritual process. Psychological, relational, and even physical healing is facilitated, and is more profound and lasting, when people heal and grow spiritually.

Malony, 1985). They also feel a sense of closeness and harmony with God and experience a sense of strength, meaning, and fulfillment from their spiritual beliefs. People who neglect their spiritual growth and well-being, or who consistently choose to ignore the influence of God's spirit and do evil, are more likely to suffer poor mental health and disturbed, unfulfilling interpersonal relationships.

Therapeutic change and healing can be facilitated through a variety of means, including physiological, psychological, social, educational, and spiritual interventions. But complete healing and change requires a spiritual process. Therapeutic change is facilitated, and is often more profound and lasting, when people heal and grow spiritually through God's inspiration in their lives. Spiritual practices such as prayer, meditation, reading sacred writings, worship and ritual, repentance and forgiveness, altruistic service, and seeking spiritual direction can give people added hope and power to cope, heal, and change (Benson, 1996; Richards & Bergin, 1997).

Theistic View of Psychotherapy

The sacred writings of all of the major theistic religious traditions affirm God's power to inspire, comfort, and heal. Our theistic orientation assumes that clients who have faith in God's healing power and draw on the spiritual resources in their lives during psychological treatment will receive added strength and power to cope, heal, and grow (Richards & Bergin, 1997, p. 100). Theistic psychotherapists, therefore, may encourage their clients to explore how their faith in God and personal spirituality may assist them during treatment and recovery. In this sense, our theistic orientation offers a unique view of psychotherapy. No other mainstream psychotherapy orientation makes faith in God's loving and healing influence the foundation of its theory and approach (Bergin, 1980a; Jones, 1994).

Another distinctive view of our orientation is that it asserts that a theistic moral framework for psychotherapy is possible and desirable. By a moral framework, we do not mean a detailed list of moral instructions. We mean that there are general moral values and principles that influence healthy human development and functioning and that can be used to guide and evaluate psychotherapy (Bergin, 1980a, 1985, 1991). Theistic psychotherapists appeal to the world's great religious traditions for insight into what are these moral values and principles. They also seek to cross-validate and deepen their understanding of health and human welfare values by gleaning insights from mental health professionals, ethicists, moral philosophers, and behavioral scientists (Bergin, 1985, 1991; Richards, Rector, & Tjeltveit, 1999).

Although there is great diversity between and within the theistic religious traditions regarding their beliefs and practices, they agree that human beings can and should transcend hedonistic and selfish tendencies to grow spiritually and to promote the welfare of others. There is also general agreement among the world religions about what moral principles and values promote spiritual enlightenment and personal and social harmony. According to Ninian Smart (1983), a respected world religion scholar, "The major faiths have much in common as far as moral conduct goes. Not to steal, not to lie, not to kill, not to have certain kinds of sexual relations—such prescriptions are found across the world" (p. 117).

A variety of moral values and principles grounded in the theistic religious traditions are associated with better mental and physical health and harmonious interpersonal relationships. These include values and principles such as integrity, honesty, forgiveness, repentance, humility, love, spirituality, religious devoutness, marital commitment, sexual fidelity, family loyalty and kinship, benevolent use of power, and respect for human agency (Bergin, 1985, 2002; Richards & Bergin, 1997). These theistically based moral values provide theistic psychotherapists with a framework for evaluating whether their clients' lifestyles are healthy and mature and for deciding what therapeutic goals to endorse. We think it is noteworthy that there is substantial overlap of these theistically based values with health values endorsed by most mental health professionals, ethicists, and moral philosophers (Jensen & Bergin, 1988).

Although there are moral values that do more than others to promote mental health, harmonious relationships, and spiritual growth, the application and prioritization of these values may vary somewhat depending on the time, context, and other competing values. For example, even a seemingly absolute value such as "It is wrong to kill another human being" may depend on the context for its application and validity. Thus, in endorsing the idea that certain values are moral and beneficial, and that therapists should share their understanding with clients about these values, this does not mean therapists should tell their clients how to apply them in a given situation. Ultimately, therapists must permit clients to make their own choices about what they value and how they will apply these values in their lives, but it would be irresponsible for therapists not to share what wisdom they can about values when it is relevant to clients' problems (Bergin, 1991; Richards et al., 1999).

A third contribution of our theistic orientation is that it provides a body of spiritual interventions that psychotherapists can use to intervene in the spiritual dimension of their clients' lives. No mainstream psychotherapy tradition has interventions designed for this purpose. Spiritual interventions that may be used by theistic psychotherapists include praying for clients, encouraging clients to pray, discussing theological concepts, making reference to scriptures, using spiritual relaxation and imagery techniques, encouraging repentance and forgiveness, helping clients live congruently with their spiritual values, self-disclosing spiritual beliefs or experiences, consulting with religious leaders, and recommending religious bibliotherapy (Ball & Goodyear, 1991; Kelly, 1995; Richards & Bergin, 1997; Richards & Potts, 1995). Most of these spiritual interventions are actually practices that have been engaged in for centuries by religious believers. They have endured because they express and respond to the deepest needs, concerns, and problems of human beings.

Research evidence indicates that there is significant healing potential in many spiritual practices (e.g., Benson, 1996; Borysenko & Borysenko, 1994; Miller, 1999; Richards & Bergin, 1997, 2000). Benson (1996) concluded that interventions for promoting the relaxation response are more powerful when they draw on people's deepest spiritual convictions. He referred to this as the "faith factor" and indicated that it appears that people's faith in an "eternal or life-transcending force" enhances "the average effects of the relaxation response" (pp. 151, 155). Spiritual interventions that help clients access the resources of their faith in God and personal spirituality may enhance the effects of other forms of medical and psychological treatment. Bergin (1991) suggested that

> some religious influences have a modest impact, whereas another portion seems like the mental equivalent of nuclear energy . . . the more powerful portion can provide transcendent conviction or commitment and is sometimes manifested in dramatic personal healing or transformation. When this kind of experience is also linked with social forces, its effect can be extraordinary. (p. 401)

Such experiences often alter people's worldviews, positively change their sense of identity, heal their feelings of shame, and reorient their values from materialistic to spiritual ones (Bergin et al., 1994; Emmons, 1999; Miller & C'deBaca, 1994; Richards, 1999). These inner changes in beliefs and values can lead to outer changes in lifestyle, which can thereby lead to healthier behaviors and reductions in psychological and physical symptoms and problems. Thus, spiritual interventions may help set people on a path that is more conducive to physical and mental health.

A fourth element of our viewpoint is that both therapists and clients may seek, and on occasion obtain, spiritual enlightenment to assist in treatment and recovery (Chamberlain, Richards, & Scharman, 1996; Richards & Bergin, 1997). By entering into meditative or prayerful moments before, during, or after sessions, therapists and clients may experience inspired insights. These experiences are usually not dramatic but may come as quiet, gentle impressions to the mind and heart of the therapist and client. Genuine spiritual impressions can give therapists and clients important insight into problems as well as ideas for interventions or healing strategies that may be effective. If heeded, such impressions can facilitate clients' therapeutic growth. Some of the most powerful healing moments in therapy happen when this occurs. Table 1.4 provides a summary overview of some of the important components and processes of our theistic psychotherapy approach.

Process Guidelines for Theistic Psychotherapy

A variety of important process issues and principles need to be kept in mind when implementing spiritual interventions in treatment. The follow-

TABLE 1.4
Summary of Important Components and Processes of Theistic Psychotherapy

Goals of therapy	Therapist's role in therapy	Role of spiritual techniques	Client's role in therapy	Nature of the therapy relationship
Spiritual view is part of a multisystemic view of humans and therapy and so therapy goals depend on the client's issues. Goals directly relevant to the spiritual dimension include (a) help clients affirm their eternal spiritual identity and live in harmony with the Spirit of Truth; (b) assess what impact religious and spiritual beliefs have in clients' lives and whether they have unmet spiritual needs; (c) help clients use religious and spiritual resources to help them in their efforts to cope, change, and grow; (d) help clients resolve spiritual concerns and doubts and	Adopt an ecumenical therapeutic stance, and when appropriate, a denominational stance. Establish a warm, supportive environment where the client knows it is safe and acceptable to explore their religious and spiritual beliefs, doubts, and concerns. Assess whether clients' religious and spiritual beliefs and activities are impacting their mental health and interpersonal relationships. Implement religious and spiritual interventions to help clients more effectively use their religious and spiritual resources in their coping and growth process. Model	Interventions are viewed as very important for helping clients understand and work through religious and spiritual issues and concerns, and for helping clients draw upon religious and spiritual resources in their lives to assist them in better coping, growing, and changing. Examples of major interventions include cognitive restructuring of irrational religious beliefs, transitional figure technique, forgiveness, meditation and prayer, scripture study, blessings, participating in religious services, spiritual imagery, journaling about spiritual feelings, repentance, and	Examine how their religious and spiritual beliefs and activities affect their behavior, emotions, and relationships. Make choices about what role religion and spirituality will play in their lives. Set goals and carry out spiritual interventions designed to facilitate their spiritual and emotional growth. Seek to use the religious and spiritual resources in their lives to assist them in their efforts to heal and change. Seek God's guidance and enlightenment about how to better cope, heal, and change.	Unconditional positive regard, warmth, genuineness, and empathy are regarded as an essential foundation for therapy. Therapists also seek to have charity or brotherly and sisterly love for clients and to affirm their spiritual identity and worth. Clients are expected to form a working alliance and share in the work of change. Clients must trust the therapist and believe that it is safe to share their religious and spiritual beliefs and heritage with the therapist. Clients must know that the therapist highly values and respects their autonomy and freedom of choice,

continues

TABLE 1.4 (Continued)

make choices about role of spirituality in their lives; and (e) help clients examine their spirituality and continue their quest for spiritual growth.	and endorse healthy values. Seek spiritual guidance and enlightenment regarding how best to help clients.	using the client's religious support system.	and that it is safe for them to differ from the therapist in their religious and spiritual beliefs and values, even though the therapists may at times disagree with their values and confront them about unhealthy values and life-style choices.

Note. From *A Spiritual Strategy for Counseling and Psychotherapy* (pp.140–141), by P. S. Richards & A. E. Bergin, 1997, Washington, DC: American Psychological Association. Copyright 1997 by the American Psychological Association. Adapted with permission of the authors and publisher.

ing process recommendations are summarized from our book (Richards &
Bergin, 1997).

Multicultural Spiritual Sensitivity

The capacity to adopt an ecumenical therapeutic stance—one that is
sensitive and open to diverse spiritual perspectives—is essential for therapists who work with religious and spiritual clients. The foundations of an
ecumenical therapeutic stance are the attitudes and skills of effective
multicultural therapists (e.g., Sue & Sue, 1990; Sue, Zane, & Young, 1994),
but it goes beyond most contemporary multicultural approaches to include
training and competency in working with religious and spiritual issues.

Therapists with good ecumenical skills are aware of their own religious
and spiritual heritage and values and are sensitive to how they could affect
their work with clients from different religious and spiritual traditions. They
are capable of communicating interest, understanding, and respect to clients
who have spiritual beliefs that are different from their own. They seek to
learn more about the spiritual beliefs and cultures of clients with whom they
work. They make efforts to establish trusting relationships with members
and leaders in their clients' religious communities and seek to draw on these
sources of social support when it seems appropriate. They use spiritual resources and interventions that are in harmony with their clients' beliefs when
it appears that this could help their clients cope, heal, and change. Therapists should use an ecumenical therapeutic approach during the early stages
of therapy with all clients and over the entire course of therapy with clients
whose religious affiliation or beliefs differ significantly from their own.

Therapists may also adopt a denominational therapeutic stance with
some clients. A denominational stance is one that is tailored for clients who
are members of a specific religious denomination. A denominational approach
builds on the foundation laid earlier in therapy by the therapist's ecumenical
stance but differs from it in that the therapist uses assessment methods and
interventions that are tailored more specifically to the client's unique denominational beliefs and practices. Therapists should use a denominational
approach only with clients who view them as able to deeply understand and
respect their spiritual beliefs. Such an approach can give therapists added
leverage to help clients because it can help them more fully address the fine
nuances of a client's religious and spiritual issues as well as tap into the spiritual resources of the client's spiritual tradition.

Establish a Spiritually Open and Safe Relationship

Establishing a spiritually safe and open therapeutic relationship is crucial for the effective and ethical exploration of religious and spiritual issues.
Spiritual beliefs and feelings are often very private and sacred to people. If
clients do not feel a great deal of trust for their therapists, they are unlikely to
freely discuss and work through such sensitive matters. In addition, because

many psychotherapists have traditionally been reluctant to discuss religious and spiritual issues (Bergin, 1980a; Henning & Tirrell, 1982), clients may not believe it is appropriate to do so.

We recommend that therapists explicitly let their clients know it is permissible and appropriate to explore spiritual issues should they so desire. Therapists can do this in the written informed consent documents they give clients at the beginning of treatment or they can do so verbally at appropriate times during the course of therapy. Fears that clients may have that the therapist might view their spiritual beliefs as pathological could also be allayed in the informed consent document. Therapists can also open the door to discussions about spirituality by including questions about clients' religious and spiritual backgrounds on an intake questionnaire.

In therapeutic settings where clients from a diversity of religious traditions receive treatment, therapists should usually avoid disclosing details about their religious beliefs unless clients directly ask for such information. Prematurely disclosing details about one's affiliation or beliefs may "turn off" clients whose religious affiliation and beliefs are different. By communicating willingness to explore spiritual issues without prematurely disclosing specific details about their own religious beliefs, therapists will probably be more successful at establishing trust with a wider range of clients.

Psychotherapists should communicate interest and respect when clients self-disclose information about their religious tradition and spiritual beliefs. Therapists may also sometimes acknowledge that it is not necessarily easy to discuss spiritual matters, and that they respect the client for having the courage to do so. Letting clients know that you do not view them as foolish or disturbed for having such beliefs might also be appropriate and necessary on some occasions, even including those where the beliefs may be psychologically dysfunctional.

Therapists should also deal with religious differences and value conflicts with clients in a respectful and tolerant manner. Differences in religious affiliation and disagreements about specific religious doctrines or moral behaviors can threaten the therapeutic alliance if they are prematurely disclosed or inappropriately addressed. When such value conflicts become salient during therapy, it is important for therapists to openly acknowledge their values while also explicitly affirming clients' rights to differ from therapists without having their intelligence or morality questioned. Therapists should also openly discuss with clients whether the belief or value conflict is so threatening that referral is advisable.

Attend to Potential Ethical Concerns

Psychotherapists who implement a spiritual perspective in their professional practices are faced with several potentially difficult ethical questions and challenges. Dual relationships (religious and professional), displacing or usurping religious authority, imposing religious values on clients, violating work setting (church–state) boundaries, and practicing outside of the boundaries of professional competence are all potential ethical pitfalls.

It is beyond the scope of this chapter to specifically discuss each of these ethical issues, however this has been done in other publications (Bergin, Payne, & Richards, 1996; Richards & Bergin, 1997; Richards & Potts, 1995; Tjeltveit, 1986; Younggren, 1993). We encourage therapists to read these publications so that they can keep these ethical dangers in mind and take steps to minimize and avoid them. We also encourage therapists to always consult with professional colleagues when these or other ethical or legal dilemmas and issues arise. This will not only help safeguard therapists from lapses in judgment or ethical oversights but also may lessen their legal liability should they get sued. Most important, it will help protect clients from harm.

We do not believe that therapists who use a spiritual approach are more likely to violate ethical or legal guidelines than are other therapists, and in some ways they may be less likely to do so. Nevertheless, therapists face additional ethical complexities when integrating spiritual perspectives into their work. Thus, it is crucial for them to be aware of these complexities and do all that they can to implement spirituality into treatment in an ethical and effective manner.

Conducting a Religious and Spiritual Assessment

A religious–spiritual assessment should be imbedded in a multisystemic assessment strategy. We recommend that when therapists first begin working with clients that they quickly and globally assess the following systems or dimensions of human functioning: physical, social, behavioral, intellectual, educational–occupational, psychological–emotional, and religious–spiritual. During this phase of the assessment process, therapists can rely primarily on client self-descriptions and their own clinical impressions about how clients are functioning in each system.

Depending on clients' presenting problems and goals, and the information obtained during the initial global phase of assessment, therapists can then proceed with more in-depth assessments of only those systems where it seems clinically warranted. More focused, probing questions can be asked during clinical interviews, and therapists might also wish to have clients complete some standardized assessment measures. During this second phase of the assessment process, therapists need not rely primarily on clients' self-descriptions of their problems and functioning, but they can draw more heavily on objective assessment measures, diagnostic criteria, and clinical theory.

During the initial global phase of the assessment process, we recommend that therapists collect only that information which will help them understand whether their clients' spiritual background and status may be relevant to their presenting problems and treatment planning. Seeking insight into the following questions may help therapists make such a determination.

1. Is the client willing to discuss religious and spiritual issues during treatment? If not, this must be respected, although the issue may be revisited if new information warrants it.
2. If the client is willing to discuss religious and spiritual issues during treatment, then what is the client's current religious–spiritual affiliation? How important is this affiliation to the client?
3. What were the client's childhood religious–spiritual background and experiences?
4. Does the client believe his or her spiritual beliefs and lifestyle are contributing to his or her presenting problems and concerns in any way?
5. Does the client have any religious and spiritual concerns and needs?
6. Is the client willing to participate in spiritual interventions if it appears that they may be helpful?
7. Does the client perceive that his or her religious and spiritual beliefs or community are a potential source of strength and assistance?

Generally speaking, a more in-depth assessment of religious and spiritual issues is indicated for clients who are religious or spiritual, perceive that their spiritual beliefs are relevant to treatment, and wish to explore spiritual issues during treatment. The objective of a second phase spiritual assessment is to determine whether a client's spiritual orientation is healthy or unhealthy, and what impact, if any, it is having on his or her presenting problems and psychological functioning. Listed below are some specific assessment questions that we have found are often clinically useful to pursue during the second phase of a spiritual assessment.

1. How orthodox is the client in his or her religious beliefs and behavior?
2. What is the client's religious problem-solving style (i.e., deferring, collaborative, self-directing)?
3. How does the client perceive God (e.g., loving and forgiving vs. impersonal and wrathful)?
4. Does the client have a sound understanding of the important doctrines and teachings of his or her religious tradition?
5. Is the client's lifestyle and behavior congruent with his or her religious and spiritual beliefs and values?
6. What stage of faith development is the client in?
7. Does the client feel a sense of spiritual well-being (e.g., is the client's relationship with God a source of comfort and strength)?

8. Is the client's religious orientation predominantly intrinsic, healthy, and mature, or is it extrinsic, unhealthy, and immature (and in what ways)?
9. In what ways, if any, are the client's religious and spiritual background, beliefs, and lifestyle impacting her or his presenting problems and disturbance?

The most viable method for seeking insight into second-phase assessment questions is the clinical interview. There are also a growing number of objective religious and spiritual research measures that have been developed, mostly from within a Christian theological framework (Hill & Hood, 1999). Because most of these research measures have not been validated in clinical situations, therapists should only use them after they have carefully examined them and verified in their own minds that they are suitable for their clients. Even then, therapists should interpret these measures tentatively.

Set Appropriate Spiritual Therapy Goals

The overall purpose of psychotherapy is to help clients cope with and resolve their presenting problems and concerns and to promote their healing, growth, and long-term well-being. Although not all clients wish to explore religious issues or pursue spiritual goals, many do. We think there are five general spiritual goals that may be appropriate for therapy, depending on the unique concerns and issues of the client. These goals, of course, should only be pursued with clients who wish to do so and should be tailored to best meet the unique needs and preferences of individual clients.

1. Help clients experience and affirm their eternal spiritual identity and live in harmony with their understanding of God's will.
2. Help clients examine and better understand what impact their religious and spiritual beliefs may be having on their presenting problems and their lives in general.
3. Help clients identify and use the religious or spiritual resources in their lives to assist them in their efforts to cope, heal, and change.
4. Help clients examine and resolve religious and spiritual concerns that are pertinent to their disorders and make choices about what role religion and spirituality will play in their lives.
5. Help clients examine how they feel about their spiritual well-being and, if they desire, help them determine how they can continue their quest for spiritual growth.

Therapists need not necessarily be religious or spiritually oriented themselves to pursue these goals. Therapists who have expanded their multicultural competency into the spiritual domain can often assist clients with these important goals. We recognize that some therapists may feel uncomfortable working on spiritual issues with clients because of lack of training or their personal views about religion and spirituality. In such circumstances, it would be appropriate and ethical for them to refer clients who wish to work on spiritual issues during treatment.

Appropriately Implement Spiritual Interventions

In our view, spiritual interventions should not be used exclusively but combined with mainstream psychological and medical approaches in a multidimensional, integrative treatment strategy. In addition, spiritual interventions should not be used rigidly or uniformly with all clients but in a flexible, treatment-tailoring manner.

At the beginning of treatment, we recommend that therapists tell clients that they approach therapy with a spiritual perspective and, when appropriate, use spiritual interventions along with standard psychological ones. Therapists should not implement spiritual interventions in treatment until they have assessed their clients' psychological functioning, spiritual background and beliefs, and attitude about exploring spiritual issues during treatment. If therapists perceive that spiritual interventions are indicated for a given client, we suggest that they clearly describe the spiritual interventions they wish to use and make sure clients feel comfortable with them. Therapists should work within the value frameworks of clients, making sure that the interventions used are in harmony with their religious beliefs. Finally, therapists should use spiritual interventions in a respectful manner, remembering that many religious believers regard these interventions as sacred religious practices.

We encourage therapists to keep in mind that there are many variables that could influence whether spiritual interventions will be appropriate and effective. We think there are at least five situations in which spiritual interventions are nearly always contraindicated: (a) when clients have made it clear they do not wish to participate in such interventions; (b) when clients are delusional or psychotic; (c) when spiritual issues are clearly not relevant to clients' presenting problems; (d) when clients are minors and their parents have not given the therapist permission to use spiritual interventions; and (e) when therapy takes place in a public, tax-supported setting that requires exclusion of religious concerns.

There may also be other situations in which spiritual interventions are not clearly contraindicated but in which they may be ineffective or perceived unfavorably by clients. For example, spiritual interventions are probably more risky and less likely to be effective when clients are young (children and adolescents), severely psychologically disturbed, antireligious or nonreligious, spiritually immature, view their spirituality as irrelevant to their presenting problems, or perceive God as distant and condemning. Spiritual interventions are also probably more risky in public and state settings than in private and religious settings. Furthermore, spiritual interventions are less likely to be effective if there is low therapist–client religious value similarity. We encourage therapists to keep these possibilities in mind as they consider whether it would be appropriate to use spiritual interventions with their clients.

PLAN OF THE BOOK

We have assembled an impressive group of contributors and a fascinating variety of cases for this book. The authors are mental health practitioners whose therapeutic approaches have been influenced by various theistic religious traditions including Islam (Sufism), Orthodox and Reform Judaism, and a variety of Christian denominations (Roman Catholic, African Methodist Episcopal, Quaker, Presbyterian, Evangelical Protestant, Seventh-day Adventist, Latter-day Saint, etc.).

Although the religious backgrounds and theoretical orientations of the contributors are relatively diverse, as are the clients described in the case studies, the contributors hold in common the view that responding sensitively to their clients' religious and spiritual issues is essential for effective treatment. The variety of ways that this can be done will become apparent as you read the case studies.

We would have liked to include an even greater diversity of theistic viewpoints in the book. Given the fact that there are more than 160 Christian denominations and numerous non-Christian theistic traditions and groups in North America (Melton, 1996), it was impossible to represent all of them. Despite space limitations, and the pragmatic difficulty of locating authors from some traditions to write chapters, we hope we have at least provided a sample of theistic therapeutic perspectives that will be useful to clinicians.

We asked each of the contributors to do their best to explicitly describe how they and their clients' theistic beliefs influenced the processes and outcomes of treatment. We also asked the contributors to provide a description of all essential aspects of their case, including client demographics, presenting problems and concerns, client history, diagnosis and assessment, treatment setting, treatment process and outcomes, and therapist commentary. We hope that this information will give you considerable insight into the dynamics, processes, and outcomes of each case.

We have grouped the case reports into three categories: (a) Programmatic, Group, and Marital Therapies, (b) Individual Denominational Therapies (Within Faiths), and (c) Individual Ecumenical Therapies (Across Faiths). This organizational scheme was a pragmatic decision to simplify and highlight some important features of the cases (i.e., what treatment modality was used and whether the spiritual approaches were applied within faiths or across faiths).

Within Part II of the book, Programmatic, Group, and Marital Therapies, cases are presented that illustrate a theistic treatment community program for a conduct-disordered adolescent girl (chap. 2, by Slife, Mitchell, & Whoolery), a theistic inpatient treatment program for a Latter-day Saint woman with an eating disorder (chap. 3, by Hardman, Berrett, & Richards), a group, interpersonal-theistic approach for adolescent, depressed Christian mothers (chap. 4, by Miller), and a theistic-marital-therapy approach for a Lutheran and Roman Catholic couple experiencing religious discord and marital conflict (chap. 5, by Krejci).

Within Part III, *Individual Denominational Therapies*, cases are presented that illustrate a psychodynamic-cognitive-theistic approach for a Protestant woman with alcohol problems (chap. 6, by Dobbins), a psychodynamic-cognitive-theistic approach as applied with several different Orthodox Jewish clients (chap. 7, by Rabinowitz), a biopsychosocial-theistic approach with a Roman Catholic woman who was struggling with perfectionistic and obsessive-compulsive tendencies (chap. 8, by Sperry), and a psychodynamic-theistic approach with a Roman Catholic woman suffering from stress and migraine headaches (chap. 9, by Shafranske).

Within Part IV, *Individual Ecumenical Therapies*, cases are presented that illustrate a person-centered, multicultural-theistic approach with a Baptist woman who was struggling with career-related stress, burnout, and identity issues (chap. 10, by Cook), a psychodynamic-cognitive-theistic approach with a Southern Baptist man who had a sexual addiction and problems relating with women (chap. 11, by Rayburn), a cognitive-psychodynamic-theistic approach with a Muslim (Sufi) convert who was experiencing conflict with his work supervisor and identity issues (chap. 12, by West), a Rational Emotive Behavior Therapy (REBT) theistic approach with a Muslim woman who was experiencing discrimination and unresolved issues from being raped (chap. 13, by Nielsen), a psychodynamic-theistic approach with a woman who was not affiliated with a religious tradition but who believed in God—and who was suffering from posttraumatic stress disorder due to catastrophic medical complications associated with a pregnancy (chap. 14, by Hedayat-Diba), a REBT-theistic approach with a Protestant adolescent boy struggling with depression about homosexual concerns (chap. 15, by Johnson), a psychodynamic-theistic approach with a Protestant man experiencing marital dissatisfaction and another psychodynamic-theistic approach with two children who were experiencing learning, impulsivity, and identity problems (chap. 16, by Lovinger & Lovinger).

As you read the case reports, we encourage you to keep in mind and reflect on the following questions:

1. How did the therapist's spiritual beliefs influence the processes and outcomes of treatment?
2. How did the client's spiritual beliefs influence the way he or she presented problems as well as the processes and outcomes of treatment?

3. How might have the processes and outcomes of this case been different if the therapeutic work had not been informed and influenced by theistic spiritual perspectives?
4. How might you have approached this case given your personal spiritual beliefs and theoretical orientation?

As you reflect on these questions and others that may be important to you personally, we anticipate that you will gain greater insight and appreciation into the variety of ways that theistic perspectives can influence psychotherapy. Of course, we do not expect you to agree with all of the ways in which theistic perspectives and interventions were applied in treatment. We did not agree with every approach that was used or therapeutic decision that is described in this book. However, if we had wanted every case report to reflect our own theistic approach, this book would have contained only our cases. That was not our desire.

We are grateful for all that we have learned through the religious and therapeutic diversity that is represented in the case reports. We hope that this will also be your experience. We feel optimistic that the cases will give you much insight into how you can more fully and effectively incorporate theistic perspectives into your own practice.

REFERENCES

American Psychiatric Association. (1994). *Diagnostic and statistical manual of mental disorders* (4th ed.). Washington, DC: Author.

Ball, R. A., & Goodyear, R. K. (1991). Self-reported professional practices of Christian psychologists. *Journal of Psychology and Christianity, 10*, 144–153.

Barbour, I. G. (1990). *Religion in an age of science: The Gifford lectures 1989–1991* (Vol. 1). San Francisco: Harper & Row.

Barbour, I. G. (1997). *When science meets religion: Enemies, strangers, or partners?* San Francisco: HarperCollins.

Barrett, D. B., & Johnson, T. M. (1998). Religion: World religious statistics. In *Encyclopaedia Britannica book of the year* (p. 314). Chicago: Encyclopaedia Britannica.

Benson, H. (1996). *Timeless healing: The power and biology of belief.* New York: Scribner.

Bergin, A. E. (1980a). Psychotherapy and religious values. *Journal of Consulting and Clinical Psychology, 48*, 75–105.

Bergin, A. E. (1980b). Religious and humanistic values: A reply to Ellis and Walls. *Journal of Consulting and Clinical Psychology, 48*, 642–645.

Bergin, A. E. (1983). Religiosity and mental health: A critical reevaluation and meta-analysis. *Professional Psychology: Research and Practice, 14*, 170–184.

Bergin, A. E. (1985). Proposed values for guiding and evaluating counseling and psychotherapy. *Counseling and Values, 29*, 99–116.

Bergin, A. E. (1988). Three contributions of a spiritual perspective to counseling, psychotherapy, and behavior change. *Counseling and Values, 32,* 21–31.

Bergin, A. E. (1991). Values and religious issues in psychotherapy and mental health. *American Psychologist, 46,* 394–403.

Bergin, A. E. (2002). *Eternal values and personal growth: A guide on your journey to spiritual, emotional, and social wellness.* Provo, UT: Brigham Young University Studies.

Bergin, A. E., Masters, K. S., Stinchfield, R. D., Gaskin, T. A., Sullivan, C. E., Reynolds, E. M., et al. (1994). Religious life-styles and mental health. In L. B. Brown (Ed.), *Religion, personality, and mental health* (pp. 69–93). New York: Springer-Verlag.

Bergin, A. E., Payne, I. R., & Richards, P. S. (1996). Values in psychotherapy. In E. Shafranske (Ed.), *Religion and the clinical practice of psychology* (pp. 297–325). Washington, DC: American Psychological Association.

Borysenko, J., & Borysenko, M. (1994). *The power of the mind to heal.* Carson, CA: Hay House.

Chamberlain, R. B., Richards, P. S., & Scharman, J. S. (1996). Spiritual perspectives and interventions in psychotherapy: A qualitative study of experienced AMCAP therapists. *AMCAP Journal, 22,* 29–74.

Collins, G. R. (1977). *The rebuilding of psychology: An integration of psychology and Christianity.* Wheaton, IL: Tyndale House.

Collins, G. R. (1988). *Christian counseling: A comprehensive guide* (Rev. ed.). Dallas, TX: Word Publishing.

Eccles, J., & Robinson, D. N. (1984). *The wonder of being human: Our brain and our mind.* New York: Free Press.

Elkins, D. N. (1995). Psychotherapy and spirituality: Toward a theory of the soul. *Journal of Humanistic Psychology, 35,* 78–98.

Emmons, R. A. (1999). *The psychology of ultimate concerns: Motivation and spirituality in personality.* New York: Guilford Press.

Epstein, M. (1995). *Thoughts without a thinker: Psychotherapy from a Buddhist perspective.* New York: Basic Books.

Faiver, C., Ingersoll, R. E., O'Brien, E., & McNally, C. (2001). *Explorations in counseling and spirituality.* Belmont, CA: Wadsworth Group.

Griffin, D. R. (2000). *Religion and naturalism: Overcoming the conflicts.* Albany: State University of New York Press.

Griffin, D. R. (2001). *Reenchantment without supernaturalism.* Ithaca, NY: Cornell University Press.

Griffith, J. L., & Griffith, M. E. (2002). *Encountering the sacred in psychotherapy: How to talk with people about their spiritual lives.* New York: Guilford Press.

Hedayat-Diba, Z. (2000). Psychotherapy with Muslims. In P. S. Richards & A. E. Bergin (Eds.), *Handbook of psychotherapy and religious diversity* (pp. 289–314). Washington, DC: American Psychological Association.

Helminiak, D. A. (1996). *The human core of spirituality: Mind as psyche and spirit.* Albany: State University of New York Press.

Henning, L. H., & Tirrell, F. J. (1982). Counselor resistance to spiritual exploration. *The Personnel and Guidance Journal, 61*(2), 92–95.

Hill, C. H., & Hood, R. W. (1999). *Measures of religiosity.* Birmingham, AL: Religious Education Press.

Jensen, J. P., & Bergin, A. E. (1988). Mental health values of professional therapists: A national interdisciplinary survey. *Professional Psychology: Research and Practice, 19,* 290–297.

Jones, S. L. (1994). A constructive relationship for religion with the science and profession of psychology: Perhaps the boldest model yet. *American Psychologist, 49,* 184–199.

Keller, R. R. (2000). Religious diversity in North America. In P. S. Richards & A. E. Bergin (Eds.), *Handbook of psychotherapy and religious diversity* (pp. 27–55). Washington, DC: American Psychological Association.

Kelly, E. W. (1995). *Religion and spirituality in counseling and psychotherapy.* Richmond, VA: American Counseling Association.

Larson, D. B., & Larson, S. (1994). *The forgotten factor in physical and mental health: What does the research show?* Rockville, MD: National Institute for Healthcare Research.

Lovinger, R. J. (1984). *Working with religious issues in therapy.* New York: Jason Aronson.

Malony, H. N. (1985). Assessing religious maturity. In E. M. Stern (Ed.), *Psychotherapy and the religiously committed patient* (pp. 25–33). New York: Haworth Press.

Melton, J. G. (1996). *Encyclopedia of American religions.* Detroit, MI: Gale Research.

Miller, W. R. (1999). *Integrating spirituality into treatment: Resources for practitioners.* Washington, DC: American Psychological Association.

Miller, W. R., & C'deBaca, J. (1994). Quantum change: Toward a psychology transformation. In T. Heatherton & J. Weinberger (Eds.), *Can personality change?* (pp. 253–280). Washington, DC: American Psychological Association.

Nielsen, S. L., Johnson, W. B., & Ellis, A. (2001). *Counseling and psychotherapy with religious persons: A Rational Emotive Behavior Therapy approach.* Mahwah, NJ: Erlbaum.

Peck, M. S. (1978). *The road less traveled: A new psychology of love, traditional values, and spiritual growth.* New York: Simon & Schuster.

Provine, W. (1988). Progress in evolution and meaning in life. In M. H. Nitecki (Ed.), *Evolutionary progress* (pp. 49–74). Chicago: University of Chicago Press.

Rabinowitz, A. (2001). *Judaism and psychology: Meeting points.* New York: Jason Aronson.

Richards, P. S. (1999, August). *Spiritual influences in healing and psychotherapy.* Paper presented as the William C. Bier Award Invited Address, Division 36 (Psychology of Religion) at the 107th Annual Convention of the American Psychological Association, Boston.

Richards, P. S., & Bergin, A. E. (1997). *A spiritual strategy for counseling and psychotherapy.* Washington, DC: American Psychological Association.

Richards, P. S., & Bergin, A. E. (Eds.). (2000). *Handbook of psychotherapy and religious diversity.* Washington, DC: American Psychological Association.

Richards, P. S., & Potts, R. W. (1995). Using spiritual interventions in psychotherapy: Practices, successes, failures, and ethical concerns of Mormon psychotherapists. *Professional Psychology: Research and Practice, 26,* 163–170.

Richards, P. S., Rector, J. R., & Tjeltveit, A. C. (1999). Values, spirituality, and psychotherapy. In W. R. Miller (Ed.), *Integrating spirituality in treatment: Resources for practitioners* (pp. 133–160). Washington, DC: American Psychological Association.

Rubin, J. B. (1996). *Psychotherapy and Buddhism: Toward an integration.* New York: Plenum Press.

Schroeder, G. L. (2001). *The hidden face of God: How science reveals the ultimate truth.* New York: Free Press.

Shafranske, E. P. (Ed.). (1996). *Religion and the clinical practice of psychology.* Washington, DC: American Psychological Association.

Sharma, A. R. (2000). Psychotherapy with Hindus. In P. S. Richards & A. E. Bergin (Eds.), *Handbook of psychotherapy and religious diversity* (pp. 341–365). Washington, DC: American Psychological Association.

Slife, B. D. (2003). Theoretical challenges to therapy practice and research: The constraint of naturalism. In M. J. Lambert (Ed.), *Bergin and Garfield's Handbook of psychotherapy and behavior change* (5th ed., pp. 44–83). New York: Wiley.

Slife, B. D., Hope, C., & Nebeker, R. S. (1999). Examining the relationship between religious spirituality and psychological science. *Journal of Humanistic Psychology, 39,* 51–85.

Smart, N. (1983). *Worldviews: Crosscultural explorations of human beliefs.* New York: Scribner.

Smart, N. (1994). *Religions of the West.* Englewood Cliffs, NJ: Prentice Hall.

Spero, M. H. (Ed.). (1985). *Psychotherapy of the religious patient.* Springfield, IL: Charles C Thomas.

Sperry, L. (2001). *Spirituality in clinical practice: Incorporating the spiritual dimension in psychotherapy and counseling.* Philadelphia: Brunner-Routledge.

Sue, D. W. & Sue, D. (1990). *Counseling the culturally different: Theory and practice* (2nd ed.). New York: Wiley.

Sue, S., Zane, N., & Young, K. (1994). Research on psychotherapy with culturally diverse populations. In A. E. Bergin & S. L. Garfield (Eds.), *Handbook of psychotherapy and behavior change* (4th ed., pp. 783–817). New York: Wiley.

Swinton, J. (2001). *Spirituality and mental health care.* London: Jessica Kingsley.

Templeton, J. M., & Herrmann, R. L. (1994). *Is God the only reality? Science points to a deeper meaning of the universe.* New York: Continuum.

Tjeltveit, A. C. (1986). The ethics of value conversion in psychotherapy: Appropriate and inappropriate therapist influence on client values. *Clinical Psychology Review, 6,* 515–537.

Vaughan, F., Wittine, B., & Walsh, R. (1996). Transpersonal psychology and the religious person. In E. Shafranske (Ed.), *Religion and the clinical practice of psychology* (pp. 483–509). Washington, DC: American Psychological Association.

West, W. (2000). *Psychotherapy and spirituality: Crossing the line between therapy and religion.* London: Sage.

Younggren, J. N. (1993). Ethical issues in religious psychotherapy. *Register Report, 19,* 1, 7–8.

II

PROGRAMMATIC, GROUP, AND MARITAL THERAPIES

2

A THEISTIC APPROACH TO THERAPEUTIC COMMUNITY: NON-NATURALISM AND THE ALLDREDGE ACADEMY

BRENT D. SLIFE, L. JAY MITCHELL, AND MATTHEW WHOOLERY

Although the short tradition of theistic therapy has emphasized the individual client, the long tradition of theism itself has often emphasized the community. The Hebrew tradition of theism, for instance, emphasizes community almost exclusively (Boman, 1960; Dueck, 1995; Lohfink, 1984). It includes not only community-based "interventions"—divine and mortal—but also community discernment of the Spirit and even community salvation. Consequently, the formulation of a theistic approach to therapeutic communities, as described herein, is an obvious and a necessary extension of this long theistic tradition (a tradition that says God is actively involved in the events of the world).

The problem is that most therapeutic communities have been founded on the secular philosophy of naturalism. The popularity of this philosophy is understandable. Many psychotherapists view it as an advance over the mystical and magical paradigms of the premodern era, and many view it as a relatively nonpartisan and objective philosophy regarding religion. Although we agree, in some sense, with the first view, we cannot agree with the second. Indeed, we agree with Richards and Bergin (1997) that the philosophy of naturalism is incompatible with theism. If this is true, then a theistic approach to therapeutic communities cannot be naturalistic.

The purpose of this chapter is to describe a particular client's therapeutic path through a *non*-naturalistic therapeutic community. We begin by outlining briefly the problematic nature of naturalism for theistic therapy. We next compare and contrast five of the major assumptions of naturalism to a non-naturalistic philosophy—one that we believe clears a conceptual space for a true theism to be practiced. As an illustration of this non-naturalistic philosophy, we then describe a particular theistic therapeutic community—the Alldredge Academy—and report one client's therapeutic journey through the Academy.

NATURALISM AND THERAPEUTIC COMMUNITY

Several scholars and therapists have recently noted how problematic the philosophy of reductive naturalism (hereafter, naturalism) is for psychology, especially as the field attempts to incorporate theistic interventions (Collins, 1977; Gunton, 1993; Leahey, 1991; Richards & Bergin, 1997; Slife, 2003; Slife, Hope, & Nebeker, 1999; Smith, 2001). However, this philosophy is increasingly fueled by the perceived need to make the field more scientific and biological. As Leahey (1991) notes, naturalism is "science's central dogma" (p. 379). Consequently, as psychotherapy has moved increasingly toward natural sciences such as medicine, this "central dogma" has become increasingly influential. Indeed, this dogma has, like many other dogmas, foreclosed many conceptual and clinical options that were once open to exploration (Slife, 2003), including theistic options. What is this foreclosing philosophical "dogma?"

The philosophy of naturalism essentially postulates that laws or principles ultimately govern the events of nature, including human nature (cf. Griffin, 2000; Honer & Hunt, 1987; Leahey, 1991; Richards & Bergin, 1997; Slife, 2003; Smith, 2001; Viney & King, 2003). From laws of gravity to principles of pleasure (psychoanalysis), reinforcement (behaviorism), and organismic enhancement (humanism), these types of natural laws and principles supposedly govern all aspects of human beings, including our bodies, minds, and even spirits. Unfortunately for theism, this secular philosophy implies that other entities, such as God, do not govern these aspects of humanity. Natural laws and theoretical principles essentially fill up the conceptual space where God might be, explaining human behavior and cognition without requiring a God of any kind (Whoolery, Slife, & Mitchell, 2002). Because theism does require a God, by definition, naturalism and theism are often viewed as incompatible philosophies in principle (cf. Griffin, 2000).

Naturalism is so prevalent, however, that many theists attempt to make naturalism compatible with theism. The most popular attempt at compatibility is deism—the claim that God created the natural laws. However, naturalism assumes that the operation of these laws is independent of any deity or Supreme Being. Although a deity may have originally created the laws, the laws now operate on their own. Moreover, the laws and principles must be universal and unchangeable in order to be lawful. If a deity is assumed to exist at all, then it cannot disrupt or suspend these laws on any particular or regular basis, or the laws would no longer be lawful (Griffin, 2000). Most theisms are thus impossible in this naturalistic account. A deity may exist, to be sure, but it is rendered passive and effectively nonexistent because naturalism does not permit it to actively change or disrupt the regular, autonomous operation of these laws. The universe is assumed to work as it always has, whether or not this god exists.

COMPARING NATURALISTIC AND NON-NATURALISTIC ASSUMPTIONS

We believe that the best way to make these issues clear, particularly for therapeutic communities, is to explicate the assumptions involved. Assumptions are taken-for-granted beliefs about the world. All therapists make assumptions because they postulate a world in which their techniques are effective. Slife (2003) has described the role of five of naturalism's major assumptions in individual psychotherapy (as well as each assumption's problems and alternatives): objectivism, materialism, hedonism, atomism, and universalism. Although the labels have sometimes differed, other scholars have concurred with these five assumptions and noted others: determinism (Baldwin & Slife, 2003; Richards & Bergin, 1997), rational order (Rychlak, 1988; Slife, 2001), reductionism (Griffin, 2000; Slife & Williams, 1995), and empiricism (Collins, 1977; Viney & King, 2003).

Unfortunately, the implicit status of these assumptions means that few therapists *explicitly* claim or acknowledge them in their practices. Many therapists are unfamiliar with the subtle nature of assumptions and often do not recognize their own assumptions or the assumptions of therapeutic practices across the field. These therapists will undoubtedly need more explanation (and space) than is permitted in this chapter (cf. Valentine, 1992). We ask the reader's indulgence here and refer them to the references provided as well as the introductory chapter of this volume. Our purpose here is to briefly compare and contrast five naturalistic and five non-naturalistic assumptions that specifically pertain to therapeutic community (see Table 2.1). As we shall show, these assumptions are pivotal to the formulation and practice of therapeutic community.

We anticipate that many mental health professionals will resist the implied "versus" (either–or) of the items in Table 2.1, which is rendered

TABLE 2.1
Comparison of Assumptions in the Therapeutic Community

Naturalistic assumptions	Non-naturalistic assumptions
Objective: To obtain a true understanding of natural objects, including humans, therapeutic and scientific methods should strive for and can be value-free.	**Value-laden:** To obtain a true understanding of humans, therapeutic and scientific methods should embrace the inescapability of values.
Hedonic: The chief good and *ultimate* constant motivation of all natural beings, including humans, is self-benefit.	**Altruistic:** The chief good and *ultimate* motivation of all humans can and should be the benefit of others.
Determined: Natural laws and/or principles govern the actions of humans, preventing them from acting otherwise.	**Agentic:** Natural laws and/or principles do not govern human action, allowing them to act otherwise than they did.
Rational: The order of natural events and human understanding is rational and thus evidences logical consistency.	**Dialectic:** The order of human events and understanding is not solely rational but also inconsistent and even paradoxical.
Atomistic: The qualities of all natural objects, including humans, are self-contained within the objects themselves.	**Holistic:** The qualities of humans are not self-contained, but instead stem from their relationships to other humans.

more explicit in our narrative description of the comparison that follows. However, assumptions are peculiar beasts. They are not factors that can be combined, nor are they variables that interact; they are foundational philosophical conceptions that rule out, in principle, other foundational philosophical conceptions. This is not to say that some assumptions are not compatible with other assumptions. It is only to say that all assumptions rule out, and are incompatible with, *some* other assumptions. In the case of the naturalistic assumptions of Table 2.1, the *ideas* of their non-naturalistic counterparts (and not the *labels* per se) are disjunctive—incompatible by definition (Slife, 2003; Slife & Williams, 1995). Consequently, we compare each pair of assumptions, in turn, and then describe a therapy case in which the non-naturalistic assumptions were applied successfully at the Alldredge Academy.

Objective Versus Value-Laden

Objectivism is the naturalistic notion that all worthy methods, including therapeutic techniques and scientific methods, should *strive* to be objective and value-free (Bernstein, 1983; Richardson, Fowers, & Guignon, 1999; Slife, 2003). Although professionals are themselves biased by their values, the logic of objectivism is that removing biases as much as possible removes distortions of our knowledge of the natural world, including the natural world of therapy. As applied to therapeutic communities, therapeutic techniques should be derived from value-free scientific methods as much as possible. Also, such techniques should not themselves have implicit values that bias them against client value systems (e.g., religions, traditions, ethnicity, and gender).

The position of the Alldredge Academy, by contrast, is that values are not only inescapable but also necessary for understanding. All therapeutic communities (including the naturalistic) accept and reject, and promote and discourage particular values, whether or not they acknowledge it (Slife, Smith, & Burchfield, 2003). This position implies that the therapists of such communities should identify and prominently present their values (and assumptions) for the purposes of informed consent—*especially* regarding their methods and strategies (Slife & Richards, 2001). Another crucial task (value) of any such community is helping clients to discern the values that are best suited for them and their circumstances. Therapists will purvey values, and clients will adopt them, regardless of the therapeutic system, so this process of purveying and adopting should occur deliberately rather than by default.

Hedonic Versus Altruistic

Hedonism is the notion that the chief good and ultimate motivation of all natural beings is self-preservation and self-benefit (Webster's New Collegiate Dictionary, 1981; Slife, 2000, 2003). If a species consistently seeks pain instead of pleasure, then this pain seeking invites evolutionary extinction. As applied to a therapeutic community, this assumption implies that the chief good and most important motivator for therapeutic communities is client benefits (in exchange for therapist benefits; Fisher-Smith, 2000). Client self-benefit is the primary goal (even if helping others is the means) and self-benefit is the primary client motivator (e.g., self-actualization) for achieving this goal.

The altruistic position of the Alldredge Academy, however, assumes that all people can be ultimately motivated by and for others (e.g., other-actualization). The "can" here is important because this particular altruistic position focuses on capability. It does not obviate the possibility of self as a motivator; it merely claims that self-benefit is not the most natural (fundamental) or only motivator. As applied to therapeutic communities, the end of any action (by therapist or client) should not be the self, with the means being other people (as with hedonism). The end must be others, with the means being the self. Benefits can *ensue* from the caring of others, but true self-benefit cannot be *pursued* (Slife, 1999; Yalom, 1980).

Determined Versus Agentic

Because naturalism assumes that physical laws and principles govern the real world—including the human world—human behavior and cognition are determined (Richards & Bergin, 1997). We may not yet know the principles that are responsible for determining behavior (e.g., biological or social principles), but they determine it nevertheless. Determinism is not about limits here but about what is *responsible for* things and events. As applied to therapeutic communities, physical and social laws are responsible for human behavior. Therefore, the psychotherapist's job is to discern those laws (or postulate them through theory), as much as possible, and manipulate them in instrumental ways that benefit the client (determinism plus hedonism; Richardson & Bishop, 2002).

The Alldredge Academy assumes that the clients themselves contribute intentionally to their own behavior (agency) (Howard, 1994; Rychlak, 1988). This assumption does not exclude the contextual importance of the environment and biology, but it does reorient the notion of ultimate responsibility and thus modifies conceptions of causality and intervention (Slife, 2002; Slife & Fisher, 2000). As applied to therapeutic community, it means that clients can and should be held responsible for their own actions, and interventions can only *facilitate* healing experiences (an introspective perspective) and not *cause* behavior change (an extraspective perspective) (Rychlak, 1981).

Rational Versus Dialectical

The lawfulness of natural laws is thought to imply their rational consistency (Gunton, 1993; Rychlak, 1988; Smith, 2001). The laws and principles of a therapeutic community must also occur in an orderly and even logical fashion. They are not disorderly or irrational, implying that the most effective therapeutic interventions are themselves logical and consistent. For example, interventions should be consistent, rather than inconsistent, with the stated goals of therapy. Because clients are typically encouraged to frame their goals hedonistically (e.g., self-benefit), the assumption of rational consistency is often combined with hedonism to mean "consistent with self-benefit" (Shaver, 1999).

At the Alldredge Academy, however, rational consistency, in this sense, is intentionally violated to enhance dialectical relations (and altruistic relations). Instead of assuming that the primary relations among therapeutic events are (or should be) relations of rational consistency (Rychlak, 1988), this position implies that "inconsistency" and paradox are just as important as consistency and rationality, particularly in a therapeutic community. For example, particular learning opportunities are facilitated through paradoxical interventions in which clients are jolted from their typical ways of thinking and reasoning.

Atomistic Versus Holistic

The philosophy of naturalism assumes that the qualities of all objects (e.g., the atom) are inherent in the objects themselves. That is, if we want to understand a particular object, we must study the object itself and not the objects that surround it (atomism). In the behavioral sciences, atomism has implied that the basic unit of study is the self-contained individual, not the group or culture (Richardson et al., 1999). If a therapeutic group or community is studied at all, it is often viewed as a collection of individuals, each with his or her own self-contained qualities (e.g., reinforcement history, cognitive schema, or intrapsychic structure).

The Alldredge Academy, conversely, believes the focus should be the relationships among the individuals of a therapeutic community (i.e., the community itself). This focus was, in fact, the original impetus for healing theistic communities. Just as any part of a whole gets many of its qualities from its relation to other parts, so too individuals of a community get many of their qualities from their relationships to other individuals (Slife et al., 1999). As applied to a theistic therapeutic community, the group or team is as important as the individual, and meaningful relationships are more important than individual self-benefits.

TREATMENT PROCESS AND OUTCOME

Therapeutic Setting

The Alldredge Academy is a rare example of an authentically non-naturalistic treatment philosophy that is compatible with theism. As discussed previously, naturalistic assumptions do not require divine beings. These assumptions are themselves naturalistic principles (e.g., hedonism) that operate much like natural laws—autonomously and automatically (mechanistically). The Alldredge Academy, by contrast, assumes that none of the assumptions of non-naturalism are possible or helpful without the *Source*—the Academy's term for God or Spirit. True altruism, for example, is not attainable without the inspiration of this divine entity. Although this philosophy–theology is obviously compatible with theism, the Academy is not typically viewed as a religiously based community per se. It is, instead, more ecumenical, accommodating several widely varying theistic traditions and worldviews, from Christian to Jew to Muslim.

The Alldredge Academy is located in the mountains of West Virginia, where rugged terrain and beautiful vistas are commonplace. Alldredge is an accredited school with more than 500 graduates to date, typically of the one-semester (3-month) program. At full capacity, the academy can accommodate 72 students along with 71 staff members. All counselors receive an initial 4 week, 10 hour per day course of training in the non-naturalistic Alldredge model. In addition to regular weekly supervision, they receive a 4-hour training session every second week, with another 4-week training stint every year. The owner/director of the Alldredge Academy (L. J. Mitchell) developed

Client Background

To bring the academy alive, we follow the experiences of a recent resident and "student," Laura (a pseudonym). We reconstruct salient aspects of her therapeutic journey through Alldredge with the help of an extensive collection of treatment notes and a three-inch pile of Laura's own journal entries. Laura is a 16-year-old Caucasian girl with no particular denominational affiliation and custodial grandparents. Both her birth mother and father were addicted to drugs, and neither parent was currently active in Laura's life. Prior to attending Alldredge, Laura was admitted to an inpatient psychiatric ward for a series of incidents, including running away, heavy drug use, and misdemeanor convictions for shoplifting and truancy. She was diagnosed in this hospital as having attention-deficit/hyperactivity disorder (ADHD) with secondary depression and placed on Prozac, but her problematic behaviors continued. Therefore, an educational consultant, with expertise in the special needs of youth, referred her to the Alldredge Academy.

Laura arrived at the academy in May and joined a group of eight other adolescent students for at least a 3-month (semester) experience, including at least 1 month in "mountain search and rescue," 1 month in the "village," and 1 month in the "school." Her custodians asked that Alldredge help her to stop the drug and antisocial behavior, develop new learning strategies, and diminish her depression. The other adolescents of her group had similar profiles, with the group moving together through the 3-month journey and sharing experiences with similar size groups along the way.

Mountain Search and Rescue Phase

On arrival, members of the group were taken to the Canaan Valley, which consists of high elevation mountainous terrain. They were outfitted for continuous camping and told they would be trained as a search and rescue team, with all the technical, emotional, and physical skills necessary to save someone's life. Laura was "absolutely shocked," as she writes in her journal, by the notion that she was not there primarily for herself. In fact, this was her first exposure to the concept of true altruism, real teamwork, and a life based on service (though initially the staff never mentioned these concepts). Even at this early stage, the instructional staff was clearly led by two violations of the philosophy of naturalism. First, students are not there for their own benefit (hedonism); they are there for someone else's benefit entirely (altruism). Second, as Laura will learn, she is not there to cultivate her individuality (atomism); she is there to cultivate the team (holism).

These concepts are foreign to Laura, so she resists them. However, the "instructors" do not attempt to convince or persuade her of anything (except that she will successfully complete the program). Indeed, this is one of the salient features of Alldredge. Although the instructors are committed to an explicit set of broad values such as love, integrity, hope, and valor, there is no preaching or proselytizing. Instead, the instructors model these values and facilitate experiences that aid the students in coming to *their own values* by and through the Source. In fact, there is considerable evidence that the Mountain Search and Rescue phase facilitates the students' desire to explore different values and seek inspiration to come to their own value systems.

How do the instructors facilitate such experiences? Two of the main guiding principles are themselves violations of naturalism: agency and the dialectic. In the case of agency, Laura is expected to be responsible for herself, because she is the agent of her own actions. She learns quickly that important wilderness skills are required to care for others (as a member of the rescue team) and herself. For the first time in many years, she seeks the advice of adults (because they volunteer very little)—and she listens. Hedonists may assume that progress here is the result of natural reinforcement contingencies, but the entire thrust of the group is precisely the opposite. Although it is true that the staff is supportive of Laura taking responsibility for her needs, her needs are only important insofar as she can be trusted as a team member to save the life of another. In other words, even her responsibility (and agency) is holistic and altruistic. She is not the individualistic end; she is the relational means to serving others.

Of course, Laura has many old thought and behavioral patterns that help her avoid personal responsibility and meaningful relationships. Again, however, the instructors never cajole or preach. They instead help her to generate her own lessons dialectically. That is, they act inconsistently with Laura's "logic," even (seemingly) the logic of the program itself. At one point, for example, Laura became frustrated with "doing all the stupid stuff everyone else is doing," because she was "not like them." Rather than the instructors urging her to "stay with the program" or "take care of herself" (consistent with the logic of their seeming purpose), they apologized for not recognizing her uniqueness, moved her bedroll away from the group, and had her turn her sweater inside out to honor her uniqueness. After all, she could not be part of a group to which she did not belong. After 3 days, Laura tearfully requested that the group accept her back, but there were tense moments as the group sincerely considered her request. Laura responded to their eventual acceptance with cheerful enthusiasm for all her personal and team duties.

Such dialectical interventions have sometimes been labeled "paradoxical" (e.g., Watzlawick, 1984). However, they are only paradoxical from a deterministic, naturalistic perspective. When agency is truly incorporated into the philosophy of treatment, dialectical interventions are a logical consequence. In other words, the dialectic does not tell the instructors to be inconsistent with their values; the dialectic merely recognizes that contrasting meanings are intimately related to one another. When clients have agency, especially adolescents, therapists will rarely persuade them with logic and rationality, particularly if their patterns of decision making are ingrained and longstanding. Therapists must therefore help clients to experience the contrast of their treatment goals so they can truly understand and desire the goals for themselves.

Consider another of the many small and large dialectical interventions with Laura. Although Laura worked more responsibly and cooperatively, she resisted the search and rescue training in other ways. For instance, she constantly interrupted instructors with wisecracks and invited other students to join in. Instead of the instructors chastising or attempting to extinguish this behavior, they "reinforced" it. They lauded Laura for her comedy and gave her the team responsibility for being funny, an "important responsibility" when the "going gets tough" (e.g., in a steady rain). This reframed her individualistic (and thus atomistic) behavior as a service to the team (holism) and their altruistic tasks, and Laura rapidly tired of her responsibility. Not only did she find it hard to provide wisecracks during these tough times, she also found very few people laughing with her. She solemnly asked the group for a release from her responsibilities, abandoned her "clown" pattern, and never interrupted anyone again.

Laura generally found herself "confused" by these experiences, as she wrote in her journal. For some reason, her usual "games" were not getting their usual result. In addition, she was experiencing other feelings that seemed odd yet positive—feelings of belonging, camaraderie, caring, and a willingness to be taught. As she reports, a particular incident helped these positive feelings overcome her negative confusion. The local sheriff asked the team to find a battered woman who had apparently taken refuge in the mountains from her drunken husband. The woman's relatives were convinced that she was lost and were afraid her husband would find her before anyone else and abuse her again. Laura and her team worked like a well-oiled machine, not only locating the woman and providing first aid but also shielding her at one point from her threatening husband.

Laura recalls being completely unafraid for herself during this incident, although she was voluntarily taking personal risks. She was so involved in caring for and protecting the woman that she now believes she found herself through this service. Not coincidentally, all five of the factors of non-naturalism were included in this growth-producing incident. In other words, she found herself in a moral (value-laden) situation that led her to choose (agentically) to cooperate with the team (holistically) and give of herself (altruistically) for the sake of another. The paradox (dialectic) of the situation is that Laura may have benefited most from an incident that was not, ostensibly, for her sake at all.

There is, of course, much more to the wilderness experience. However, the net effect for Laura, like so many other students, was that she now yearned for something more substantive than her "silly games," as she came to call them. After an emotional but productive visit with her family (during the Alldredge parent–student program), her journal indicates that she wanted to know how to be a good friend, how to best help others, how to be respectful, and how to love (altruism).

The Village Phase

In the village phase of her journey, Laura often turned to her instructors for easy answers. However, the village is not set up to provide easy answers; it is set up dialectically for Laura to experientially discover these answers for herself. Although specific virtues such as love, hope, integrity, and forgiveness are extolled and discussed in the village, these virtues are not viewed as ends in themselves; they are viewed as the means for Laura to arrive at her own answers and own moral system in relation to her community (value ladenness). The hope is that students will find a more productive and loving identity. The village is designed to help them choose to change their irresponsible victim image by connecting to the Source, discovering a sense of mission and life purpose, and living more virtuously.

The village is a group of primitive hutlike structures nestled between two rivers. Yet, the village was "luxury" to Laura after her monthlong camping and hiking experiences (a dialectic appreciation for "what I usually take for granted"). Village experiences are divided into four "Journeys," with each journey essentially representing a different system of theistic values from a particular primitive culture. The four Journeys together form a dialectic, through contrasts and oppositions, bringing hidden life meanings to each student's awareness.

As the students enter each Journey, they enter a culture—living like, thinking like, and basically trying on the values and spirit of each culture. For Laura (as she reports in her journal), this dialectic helped her to gain a "perspective" on her teenage culture, beliefs, and spirit. Relationship issues are a main focus (holism), with students counseling each other to trod the "path of virtue" (value ladenness). Each night there is a truth circle where a truth stick is passed to each student and feelings are expressed. As problems are identified, students must take personal responsibility for solving their problems rather than blaming others (agency).

The Journeys also provide students with value-clarifying experiences. For example, part of the South Journey is the theme of the Shadow (a somewhat Jungian conception). Laura learned that her greatest fear and pain came from her Shadow. On one occasion, she made a list of three people whom she "most hated," listing two characteristics of each that were particularly disgusting. As she described these characteristics and her loathing for them in the group, her peers and instructors began to help her see her loathing for these characteristics in herself. She began to see these characteristics as part of herself, her Shadow, in relation to the community (holism). She learned as she reclaimed, examined, and released them that she was less harsh with herself and others.

The students spent the entire week of the South Journey noting how each other's shadows waxed or waned. One of the wonders of the village is one of the missing elements of our society—constant, loving, but brutally honest, feedback to one another. Students and instructors can deliver this type of feedback because the students themselves invite it. Indeed, they hunger for it. As a culminating South Journey experience, Laura vividly reports that she and her group entered a "deep and mysterious" cave called the "den of the serpent." One by one, the members of her group shared their shadows, discussed how they affected their friendships, and then "left" them in the cave chamber. Laura was "deeply moved" by this experience and felt considerable relief from "unloading my 'shadowy' burdens." More important, she found herself "a better friend," a "better leader," and a "better listener"— again, the Alldredge emphasis on altruistic relationships rather than self.

Uniting all the Journeys is the Source. Indeed, the Alldredge instructors see the Source as uniting all their therapeutic interventions, from the Mountain Search and Rescue phase to the end of the program (holism). However, the notion of a Source is made less explicit in the wilderness because the students are typically not ready (i.e., they may not initially desire the guidance the Source can bring). Still, the instructors attempt to facilitate student experiences of the Source. They assume the Source is already present; their only job is to facilitate "spiritual" experiences and loving relationships that help the students to sense and acknowledge the Source (however they might conceive of it).

Before leaving a campsite, for example, the instructors routinely assemble the group for a moment of silence—a silence that can only be appreciated if one has been in the mountains of West Virginia. Students are also asked to go "solo," camping (under the watchful eye of the instructor) alone. The hunger here for any mind-occupying activity is deep, so students are given short novels that bristle with "Source" themes. As Laura says in her journal, "I was pulled into the book at the start—the love, the conflict, the caring. I had forgotten the awesome feeling books had always given me." Laura also discussed the "religious" experience of her "team" rescuing the woman (both in group discussion and her journal)—how she felt empowered by "something," how she felt prompted by "something," how "something" helped her "to care more about her than me."

In the Village, the Source is discussed more explicitly and directly. If students show an interest in the Source, they are directed to consider their own experiences. Spiritual experiences are described and students are asked if they have ever felt anything like these. Without exception (particularly when students have already shown an interest), they reply that they have experienced similar "communications" with the Source. The students are then asked if they would like to enhance and deepen these communications. For example, the North Journey—the Finder of the Truth—is a series of exercises/experiences to accomplish this enhancement, including (for Laura) a realization of her history with the Source, an acknowledgment of the Source's reliability, and some skills in distinguishing counterfeit sources. She eventually learned that deepening this communication meant letting go of the "image management" and "personal agenda" that she believed originally led to her addiction.

At one point, Laura asked her instructors for advice about "praying." In keeping with the Alldredge lack of explicit direction, the instructors offered several options (dialectic), with Laura choosing one (agency). As she put the experience in her journal, "I asked Carrie [the instructor] to show me, Brad, and Julie how to create Indian prayer ties. She gave each of us five squares of fabric and a string. We picked a pinch of ashes out of a bowl, held it up, silently thought our prayer, held it to our hearts, then wrapped it and tied it to our strings. It was one of the coolest things I'd ever done. I told Julie I was glad we shared this together and gave Brad and her hugs." Laura later connects these good feelings to the wholeness and relationships she felt, which "could only have come from the Source."

Well known to all present and former students of the Alldredge Academy is that no one, but no one, ever wants to leave the village. Its soil is considered almost sacred and holy. It is viewed as a place of vital discoveries as well as a location of deep security and incredible relatedness to the instructors, the other students, the land, and perhaps most of all, the Source who unites them all. Laura reported the same feelings in her journal. However, she also admitted considerable fear and anxiety. How was she going to leave this "womb?" How could she face "school" and all the "crap" that this might bring with it? She felt she had "new wings," but now they would really be tested. Could she fly?

The School Phase

The school phase is intentionally more "school" oriented to provide a more realistic transition from the academy. After another 4-day round of family therapy, more traditional coursework is studied and more conventional schedules are kept. However, school counselors are plentiful, and considerable time is allotted for "conversation" and the "future." Here, the goal is to consolidate the often incredible emotional and relational gains made and provide a means by which these gains can be translated into a life of service "on the outside" (altruism). Although this transition is a familiar problem to any counselor in a therapeutic community, the main academy tool for solving this problem is perhaps less familiar, at least less profession-ally familiar—the Source.

As an explicitly non-naturalistic, theistic model, the Alldredge Acad-emy recognizes that the only part of the students' therapeutic context that they will always be able to take with them is the Source (along with the sense of life purpose and virtue that accompanies the Source). Few, if any, students will end up in a place as beautiful as the mountains of West Virginia. Few, if any, students will ever experience again the magic associated with saving a life. Few, if any, students will experience another "village," with its loving relationships, mysterious caves, and constant personal feedback. Still, from the perspective of the Academy instructors, all these things were produced by and are presently available in the Source (holism). Moreover, the Source can never be stolen, mutilated, or deceived. It can only be rejected, in spite of its imminent and universal accessibility.

Consequently, the mission of the "school" is to transfer and consolidate the experiences and insights related to the Source. Instructors accomplish this task by continuing the spiritual scaffolding and dialectic begun by the Journeys (and their dialectical relations). What lessons did you learn? How are you applying them in this new context? How are they fading, conflicting, hurting you? How can they be enhanced? With Laura, the West Journey had always been her Achilles heel. Reasoning dialectically, she also knew that this was her greatest opportunity for relational growth. She also had the fervent wish to serve the Source and somehow this challenge was her best way to effect this service (altruism). Therefore, she and her counselor set their sights on understanding and overcoming her struggles with the West Journey.

Although the West Journey is adorned with important symbols of primi-tive cultures such as the Invisible Warrior, its main theme (or virtue) is for-giveness (value ladenness). Laura admitted to having many problems with this virtue, problems in forgiving herself and problems in forgiving others. She knew and endorsed the concept intellectually, but she also knew that she did not "know it in my heart." She also knew that the Source would not be wholly available to her when she left the Alldredge Academy if she did not work through her struggles with this virtue. Rather than her usual "games" with such struggles—isolating herself and avoiding the things that really mattered—she turned to the members of her group (along with the school counselors) and made a point of asking their help in investigating her prob-lems with forgiveness (agency and holism).

Through an honest, forthright, and courageous give-and-take with her peers and instructors, Laura realized that she had several preconceptions about the notion of forgiveness from her journal:

1. Forgiveness means giving someone permission to continue
    their wrong behavior.

2. Forgiveness is only a verbal statement, which cannot be trusted.
3. Forgiveness can only come after forgetting.
4. Forgiveness can only be given when someone deserves to be forgiven.

Of course, to recognize these preconceptions as faulty is to realize at some level what is true (the dialectic). However, Laura knew that she was still struggling with the heartfelt forgiveness of someone. Her instructors then provided her with empathy exercises, allowing her to step into the identity, beliefs, and history of another person. At the same time, she asked the Source for the "spirit of forgiveness," and to her utter surprise, she realized her request had been granted. She learned that she had always had a gift for understanding what people were going through, though this gift had somehow been blocked. As she developed this gift, however, she found compassion for others and the desire to forgive even people who had wronged her, like her parents (holism). By empathically understanding the vulnerability of another, even when they seemed strong, she found she wanted to forgive, indeed forgive herself.

She realized that the Source had provided; the Source had granted her request. Indeed, her discovery of the forgiveness virtue and all that she gained through more fulfilling relationships indicated to her that the Source would always provide. Suddenly, her fears about leaving the village "womb" were gone, and her hopes for the future "outside" brightened considerably. She realized that she would have to give up much of what she once thought she had, including her old "druggie" friends, her old images of her grandparents (and parents), and her need for approval. However, she knew that with the help of the Source she could belong somewhere else, minister to others somewhere else, and continue to grow somewhere else.

As of this writing—2 years after her Alldredge experience—Laura's parents report that she is doing well in college, with no drug abuse or bouts of serious depression. They also report that she is currently searching for a major that will maximize her service to others.

Therapist–Author Commentary

How would a naturalistic, and thus nontheistic, treatment have led Laura on a different therapeutic journey from the one above? How would the five assumptions of naturalism have coalesced into a different experience for Laura? In answering these questions, we would first contend that naturalistic assumptions are not only used in many systems of treatment but also frequently considered axiomatic across the field. Many familiar notions of mental health care owe their existence and widespread endorsement to these assumptions. We realize that some researchers would claim empirical support for many of these assumptions (e.g., Higgins, 1997), but the fact is that their efficacy and effectiveness have rarely, if ever, been directly compared to non-naturalistic assumptions. Consider the following common notions of therapeutic community (with the main naturalistic assumption in italics) along with their comparison to Laura's actual treatment:

1. *The best or ultimate motivator of clients is their own self-benefit (e.g., reinforcement, happiness, satisfaction, well-being).* Because the human nature of clients is ultimately *hedonistic*, all strategies for motivating clients should take advantage of this nature. Even the helping of other people should not be encouraged unless it results in client fulfillment and thus self-benefit. However, this common understanding of motivation is belied by perhaps the primary turning point in Laura's treatment—her risking her life (and perhaps suffering) for the sake of someone she barely knew. Laura believed that the altruism of the Source, as learned through her interactions with the team, led to her altruism with the rescued woman. This altruism, in turn, resulted in her service orientation toward the team and her counselors.

2. *The core therapeutic principles of a mental health community should be objective—as free from bias as humanly possible.* This *objectivity* usually has two implications for therapeutic communities. First, only therapy strategies that are supported by supposedly bias-free research are permitted (e.g., empirically supported treatments; Nathan & Gorman, 1998). Second, all residents— regardless of their value systems—are thought to be treatable by the objective techniques and strategies of the community. With Laura, however, instructors at the Alldredge Academy were up front and constant in their promotion of her virtue and character. (The academy also holds that no research is bias-free; see Slife & Williams, 1995.) Laura was encouraged to arrive at her own values, through the value-laden experiences of the three phases of the academy. However, not all values are considered equal or correct, so she was gently guided by her counselors to consult the Source as she did so.

3. *Changes in environmental and/or biological factors are responsible for changes in client behavioral patterns.* In other words, the setting, structure, and interventions of the therapeutic community itself, along with medications, are responsible for client changes. However, if these factors are responsible for these changes—factors that are, for the most part, outside the personal control of clients—then the clients themselves are not responsible for them; the intervention is *deterministic*. The Alldredge Academy, by contrast, did not view Laura's biol-

ogy or her environment in this fashion. Although these factors undoubtedly play a role in Laura's behavior, she is also the agent of her actions, permitting her to do otherwise than her nature and nurture would dictate. In this sense, Laura was helped to *desire* change. Although nothing can force her to desire change, dialectical and relational experiences with the Source can facilitate her evaluation of her current desires and offer options she did not have before.

4. *Therapeutic systems and interventions should be applied rationally and consistently.* Clients should be taught how each portion of the healing process is *consistent* with the treatment goals of long-term, hedonistic self-benefit. Laura, however, was not motivated by her long-term self-benefit; she was motivated by the benefit of others (e.g., her team and the woman she rescued). Moreover, many interventions seemed quite paradoxical to Laura, and thus inconsistent with her long-term self-benefit. That is, her usual patterns or "games" were challenged in such a way that she sincerely began to give up the selfish ends of her games (using others for pleasure or power). She gave up these games because they were incompatible with the relationship she discovered with the Source (and others).

5. *The individual is the primary unit and concern of a therapeutic community.* Because individuals supposedly carry around with them their unique, self-contained qualities (e.g., intrapsychic conflicts, reinforcement histories, cognitive schemas), these *atomistic* qualities are the primary reason for client problems and the primary focus of client treatment. This focus does not preclude interactions with others, but it does fundamentally isolate the individual. The therapeutic community becomes a collection of autonomous individuals with their own self-contained problems. Therapeutic strategies are limited to the effect of outside factors (e.g., people and environment) on the individual's self-contained problem. By contrast, the primary unit and concern of the Alldredge Academy is the relationship, including relationships between people, between people and nature, and most important between people and the Source. Consequently, relationships, not individuals, are nurtured and guided. Treatment goals are not so much about individual fulfillment as they are about relational caring and true intimacy.

CONCLUSION

At this point, we should reunite important aspects of the case presented here. Our case is, in some sense, the field of therapeutic communities, with its emphasis on a secular and naturalistic philosophy. Without some non-naturalistic philosophy, we contend that it will be difficult to formalize theistic interventions. Our case is also a particular therapeutic community, the Alldredge Academy. This unique institution has pioneered not only a relatively unfamiliar philosophy (for therapy) but also many of the practices that would seem to follow from it. We believe that secular psychotherapy—restricted as it is by its naturalistic dogma—can learn a great deal from a therapeutic community such as the Alldredge Academy. Finally, our case is Laura, who was privileged not only to solve her problems and reconstitute her relationships but also to discover the greatest gift of all—the fellowship of the Source.

REFERENCES

Baldwin, S., & Slife, B. D. (2003). *Three "silent assumptions" of cognitive–behavioral therapy.* Unpublished manuscript.

Bernstein, R. J. (1983). *Beyond objectivism and relativism: Science, hermeneutics, and praxis.* Philadelphia: University of Pennsylvania Press.

Boman, T. (1960). *Hebrew thought compared with Greek.* New York: Norton.

Collins, G. R. (1977). *The rebuilding of psychology: An integration of psychology and Christianity.* Wheaton, Il: Tyndale House.

Dueck, A. (1995). *Between Jerusalem and Athens: Ethical perspectives on culture, religion, and psychotherapy.* Grand Rapids, MI: Baker Books.

Fisher-Smith, A. M. (2000). Limitations in the psychotherapeutic relationship: Psychology's implicit commitment to hedonism. *General Psychologist, 35,* 88–91.

Griffin, D. R. (2000). *Religion and scientific naturalism.* Albany, NY: SUNY Press.

Gunton, C. E. (1993). *The one, the three, and the many: God, creation, and the culture of modernity.* Cambridge, England: Cambridge University Press.

Higgins, E. T. (1997). Beyond the pleasure principle. *American Psychologist, 52,* 1280–1300.

Honer, S. M., & Hunt, T. C. (1987). *Invitation to philosophy: Issues and options* (5th ed.). Belmont, CA: Wadsworth.

Howard, G. S. (1994). Some varieties of free will worth practicing. *Journal of Theoretical and Philosophical Psychology, 14*(1), 50–61.

Leahey, T. H. (1991). *A history of modern psychology.* Englewood Cliffs, NJ: Prentice Hall.

Lohfink, G. (1984). *Jesus and community: The social dimension of Christian faith.* New York: Fortress Press.

Richards, P. S., & Bergin, A. E. (1997). *A spiritual strategy for counseling and psychotherapy.* Washington, DC: American Psychological Association.

Richardson, F. C., & Bishop, R. (2002). Rethinking determinism in social science. In H. Atmanspacher & R. Bishop (Eds), *Between chance and choice: Interdisciplinary perspectives on determinism* (pp. 425–446). Charlottesville, VA: Imprint Academic.

Richardson, F. C., Fowers, B. J., & Guignon, C. B. (1999). *Re-envisioning psychology: Moral dimensions of theory and practice.* San Francisco: Jossey-Bass.

Rychlak, J. F. (1981). *Introduction to personality and psychotherapy: A theory-construction approach* (2nd ed.). Boston: Houghton Mifflin.

Rychlak, J. F. (1988). *The psychology of rigorous humanism* (2nd ed.). New York: New York University Press.

Shaver, R. (1999). Rational egoism. Cambridge, England: Cambridge University Press.

Slife, B. D. (1999). Values in Christian families: Do they come from unrecognized idols? *Brigham Young University Studies, 38*(2), 117–147.

Slife, B. D. (2000). Hedonism: A hidden unity and problematic of psychology. *General Psychologist, 35*(3), 77–80.

Slife, B. D. (2001). *Applying a non-naturalistic philosophy/theology.* Paper presented at the Alldredge Academy, West Virginia.

Slife, B. D. (2002). Time, information, and determinism in psychology. In H. Atmanspacher & R. Bishop (Eds.), *Between chance and choice: Interdisciplinary perspectives on determinism* (pp. 469–484). Charlottesville, VA: Imprint Academic.

Slife, B. D. (2003). Theoretical challenges to therapy practice and research: The constraint of naturalism. In M. J. Lambert (Ed.), *Bergin & Garfield's Handbook of psychotherapy and behavior change* (pp. 44–83). New York: Wiley.

Slife, B. D., & Fisher, A. M. (2000). Modern and postmodern approaches to the free will/determinism dilemma in psychology. *Journal of Humanistic Psychology, 40*(1), 80–108.

Slife, B. D., Hope, C., & Nebeker, S. (1999). Examining the relationship between religious spirituality and psychological science. *Journal of Humanistic Psychology, 39*(2), 51–85.

Slife, B. D., & Richards, P. S. (2001). How separable are spirituality and theology in psychotherapy? *Counseling and Values, 45,* 190–206.

Slife, B. D., Smith, A. M., & Burchfield, C. (2003). Psychotherapists as crypto-missionaries: An exemplar on the crossroads of history, theory, and philosophy. In D. B. Hill & M. J. Kral (Eds.), *About psychology: Esssays at the crossroads of history, theory, and philosophy* (pp. 55–72). Albany, NY: SUNY Press.

Slife, B. D., & Williams, R. N. (1995). *What behind the research? Discovering hidden assumptions in the behavioral sciences.* Thousand Oaks, CA: Sage.

Smith, H. (2001). *Why religion matters: The fate of the human spirit in an age of disbelief.* San Francisco: Harper.

Valentine, E. R. (1992). *Conceptual issues in psychology* (2nd ed.). London: Routledge.

Viney, W., & King, D. B. (2003). *A history of psychology: Ideas and content* (3rd ed.). New York: Allyn & Bacon.

Watzlawick, P. (1984). *The invented reality*. New York: Norton.

Webster's new collegiate dictionary. (1981). Springfield, MA: G & C Merriam.

Whoolery, M., Slife, B. D., & Mitchell, L. J. (2002, February). *Creating a theoretical space for spiritual interventions*. Paper presented at the meeting of the American Association for Behavorial and Social Sciences, Las Vegas, NV.

Yalom, I. D. (1980). *Existential psychotherapy*. New York: Basic Books.

3

A THEISTIC INPATIENT TREATMENT APPROACH FOR EATING-DISORDER PATIENTS: A CASE REPORT

RANDY K. HARDMAN, MICHAEL E. BERRETT, AND
P. SCOTT RICHARDS

Despite indications that religion and spirituality may be important in the treatment of eating disorders (Hall & Cohn, 1992; Hsu, Crisp, & Callender, 1992; Mitchell, Erlander, Pyle, & Fletcher, 1990; Rorty, Yager, & Rossotto, 1993; Smith, Richards, Fischer, & Hardman, 2003), spiritual interventions are rarely used in contemporary treatment programs. We have described elsewhere why we believe that spiritual treatment approaches and interventions hold promise for enhancing the effectiveness of eating disorder treatment programs (Hardman, Berrett, & Richards, in press; Richards, Hardman, Frost, Berrett, Clark-Sly, & Anderson, 1997). Briefly, we believe that some of the core issues that eating-disorder patients struggle with are spiritual in nature (e.g., lack of spiritual identity, negative images of God, feelings of spiritual unworthiness and shame, etc.), and that the most powerful way to resolve these issues is through spiritual interventions (Richards et al., 1997).

In this chapter, we describe an integrative, multidisciplinary inpatient treatment program for women with eating disorders. Undergirding the Center for Change (CFC) treatment philosophy and approach is the belief that faith in God and spiritual self-understanding and growth can be crucial for those recovering from eating disorders (Richards et al., 1997). To more clearly illustrate the processes and potential outcomes of our nondenominational theistic treatment approach, we share the treatment history of one patient, Jan, whose faith in God and personal spirituality played a crucial role in her healing and recovery.

DESCRIPTION OF THERAPISTS

Randy K. Hardman

I completed a PhD in counseling psychology in 1984 at Brigham Young University (BYU). Since 1984, I have worked as a program director and clinical practitioner in university, hospital, specialized treatment center, and private practice settings in Indiana, Colorado, and Utah. I served as an adjunct faculty member at BYU in the Counseling Psychology program. I am currently an owner and codirector of Center for Change, an inpatient specialized eating disorder treatment center, in Orem, Utah.

I am a committed and active member of the Church of Jesus Christ of Latter-day Saints (LDS). I grew up on a farm in rural Idaho, and my own religious upbringing was without regular church attendance or participation by either my parents or by our family. In a real sense, I was on my own a great deal in both a literal and in a religious–spiritual way. I spent many hours alone in farming responsibilities, and in the quietness and isolation of this rural setting, I communed with God in personal prayer on a regular basis. I was a believer in God, and as a boy felt a connection with God spiritually before I became acquainted with and fully engaged in the religious teachings and tenets of my church as an older teenager.

Over the years, in many thousands of hours of face-to-face interactions with individuals, couples, and families, I have become more in tune with how relationships with self, God, and others are interconnected and need to be addressed and included together in successful therapeutic change. I believe that these relationship experiences, whether perceptual, emotional, or spiritual, have the greatest long-term impact on healing, change, and recovery. I listen closely to clients to understand where they are willing to go in the spiritual–religious experiences of their relationships. I have become more willing over the years to openly and directly discuss spiritual concerns and needs because clients are so eager to explore them. I have found spiritual recovery as the key for bringing hope, healing, and recovery for women with eating disorders.

Michael E. Berrett

I completed my doctorate in counseling psychology at Brigham Young University. I also completed a formal doctoral minor in marriage and family therapy as well as a master's degree in school psychology. I began working in the field as a school psychologist and then as a high school counselor. Following these positions, I worked as a primary therapist in adult and adolescent acute inpatient treatment and in an inpatient specialty eating disorder program. In the more recent years of my career, I have served as a business consultant, taught college courses in clinical and counseling psychology, directed a clinical wilderness treatment program for troubled adolescents, operated a successful private practice, and cofounded and codirected an intensive inpatient treatment program for anorexia, bulimia, and coexisting emotional disorders.

Throughout my career, I have noticed that those with spiritual beliefs, and especially those who live congruent with their spiritual beliefs, seemed to make more dramatic gains in the recovery process and in maintenance of treatment gains. I have repeatedly heard from patients that their own focus on religious and/or spiritual issues in treatment, whether within the therapeutic relationship or "on their own," including their faith in their own spiritual tenets and consequent life activities and choices, were some of the most powerful catalysts for positive change.

As a result of this "personal learning" over time, which I consider a blessing to me from the clients I have worked with, myself and several colleagues began conceptualizing those spiritual themes that were both recurrent and most powerful in our patients' lives. This led to designing a spirituality workbook, a spirituality group in treatment, spiritual interventions in treatment, research on the efficacy of spiritual interventions in treatment outcome, and several professional publications about spirituality and eating disorders.

Although I believe that the spiritual approach is not the only worthwhile modality of treatment and indeed that the best treatment is multimodal and multidisciplinary, I strongly believe that the spiritual is the most important aspect of healing and recovery. I intend to continue to attend to this understanding, and I hope that attending to it will help many individuals in their road to recovery, healing, and peace.

TREATMENT SETTING AND PROGRAM

CFC is a private inpatient care facility for women with eating disorders. Some staff members also provide outpatient psychotherapy services to women and men with a wide variety of other psychological and relationship concerns. The multidisciplinary inpatient treatment staff includes 2 medical doctors, 2 psychiatrists, 5 PhD psychologists, 1 PhD marriage and family therapist, 2 clinical social workers, 2 PhD psychology residents, 3 PhD psychology interns, 1 director of nursing and health services, 9 registered nurses, 3 registered dieticians, 1 dietary technician, 1 PhD instructional psychologist/education director, 5 experiential therapists, 18 care technicians, and 2 chefs; 81% of the treatment staff are women. Approximately 50% of the staff are members of the LDS church and the remaining adhere to a variety of spiritual traditions, including Protestant Christian, Jewish, and Muslim perspectives.

The CFC treatment program is grounded in current research findings and accepted clinical guidelines for treating eating disorders (American Psychiatric Association, 1993; Richards, Baldwin, Frost, Clark-Sly, Berrett, & Hardman, 2000; Yager, 1989). Treatment is customized to meet each patient's needs; thus, length of stay varies. However, as a general rule, patients and their families commit to a minimum of 12 weeks of inpatient treatment for anorexia and 8 weeks for bulimia. The treatment team continuously evaluates ongoing needs and adjusts treatment length when needed.

Once admitted to CFC, each client receives a medical assessment. The evaluation includes a complete medical history, physical assessment, necessary medical procedures, and medications. Throughout the treatment program, the physician oversees the physical aspects of recovery including the medical progress of each client, her diet, and her weight gain. In addition, at the time of admission, a psychiatrist, psychologist, or social worker gathers an eating disorder history and assesses the patient's emotional condition.

Along the recovery path, patients work their way through a four-phase treatment program. The four phases of recovery represent distinct stages of growth and change. Each phase has clearly defined guidelines, assignments, and therapy tasks, as well as increased privileges and responsibilities.

> Phase one: The patient recognizes and acknowledges the presence, reality, severity, and effect of her eating disorder and other emotional disorders. She also begins to understand herself and the development of the eating disorder.
>
> Phase two: The patient takes responsibility and ownership for her eating disorder and other difficulties; learns to take responsibility for her recovery; and regains a sense of choice, power, control, and hope.
>
> Phase three: The patient increases in desire to let go of her eating disorder, deals with her difficult feelings, and makes a personal commitment to do the work necessary to overcome her eating disorder.
>
> Phase four: The patient actively works to decrease her feelings of shame and self-criticism, and to increase patterns of self-acceptance and self-correction. She also begins to share with others some of what she has gained in treatment.

Each patient advances individually through each phase as soon as she is ready, and great care is taken to ensure that each patient progresses at her own pace. Her privileges and responsibilities increase over time as she demonstrates readiness to move ahead. This stepped-care approach to treatment gently helps patients gain confidence as they advance through the phases of change at their own pace.

Patients participate in a variety of needed therapies to assure comprehensive treatment and progress toward recovery. These include (a) individual psychotherapy sessions (4 times weekly); (b) group psychotherapy (7 times weekly) and body image group (2 times weekly); (c) experiential and expressive activities, including music, dance, movement and recreation therapies (8 to12 times weekly); (d) family counseling (frequency varies per patient needs); (e) nutrition monitoring and counseling (3 times weekly); (f) medical evaluations and treatment (frequency varies per patient needs); (g) eating disorders education classes on a variety of topics, including diet and nutrition, self-esteem, healthy exercise, assertiveness, communication skills (3 times weekly); (h) individualized academic management and tutoring (as needed depending on patient needs); and (i) spiritual exploration and growth activities, including spirituality groups (3 times per week), spiritual readings, and service activities.

SPIRITUAL COMPONENT OF THE TREATMENT PROGRAM

We believe that a spiritual component is an essential part of a multidimensional, multidisciplinary treatment approach for women with eating disorders. Our integrative, theistic approach to using spiritual interventions is consistent with the recommendations of numerous professionals that spiritual interventions should not be used alone, but integrated with standard psychological and medical interventions (Richards & Bergin, 1997; Richards & Potts, 1995; Shafranske, 1996).

We use a nondenominational spiritual emphasis that has proved helpful to patients from a wide variety of religious backgrounds. Two research studies conducted at CFC have provided evidence that spiritual growth and healing during treatment is positively associated with better patient outcomes (Richards, Berrett, & Hardman, 2001; Smith et al., 2003).

During treatment, patients are encouraged to explore their own spiritual beliefs and to draw on their faith to assist in their recovery. We believe that as patients align their behavior with their own spiritual beliefs, they will benefit from improved confidence, self-respect, and peace of mind. Patients are invited to explore spiritual issues related to their recovery if they desire during their individual psychotherapy sessions.

To further facilitate spiritual exploration and healing, patients attend a weekly 60-minute spiritual exploration and growth group, and read a self-help workbook (Richards, Hardman, & Berrett, 2000), which includes scriptural and other spiritual readings and educational materials about topics such as faith in God, spiritual identity, grace, forgiveness, repentance, faith, prayer, and meditation. Each patient utilizes the structure of the workbook and support of the group to help them come to an understanding of their own spiritual beliefs and convictions, and to include those understandings in their recovery program.

Patients also participate in a biweekly, 12-step group, adapted for women with eating disorders. Patients are also given opportunities during the treatment program to attend religious services of their choice and to engage in altruistic acts of service within the Center and community.

CLIENT DEMOGRAPHIC CHARACTERISTICS

Jan was a 19-year-old, Caucasian woman from the western United States. Before her admission to CFC, she resided with her parents and a younger sister. Jan was the second of three children. Her parents were in their first marriage. Their socioeconomic status was upper-middle class. Jan's older brother was 22 years old and her younger sister was 8 years old.

A high school graduate, Jan had enrolled as a freshman at a university in a western state, but she was unable to successfully continue in the educational program because of the severity of her anorexia. Jan and her family of origin were members of The Church of Jesus Christ of Latter-day Saints (LDS church; Ulrich, Richards & Bergin, 2000). Jan considered herself an "active" (orthodox) member of the church.

Dr. Randy K. Hardman was assigned to be Jan's individual psychotherapist during her inpatient stay at CFC. Jan met with Dr. Hardman four times per week. As the president and director of Clinical Services at CFC, Dr. Michael E. Berrett oversaw Jan's treatment during her inpatient stay. He also served as the group leader for Jan's weekly spiritual exploration and growth group.

PRESENTING PROBLEM AND CONCERNS

Jan had suffered with anorexia since the eighth grade and it had become extremely severe in the year prior to her admission. She had also had a long-standing, depressive disorder, with a general state of guilt and unhappiness. She had tried some outpatient therapy but had not persisted with it. She came to CFC following an assessment and referral by an outpatient therapist in her community. This was the first intensive therapeutic treatment that she had received.

In her first individual therapy session with Dr. Hardman, Jan said,

> I'm at a stand still. I have no social life. I don't see any way for a future family or career because of my eating disorder. My eating disorder controls everything. Health is a big concern. I'm very worried about it. I'm scared of a heart attack. I feel sick inside, tired. I'm aged. I've aged myself fifty years. I'm not okay.

CLIENT HISTORY

Significant Childhood and Family History

Jan grew up in a Latter-day Saint home, but her father was not active in the Church. Her mother was always very involved in the church. Jan described her parents' marriage as "stable." She said that her parents have never been abusive to her or her siblings.

When she was a small child (6 or 7 years), Jan was placed in the care of a babysitter, and in that placement, the father of her babysitter sexually abused her. She also witnessed the father sexually abusing his daughters, and found pornographic pictures of the father's children.

As she grew up, Jan felt like she could never please or satisfy the expectations of her mother in regards to cleanliness and behavior. She also felt that her parents were emotionally distant and rarely praised her or validated her worth and goodness.

Jan described her parents as strict and structured, but indicated that her younger sister got away with a lot of things that she and her older brother did not. Jan said that she felt like she "always had to be a good child. I was a pleaser." Jan said that this pattern has not changed in her life.

Jan said that her mother viewed her as a very emotional child. Her older brother was more oppositional than she was and tended to break the rules. Jan did not feel that she got rewarded for being the compliant and obedient child.

Jan said that her father drank every day at home and got intoxicated on a somewhat regular basis. He ran a family business and her father's relatives all consumed alcohol. As Jan got older, she had a lot of negative feelings about her father's use of alcohol and his lack of religious participation. Jan said that her father made an effort to be close to her when he became aware of the eating disorder, but she emotionally pulled away from him.

Jan described her mother as a sensitive person, but said, "She's not very sensitive to me." Jan felt an emotional disconnection from her mother most of her adolescent life. Jan explained, "I am very sensitive when I'm talking to her. Instead of responding to me and what I'm saying, she will talk about something that she is worried about." Jan described her mother as a poor listener. Jan said her mother was always worried and preoccupied with other things. Jan described herself as being "wanted, but not needed."

During the year prior to Jan's admission to CFC, Jan felt like her parents' focus was on her older brother, who was preparing for his church mission. Jan said that at one point she was afraid her parents might forget her high school graduation.

Jan said that she and her brother are close, but she believes her parents favored him. Jan admitted, "I feel selfish for saying things about that because I feel like I'm the expensive child. I go through money, braces, dance, and now I'm here with therapy." Jan said that her little sister is a worry for her, but that their relationship is good.

Jan had a good high school experience, except for her junior year when her eating disorder became extremely severe. She said that she was somewhat popular during high school. She had close friends and dated periodically, although she had no serious boyfriends. Jan was a very good student in high school, had a 4.0 grade point average, and received a scholarship to attend university.

Eating Disorder History

Jan said that she started her eating disorder when she was in eighth grade by restricting and going on a very rigid diet. When she started to lose weight, she increasingly restricted her eating. Jan would divide the food on her plate in half and eat only half of her food. She gradually eliminated all sugars, butter, peanut butter, and all fat foods from her diet. By the spring of 1996, she was eating only fruits and vegetables. Even then, she felt much guilt and self-incrimination about her eating. Jan also often fasted when she knew that she could not get out of eating a meal. She felt like she had to restrict and fast in order to feel deserving to eat. She would not eat to compensate for the times she did eat. Jan also participated in many dietary trends.

When Jan became a junior in high school, her eating disorder worsened. Jan said that school became much more difficult because her grandmother worked at the high school and she would "send her attack dogs—other teachers and administrators—out on me to make sure I'd eat. Everybody focused on my eating and my eating disorder." Jan said it was very difficult and embarrassing to have her grandmother watching over her in that way.

Jan's eating disorder continued through her senior year, although she viewed it as less severe than it was during her junior year. In her senior year, Jan was extremely unhappy, felt like her pants were too tight, and she stated that "everybody else thought I was doing great, but on the inside I was miserable. I was never happy. I felt dull inside. Because of that, I made a suicide attempt."

Jan said that as her eating disorder continued to worsen she would not eat breakfast, yet eat a small lunch and a small dinner with the family. She indicated that the amount of food she would eat continued to decrease. She hated to eat in front of other people. When she was on dates, she would only eat a salad. She stopped going to social events because she could not stand to eat in front of other people and she could not have complete control over her food.

Jan said that she became consumed by her eating disorder. Every thought was about food. She began to hide things, lie a lot, keep secrets, deny things, and tell people she was eating when she was not. She stated, "I hate lying, but I got good at it. I'd fake that I had eaten meals, but I hated the fact that I lied all the time." Jan said they she did not ever engage in laxative or diet pill abuse. She did, however, overexercise somewhat during the 2 years prior to her admission at CFC.

Jan attended university for one semester, but she had a very difficult time with the eating disorder even though she did all right with her grades. While at college, Jan said she restricted every meal: "My roommates never saw me eat. My main meal in college was a Diet Coke." Jan said that sometimes she would drink water and other times she would go days without drinking it because she hated the "full" feeling that drinking would give her. Jan dropped out of university because the eating disorder had escalated to the point where she could not function.

In spite of all of her weight loss efforts, Jan admitted on her admission to CFC that she constantly felt fat. Her hair was falling out. Her skin was pallid and white. She looked like she did not feel well physically. She lost her menses prior to her admission to CFC. She had also lost her menses for a year during high school. Jan admitted that for several months prior to her admission she was purging up to three times a day, and she continued to both restrict and purge up until the time of her admission.

ASSESSMENT AND DIAGNOSIS

When Jan was admitted to CFC, she underwent a physical and nutritional exam, and Dr. Hardman conducted a psychiatric evaluation and a mental status exam. Jan also completed a comprehensive battery of psychological tests, including the Minnesota Multiphasic Personality Inventory—2 (MMPI–2; Butcher, 1990), Eating Attitudes Test (EAT; Garner & Garfinkel, 1979), Body Shape Questionnaire (BSQ; Cooper, Taylor, Cooper, & Fairburn, 1987), Outcome Questionnaire (OQ 45.2; Lambert & Burlingame, 1996), Multidimensional Self-Esteem Inventory (MSEI; O'Brien & Epstein, 1988), Spiritual Well-Being Scale (SWBS; Paloutzian & Ellison, 1991), Religious Orientation Scale (ROS; Allport & Ross, 1967), and Spiritual Outcome Scale (SOS; Richards & Smith, 2000). She completed all of these measures again except the MMPI–2 and ROS when she was discharged from CFC. Jan's admission and discharge scores on the EAT, BSQ, OQ 45.2, MSEI, SWBS, ROS, and SOS are presented in Table 3.1.

Jan's physical exam at admission revealed that she was 5' 6" tall and weighed 94.5 lbs. Jan's physical, cardiac, and neurologic exams were unremarkable, although her heart rate was only 55. The physician also noted that Jan was "thin and somewhat cachectic appearing, occasionally gets some sharp chest pains and some constipation," and her last menstrual period was in September of 1999.

The nutritionist estimated Jan's Body Mass Index at 15.5. She also concluded that Jan's body weight and somatic protein stores were below normal limits. She noted that Jan had "poor hair growth and falling out," "skin bruises

TABLE 3.1
Jan's Scores on the Battery of Psychological Tests Completed on Admission and Discharge From Center for Change

Psychological test	Admission score	Discharge score	Normal range
EAT	80	7	< 30
BSQ	162	57	< 110
OQ 45.2			
Total score	78	26	< 63
Symptom distress	45	12	< 39
Relationship distress	15	10	< 15
Social role conflict	17	4	< 13
MSEI (Global self-esteem)	33.6	46.3	40–59
ROS			
Intrinsic	41	N/A	N/A
Extrinsic	28	N/A	N/A
SWBS			
Religious well-being	60	60	> 47
Existential well-being	53	57	> 43
Spiritual Outcome Scale			
Total	46	61	> 54
Love of God	17	22	>19
Love of others	20	23	>19
Love of self	9	16	>15

Note. For the Eating Attitudes Test (EAT), Body Shape Questionnaire (BSQ), Outcome Questionnaire (OQ 45.2), Spiritual Well-Being Scale (SWBS), and Spiritual Outcome Scale, the estimates that are considered in the normal range are based on normative data. The Multidimensional Self-Esteem Scale (MSEI) subscale scores are all *t* scores, and so the normal range is between 40 and 59. ROS = Religious Orientation Scale.

easily," "increased sensitivity in teeth and gums bleeding," "stomach pain, bloating, and gas," and "cold body temperature." She concluded that Jan is "at risk for malnutrition."

During her psychiatric interview with Dr. Hardman, Jan described her eating disorder symptoms, as well as symptoms of major depression that had been present for several years. There were no indications of psychotic features or thought disorders. Jan's *DSM–IV* Axis I diagnosis was Anorexia Nervosa (Purging Type, Severe) and Major Depression (Single Episode, Moderate). Jan's Axis II diagnosis was deferred.

Jan's MMPI–2 profile confirmed that she was suffering from clinically significant levels of a variety of psychiatric symptoms such as depression, anxiety, fearfulness, obsessive thoughts, guilt, low self-esteem, self-blame, and feelings of worthlessness. Jan also suffered from multiple somatic symptoms, including poor appetite, fatigue, insomnia, and cardiac pain. Jan's MMPI–2 configural code type was a 72. Her Pt scale was 94, D scale was 90, and her Hs scale was 86. Her F scale was also elevated at 82, although her L scale was 62 and her K scale was 46. We concluded that Jan's profile was valid, but that she had exaggerated her symptoms somewhat in a cry for help.

Jan's EAT score revealed that Jan was experiencing a clinically significant level of eating disorder symptomology, including restricting, binging, purging, anxiety about eating, and preoccupation with food. Jan's scores on the BSQ revealed that she was also experiencing a clinically significant level of distress about her body shape (e.g., feeling too fat, wanting to be thinner, and feeling ashamed of her body). Jan's scores on the OQ 45.2 revealed that she was experiencing clinically significant levels of distress and symptoms in her (a) intrapsychic functioning (depression and anxiety), (b) interpersonal relationships, and (c) social role performance (e.g., as a daughter, student, and sister). Jan's score on the MSEI global self-esteem scale revealed that Jan did not view herself in a favorable manner. More specifically, she was self-critical and self-doubting. She also viewed herself as being incompetent, unlikable, unassertive, and physically unattractive.

Jan's scores on the ROS revealed that she was intrinsically religious, which suggests that she believed in her religion and was attempting to live it in her daily life. Jan's scores on the SWBS revealed that she believed that God loved her and was concerned about the problems she was experiencing, and that she felt a sense of purpose in her life. Thus, based on the ROS and SWBS, Jan's religious faith and involvement appeared to be a potential strength and resource in her life. However, Jan's scores on the SOS subscales indicated that her feelings of love for God, others, and herself were below the normal range.

TREATMENT PROCESS AND OUTCOMES

Medical Issues and Outcomes

Jan participated in all of the aspects and components of the inpatient program at CFC. She received a medical consultation evaluation and a psychiatric evaluation. The Center's physician placed Jan on 40 mg of Prozac for her depression and also prescribed Adivan (0.5 mg) for Jan to use as needed for her anxiety.

Jan ate three meals and three snacks a day throughout her stay. Toward the end of her stay, she ate in "family style," which meant she was allowed to choose the type and portions of the food she wished to eat. Jan began menstruation in CFC and had two menses during her treatment stay. At the time of admission, she weighed 94 pounds, and at the time of discharge she weighed 117 pounds. At the time of discharge, Jan was no longer restricting her eating or binging and purging. She also reported that she rarely had thoughts about engaging in eating disorder behaviors.

Psychosocial Issues and Outcomes

Jan received individual therapy from Dr. Hardman 4 times a week, daily group therapy, and regular nutritional and dietary consultations. She took part in nutritional classes, educational classes, art therapy, dance and movement therapy, music therapy, and recreational therapy. She participated in all four phases of the treatment program and successfully completed each phase.

Jan was extremely motivated and committed to the recovery process. She worked hard and faced her fears. She challenged herself to face her issues. Jan experienced much fear, guilt, and emotional conflict at times during treatment due to the emotional and traumatic issues of her past. But she was able to talk about and emotionally work through her issues in an appropriate fashion.

Jan worked on understanding and exploring the underlying causes of her anorexia and the contributing factors of the depression. She came to realize that the sexually abusive experiences she had gone through when being babysat had been traumatic and negatively affected her. She was able to address and resolve much of the affect of these negative sexual molestation and observation experiences.

Jan participated in family therapy on two extended weekend visits with her parents and younger sister. She was able to address issues and patterns from her own family of origin that had influenced her throughout her life, including her feeling that she was never "good enough" for her mother. Fortunately, Jan's mother and father were responsive to treatment and made positive efforts and changes in their support of Jan's recovery.

Jan also addressed her intense feelings of self-rejection and self-criticism and the underlying theme that she felt like she was always in trouble and had done something wrong. Jan also addressed her constant feeling of low self-esteem, not being good enough, and feeling weak. She was able to become more self-accepting and self-forgiving.

Jan was able to take risks and face fears related to her eating disorder and her social life throughout the course of treatment. Jan also addressed some sexual fears and concerns during treatment, including dating and social involvements. During her stay at CFC, Jan went on several dates and engaged in a variety of social activities while she was on therapeutic passes.

Jan also addressed future plans and living arrangement during her treatment stay. At the time of discharge, Jan was committed to continue her recovery on an outpatient basis. She had made arrangements to live with her cousin, someone who Jan viewed as a positive, noneating-disorder support person. Jan also made plans to have periodic visits with her parents and sister to continue to receive and develop positive support from them. Jan also made plans to return to her university studies several months after her discharge.

The Role of Faith and Spirituality

Jan's faith in God and personal spirituality were frequently discussed during her individual psychotherapy sessions and spirituality group meetings and played a central role in her healing and recovery. Although Jan was active in her church and publicly expressed her belief in God, it became apparent during her individual psychotherapy that she privately harbored intense feelings of shame, irrational guilt, and unworthiness. Jan superficially or "theoretically" believed that God loved her and was concerned about her problems, but in her heart she felt that God viewed her in a disapproving, condemning manner.

During her individual psychotherapy sessions it became clear that the sexual abuse she had suffered at the hands of her neighbor was the origin and root cause of her feelings of shame and unworthiness in her relationship with God, her parents, and others. The experience of being abused had left her feeling like she had done something terribly wrong, and ever since that experience she had lived with the feeling that she was bad and unworthy. Her parents had further reinforced these feelings through their emotional distance and failure to praise and validate Jan's goodness and competence.

As these core spiritual identity issues surfaced during treatment, Dr. Hardman and Dr. Berrett implemented several spiritual interventions that they believed might help Jan address them. First, Dr. Hardman and Dr. Berrett acknowledged the spiritual nature of Jan's concerns and communicated their willingness to discuss religious and spiritual concerns with her. Once Jan understood that it was acceptable and safe to discuss her personal faith and spirituality during individual therapy and during her spiritual growth group, she frequently initiated discussions about these topics.

Second, Dr. Hardman suggested that Jan read some scriptural writings from the Bible and Book of Mormon (The Church of Jesus Christ of Latter-day Saints, 1981) about God's view of children, including God's affirmations about their innocence and His love for them. These scriptural readings proved effective in helping Jan begin to reexamine her assumptions that God held her responsible for the abuse she had experienced as a child or that God viewed her in a condemning, judgmental way.

Third, Dr. Hardman and Dr. Berrett encouraged Jan to use the private time that is provided for patients in the CFC's daily treatment schedule to engage in contemplation, prayer, and journaling about her feelings and spiritual impressions. Jan's "spiritual solo time" played a powerful role in her healing and recovery. On several occasions as she contemplated and prayed, Jan received personal spiritual witnesses that God loved her and that it was okay for her to speak the truth about the sexual abuse she had experienced, even if people chose not to believe her.

During these sacred spiritual experiences Jan felt deep reassurances of God's love come into her heart and mind. Jan said that during these times she felt comforted, uplifted and sustained, and loved and nurtured. Her feelings of hope and faith that she could face and overcome her problems were also strengthened. As Jan shared these experiences during therapy and group sessions, Dr. Hardman and Dr. Berrett communicated their belief in the value and reality of Jan's experiences, and they affirmed the validity of the personal insights about her identity, worth, and sense of life meaning and direction that came to her during these times. Over the course of her stay, Jan wrote down in her own words the spiritual impressions and feelings that came to her and these writings became a personal code of living that she used every day to comfort and encourage herself in the recovery process.

Once Jan felt safer in her relationship with God and knew in her heart that God was with her in her recovery, she became very willing to take significant risks in treatment to face her fears and to resolve issues with her family. The permission she had felt from God during her spiritual solo times to tell the truth about the sexual abuse gave her the courage to disclose what had happened to her parents. The security that Jan felt because of her growing faith that God loved her as a child and now as an adult helped her be honest and face her fears and pain. The growing sense of security about her personal spiritual identity and worth provided an anchor or foundation that enabled Jan to move forward with courage and confidence as she actively engaged in all aspects of the CFC treatment program. Jan described her spiritual healing as "bigger than her own thoughts and feelings." She came to trust in a power beyond herself to help her change and overcome the problems in her life.

Psychological and Spiritual Outcome Measures

Jan's scores at the time of discharge on the EAT, BSQ, OQ 45.2, MSEI, SWBS, and SOS confirmed our clinical judgment that Jan had improved a great deal during her stay at CFC. As can be seen in Table 3.1, Jan's scores on the EAT dropped from being in the high clinical (abnormal) range (80) into the normal range for women (7). This indicates that Jan no longer suffered from eating disorder symptoms, such as restricting, binging, purging, anxiety about eating, preoccupation with food, and so on. Jan's scores on the BSQ also dropped from the high clinical range (162) into the normal range for women (57). This indicates that Jan was no longer experiencing clinically significant levels of concern, worry, and distress about her body shape.

Jan's scores on the OQ 45.2 also dropped from being in the clinical range into normal ranges. This indicates that Jan no longer suffered from clinically significant levels of distress and symptoms in her (a) intrapsychic functioning (depression and anxiety), (b) interpersonal relationships, or (c) social role performance (e.g., as a daughter, student, sister). Jan's score on the MSEI global self-esteem scale also fell into the normal range at the conclusion of treatment, indicating that during treatment Jan became more self-accepting and self-confident. She also came to view herself as being more competent, likable, powerful, and physically attractive.

Jan's scores on the religious well-being scale of the SWBS did not change during treatment, perhaps because her admission score of 60 is the highest possible score on the SWBS. Jan's scores on the existential well-being scale of the SWBS increased from 53 to 57, staying in the high normal range. This indicates that Jan continued to believe that her life had purpose and meaning, but again because of the ceiling effect of this measure her scores may not accurately reflect how much progress she experienced in this dimension of her life. Others have raised concerns about the ceiling effect problem of the SWBS and its lack of sensitivity to change among highly religious people (Hall, Tisdale, & Brokaw, 1994). With Jan, the SWBS provided a good measure of her cognitive, doctrinal beliefs about God, but it failed to sensitively measure the changes in the inner dimension of her spirituality.

Conversely, Jan's scores on the love of God, love of others, and love of self SOS subscales all increased and fell in healthy, normal ranges at the time of discharge. Thus, it appears that the SOS was a more sensitive measure of the changes in the inner dimension of Jan's spirituality—that is, her love of God and others, as well as her growing felt conviction based on personal spiritual experiences that she is a lovable and worthy person.

Jan's Postdischarge Functioning

Follow-up phone interviews with Jan by Dr. Hardman and the CFC research staff and aftercare coordinator on periodic occasions since she was discharged 2 years ago have confirmed that Jan has continued to progress in her journey of healing and recovery. Jan did return to university several months after she was discharged from CFC and enjoyed success in her studies. During a one-year follow-up standardized phone interview conducted by a CFC research staff member, Jan indicated that she viewed herself as "mostly recovered." Jan also indicated that during the previous month she had not binged or purged. She said that she had only restricted her eating by skipping meals about once a week during this time.

Life for Jan since her discharge has not been without challenges. Jan experienced two temporary relapses into her eating disorder behaviors (some restricting, binging, and purging) after her discharge. One of her relapses occurred 8 months after discharge when she returned home to live with her parents for a summer break from school. In this situation where so many of the "old triggers" were present, Jan went back into her feelings of shame and badness and her eating disorder coping mechanisms. This relapse lasted for about 3 months. After returning to university, Jan stopped engaging in her eating disorder behaviors and enjoyed positive psychosocial functioning for about 6 months.

Jan's second relapse lasted longer—almost 6 months—and the "trigger" for this setback was an emotionally intimate relationship with a man. This relationship stirred up Jan's fears about men and sexuality, which contributed to her relapse into her old ways of thinking, feeling, and viewing herself.

During both of her relapses, Jan was ultimately able to pull out of her shame and cease her eating disorder behaviors by reaffirming her faith that God loves her, she is not alone, her life has purpose and meaning, and God will support her. Thus, by going back to the "spiritual anchors" she discovered during her treatment at CFC, Jan has been able to overcome her challenges and relapses and move forward on her journey of healing and recovery.

Jan's level of psychosocial functioning since her discharge has remained consistently higher than it was previous to her treatment, even during her relapses. Jan has enjoyed and functioned more effectively in her family and social relationships. She has dated more than she ever did before treatment, and has experienced two close dating relationships with men. Overall, Jan has reported that she is much happier and satisfied with herself and her life since her treatment. Currently, 2 years after her discharge, Jan is free of her eating disorder behaviors and is functioning well psychologically, socially, and spiritually.

THERAPIST AND AUTHOR COMMENTARY

Although we use many standard medical and psychological interventions at CFC, at the core of our nondenominational theistic treatment philosophy and approach is our conviction that God exists. Our approach is also grounded in other theistic assumptions about human nature and therapeutic change, including (a) God has the power and desire to help people cope, heal, and grow, and (b) people who have faith in God's healing power and draw on the spiritual resources in their lives during psychological treatment will have added strength and power to cope, heal, and grow (Richards & Bergin, 1997, p. 100).

As described in this case report, Jan's personal faith and the spiritual experiences she had during her stay at CFC played a crucial role in her healing and in the process of treatment and recovery. The spiritual assurances Jan received of her spiritual identity, worth, and goodness, along with the affirmations of her worth and goodness that she received from Dr. Hardman and other members of the treatment staff, helped heal her shame, guilt, and distorted sense of identity. Jan's faith in God's love and support gave her added courage to face the pain of the sexual abuse she had experienced, as well as the pain she felt over her parents' emotional neglect. It also helped her recommit to recovery and health on those occasions after her discharge when she relapsed into her old behaviors and ways of thinking.

We doubt that a secular treatment approach that did not value or honor Jan's faith in God and personal spirituality would have been as effective in helping Jan heal and recover. If Jan's individual psychotherapist had not encouraged her to engage in times of spiritual contemplation and prayer, it is unlikely that Jan would have engaged in such practices on her own. By the time Jan entered treatment, the progression of her eating disorder and self-contempt had so undermined her feelings of worthiness and acceptability to God that she would most likely not have felt deserving of seeking God's assistance in her treatment and recovery. As a result, she may not have opened her heart and mind to the spiritual experiences she had during treatment that so powerfully assured her of God's love and of her goodness. Without these powerful and emotionally healing experiences to serve as her anchor and strengthen her faith and confidence, we doubt that Jan would have engaged so courageously in the treatment process and in facing her pain and fears.

For Jan, God was the first to validate her worth and goodness in a way that made her feel and know deeply in her heart that she was lovable and good. Receiving a spiritual assurance of God's love, and of her lovability and goodness, changed the way Jan thought and felt about herself. She began to heal from the inside out. Once Jan had felt God's loving and healing validation, it became much easier for her to feel and accept Dr. Hardman's love and validation, as well as love from other treatment staff members. From our theistic perspective, God is the ultimate healing power in patients' lives. When patients open their hearts to God's love and healing presence, then psychotherapists simply become facilitators and witnesses to a healing process that transcends ordinary psychological change processes.

REFERENCES

Allport, G. W., & Ross, J. M. (1967). Personal religious orientation and prejudice. *Journal of Personality and Social Psychology, 5*(4), 432–443.

American Psychiatric Association. (1993). Practice guidelines for eating disorders. *American Journal of Psychiatry, 150*, 207–228.

Butcher, J. N. (1990). *MMPI-2 in psychological treatment.* New York: Oxford University Press.

The Church of Jesus Christ of Latter-Day Saints. (1981). *The Book of Mormon: Another testament of Jesus Christ.* Salt Lake City, UT: Author.

Cooper, P. J., Taylor, M., Cooper, Z., & Fairburn, C. G. (1987). The development and validation of the Body Shape Questionnaire. *International Journal of Eating Disorders, 6*, 485–494.

Garner, D. M., & Garfinkel, P. E. (1979). The Eating Attitudes Test: An index of the symptoms of anorexia nervosa. *Psychological Medicine, 9*, 273–279.

Hall, L., & Cohn, L. (1992). *Bulimia: A guide to recovery.* Carlsbad, CA: Gurze Books.

Hall, T. W., Tisdale, T. C., & Brokaw, B. F. (1994). Assessment of religious dimensions in Christian clients: A review of selected instruments for research and clinical use. *Journal of Psychology, 22*, 395–421.

Hardman, R. K., Berrett, M. E., & Richards, P. S. (in press). Spirituality and ten false pursuits of eating disorders: Implications for counselors. *Counseling and Values*.

Hsu, L. K., Crisp, A. H., & Callender, J. S. (1992). Recovery in anorexia nervosa—the patient's perspective. *International Journal of Eating Disorders, 11*, 341–350.

Lambert, M. J., & Burlingame, G. M. (1996). *The Outcome Questionnaire*. Stevenson, MD: American Professional Credentialing Services.

Mitchell, J. E., Erlander, Rev. M., Pyle, R. L., & Fletcher, L. A. (1990). Eating disorders, religious practices and pastoral counseling. *International Journal of Eating Disorders, 9*, 589–593.

O'Brien, E. J., & Epstein, S. (1988). *The Multidimensional Self-Esteem Inventory manual*. Odessa, FL: Psychological Assessment Resources.

Paloutzian, R. F., & Ellison, C. W. (1991). *Manual for the Spiritual Well-Being Scale*. Nyack, NY: Life Advances.

Richards, P. S., Baldwin, B., Frost, H., Clark-Sly, J., Berrett, M., & Hardman, R. (2000). What works for treating eating disorders: A synthesis of 28 outcome reviews. *Eating Disorders: Journal of Treatment and Prevention, 8*, 189–206.

Richards, P. S., & Bergin, A. E. (1997). *A spiritual strategy for counseling and psychotherapy*. Washington, DC: American Psychological Association.

Richards, P. S., Berrett, M. E., & Hardman, R. K. (2001, August). *Evaluating the efficacy of spiritual interventions in the treatment of eating disorder patients: An outcome study*. Paper presented at the 109th Annual Convention of the American Psychological Association, San Francisco.

Richards, P. S., Hardman, R. K., & Berrett, M. E. (2000). *Spiritual renewal: A journey of healing and growth*. Orem, UT: Center for Change.

Richards, P. S., Hardman, R. K., Frost, H. A., Berrett, M. E., Clark-Sly, J. B., & Anderson, D. K. (1997). Spiritual issues and interventions in the treatment of patients with eating disorders. *Eating Disorders: Journal of Treatment and Prevention, 5(4)*, 261–279.

Richards, P. S., & Potts, R. (1995). Using spiritual interventions in psychotherapy: Practices, successes, failures and ethical concerns of Mormon psychotherapists. *Professional Psychology: Research and Practice, 26*, 163–170.

Richards, P. S., & Smith, T. B. (2000, June). *Development and validation of the Spiritual Outcome Scale*. Paper presented at the Annual Convention of the Society for Psychotherapy Research, Chicago.

Rorty, M., Yager, J., & Rossotto, E. (1993). Why and how do women recover from bulimia nervosa? The subjective appraisals of forty women recovered for a year or more. *International Journal of Eating Disorders, 14*, 249–260.

Shafranske, E. P. (Ed.). (1996). *Religion and the clinical practice of psychology*. Washington, DC: American Psychological Association.

Smith, F. T., Richards, P. S., Fischer, L., & Hardman, R. K. (2003). Intrinsic religiosity and spiritual well-being as predictors of treatment outcome among women with eating disorders. *Eating Disorders: Journal of Treatment and Prevention, 11*, 15–26.

Ulrich, W. L., Richards, P. S., & Bergin, A. E. (2000). Psychotherapy with Latter-Day Saints. In P. S. Richards & A. E. Bergin (Eds.), *Handbook of psychotherapy and religious diversity* (pp. 185–209). Washington, DC: American Psychological Association.

Yager, J. (1989). Psychological treatment for eating disorders. *Psychiatric Annals, 19*(9), 477–482.

4

A SPIRITUAL FORMULATION OF INTERPERSONAL PSYCHOTHERAPY FOR DEPRESSION IN PREGNANT GIRLS

LISA MILLER

DESCRIPTION OF THERAPIST

Lisa Miller is a 35-year-old, Caucasian Jewish woman who is currently an assistant professor of psychology and education in the Clinical Psychology Program at Teachers College, Columbia University. Dr. Miller has a PhD in clinical psychology from University of Pennsylvania where she studied positive psychology under Martin Seligman, a bachelor's in psychology from Yale University and has practiced in various settings since 1994 with a spiritually informed eclectic orientation.

THEORETICAL ORIENTATION

My theoretical orientation might be described as a form of Interpersonal Psychotherapy with a spiritual foundation. Interpersonal Psychotherapy (Klerman, Weissman, Rounsaville, & Chevron, 1984) holds that irrespective of its etiology, depression is ameliorated through renegotiating our in-

terpersonal relationships. To this formulation I add that interpersonal rene-
gotiation teaches us a more spiritually enlightened form of interaction, such
that interpersonal growth culminates in spiritual growth. Suffering, including nonbiologically based depression, may happen when we break absolute
spiritual laws of living, just as we skin a knee when we ignore gravity. Many
cultures and religions endorse a set of ultimate laws, which share a great deal
in common (most obviously not to kill, steal, or commit sexual transgressions). Richards and Bergin (1997) have posited the notion of the Spirit of
Truth, which I understand to be a body of pandenominational, universal
laws for living which sustain us, and if violated, can destroy us. For example,
commitment to family and keeping our word promotes a fruitful life, and
violating these absolute laws creates turmoil. Therapy is most successful—
interpersonally, emotionally, and spiritually—when as the outcome the Spirit
of Truth is upheld.

Central to my theoretical orientation is that the life transitions that
clients experience are not random, but rather they are universal opportunities for profound spiritual evolution. A parent's death, one's marriage, or
one's becoming a parent inherently transforms individuals emotionally and
spiritually. When one embraces and attends to these transitions, one can
grow interpersonally and spiritually. If ignored or left willy-nilly, however,
these opportunities for spiritual growth can devolve into depression or destructive inclinations. Of course this is old knowledge, as ancient societies
and many current-day religious practices honor these transitions throughout
the life span. In our American society, which is relatively scarce on ceremony, one needs to be mindful, perhaps even vigilant, of the power and
ultimate spiritual significance of life transitions if one wishes for the powers
to take hold in an evolutionary way.

The current case study concerns one of life's most significant transitions—the emergence of motherhood. Many religious traditions celebrate
the profound spiritual experience around conception, gestation, childbirth,
and new motherhood. In the cases presented here I attempt to show the
effect of this enormous transforming spiritual power of motherhood on young
poor mothers in Harlem, New York.

SETTING AND DEMOGRAPHICS

Seven poor pregnant girls with depression nominated themselves to
join a group Interpersonal Psychotherapy which had been explained to them
as a treatment likely to ameliorate depression and support the transition into
motherhood. At the completion of the group, the treatment was repeated
with 7 new girls in the second semester of the school year. The adolescent
girls met in a room of a public high school exclusively for pregnant and
parenting girls located in Harlem. Inclusion in the psychotherapy group hinged

on a pregnancy beyond the third month, at least moderate symptoms of depression, no indication of functional impairment, and no history of suicidal attempts (which would suggest the necessity of individual treatment rather than group). The group met for 1 hour and 15 minutes weekly for 12 sessions.

Initially the group had been constructed as a classic interpersonal treatment. It was my first time conducting a psychotherapy group for pregnant girls, although treatment of depressed poor women has been central to my clinical research and practice for nearly 10 years. I have found that treating depression in women almost always leads to discussion of spiritual life, and that central to healing is a renewed spiritual perspective. On the basis of this previous experience, I suspected that in the course of treatment the girls might show a significant spiritual underpinning to their current situation.

CLIENT DEMOGRAPHICS

The girls in the psychotherapy group ranged from 14 to 18 years of age, were African American or of Latin descent, and all lived in economic conditions below the poverty line. Of the 14 girls in the two groups, none lived with two stable parent figures (neither a mother and father nor mother and grandparent). Seven girls lived with their mothers, of whom 4 girls were primary caretakers of younger siblings and emotional supports to mothers who could not fully function. Seven girls did not live with any parent or any biological relative; 5 of these girls lived with a boyfriend, 1 girl lived in foster care, and 1 girl lived with a friend. Several of the girls had witnessed the dissolution of their biological family through intervention from child services, had been homeless, sold drugs and prostituted to pay for food, or had escaped the perceived perils of living in a government-sponsored group home. In childhood, most of the girls had been raised within some form of Christian denomination, often taught by a member of the extended family such as a grandmother. When asked about current religious beliefs, most girls responded that they were spiritual but not currently involved in either a religious community or a religious denomination. The girls spoke in group about meaningful synchronicity, instructive dreams, and signs from the Creator. Perhaps most profound, the girls spoke of their gestating children as ultimate gifts from the Creator. Love of their child was a spiritual love.

CLIENT HISTORY

The immediate commonality between the girls was the decision to carry the fetus to term. All 14 girls had been strongly urged to have an abortion by older adults such as a mother, social worker, or school counselor. Some of the girls had insisted on keeping the child at enormous personal cost: being thrown out of their mother's home, public shaming, or dismissal from their previous high school.

Contrary to prevalent assumptions in our society surrounding pregnant girls, the decision to carry the pregnancy for most girls was not based on unrealistic assumptions about children or greed. None had illusions of marriage from the baby's father or aspirations of receiving money either from him or through public assistance. The girls raised younger siblings or shared quarters with babies and young children in foster care. On one occasion I brought my own child (about 18 months old) to the group, and felt particularly taken by the girls' level of comfort and adoration for him. The girls had few prominent illusions about motherhood. Motivating the decision to keep the child was a genuine love of children and a vital sense of the sacredness of life.

Two broad paths emerged among the girls in the group—which might be called (1) *the way of the young survivors*—who had no immediate family and often had been homeless; and (2) *the way of the childhood mother*—who throughout her own childhood had been a primary caretaker for younger siblings and steadfast support for her mother.

Among the *young survivors*, several girls had left home to escape sexual abuse from a maternal boyfriend or to flee the emotional assaults of maternal substance abuse or mental illness. Other young survivors had faced parental death or parental abandonment, in the latter case often in response to news of the pregnancy. One mother had learned of her daughter's pregnancy and then left without notice or contact information on a one-way bus to Virginia. Another mother had thrown her daughter out of the house when the girl refused to have an abortion. To find money to eat, some young survivors begged, sold drugs, prostituted, or stripped. Some girls found this solution preferable to foster care or group homes. Ultimately most young survivors moved in with a boyfriend primarily for shelter. Their choices were not without moral struggle and shame.

The *childhood mothers* stood by their own mothers and younger siblings at all costs. One girl's biological father had abandoned the family and offered no financial support or relationship. Another childhood mother guided her own mother and younger siblings through a maze of homeless shelters so that they might remain anonymous from a physically abusive maternal boyfriend. Still another childhood mother fiercely guarded her two younger brothers in a particularly dangerous segment of public housing and within her home from her alcoholic mother. Childhood mothers felt highly responsible and carried an extreme sense of duty for their younger siblings, determined to shelter their siblings from parental abandonment, parental violence, and societal abuse or neglect.

The path of both the *young survivor* and the *childhood mother*, respectively, are illustrated through the personal stories of Renee and Ilana.

CASE OF RENEE: A YOUNG SURVIVOR

Presenting Problems and Concerns

Renee's mother had died within the past year, leaving Renee without a family or home. Although Renee knew her biological father, he would not allow her to live with him and his new wife, and currently refused to speak with Renee on account of her pregnancy. He was a harsh disciplinarian but unhelpful in offering support.

Renee's boyfriend also had turned against her on account of the pregnancy. On learning that Renee was pregnant, her boyfriend had insisted that she have an abortion. When Renee indicated her desire to keep the baby, her boyfriend proposed a Faustian deal: If she kept the baby the relationship would end, if she aborted the baby he would eventually offer marriage. Renee refused the boyfriend's deal, and in the third month of pregnancy the boyfriend's mother moved him to Mississippi so that he would no longer see Renee and thus disown his child.

With no family, Renee entered foster care. She petitioned the foster care system to allow her to live with her best friend's mother. Soon after Renee moved in with her best friend, the friend threatened to kick Renee in the stomach to deliberately kill her gestating baby. Renee called the police to protect the gestating child, which eventuated in the Child Welfare Agency removing the friend from the girl's own home. The girl's mother, Renee's foster mother, became furious with Renee, henceforth disallowing Renee to use the family telephone or eat food from the refrigerator. The harsh neglect from her foster care mother particularly hurt Renee as she continued to hold out hope that she might be a loving surrogate mother.

Assessment and Diagnosis

Using a structured clinical interview, Renee met *Diagnostic and Statistical Manual of Mental Disorders* (4th ed., rev.; *DSM–IV–R*, American Psychiatric Association, 2000) diagnosis for Major Depressive Disorder. Her score on the Hamilton Rating Scale for Depression (Hamilton, 1960) was a 16, indicating a moderate to severe level of depressive symptoms. From an interpersonal perspective, Renee's depression stemmed from grief: a harsh spate of abandonment and loss including her mother's death, rejection from her foster mother, and denial of love from her boyfriend who refused to acknowledge his child.

Treatment Process and Outcomes

A very pretty and vibrant African American young woman of 16 years, Renee was 5 months pregnant at the start of group. Renee would talk to her baby *in utero*, and felt a strong relationship with him. She shared with the group that she noticed the baby kicking when she confronts people who are destructive or threatening, indicating a companionship with her baby in a world where Renee was otherwise painfully alone. Renee felt that her baby boy would have good judgment and a strong will.

Renee first presented in group with a slick and sometimes jocular tone around the events surrounding her pregnancy. In the initial two sessions she was very guarded with personal material, talking tough and retributive around her losses.

After the first few sessions, however, Renee ceased resisting the opportunity to do psychotherapy. She worked from a place of genuine emotion and became a leading contributor to the group. Renee repeatedly and emphatically reviewed the episode with her boyfriend in which he had pressured her to have an abortion under penalty of abandonment. She loved her boyfriend still, and suffered enormously for his loss. Were he to return to New York, she admitted that she would quickly take him back. Amidst this heartbreak, Renee kept reiterating her decision. She asserted, "I told him that I am not going to kill my baby. No way. This is my child."

It was at this juncture that my spiritual perspective as the therapist may have informed Renee's process and the group process. I supported Renee's decision on spiritual grounds. I supported her view that preservation of the child's life was a legitimate decision, and this conveyed that she had been clear and brave in protecting her child under unsupportive conditions. I acknowledged that indeed she must love her child very much. Because I believed that Renee genuinely loved her child (that this was not an immature illusion), Renee may have felt the first signs of support from an adult for her decision to become a mother. The group supported Renee for sticking with her conviction to carry the child and to love the child, over the great pain of romantic loss. The group process may have been validating to Renee, or supportive of her healing process, in that she shared in a subsequent group, "What kind of father says that! You know, I knew that he would leave me anyway. It hurts me he does not own his child. But this is my child and I love my child. It's me and my child in this world."

Renee also shared with the group feelings surrounding her mother's death. On one occasion Renee recounted a vicious argument from the past week in which a boy in her foster care home had touched a pillow left to her from her mother. It was her only material remain of her mother. Renee was blinded with rage, threatened the other foster care child, and throughout group could not stop venting her anger. "I told him whatever you do, don't touch my mother's pillow or I'll whip you down." It was in this episode of rage around the loss of her mother that Renee's sole support behind her pregnancy became clear. "I am having this baby for me and my mother. I know that she is looking out after me, and that she will help me." She then elaborated. "You see me and my mother, we were real close. She knew what I was thinking, and would say things before I ever said a word." Renee's mother had been a bright source of love in her difficult world, now a world plagued with abandonment. The knowledge that her deceased mother watched over her as she was becoming a mother served as the sole source of solidarity, familial commitment, and guidance in her life.

Again, at this juncture in the therapeutic process, I think that my spiritual orientation as the therapist may have informed the group process. I readily supported Renee's belief that her mother walked with her and attempted to guide her as a single young mother. My endorsement of this belief may have helped Renee separate her mother's spiritual companionship from the complicated grief surrounding her ardent wish for a physical mother. Renee's complicated grief was fostering a destructive attachment to her foster mother who continued to painfully reject and degrade Renee. After several sessions, Renee shared with the group her realization, "You know she don't love. She treats me like a second class citizen." Strikingly the tone of this realization was one of clarity and relief from the confusion of a complicated bereavement.

Renee started to realistically appraise the suitability of her current living situation to motherhood. The lack of sustenance and emotional support coming from the foster mother, the lingering physical threat to the fetus by the imminently returning friend, and the lack of opportunity for child care emerged at the forefront of her concerns. The world that she had hoped was full actually, on realistic appraisal, looked empty. In group and outside of group, Renee began to investigate how she might build her world out of her desire to be a mother; to better care for her well-being and that of the soon-to-be newborn.

Throughout the emerging realism in the intermediate phase of treatment, Renee continued to speak of the unborn child from a stance of great love and intimacy, again indicating to me that her attitude toward her child was authentic and independent of the confusion surrounding her losses. Renee started speaking about what kind of role model she hoped to set for her child. She emphatically confronted a fellow group member who was struggling to step back from fistfights saying "you cannot go around getting into fights in front of your baby, what kind of mother is that?" Renee knew that motherhood was a profound transition, one that carried absolute moral standards of conduct. Once a mother, you are accountable to your child and simply accountable in an absolute sense. I supported her (as well as fellow group mothers) in the belief that motherhood is a spiritual imperative, unaltered by youth, poverty, and confusion.

In the final phase of treatment Renee announced to the group that she had successfully secured a new living situation through seeking assistance from the school social worker (whom most girls in the high school avoided for fear of losing autonomy). Renee located a government-sponsored program that would provide her with an apartment and child care while she completed her final year of high school as well as 4 years of college. Renee explained her desire for independence as the opportunity to build a world for herself and her child far away from her old neighborhood and the people who might harm her or her child. Renee had journeyed through the distortion and pain of abandonment. She had achieved clarity about the reality of her world. Now she was setting about building a new world in which her youth and poverty did not attenuate her effectiveness and love as a mother.

At termination Renee no longer met criteria for a *DSM–IV–R* diagnosis of Major Depressive Disorder and her score on the Hamilton Rating Scale for Depression had fallen from a 16 to a 4, well below the cutoff for depression.

CASE OF ILANA: CHILDHOOD MOTHER

Whereas a young survivor builds a new world motivated by motherhood, a childhood mother attempts to heal her surroundings through changing the people in her family. A childhood mother has been handed a broken world by her own mother, and now seeks to better this collective home.

Presenting Problems and Concerns

At age 14, Ilana entered treatment as one of the youngest girls in the school. Dressed in an oversized pink sweat suit, wearing a Minnie Mouse watch, and with a childlike face, Ilana appeared young. Her living situation, however, belied any trace of blithe childishness. Ilana, her mother, and two younger brothers lived in a series of homeless shelters. The family constantly relocated from one shelter to another to hide from an abusive maternal boyfriend. Ilana had been the effective leader of the family since her father had left the family 3 years ago (out of humiliation for not providing sufficient financial support); her mother was severely depressed and abused alcohol. Despite the ongoing strains of poverty, maternal dysfunction, and danger associated with living in a homeless shelter, the chief concerns for Ilana were her boyfriend's lifestyle now that he was becoming a father, specifically his use of drugs and involvement in a gang, and her mother's harsh disapproval of the pregnancy.

In contrast to several of the girls in the group, Ilana had been truly surprised by the pregnancy and was ambivalent about becoming a mother. She stated "I would not kill my baby, but I did this so I have to live with it." Ilana described the great shock and fear she felt upon learning that she was pregnant. She described her mother's fury over the pregnancy as not stemming from anticipation of another child in the very poor family, but rather out of dismay that Ilana had been sexually active. In contrast to most girls in the group, Ilana's mother, a Catholic, agreed with her daughter that the fetus was a life and that the baby must be carried to term. To the extent that she could draw a distinction between her mother's feeling and her own, Ilana did not personally feel dismayed that she had sinned, but rather simply could not stand the enduring looks of her mother's anger and disapproval.

Because of Ilana's unstable living situation, she and her boyfriend had decided that the baby primarily would live with her boyfriend and his mother. Hence it was particularly upsetting to Ilana that her boyfriend continued to use drugs and belong to a gang despite her urging to change his lifestyle. She felt that his drug use drew him away from her, and she feared that drugs would impair his capacity to parent and expose the baby to violence. Ilana also feared that the baby would grow up surrounded by fellow gang members offering only the role models of gang membership.

Assessment and Diagnosis

Ilana showed the highest level of depressive symptoms of any girl in the treatment group. In a structured clinical interview, the Schedule for Affective Disorders and Schizophrenia for Children (K-SADS), Ilana met *DSM–IV–R* diagnosis for Recurrent Major Depressive Disorder and scored 24 on the Hamilton Rating Scale for Depression, indicating severe depression.

Treatment Process and Outcomes

In the initial session, Ilana shared with the group her upset over her mother's current rejection, and her mother's disappointment in her for being sexually active. To a large extent her mother's shame colored her own senti-ment surrounding the pregnancy.

Ilana spoke extensively about her rage over her boyfriend's ongoing use of drugs and affiliation with a gang. Although her boyfriend had long used drugs and been a gang member, she had repeatedly asked him to stop these activities since learning of the pregnancy. Her greatest upset came when he had expressed his hope that the baby could be "blessed" as a gang member soon after birth, as was the custom in his gang, for lifelong membership. Despite the unstable life her own mother had offered, Ilana wanted to be-lieve that she could make a better life for her child. That her boyfriend un-dercut her efforts produced profound defeat and depression.

From the therapist's perspective, it seemed that Ilana was unaware of her extraordinary resilience and strength that allowed her to protect and guide her family through their uncertain lifestyle. Her strong desire to make a better world for her baby indicated to me that despite her ambivalence around pregnancy, her emerging motives as mother were healthy and whole.

As in the case of Renee, the treatment process surrounding Ilana was buttressed by my belief, and the belief among group members, that carrying the child to term was a valid spiritual choice, and that motherhood as an absolute spiritual calling which inherently transforms women is not less accessible to young and poor girls. The urgent treatment goal was to empower Ilana to use the emerging powers of motherhood to make a safe world for the baby. On many subsequent occasions Ilana had exercised strength and determination as a childhood mother to protect her family. She now needed to be conscious of her great maternal strength and apply it toward her own child. As a second treatment goal, Ilana's shame and negativity surrounding her pregnancy, despite her genuine concern for the child, suggested that Ilana needed to distinguish her own spiritual convictions about carrying the child from the stigma applied to her pregnancy for signaling sexual activity, ironically amidst a community in which most girls are sexually active.

As Ilana's pregnancy advanced, her mother focused away from the issue of sexual activity and became excited about the birth of a grandchild. Her mother even purchased presents for the baby out of the limited family funds. Because of her mother's emerging enthusiasm, and potentially because of the group support as well, Ilana recognized in group that most women in her community had birthed children in adolescence, and that it was relatively normative for grandmothers to help raise babies. She noticed a prevalent disparity between the structure of motherhood in her community and the duplicitous talk given to chastity. Few people in her childhood community sexually abstained in adolescence, including her own mother who had given birth to Ilana when she was 16 years old. This paradox surrounding her pregnancy then seemed to prompt spiritual individuation in which Ilana clarified her own spiritual views from those of her mother or her community. Amidst poverty, suffering, and maternal dysfunction appeared a classic adolescent spiritual individuation process. Supporting this therapeutic process may have been my belief in the spiritual validity of keeping her child and an awareness of a universal process of adolescent spiritual individuation.

For having worked on spiritual individuation, Ilana's shame over her mother's initial reaction and community stigma lifted. Ilana now claimed that although she had initially been surprised by the pregnancy, she was now eager to be a mother. She loved children. She had taken care of children all her life, and now she was eager to have her own child. Ilana recognized her sense of responsibility, preservation, and efficacy in raising her two younger brothers; these were maternal strengths. Her maternal powers would rise to new heights as she carried her own child. "It's always been that when I walk down the street guys give me a hard time. But now someone will cut him off and say 'hey, don't talk that way to her, she's going to be a mother.' Being a mother is a better thing and they know it."

Embracing her emergent motherhood gave Ilana a sense of moral authority as a mother. She now had the confidence to confront her boyfriend's drug use and his intention to swear their newborn baby into his gang. The group helped Ilana consider ways to effectively approach him. In exploring their pattern of conflict, it became clear that Ilana's urging had been ineffective because she was perceived by her boyfriend as nagging, in part because she actually had felt powerless to change the situation for her child. The group suggested to Ilana that she might explain from a position of love that his drug use made her feel, as a mother, that he did not care about her or their baby. When Ilana framed her concerns in the context of her hope that he might love and protect the baby, the boyfriend was far more able to listen. He claimed that he would try to cut back the drug use.

The group also supported Ilana in her emerging belief that she could offer her baby a life better than that she had inherited. The newborn child need not join a gang, at least not at her bequest. Ilana worked through her latent ambivalence: on the one hand the gang would have given the baby clothes and presents—her only hope for a baby shower; on the other hand she did not know if she could face her child the day he understood that she was responsible for his "blessing" by a gang. At this point the group regarded the power and authority a mother has in the eyes of her child, and that mother is often the sole source of moral and spiritual standards. Ilana clarified her feelings by saying, "If the child someday decides to join a gang, then it is his choice. A mother does not tell her child to join a gang." She was now mothering her own child.

Ilana was the most improved of any girl in the group. At 12-week termination she no longer met *DMS–IV–R* diagnosis for Major Depressive Disorder, and her score on the Hamilton Depression Scale had dropped to 5, below the range of even mild depression. Ilana's boyfriend stopped using drugs (at least for the time being) and respected Ilana's conviction that the baby not be "blessed" by the gang on the grounds that it was her wish as the mother. Even though the baby was to live with the boyfriend and his mother, Ilana's role as the mother was more clear to all involved. I believe that Ilana's extreme improvement was due to her recognition of her spiritually endowed power through which to enact motherhood.

THERAPIST COMMENTARY

None of the pregnant girls were depressed because they were poor or homeless, lacked access to opportunity, or because they did not have an easy or protected adolescence. These girls were depressed over seemingly insurmountable challenges to their emerging motherhood, a calling which they embraced with a profound respect. Depression, from a spiritual perspective, served as the valuable guide, granting focus on the necessary changes to prepare for the arrival of the baby.

Motherhood might be understood as a spiritual developmental process that starts with conception. Against all recommendations from family and counselors, and in some cases against coercion, these girls initiated mothering by insisting on carrying the child. The inherent grace and power in motherhood emerged as profoundly transforming against each girl's material and interpersonal challenges. To the extent that each girl's world budged, it is now more supportive of her motherhood. To the extent that each girl tried but the world did not budge, the girl still is now that much more a mother. It is worth considering that ultimately motherhood protected not only the new babies but also the adolescent girls. Several girls feared that had they not become mothers, they might have been destroyed by the abuse, drugs, and relational neglects that they now sought to transform.

REFERENCES

American Psychiatric Association. (2000). *Diagnostic and statistical manual of mental disorders* (4th ed., rev.). Washington, DC: Author.

Hamilton, M. A. (1960). A rating scale for depression. *Journal of Neurology, Neurosurgery and Psychiatry, 23,* 56–62.

Klerman, G. L, Weissman, M. M., Rounsaville, B. J., & Chevron, E. S. (1984). *Interpersonal psychotherapy of depression.* New York: Basic Books.

Richards, P. S., & Bergin, A. E. (1997). *A spiritual strategy for counseling and psychotherapy.* Washington, DC: American Psychological Association.

5

FORGIVENESS IN MARITAL THERAPY

MARK J. KREJCI

DESCRIPTION OF THERAPIST

Mark Krejci is a professor and chair of the Psychology Department at Concordia College in Moorhead, Minnesota, where his primary teaching responsibilities fall in the area of mental illness and psychotherapy. Dr. Krejci received his PhD in counseling psychology from the University of Notre Dame and completed a clinical psychology internship at the Norfolk Regional Center in Norfolk, Nebraska. For the past 14 years he has been seeing clients through a part-time private practice at a local Roman Catholic church. Dr. Krejci is a practicing Roman Catholic whose therapeutic orientation is influenced by both humanistic and cognitive–behavioral approaches to psychotherapy. He became interested in the use of religious coping in the lives of his clients beginning in graduate school. His research, investigating the acceptance of nontraditional (female) God images, developed as he worked with clients whose use of male God imagery reinforced traditional female/male stereotypes. Dr. Krejci recently served as editor of the *Psychology of Religion Newsletter*, a publication of Division 36 (Psychology of Religion) of the American Psychological Association.

SETTING

The clients were seen through the author's part-time (5 hours per week) private practice located at a Roman Catholic church in a moderate-size urban area in the upper Midwest. Parish staff members refer clients to the practice with self-referrals also accepted from within the parish. In addition, some clients are referred from the local Catholic diocese and other area priests. Clients are not charged for therapy. Individual, marital, and family therapy are provided for a range of issues although referrals with severe, acute mental illness are at times referred to other agencies that are able to provide more comprehensive care. The majority of cases deal with marital therapy or developmental and life adjustment issues.

CLIENT DEMOGRAPHIC CHARACTERISTICS

Mary and John were both 34 years old and married for just more than 10 years when they came in for marriage therapy. At the time of their first session, their two children were ages 8 (daughter) and 3 (son). Mary was raised Roman Catholic (RC), whereas John was raised in the Lutheran Church–Missouri Synod (LCMS) by orthodox parents. Her family of origin were devout and liberal Catholics, and Mary was always a very active church member. John, after moving to college, dropped out of active participation in the LCMS much to the consternation of his parents who feared he would not remain a Christian. At the time of their wedding, John professed a belief in God but was indifferent to active participation in a denomination although he did attend Catholic services with Mary during their courtship. Their wedding was in a Catholic church, which was fine with John, Mary, and her family, but distressed his parents. They stated a fear that this was another sign that their son was rejecting his faith, a concern that John and Mary dismissed.

Mary and John received college degrees and he worked in a professional position that required travel and long hours. Mary worked a part-time (less than 10 hours per week) retail job while the children were in school and preschool. They lived an upper-middle-class lifestyle but acknowledged that they did not have enough income to meet their perceived needs. They were devoted parents and recognized this in each other. He stopped attending RC services after approximately 2 years of marriage to take care of the baby while Mary attended services. Approximately 1 year before first contact, John started to develop a renewed interest in participating in the LCMS. John had formally joined an LCMS congregation 10 months before their first session, a move that Mary supported.

PRESENTING PROBLEMS AND CONCERNS

The couple came in for marriage therapy because of the excessive anger they felt toward each other that manifested itself in daily verbal fighting over whatever topic came up that day. The fighting included calling each other names, raising their voices to the point that the children could hear their shouting, and arguing with each other. They acknowledged that they did not listen to each other, but they justified this by their belief that the other person was wrong.

When asked what were some specific things over which they fought, they each had a very different list of topics. She said that he was condescending toward her for many reasons. According to Mary, John thought that she was not as intelligent, that she did not contribute enough to financial security by not making enough money at her part-time job and by spending too much money, and that she demanded too much from him. She further complained that he was emotionally isolated and that he put her down for having emotions. Mary felt very alone in the marriage because of her emotional isolation, and she wanted a spouse who would be able to cue in to her emotions and meet her emotional needs.

John said that he and Mary fought when she was "needling" him about what was going on in his life. He saw Mary as always checking up on him, wanting to know what he was doing every minute of his day. He used the phrase "I want a wife, not a mother" to describe how he perceived Mary as being too controlling. He also complained that she became emotional "about everything" and that she "refused" to step back and look at issues from a more logical perspective. John claimed that he was open to her emotions but that it was too draining to have her become emotional about everything in their marriage.

During the initial session when John and Mary presented their concerns, while one person was talking the other person wanted to interrupt to give the "correct" view. For example, Mary said that she was not "needling" John but only wanted to know about his life and be involved with him. John said that he never complained about Mary not making enough money but did acknowledge that he questioned her spending habits.

The couple detailed a series of past hurts that continued to be a source of anger in their lives. They listed several behaviors, perceived thoughts, and behavioral omissions that they observed in the other person that stretched over the entire marriage. For example, both individuals were able to talk about a specific incident in the first year of their marriage that continued to anger them. The anger was apparent while they recounted the incidents. The couple even attempted to argue about the details of these events that had occurred more than 10 years ago.

Thus, anger was the obvious presenting issue and the couple readily acknowledged that they did not deal well with anger or disagreements in their relationship. They did not possess good listening skills and reported that they viewed conversation with apprehension because of their common fear that any verbal exchanges would deteriorate into an argument. Because they each tended to believe that they were "correct" while their spouse was "wrong," they had very little empathy for the other's beliefs and subsequent emotional experience.

The lone area in which they could and did communicate in a positive manner was about the children. In fact, the marriage had reached a point at which the only tender exchanges between John and Mary were in relation to the children, and they stated that one motivation for keeping the marriage going was for the sake of the children. Although they acknowledged that this was not the best motivation for keeping a marriage together, they admitted that this was probably the most effective motive at that point in time. They also expressed remorse for having their children observe their arguments.

During the first session, the couple also presented that religion was becoming an increasingly contentious issue in the relationship. He stated a long-standing resentment to Mary's suggestions that he convert to RC. Mary acknowledged that early in the marriage she hoped that his nonparticipation in the LCMS and his attendance at RC services would result in him joining the RC church. She began to explicitly ask him if he wanted to join the RCIA (the Catholic church's Rite of Christian Initiation for Adults) process after the birth of their first child. His initial response was that he would "think about it" yet he admitted that he said this to give her an answer that would make her happy. He felt he could not convert because it would upset his parents and because he did not agree with some Catholic doctrine. He began to resent what he perceived as Mary's regular overtures toward him on the topic. For example, when Mary came home from mass and talked about the sermon or music at the service, John interpreted this as her attempts to make him feel guilty for not attending services and as an attempt to get him to join RCIA. Mary commented that she was only trying to share her faith experience with her husband. This behavior pattern culminated in a Sunday afternoon argument about the topic, which concluded by John stating his interest in going back to the LCMS. Mary saw this statement as an attempt to emotionally hurt her in the situation and accused John of just this, which he denied. The next day, John sought out an LCMS congregation and pastor. He joined the congregation and religious doctrine became a new source of argument for the couple. When John perceived Mary as suggesting he join the RC church, he now presented the idea that she, and the children, should join the LCMS. This type of argument had just emerged before their initial therapeutic contact and during the initial contact they acknowledged that each should be able to pursue their own denominational identity and that the children would remain RC.

CLIENT HISTORY

Mary and John were raised by married parents who stressed the virtue of a religious life. The couple had similar families of origin in that both fathers worked outside of the home, both mothers stayed at home and took care of all of the domestic responsibilities short of yard work, and both had a similar number of brothers and sisters. Neither John nor Mary could remember their parents fighting. John reported that when his mother and father disagreed, she would state her opinion and then become silent with his father's opinion prevailing. Mary did not have any insight into parental disagreements and believed that her parents just agreed on everything. The only instance when she saw anything to the contrary was when Mary and her sisters started to date. Mary's father would at times pronounce a strict rule for the evening date (e.g., to be in by 9:00 p.m.), Mary's mother would gently tease the father about his strictness, and then Mary's father would change his mind and allow more leniency. Mary and John's parents had a family structure in which the father had a greater amount of actual power in the marital relationship and the mother exerted a more subtle power.

Both John's and Mary's families of origin stressed the importance of family activities and centered many of their activities on church. The fathers were involved in leadership positions in their church yet the mothers were the ones identified by John and Mary as being more religious. One noticeable difference had to do with their ability to express religious doubt with their parents. Whereas Mary's parents accepted religious doubts and engaged her in conversation about her doubts, John's parents punished religious doubt by engaging him in what he described as "indoctrination" sessions. In the end, neither John nor Mary were rebellious about religious beliefs and participated in their respective denominations throughout their time at home.

Mary and John met in college during their senior year and saw each other daily after their first few dates. They reported that they were physically attracted to one another on first sight and that their first months of courtship were filled with only happy times, no fighting, and a general feeling of euphoria. They talked about religion early in their relationship because they believed they wanted to only get serious with a Christian who strongly believed in their faith. It was at this time that John began to go on "church dates" with Mary, going with her to Sunday mass nearly every week. As the end of their senior year approached, they talked about marriage and used school breaks to introduce each other to their families of origin. On graduation, they found jobs in their professions at companies located in major cities that were within 50 miles of each other. At first, they believed it would be easy to maintain a relationship by meeting every weekend and talking on the phone during the week. Within a year, this proved to be unsatisfactory for the couple and they decided to live in the same city. At this time, they also became formally engaged. While they looked for different employment, Mary finally moved and was employed in a lower paying job. She moved into an apartment in the same building as John to keep an illusion of separate residences for the sake of the parents, but in actuality Mary lived with John. The couple reported avoiding arguments during this period because they wanted their time together to be pleasant.

Planning for the wedding was difficult given that they were to be married in Mary's hometown but they were living in a distant city. Thus, Mary's mother made many of the arrangements, carefully checking with the couple on any needed decisions. The couple stated that this was a stress-free arrangement because all they needed to do was arrive in Mary's hometown one week before the ceremony and everything was prepared. However, the couple reported that their first argument developed over wedding plans. John's mother expressed to him that she felt left out of the preparations. John related this concern to Mary but did not suggest any resolution. Mary saw this as criticism of her and her mother and became upset that John "would think that I was trying to hurt your mother." John felt that the accusation was unjustified but did not share this view with Mary. Rather, they gave each other the "silent treatment" but ended this the next day. They never did go back and discuss the issue that created the original rift until it was brought up during therapy.

After their wedding, Mary and John continued to pursue careers until Mary became pregnant with their first child. They believed that the mother should stay at home with the children and so Mary was not employed outside of the home until 4 months prior to their first session when their son had started preschool.

ASSESSMENT AND DIAGNOSIS

The initial therapy sessions involved time devoted to assessment of the marital condition and taking a complete history of the individuals and the marriage. As part of these initial assessment interviews, couples are routinely asked about their religious beliefs and if they think that their religious beliefs could assist them as they work on their marriage. Given that both believed this to be the case, Mary and John were asked several questions about their religious beliefs, how religion influences their lives, and how they think their faith helped them deal with their marriage. The religious issues presented in this chapter were highlighted as a result of these questions. Given their denominational differences and the stress associated with their religious views, the couple completed the Christian Orthodoxy Scale (Fullerton & Hunsberger, 1982). This scale measures acceptance of core beliefs found across Christianity. Mary and Jack had very similar scores that reflected a moderate to strong agreement with the tenets of Christianity measured by the scale. As a general evaluation of the degree of conflict in the marriage, the couple also completed the Marital Satisfaction Inventory (Snyder, 1979). This assessment revealed elevations on the subscales of Affective Communication, Problem-Solving Communication, and Disagreement About Finances.

Mary and John's marriage was dysfunctional in many ways. The most obvious difficulty was the extreme and constant anger that set a negative emotional and relational tone in the marriage. The anger developed from sources of frustration that appeared early in the relationship but were never resolved through honest problem-solving communication. Rather, the couple established a pattern in which they ignored differences to avoid the ill will that developed in the short term as they coped with the issues. By ignoring the issues, the frustration grew to anger and the couple would then deal with their differences when motivated by their anger. The anger was compounded over many years given that they did not forget about their spouse's past offenses.

The marital relationship was also hurt by the lack of commonality between Mary and John. The couple did not continue to develop their relationship after their marriage. The couple fell out of the practice of talking with each other about positive topics, of developing activities that they could share, and in spending time with each other. As a result, John and Mary found themselves sharing very little with each other except for anger.

Given that the couple's agenda for therapy was to talk only about the anger, it was important for them to also spend time in sessions talking about something positive that could assist the growth of the marriage. There were two areas of agreement that existed when they first came in for therapy. One had to do with their views of the children. They agreed that the other was a good parent and that they shared love for the children. However, the children were not a good choice for building marital cohesion because they could become entangled in an emotional triangle with their parents. Also, the focus of therapy would then be on their roles as parents and not on their roles as marital partners.

The other area in which they shared some commonality was their faith in God. Given what has been discussed to this point, this may seem contradictory because John and Mary seemingly had much disagreement regarding this topic. Although it was true that they identified with different religious denominations and manifested their religious life differently, they shared a deep and genuine belief in God. They believed that their Christian beliefs were central to their lives and recognized the same in the life of their spouse. Both wanted to share their faith in their marriage but did not know how to do this. Religion had become something that they pursued individually, not something that was part of the marriage, and not something to be shared within the context of the relationship.

Marital therapy with John and Mary became primarily focused on two issues. One was the need to resolve the anger and change the basic dynamic governing interaction in the relationship. This meant developing appropriate communication, which included empathic listening, and developing problem-solving abilities. Ultimately, to resolve the lingering anger, John and Mary needed to engage in a process of forgiveness to end the sustained state of anger.

The second issue was to develop a greater sense of commonality in the relationship. This was accomplished by having the couple focus on sharing their spiritual life with each other rather than having it be a source of division. It was hoped that the couple would use the sharing of their faith life as a base from which they would begin to develop other things that they could share. Also, by focusing on their spiritual life in therapy, the couple would be examining an emotional issue in their life and sharing a positive emotion in their relationship. Finally, the two goals were connected because the couple's working image of forgiveness came from their belief in God's unconditional forgiveness.

Tan (1996) described a model in which therapists need to consider whether spiritual issues will be integrated into therapy at either an implicit or explicit level. In implicit integration, religion is not discussed as a topic during sessions but the therapist remains mindful of the clients' religious views and beliefs. In contrast, explicit integration is when the therapist and clients openly talk about religious issues from the perspective of the clients' spiritual life. Given that this couple welcomed an explicit integration, religious issues became a focus in the therapeutic process as a way for the couple to work toward improving the state of their marriage. For those couples who have an active faith life, the development of a shared spiritual life serves as a means of bringing in a positive force to their relationship. Couples can search for their roles in their marital vocation by incorporating their sense of Christian vocation into the relationship. As a Christian is called to love others, by pursuing their marital vocation within the context of their Christian vocation, the couple can share deeper love, can sacrifice with love, and can learn to forgive. When this type of love is mutual, the couple develops a deeper and more satisfying relationship.

In sum, John and Mary strongly identified with the principles of Christianity but failed to manifest these principles in their marriage. Therapy served the purpose of helping them to reflect on how to share their spiritual lives with each other and to facilitate the development of behaviors and thoughts that allow them to live Christian values with each other. This approach facilitated the work needed in forgiveness and allowed them to share a positive force in their lives.

TREATMENT PROCESS AND OUTCOME

The initial sessions involved assessment, taking complete histories, and developing goals for therapy. During these sessions, the couple repeatedly expressed anger toward their spouse every session and attempted to re-argue disagreements with the hope that the therapist would agree with their side. Not allowing this to happen, but wanting to gauge the depth of the anger, I interviewed Mary and John separately on the topic. This allowed them to be less defensive and more open about their emotions related to the marriage as well as more reflective on their own role in the marital discord. The couple kept an interaction log for 3 weeks, noting the nature of their exchanges at home. This revealed that the couple had an argument at least one time per day and that harsh words were exchanged, on average, three times per day. This number could have been higher but their overall number of interactions averaged only five per day. The only positive exchanges concerned the children.

The assessment phase revealed their strong personal commitment to their Christian faith and their desire for sharing spirituality in the marriage. Although they had areas of disagreement and argued about religious issues, the orthodoxy scale showed the couple that they shared the same basic beliefs. Their areas of religious disagreement, related primarily to denominational identity, were discussed. As mentioned previously, John had concerns that Mary wanted him to become RC and, though she initially denied this, she did admit that for several years after the birth of their first child she wanted him to convert. Mary consciously supported John's membership in his LCMS church, but he needed to reflect on schemas she developed while attending Catholic school that suggested that the RC Church was the "one true church" and that other Christian denominations were not. Mary modified these schemas after consulting with a priest about the teachings of the RC Church and by coming to the realization that her emotional allegiance to the RC Church interfered with a true acceptance of the LCMS.

John reflected on the timing of his return to the LCMS. He developed the insight that he initially returned to the LCMS as a way to punish Mary and prove to her that she was not "better" than him. He thought Mary flaunted her church participation to make John believe he was not as good as her. When John returned to the LCMS, he attended to church dogma that allowed him to use the LCMS's teachings to support him in his arguments with Mary. He told Mary that the LCMS held that men should be the authority in the family as they were in the LCMS and that this was official church teaching. The fallacy of his beliefs was dealt with in a visit with an LCMS pastor who told John that Christ teaches all Christian men to love their wives and treat them with dignity and respect. John developed an awareness that while he initially used his reconnection with the LCMS in an attempt to hurt Mary, the time back in the church awakened a new interest in congregational religious life and that he wanted to continue to participate in the LCMS for the sake of his own faith journey.

Because mutual respect of each other's denominations was established, spirituality could be used as a means for unifying the couple. The couple agreed to common goals for marriage related to their religious life. They would work toward ending their anger by attempting to forgive each other, a forgiveness motivated by the image of Jesus Christ forgiving sins. They would also work toward developing a shared spiritual, but not denominational, life as a means toward building a more positive relationship. The goals were dealt with in parallel during the course of therapy but for the sake of this chapter the topic of forgiveness in their relationship will first be addressed followed by how the couple built commonality by sharing their spiritual lives.

After completing an assessment phase and agreeing on common goals for therapy, Mary and John began to consider what they needed to do to forgive each other. They believed that, as Christians, they were expected to forgive each other and initially they thought they had forgiven the other. Yet, their forgiveness was short lived and was entirely a cognitive process. They described numerous instances when they were offended by the actions of the other, had made a conscious decision to "forgive and forget," yet when the next transgression occurred the memory and emotions of the previous events came flooding back with accompanying anger.

I presented a model of forgiveness informed by the work of Worthington (McCullough, Worthington, & Rachal, 1997; Worthington, 1998) and Enright (Enright, Freedman, & Rique, 1998) to the couple. Forgiveness was described as a process that was initiated when a decision was made to stop resenting the other person for what they had done, moving toward a process of understanding the other person with greater empathy, and finally being able to treat the offending person with a spirit of altruism. This phase of therapy focused on the couple gaining greater insight into their motivation to forgive and in stating an apology to each other.

John and Mary worked toward apologizing to their spouse by writing a letter to their spouse asking for forgiveness. These letters described what John and Mary believed they needed to be forgiven for and were worked on during individual sessions with the spouses. The apologies initially reflected senti-ments that tended to communicate "I am sorry for hurting you but I would not have done these things if you were not the person who you are." In effect, they were claiming that the actions of the other were the sole motivation for their inappropriate behavior. The couple eventually developed an apology reflective of their sorrow for hurting the other person and taking responsibil-ity for their hurtful actions. The apologies were formally exchanged and their reactions to these were processed during sessions.

After the apologies and request for forgiveness were exchanged, they struggled with the concept of making a decision to give up their resentment toward the other person. Mary and John felt justified in harboring resent-ment toward the other and the resentment was a major block to forgiveness. As part of the attempt to address their resentment, the couple was given an assignment to find religious stories and images that showed someone who forgave in spite of grievous circumstances. Such images as Christ forgiving while on the cross and God forgiving the people of Israel were used as ex-amples of God's ability to forgive all. These images were helpful models to John and Mary as they worked toward ending their resentment.

This approach resulted in the couple reflecting on their human inability to give up their resentment as God does for us, an inability that they saw as indicating sinfulness. John and Mary developed a common insight that the way they treated each other when angry represented sin in their lives. I was nondirective during this time to allow the couple to develop their own insights into the lingering anger. Mary thought that one way she could cope with her continuing resentment was to participate in the RC sacrament of Reconciliation, or more commonly called confession. John became upset with this because he thought that Mary did not need to see a priest to realize she harbored resentment toward him just as he did not need a priest to recognize the same about her. John held a common misconception about Reconciliation—that Catholics can only ask for God's forgiveness within the sacrament of Reconciliation. He learned that this was not true and that Mary wanted to experience a ritualized forgiveness, a process that he entered via prayer. Although Mary eventually went to Reconciliation, John accompanied her and prayed in the church for his own forgiveness.

The important thing at this stage of therapy was to keep the couple focused on the amount of work they needed to do within themselves and the relationship and that the Reconciliation ceremony or focused prayer was not going to be sufficient in ending all of the anger in the relationship. By turning to their religious beliefs in an attempt to end resentment, neither could expect a miraculous cure. Mary and John continued to struggle with the issue of lingering resentment as they worked toward developing empathy for their spouse.

As this topic emerged in therapy, the couple was asked to reflect on the emotions, thoughts, and motivations of their spouse. The couple started therapy with very little empathic understanding of their spouse's experience of the marriage and so they needed to hear this from each other. This also afforded the couple an opportunity to work on their active listening, which would improve marital communication. Initially, as they listened to their spouse, they would think through counterarguments. Thus, while Mary was talking about how John had hurt her when he talked to her in a condescending way, John was thinking, "What I said wasn't condescending, she is just being overly emotional." Likewise, while John was describing his view that Mary was overly emotional, Mary was thinking "he thinks he has it bad, while I could be much more emotional but I have to hold my full emotions back from him." As this tendency to cognitively counterargue was recognized, the couple was asked to identify an empathic response to their spouse's comments. Both needed to develop more of the idea that the first goal of conversation was listening versus simply talking. They also used this phase of therapy to work on their own ability to clearly communicate their thoughts and not expect the other to infer them.

Mary and John developed an ability to recognize their spouse's view of their marriage and in that process also see their own view. To deepen the understanding of the other, they worked on reframing their reactions to their spouse's statements into a more empathic reaction. They learned to listen to and accept the emotion in each other. For example, John worked toward accepting that Mary's emotions could be a rich source of energy in the relationship and Mary grew to see John's emotional indifference as reflecting an inability to understand his own emotional life.

By this point in therapy, the couple reported a decrease in the amount of fighting at home and more "civil" conversations with some positive emotional exchanges taking place. As they grew to better empathize with each other, they developed a more compassionate reaction to each other. To develop the compassion, the couple worked toward giving altruistic gifts to each other. The gifts were to be given in such a way that the spouse did not know it had happened. The issue of trust came up at this time as John and Mary were willing to give to the other but wanted to make sure the other was giving back. It was acknowledged that if only one approached the other in an altruistic spirit, the forgiving would not continue and the work they had done up to this point would slowly regress back to more arguing.

Some of the altruistic gifts were acts such as doing the other's chores, spontaneously saying words of affection, and taking care of the children to allow the other person some time alone. Another altruistic gift that the couple introduced was the idea of praying to God for blessings for their spouse. Mary and John became very interested in the idea of praying for their spouse. It was agreed that they would not be praying about the faults found in their spouse (e.g., "Oh God, make my spouse less of a complainer") because this type of prayer was ultimately seen as benefiting themselves. Rather, they prayed to God to grant positive emotional states ("Dear Jesus, bless my spouse with joy"), in thanksgiving for their spouse ("God, thank you for bringing Mary/John into my life"), or in personal petitions ("Holy Spirit, guide me so that I can be a better spouse for John/Mary"). These prayers were written together by Mary and John outside of therapy sessions and were privately prayed as part of their daily prayer life.

Even though Mary and John developed a deepening sense of forgiveness over the later sessions, the process of forgiveness was not linear as they needed to rework several issues. They recognized that forgiveness falls along a continuum and is not a yes or no issue as it is for their God. They also saw God's forgiveness as spiritual but worked toward recognizing that their own forgiveness had to also be cognitive and emotional. Mary and John, through all of the ups and downs of their marital forgiveness journey, were sustained by the image of God's forgiveness. The image of Jesus forgiving those who crucified him while still hanging on the cross became a very powerful motivator for the couple.

Gradually, forgiveness became a regular occurrence in the relationship. When new offenses emerged, forgiveness was revisited and, though the couple initially had difficulty accepting the idea that forgiveness had to be ongoing, they grew to appreciate that they were committed to seeking as well as granting forgiveness into the future. They began to say they were sorry for losing their temper in the middle of an argument. They recognized when an unresolved issue was still bothering them and sought out the other to discuss it so that anger would not develop. This resulted in a spirit of reconciliation in the relationship manifested by a decrease in arguments (averaging one argument per week at the end of therapy) and the near elimination of the exchange of harsh words. At the end of the therapeutic contact, the couple had learned to forgive each other of the past offenses, which allowed them to develop a stronger relationship focused on the positive dynamic of forgiveness and reconciliation rather than anger.

While dealing with issues related to forgiveness, the couple also began to consider how they could share their spiritual life with each other. In addition to the spiritual focus of their forgiveness work, other means to share their spiritual lives were introduced given that the couple identified this as a means to increase positive interaction in their marriage.

Initially, this was manifested by the couple praying with each other on a daily basis. This prayer was begun before the previously mentioned altruistic prayer created in response to the development of forgiveness. For prayers used early in therapy, it was suggested that they find a brief prayer that they would together offer to God for blessings on their marriage. Mary and John debated whether to construct their own prayer or use one that they knew. The couple agreed to pray the Lord's Prayer with each other just before bed. As they discussed this issue in therapy, the couple worked on developing listening skills and reflected on how they reacted to their spouse's statements.

At the beginning of the next session, anger between the two was evident when the couple reported getting into a major argument before the first time they prayed. Given his LCMS background, he wanted to include the doxology (For Thine is the kingdom, and the power, and the glory, forever and ever, Amen) as part of the Lord's Prayer. Except as used in the mass, Catholics do not commonly pray the doxology. The argument became heated and resulted in the couple not praying together that evening, not talking about the argument the next day nor praying on subsequent days, and bringing up the topic early in their next session. The couple, when reflecting on the idea that they had actually argued about how to pray the Lord's Prayer, gained greater insight into how much they were locked into an argument mode for most of their interactions. Eventually, they agreed to and did write their own prayer that they prayed on a daily basis.

As therapy continued, the couple worked toward actively sharing their religious lives in other ways. They participated in a nondenominational bible study for couples. They began to attend services in both the LCMS and RC churches together and with the children. Mary and John also reported more conversations focused on sharing their spiritual journeys with the other. The resulting positive exchanges became a means for the couple to improve their communication skills and increase the overall number of positive conversations that were now happening in their relationship.

The forgiveness and the mutual exchange of their spiritual lives resulted in the couple developing a stronger marriage. They were able to generalize the positive emotions developed from forgiveness and spiritual exchanges to other areas of their relationship. For example, going to the bible studies resulted in them realizing that they needed to spend time with just each other. That led to Mary and John occasionally going out together as a couple for meals or entertainment. Also, when disagreements now arose, they approached each other with what they described as "Christian love," which meant that they were not interested in fighting about the issue but compromising toward a solution. In general, a more positive relationship was built on the foundation of their Christian beliefs.

THERAPIST COMMENTARY

This couple's spiritual life affected therapy more than any other couple with whom I have worked. They came to therapy wanting me to settle their arguments and not thinking about their difficulties within the context of their Christian beliefs. Their anger toward each other was so strong that I found myself looking for common areas in their lives on which positive interactions could be built. It has been my experience that refighting previous arguments is not therapeutic and that anger-filled couples need to build something positive into their marriages. John and Mary expressed that they each had a spiritual life and that they wanted to share this with each other. It seemed important that the couple quickly start to have some positive interactions so that they would continue to be motivated to remain in what had become an entirely negative relationship. Thus, sharing their spiritual lives became a major theme in therapy.

I have worked with many couples on forgiveness issues. Although most of my clients express a belief in Christianity, all do not see marital forgiveness as an issue related to their spiritual lives. Mary and John did and I think this gave them additional resources on which to draw for the forgiveness they needed to give and receive. They drew hope and energy by approaching their forgiveness from a spiritual perspective because they had numerous models of forgiveness reflected in Christianity. This allowed them to move beyond a mere cognitive forgiveness to a spiritual and emotional forgiveness. An issue that needs to be addressed with some couples is the idea that they do not have to forgive. Some Christians believe that because God forgives, they do not have to. Invariably, these people turn the forgiveness over to God but keep harboring their own resentment. This couple not only realized that God would forgive their inappropriate marital behavior, but that their spouse would forgive as well.

Sharing their spiritual lives became a very effective means for this couple to develop positive emotional exchanges. If a couple tells me that they have any kind of spiritual beliefs, I will ask them to pray together for the sake of their marriage. Many couples report that they do not know how to do this and some, like John and Mary, have difficulty in agreeing how to pray. Yet, when couples work on this and develop their ability to pray, it has commonly been cited by the couple as something very unifying and positive during their therapy.

It is important that religion is not used as some type of marital panacea by the therapist and by the couple. I have worked with people in abusive relationships that believe God calls them to forgive their abuser, which they interpret to mean as needing to put up with the abuse. These individuals need to recognize the dynamics of the abusive relationship and protect themselves from further abuse. John and Mary, just like all couples who develop their spirituality within the context of marriage therapy, still needed to gain insight into their relationship that extended beyond a religious understanding. Their work went beyond developing their spiritual lives. However, using a theistic perspective allowed for therapeutic issues to be addressed and avenues to be explored that might otherwise have been overlooked. A therapist working with this couple without this perspective may not have recognized that their religious beliefs could serve as a potential source of unity in a relationship dominated by discord. Further, the forgiveness issues they addressed may not have been raised in the context of their religious faith. This religious context proved to be a motivating factor as the couple sought reconciliation in their relationship. Further, prayer would likely not have been approached as a means of increasing positive communication in the relationship. Considering therapy from a theistic perspective allowed for these issues to be raised in therapy and actively used by Mary and John as they worked to better their relationship.

As a final point of reflection, I needed to be aware of my own spirituality as I worked with this couple. First, given that I am RC, I needed to be checking my own reaction to John's and Mary's view of Catholicism. They had views different from my own and I needed to keep this in mind so as not to unconsciously attempt to shape their views toward my own. For that matter, because I pray and work toward forgiving others, both issues central to my identity, I was more nondirective during my sessions with John and Mary when the topic of religion arose. This was to ensure that they developed a shared spirituality that reflected their individual religious lives and not influenced by my own. For example, when they regularly referred to the forgiveness image of Christ on the cross, they were, in effect, using the cross as a metaphor for their marriage. My own spiritual journey would not lead me to this image, but it was very effective for John and Mary as they worked toward understanding how to forgive in their marriage.

Clients' faith beliefs can be a tremendously powerful tool for coping with issues addressed in therapy. Christian beliefs are, at their core, positive and affirming in a person's life. Even though religion, as it was initially in this case, can have a potentially negative effect, it has ultimately proven to be a positive force when individuals search for the core beliefs and values of their spiritual traditions. Although most of my clients have been Christian, I found this to also be the case with Hindu, Buddhist, and Native American clients with whom I have worked.

REFERENCES

Enright, R. D., Freedman, S., & Rique, J. (1998). The psychology of interpersonal forgiveness. In R. D. Enright & J. North (Eds.), *Exploring forgiveness* (pp. 46–62). Madison: University of Wisconsin Press.

Fullerton, J. T., & Hunsberger, B. (1982). A unidimensional measure of Christian orthodoxy. *Journal for the Scientific Study of Religion, 21*, 317–326.

McCullough, M. E., Worthington, E. L., & Rachal, K. C. (1997). Interpersonal forgiving in close relationships. *Journal of Personality and Social Psychology, 73*, 321–336.

Snyder, D. K. (1979). *Marital Satisfaction Inventory*. Los Angeles: Western Psychological Services.

Tan, S. Y. (1996). Religion in clinical practice: Implicit and explicit integration. In E. P. Shafranske (Ed.), *Religion and the clinical practice of psychology* (pp. 365–387). Washington, DC: American Psychological Association.

Worthington, E. (1998). An empathy-humility-commitment model of forgiveness applied within family dyads. *Journal of Family Therapy, 20*, 59–76.

III

INDIVIDUAL DENOMINATIONAL THERAPIES (WITHIN FAITHS)

6

SPIRITUAL INTERVENTIONS IN THE TREATMENT OF DYSTHYMIA AND ALCOHOLISM

RICHARD DOBBINS

DESCRIPTION OF THERAPIST

Richard Dobbins is a 75-year-old White man who is a traditional Pentecostal. Dr. Dobbins holds a doctorate with dual credentials as a psychologist and ordained minister with the General Council of the Assemblies of God. He has been in practice as a therapist for 37 years. His theoretical orientation is eclectic, with a heavy emphasis on dynamic and cognitive approaches to therapy. He founded EMERGE Ministries, an Evangelical Christian Mental Health center in 1974 and has remained there as director and chairman of the board. He also is a professor in a graduate program of counseling in which EMERGE Ministries partners with Ashland Theological Seminary, a Brethren seminary located in Ashland, Ohio, approximately 40 miles from EMERGE. This 2-year cohort program is now in its 27th year and satisfies the legal academic requirements for preparing students to take the licensing exam for counseling in Ohio.

TREATMENT SETTING

Kathy was seen at EMERGE Ministries where 1 psychiatrist, 4 other psychologists, and 14 master's level therapists see between 300 and 400 people per week. The clients seen at the center range from preschool children to senior citizens and present a full array of mental health problems: childhood physical and sexual abuse, learning disabilities, addictive disorders, individual adjustment problems, conjoint marital, divorce, and so forth.

CLIENT DEMOGRAPHIC CHARACTERISTICS

Kathy, a 51-year-old female Caucasian homemaker, was seen at EMERGE, an evangelical Christian mental health center in Akron, Ohio. After graduating from college Kathy met and married her husband Bert while he was still in medical school. When she came for therapy he was a 59-year-old medical doctor. They had been married 29 years and had two sons: Raymond, age 27, and Robert, age 24. Bert and Kathy were active members of a traditional Pentecostal church (Assemblies of God) when they initially presented for marriage counseling.

PRESENTING PROBLEMS AND CONCERNS

Bert and Kathy had grown apart through the years and expressed a desire for conjoint marital counseling to revitalize their relationship. However, during the intake process Kathy acknowledged she had struggled with depression for more than 20 years. Her attempts to find relief in alcohol finally resulted in her becoming addicted. Her alcohol addiction was very disruptive to her family so they focused on dealing with that while her depression had been left undiagnosed and untreated for years.

Kathy had found periodic help for her alcoholism through Alcoholics Anonymous (AA). However, because the traumas underlying her depression were never dealt with she would inevitably turn again to alcohol for relief. So, she wondered whether it would be better for her if she were to be seen in individual therapy before any attempt at marriage counseling was made. The therapist agreed that this would be a wiser procedure.

CLIENT HISTORY

Kathy's depression was rooted in a very sad and tragic family history. She was the youngest of four siblings: two brothers and a sister. All of them were deceased at the time she entered treatment.

Kathy recalled no display of affection or other evidence of an emotional bond between her parents during the years she was in the home. She recalled no evidence of an emotional bond between her mother and any of her siblings, including herself.

During her childhood Kathy was closer to her father than her mother, but she seemed to be the child both parents chose as a confidant. She had to listen to both of them express dissatisfaction with their troubled marriage. This role became deeply traumatic for Kathy when, at age 6, her father told her about his girlfriend. Of course she was expected to keep this information from her mother.

From the time she was age 10, her father used Kathy as a courier to send his lover money for her house payment. Kathy's mother knew about the affair, but she did not know about the money Kathy's father was giving to his lover. Keeping this secret from her mother was a major source of guilt for Kathy. It was the root of much of her hatred of her father.

The woman in her father's life was very affectionate with Kathy. So Kathy reached out to her to compensate for the absence of affection in her relationship with her mother. Often, her father would use Kathy as a liaison between him and his girlfriend. She would carry notes from one of them to the other. As a child, Kathy was torn between her need for the affection she received from her father and his girlfriend and her guilt over betraying her mother in protecting their secret.

One day, while Kathy's mother was lamenting about the affair her father was having, Kathy learned that earlier her father had infected her mother with a sexually transmitted disease he acquired from other promiscuous relationships. That disease resulted in the loss of vision in her mother's right eye. Kathy knew her mother could not see out of her right eye, but until then never knew why.

This incident intensified the ambivalence Kathy felt toward both her mother and her father. She despised her father for doing something so despicable and lost respect for her mother because she tolerated it and stayed in the marriage.

ASSESSMENT AND DIAGNOSIS

Kathy was administered the Minnesota Multiphasic Personality Inventory (MMPI) and the Sentence Completion Blank (SCB). The validity scales on the MMPI were within normal range. There were significant elevations on the 2, 4, 6, and 7 scales. Several responses to the SCB reflected the "helpless-hopeless" syndrome often seen in depressed and addicted clients.

Testing and evaluation resulted in the following *Diagnostic and Statistical Manual of Mental Disorders* (4th ed., *DSM–IV*; American Psychiatric Association, 1994) diagnosis:

Axis I: 300.40 Dysthymic Disorder
       305.00 Alcohol Abuse
Axis II: V 71.09
Axis III: V 71.09
Axis IV: Marital Stress
Axis V: GAF 55

TREATMENT PROCESS AND OUTCOME

After her initial session Kathy was referred to her medical doctor for antidepressant medication. She adjusted well to it and this enhanced her ability to participate in the therapeutic process.

Beginning Phase of Therapy

Kathy's alcoholism precipitated the crisis that brought her to counseling. Therefore our first goal was keeping the addiction under control so Kathy could effectively engage in therapy.

I took a complete history of Kathy's addictive behavior. Succumbing to peer pressure, Kathy began to drink as a sophomore in high school. By the time she and Bert got married she had learned to disguise her drinking so well he was not aware of it. During her pregnancies Kathy managed to stay sober but not long enough to nurse her babies. After I took the history of her addiction, I showed her a four-stage cognitive–behavioral model for "putting off the old self . . . putting on the new self," based on the Apostle Paul's admonition to Ephesian Christians (see Figure 6.1).[1] Then I explained the four stages somewhat as follows:

> As you can see, the horizontal plane represents the time when you are free from temptation. This is why it is called the Plane of Rest. The vertical plane represents the rising intensity of your need to drink. So it is referred to as the Plane of Intensity. As you move up the Plane of Intensity you reach a point beyond your control. The only successful way you have learned to relieve this intensity is to drink alcohol. So you "act out." This does succeed in relieving the intense turmoil you are experiencing, but at the expense of deepening your addiction and lowering your self-esteem. Inevitably, once the effects of the alcohol diminish you evaluate yourself and feel defeated by the addiction. Notice the calibrations on the vertical plane of intensity. Try to define the urgency of your temptation to drink by identifying it with a number on this vertical plane.

---

[1]Ephesians 4:20–24

Now look at the window of escape introduced in Stage 2. It represents a period of time you have to engage in some other kind of behavior approved by your conscience that also will break the intensity of your craving for alcohol and turn it back toward the plane of rest, enabling you to avoid reaching the point of inevitable acting out. The discovery that this plane of intensity can be broken by some behavior other than drinking results in tremendous relief and a positive self-evaluation.

At this point, it is important that you mentally compare the way you remember feeling about yourself when you resorted to alcohol to break this tension with how you feel about yourself when you use some other behavior, consistent with your conscience, to break it. However, it is important for you to understand that once the intensity builds beyond the upper limits of this window of escape, you will lose control and proceed toward the point of inevitable acting out. This is when your addiction takes control of you and acting out becomes inevitable.

Then, I explained the two things that must happen if successful treatment is to occur. Kathy would have to define the following:

1. The triggering mechanisms that compelled her to alcohol. Was it loneliness, depression, stress and conflict, things not going well in the marriage, and so forth? She would need to identify as many of these triggering mechanisms as possible.
2. Substitute behaviors consistent with her value system that would help her turn the rising intensity of temptation back toward the plane of rest.

Kathy was told to notice the time intervals on the plane of rest and estimate the time it took her to process her temptation through the window of escape and return to the plane of rest. I explained that she should be able to trace her recovery by noticing the number of times she was able to anticipate the triggering mechanisms and to implement her substitute behaviors. I reviewed with her a printed copy of the typical homework assignments for Stage 1, which are as follows:

1. Bring to the next session a list of triggering mechanisms.
2. See how early you can detect the rising level of intensity.
3. Discover some substitute behaviors that work for you.
4. Hold yourself responsible for being honest and accountable to your counselor and at least one other person in reporting temptations, failures, and successes.
5. Memorize at least one verse of Scripture from the recommended list each day.
6. Carry your accountability card with you all the time and read it during your devotions each day.
7. Daily rate your feelings about yourself on a 10-point scale ranging from 1 (*worst*) to 10 (*best*).

A

Putting Off the Old Self/Putting On The New Self
Ephesians 4:22–24

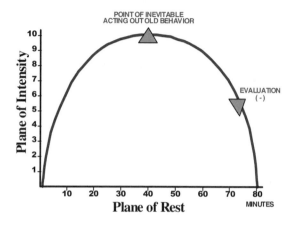

B

Putting Off the Old Self/Putting On The New Self
Ephesians 4:22–24

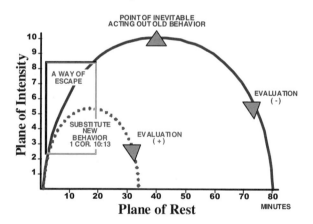

Figure 6.1. Four-stage cognitive model for putting off the old self and putting on the new self (Ephesians 4:22–24).

continues

C

"You were taught, with regard to your former way of life, to put off your old self, which is being corrupted by its deceitful desires; to be made new in the attitude of your minds; and to put on the new self, created to be like God in true righteousness and holiness." (Ephesians 4:22-24, NIV)

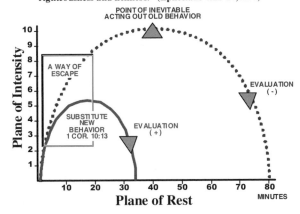

D

Putting Off the Old Self/Putting On The New Self
Ephesians 4:22–24

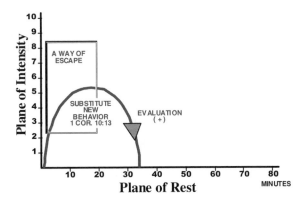

Figure 6.1. Continued.

I explained that the solid line in Stage 2 indicates that acting out would still be the most frequent way of dealing with the buildup of stress. However, there would be times when substitute behaviors would work to bring the plane of intensity back to the plane of rest. Kathy was encouraged to compare the way she felt about herself when she acted out with the way she felt about herself when she took the way to escape temptation.

By contrasting these feelings, Kathy would learn the relationship between the new spiritual disciplines she was learning and her ability to choose the way to escape rather than acting out as a means for relieving the stress of temptation. The following is a set of typical homework assignments for Stage 2:

1. Review triggering mechanisms and add any new ones you have discovered.
2. Report any improvement in becoming aware of the rising level of intensity earlier in the process.
3. Report which substitute behaviors are most helpful and indicate any new ones you may have discovered.
4. Continue to hold yourself responsible for being honest and accountable to your counselor and at least one other person in reporting temptations, failures, and successes.

I called attention to the progress that would be indicated in recovery by showing Kathy that in Stage 3 the solid line of "acting out" is now a broken line and the line of the "way to escape" is now solid (see Figure 6.1, Panel C). This indicates that, most of the time, at this stage in her recovery she would be able to identify the triggering mechanisms and put the substitute behaviors into place so that she would find the way to escape and avoid the need to act out. Instead of feeling defeated, she would feel victorious over a bondage that had left her feeling defeated for years.

I then called her attention to the final stage of treatment. Here the old behavior has been replaced by the new behavior. The "old self" has been put off. The "new self" has been put on. I urged her to have patience with herself in the process of recovery, reminding her that this usually involves a period of 6 to 18 months.

Putting off the old person and putting on the new person was a Bible teaching that Kathy had been familiar with for years. She knew she ought to be able to do this, but she did not know how to do it. I reminded her that Christ was living in her mental process and as she demonstrated a willingness to break free from her addiction, she could count on Him to strengthen her will. She welcomed this practical application of her faith and found that when joined with weekly group meetings at AA it was very affective in helping her successfully battle her addiction. Eventually Kathy became an AA sponsor.

Intermediate Phase of Therapy

Within 4 months Kathy had made sufficient progress in overcoming her problem with alcohol to begin working on reframing some of the major traumas in her history. This was signaled by her announcing at the beginning of one session, "I was able to drive myself here today. Up until now, I have had to depend on someone else to bring me. This is the first time in months I have had the courage to drive on the interstate."

The intake interview had surfaced several major goals for Kathy's therapy: her self-image (which greatly improved as she recovered from alcoholism), her relationship with her father, and her relationship with her mother. So, Kathy chose to focus first on her relationship with her father.

I have found "praying through" to be an effective way of helping believers cognitively restructure or reframe traumas in their history. I explained to Kathy that none of us lives with the facts of our history. We live with the feelings generated by the way we interpret the facts of our history. These interpretations become stories we use to explain our life to ourselves and others. The facts of our history cannot be changed, but these facts are subject to a variety of interpretations ranging from very destructive ones suggested by Satan to very creative ones suggested by the Lord.

Kathy was very familiar with the term *spiritual warfare*. Hence, I shared my belief with her that spiritual warfare is the ongoing battle between the urges, fantasies, and ideas stimulated in her mind by the Lord and those stimulated by Satan. This battle is fought for control of how the believer explains life to herself.

Although we cannot change the facts of our history, the stories we tell ourselves about the facts of our history can be edited. When we learn to talk to ourselves differently about the traumas in our history we learn to feel differently about them. I explained to Kathy that mental processes are not simply driven by neurohormones or neurotransmitters, but spiritual intrusions influence the interpretations we impose on events in our history. Invisible spiritual powers are at least as active in shaping our interpretations of the events of our world as invisible, natural forces are in shaping the physical world. Christ wants to use His healing influence to suggest more redemptive ways of interpreting our painful experiences while Satan wants to maximize their crippling impact upon us.[2]

I shared with Kathy that the most effective way I have found for facilitating this editing process is by "praying through." Of course, she wondered what was involved in "praying through." I explained this circular four-step process to her, adding that in some ways "praying through" is like peeling an onion. The pain of the past is dealt with one layer at a time . . . and you may cry a lot.

---

[2]John 10:10

Step 1: Talk to God Honestly About What Hurts You

The painful parts of Kathy's history with her father were stored in her memory when she was very young. There are ideational and emotional components to these memories. Often, the ideational dimension fades over time, but the painful emotional residual continues to intrude on and color our current view of life. The Apostle Paul seems to refer to this as "dark glass," or the distorted lens through which each of us views life.[3]

If we can identify these painful feelings and talk about them, we can modify them. But if we cannot identify them and articulate them we may not be able to modify them. "Praying through" is designed to help a person get in touch with painful feelings from their past by recalling the underlying historic events and any relationships involved with them.

A therapeutic letter is often useful in bringing the ideational and emotional components of our history together. I asked Kathy to begin writing her father a letter that she never intended to mail. I suggested that she probably would not be able to get everything she wanted to say written in the first installment, but this would give her something she could read to God in prayer as this first step.

By way of helping her talk to God honestly I asked her to read several of David's imprecatory Psalms (e.g., Psalms 35; 54–59) in which he tells God just how he feels toward his enemies.[4] Sometimes, a person finds this difficult especially if he or she is uncertain about how God feels toward him or her, but Kathy seemed to welcome the opportunity. Reading such a letter to God encourages the person to familiarize himself or herself in prayer with God. Expressing himself or herself to Him in prayer becomes an important part of the therapeutic process.

Step 2: Emotionally Respond to the Contents of Your Letter

In this second step in "praying through," Kathy was encouraged to allow the feelings originally generated by this hurtful history to surface and be expressed to God in a cathartic prayer. She was to plan her time for "praying through" when she would be alone. Such intense prayer and emotion can be upsetting for children or confusing to adults who might not understand.

Because Kathy's ego defenses were strong enough to support such a catharsis, I encouraged her to weep and pray intensely so that the underlying emotions could be discharged and not interfere with her entertaining less painful ways of interpreting the events and relationships referred to in the letter.

Kathy was instructed to remain in prayer until she received recognizable emotional relief . . . until the emotional burden lifted. At this point she was encouraged to take the next step in this process.

---

[3] I Corinthians 13:12
[4] Psalms 35; 54–59

Step 3: Meditate and Wait for God to Give You a New and Less Painful Interpretation of This Damaging Chapter in Your Life

I drew a continuum representing the many ways her history could be interpreted ranging from very destructive to very creative. I assured Kathy that as she waited on the Lord she could trust the Holy Spirit to help her formulate increasingly more redemptive and healing understandings of her painful history with her father, moving her more and more from the destructive side of the continuum toward the creative side.

The more often she would expose this painful part of her history to her loving Heavenly Father the more redemptive ways He would give her for interpreting it. I assured her that God loved her and wanted to heal her mind of this crippling pain.

Step 4: Thank God for Helping You Store in Your Memory This New Way of Looking at Your Old Hurt

Kathy was to thank and praise God for new interpretations of the old experiences received in Step 3. It is important to spend time mentally rehearsing the new interpretations so they are seated in memory in such a way as to override the old way of looking at it. Kathy was to write this new view of her old hurt down in her Bible and date the time when she received it.

She was instructed to repeat this four-step process until she could recall nothing else to write. When she was no longer troubled by her memories of her relationship with her father, I asked her to design a symbolic way of destroying what she had written in the presence of her pastor or someone she trusted, thus bringing closure to this process.

Over the next 6 months Kathy worked hard in therapy dealing with the destructive history of her relationship with her father. Her self-esteem began to recover as she dealt honestly with these feelings from her past. The higher her self-esteem rose the more effectively she worked at "praying through."

Finally, this circular process brought her to the place where she was able to forgive her father. She arranged a meeting with him to share her disappointment in him and to express her forgiveness to him. Then she was ready to destroy her therapeutic letter.

The way she chose to do that was very interesting. She asked me if I would observe her tearing the letter up in tiny pieces and flushing it down the commode, "as so much waste in my life." It was gratifying to experience the elation of that moment with her.

Over the next 3 months we targeted her history with her mother for "praying through." As Kathy got in touch with the contempt she felt toward her mother for being so dependent as to stay in such a destructive relationship, she began to get insight into why vulnerability was so frightening for her. She also began to understand why she detested any hint of weakness in herself.

She experienced more ambivalence in dealing with her relationship with her mother than she did in dealing with her father. There were no redeeming virtues to temper her rage toward her father. However, the thought that her mother might have stayed in the relationship to keep the home together for the children was very disturbing for her.

Finally, she was able to vent her anger toward her mother for the pain she experienced from feeling no maternal love. She forgave her. Even though her mother had died several years before Kathy came into therapy, the use of a therapeutic letter and the process of "praying through" proved to be an effective way of helping her put closure on this painful part of her past. She chose to destroy this letter by burning it in a metal container symbolically offering it to God as a burnt sacrifice.

Final Phase of Treatment

The last few months of therapy focused on Kathy's self-esteem. Effectively dealing with the traumatic history of her childhood had relieved much of her depression. Her medical doctor was able to reduce her antidepressant medication.

Successfully sponsoring another member of AA added to her growing sense of self-worth. However, there were two junctures in her history that were still very painful for her. One had to do with allowing herself to receive affection from her father's lover. This became especially painful when, at about 12 years of age she learned the cause of her mother's blindness in her right eye. Then, guilt for betraying her mother by keeping her father's secret began to haunt her. She hated herself for allowing herself to receive affection from "that woman."

The other trauma she had to deal with occurred when she fell in love for the first time with a man who betrayed and rejected her. As a devout person, Kathy construed this to mean that God was visiting some kind of divine retribution on her for betraying her mother.

Obviously, the condemnation she felt was self-imposed. I asked her if she had ever asked God to forgive her for hating her father and betraying her mother. She assured me she had. So, I asked if she believed God had forgiven her. She said, "Oh, yes. I believe God forgave me the first time I asked Him, but how can I ever forgive myself."

I then asked her on what basis she believed God was able to forgive her. She replied, "Jesus died for my sins. So, God can forgive me." Then I asked, "If God can forgive you because Jesus died for your sins, shouldn't Jesus's death for your sins allow you to forgive yourself?"

This insight proved to be liberating for Kathy. We revisited this exchange several times during the termination phase. Her new attitude toward herself is reflected in this excerpt from a letter I received from her a year after termination.

Three and a half years ago I could not write a thank you note much less a letter. There is so much I have thought of saying to you, but words just fail me. I think of myself when I came to your office as merely being like a picture frame with so many pieces of the picture outside the frame. I guess a jigsaw puzzle with nothing much put together would be more like it, just a fragmented personality. Time has dulled the memory of that devastating emotional pain and I continue on the road to being a whole person. This is a far cry from the person who felt unworthy to even go to church. This letter is just trying to thank you for directing me on the road to mental health.

THERAPIST COMMENTARY

Sharing a common faith with Kathy created a trust that enabled her to build a therapeutic relationship quickly with me. By using spiritual interventions such as "Putting off the Old Person and Putting on the New Person" and "Praying Through," Kathy found help and healing through concepts that were familiar to her. These were critical in helping Kathy deal with the complexities of dysthymia and alcohol addiction. The therapeutic use of Scripture and prayer proved to be important parts of each session I had with Kathy.

When the therapist shares common spiritual resources of faith with the client they can become powerful tools in the therapeutic process. They assist in building rapport and facilitate the treatment process necessary for helping believing clients experience healing from life's hurts and deliverance from crippling addictions.

REFERENCE

American Psychiatric Association. (1994). *Diagnostic and statistical manual of mental disorders* (4th ed.). Washington, DC: Author.

7

JUDAIC THERAPEUTIC SPIRITUAL COUNSELING: GUIDING PRINCIPLES AND CASE HISTORIES

AARON RABINOWITZ

This chapter describes the attempts of one psychologist, myself, in alleviating psychological distress and emotional pain. The uniqueness of this chapter, as of the other chapters in this book, is that the focus is on the religious and spiritual dimensions of the problems and the therapy. Psychological pain may be rooted in (a) the client's dissatisfaction with his or her fulfillment of religious obligations, and (b) in situations in which the presenting problem does not have discernible religious characteristics, but, nevertheless, hints at spiritual aspects that bear examining. Another feature of this chapter is the presentation of spiritual and theistic material that can be used in the therapeutic encounter with almost all patients.

The theoretical basis and the techniques used in therapy that includes spiritual counseling are no different than the principles that guide me and the methods I use in my usual practice of psychotherapy. There are, however, problems and patients for which the inclusion of spiritual goals and the discussion of religious material contribute greatly to successful therapy. In this respect, my approach is similar to that advocated by Richards and Bergin (1997, p. 116). Inclusion of spirituality is naturally appropriate for religious or spiritually inclined patients. There are also instances in which this novel therapeutic approach is suited for nonreligious clients as well. Furthermore, I believe that some of the material is useful for non-Jewish clients, emphasizing as it does, universally accepted ethical and moral values. Source materials are the Bible, Talmud, Midrash, and the teachings of Jewish sages from the distant past to the present generation. This integrative, multifaceted therapy strives to present the spiritual viewpoint and values so that they are perceived as an integral part of the therapy. This requires attuning the religious teachings with my understanding of personality. I feel most comfortable with the dynamic approach assigning a prominent place to unconscious motivational forces. I do not, however, accept instinct theory as the prime mover of behavior. I am convinced that the two, the concept of the unconscious and instinct theory, are not inseparably linked. Interpersonal relations theory, object relations theory, seem to me as more accurately portraying the human condition. In addition, the concept of the self-image, both as an energizer and as a barometer of one's functioning, seems to me an important component both of personality and of the therapeutic process. Combining psychotherapy with spiritual counseling also implies, in my view, a fusion of methodologies. Cognitive therapy seems appropriate for spiritual counseling that sometimes deals with analysis of theistic doctrines and their relevance to the patient, joining cognitive and dynamic therapy to form what is perhaps a new entity—therapeutic spiritual counseling. This unique combination ensures that the spiritual facets touch on people's deepest emotions and burrow deep into their hidden recesses.

Introspection regarding the steps taken in my development as a clinician leads me to conclude that my orthodox Jewish beliefs directed me to view the unconscious as a vital cog in the structure of personality. This process seems to have operated as well for other principles to which I subscribe. In this respect, my religious beliefs, psychological orientation beliefs, and personality are congruent. It is generally accepted that all clinicians choose a therapeutic approach in accordance with their philosophy and personality. My studies seem to confirm what others have said as well, that Jewish thought accepts and anticipates the impact of the unconscious on behavior and personality, but it does not view instinct theory as the basis of personality (Rabinowitz, 1999, pp. 41–95).

My clinical work is in addition to my teaching load at Bar-Ilan University from which I recently retired. The majority of my clients are Israeli, but I have also treated Americans and others who have come to Israel for either an extended or limited period of time. Sessions are held in my office at home. I was born in 1931 in the United States where I attended yeshivot (rabbinical academies) and City College in New York (where I earned a bachelor's and a master's degree). My doctorate is from Bar-Ilan University. I am an orthodox Jew and follow *Halacha* (Jewish law). It affords me great pleasure that I lecture daily in Talmud at the local synagogue.

The following points need to be addressed before proceeding. Advocates of a rapprochement between religion and psychiatry–psychology are increasingly discontented with mere accommodation between the two and instead promote dialogue which, hopefully, will lead to integration (Blazer, 1998, chap. 2; Richards & Bergin, 1997, Part II). There are many issues pertinent to the dialogue. I want to note two points that should be discussed to avoid misleading therapists who use theistic–spiritual material. Blazer (1998), in a critique of popular books on Christian counseling, appreciated their strong points but criticized what he considered weak points. An example is his critique of proposed facile formulas to deal with depression. He writes,

> Though he (the author) quotes Scripture frequently, he usually extracts passages to support his formula, as opposed to searching the Scriptures themselves for a deeper understanding of the pain of depression. The ancient biblical writings are filled with wisdom relevant to the depressed in the 20th century. The ancient writers both expressed and empathized with persons suffering emotional pain. No formulas were provided to guarantee freedom from depression. (p. 119)

I fully concur with his statements (Rabinowitz, 2001).

This leads to the second point. Blazer is disturbed that psychiatry and religion have not grappled with the angst that pervades Western society. The following is his analysis of why this is so:

> We live in a disturbingly narcissistic society, a society that demands instant gratification, including the right to emotional well-being. . . . Anti-intellectualism also pervades psychiatry and Christianity. . . . Christianity is not about instant relief, immediate gratification and the power of positive thinking. . . . The Christian life is a goal-directed life given meaning by the fullness of the Judeo-Christian heritage, a life that struggles every step of the way, a life that often suffers emotionally. (p. 97)

This perception of religion has been articulated by Rabbi Dr. Soloveitchik (1983): "The popular ideology contends that the religious experience is tranquil and neatly ordered, tender and delicate. . . . If you wish to acquire tranquility without paying the price of spiritual agonies, turn unto religion" (p. 141). He repudiates this as anti-intellectual:

> This ideology is intrinsically false and deceptive. That religious consciousness in man's experience which is most profound and most elevated . . . is not simple and comfortable. On the contrary, it is exceptionally complex, rigorous, and tortuous. Where you find its complexity, there you find its greatness. Religion . . . (is) a raging clamorous torrent of man's consciousness with all its crises, pangs, and torments. (Soloveitchik, 1983, p. 141)

Therapists practicing therapeutic spiritual counseling will do well to heed the cautionary note inherent in the previous passage. This does not negate using spiritual material to foster serenity and other traits described in the book edited by Miller (1999). It does mean that therapists should not expect spiritual counseling to be a panacea.

THREE GUIDING PRINCIPLES IN THERAPEUTIC SPIRITUAL COUNSELING

Efficacious use of the concept of the unconscious in therapeutic spiritual counseling is enhanced by introducing it as having been promulgated by one of the great talmudists and ethicists of the 19th century, Rabbi Israel Lipkin (Yisroel Salanter). He related the following hypothetical story. A scholar has an apt student to whom he is strongly attached, and a son, a wastrel whom he despises. They all reside in the same town and are asleep when fire erupts. The scholar, awakened from a deep sleep and informed that his son and student are in danger, will instinctively hasten to his son's rescue rather than to his student. This is so because not being fully awake, he is not in complete possession of his rational cognitive faculties. In this state the instinctual "inner" forces are dominant and the rational "outer" forces are unable to influence behavior. The concepts of inner and outer forces are used to explain two apparently contradictory sayings of the sages recorded in the *Midrash* (the non-Halachic, non-legal teachings found in the Talmud and similar books, also called *Aggadah*). Abraham is described in one saying as eagerly and joyously obeying God's command to sacrifice his son Isaac. In a different saying, he is depicted as weeping. Rabbi Salanter resolves the contradiction by explaining Abraham's behavior as a function of both inner unconscious forces and outer conscious forces. On the conscious level he cheerfully prepared to carry out God's wish, but inner instinctual forces caused his weeping; they could not be denied their measure of grief. Inner unconscious components of personality cannot be eliminated or controlled to the extent that they will not be experienced. The inner forces are "unclear" forces; the outer are "clear" forces. This distinction explains why the inner forces are more powerful than the outer forces; they are not familiar and seem to emerge from nowhere and overwhelm the unwary. My clients, especially those who are familiar with the Talmud and its dialectical method of reasoning, are usually receptive to the concept of the unconscious. Its use as a tool for uncovering hidden material by paying attention to subtleties of thinking and slight variations of behavior is similar to their method of textual analysis (Handelman, 1981; Jennings & Jennings, 1993).

Introspection also reveals that my predilection for the other principles guiding me, the importance of interpersonal relations and the concept of the self-image, is also rooted in my religious philosophy. The very basis of Judaism is communal. It can be reasonably argued that in this respect, Judaism is closer to the Far Eastern concept of communal cohesion than to Western individuality, although the individual is of paramount importance.

Mine ordinances shall ye do, and My statutes shall ye keep, to walk therein: I am the Lord your God. Ye shall therefore keep My statutes . . . ." (Pentateuch Leviticus 18:4,5, Hertz translation, 1941)

The verses are in the plural, indicating that the nation, as a nation, is to follow the Torah's ordinances. The individual (in this sense) is of consequence only when part of the community (Meshoch Chochma in his commentary). In his comments on Leviticus 23:21, he writes that mitzvot (commandments) associated with the holidays bind individuals to one another forming a community to serve Him. This is contrasted to the Sabbath mitzvot that serve to bind each individual to God. We are taught that both the community and the individual play important roles in life's mosaic. The Ramban—Nachmanides (a major medieval Talmudist and Bible commentator) focuses on the language of the Ten Commandments. The Torah phrases the prelude to the Decalogue in plural language, whereas the Decalogue itself is in the singular. His interpretation is that the singular is used to emphasize personal responsibility. One should not be deluded into thinking that punishments for transgressions will be meted out only to the community as a whole and not to individuals. It is striking to entertain the thought that perhaps individuals would not be punished for personal transgressions. This attests, on one hand, to the importance of the community, and on the other hand that nevertheless each individual is held liable for himself or herself.

Rabbi Dr. Soloveitchik (1965), a foremost Talmudist and profound philosopher, develops the theme that prophecy is a communal phenomenon. The prophet must bear in mind that he or she is only a messenger. Moreover, the prophecy must contain a normative ethical message. Only then is prophecy considered a manifestation of the covenant between God and Israel. I presume that is also the sages' intent in their reading of God's command to Moses to descend from Mt. Sinai when Israel sinned by adoring the golden calf. They interpreted this to indicate that Moses may lose his special status. Rashi (the most prominent medieval Jewish biblical commentator) quotes the sages, "I bestowed greatness upon you only for Israel's sake" (Exodus, 32:7). The phenomenon of God's revelation to all the Israelites on Mt. Sinai is compelling evidence of the importance of the concept of the community. It is unique as a manifestation of a religious experience in that it is a national experience in contrast to the individual religious experiences reported in the literature. Clients having poor interpersonal relationships that interfere with behavioral functioning and/or positive inner feelings benefit from therapeutic spiritual counseling, drawing on the previously noted and similar material culled from religious sources.

Patients whose self-image is flawed benefit from therapeutic spiritual counseling stressing the uniqueness and worth of each individual as a consequence of having been created in His image. Internalizing this rudimentary principle fortifies the person's healthy inclination to follow a path he or she chooses. It banishes frustration spawned from the feeling that one's fate is dependent on preordained circumstances. This perception imposes a set of values, a way of thinking, an approach to people that has as its core enormous respect for the person. It also affects the relationship between therapist and patient, defining it as an encounter between two people and not as a doctor–patient or expert–client relationship. This may be so for nonspiritual therapy as well, but it is mandatory for Judaic therapeutic spiritual counseling. This modus operandi is not confined to the spiritual facets of the person; it recognizes that the earthly aspects are fully human. The Almighty saw fit to combine spiritual and earthly entities into a complete whole. This engenders empathy in that it highlights the complexity of personality which is a joining of two opposites, spiritual and material. This juxtaposition was noted by the sages (Midrash Rabbah, Tazria 14A). They write that the human spirit was created on the first day, whereas the body was formed on the sixth day after all other forms of life were created. This teaches us that if humans prove themselves worthy, they are considered the pinnacle of creation; if, however, they do not conduct themselves properly, they are reminded that the lowly gnat was created before humans.

The Talmud (Sanhedrin 37A) states that each individual is required to feel that the world was created for his or her benefit. This is to impress on individuals the value of each human life and the magnitude of one's ethical and religious obligations. Hillel taught that "If I will not help myself, who will help me?" (Sayings of the Fathers, chap. 1), referring to spiritual attainments and fulfillment of ethical obligations. To this Hillel adds, "but of what significance are they vis-à-vis my spiritual obligations?"—a gentle reminder intended to curb one's arrogance.

The two principles, the concept of a communal religious experience and the stress on the person's uniqueness, serve to modify one another. In concert, they dictate the religious philosophy and world outlook of the orthodox Jew. He or she strives to develop and feel a personal bond or covenant with God, but this sentiment is tempered by the knowledge that the bond has already been formed. The Torah, which was given to the community, has given substance to the shape and direction of the bond. Aspiring to achieve holiness does not include, in the current era, developing a personal dialogue with God. This possibility ceased to be shortly after the destruction of the first Solomon's temple. A present-day Jew views his or her relationship with the Almighty as being realized by heeding His commandments. Studying Torah and following its precepts should be an all-consuming passion fulfilling one's spiritual longings and needs. Judaic therapeutic spiritual counseling has to mold itself to this perception. This entails dealing therapeutically with material related to Torah ideals and observance, thereby touching on the client's belief and trust in God. The two—spirituality and Torah observance—are inseparably linked. This should be reflected in therapeutic spiritual counseling. The therapeutic spiritual goal is to achieve a harmonious balance between the two factors. The therapist, and he or she can be Jewish or non-Jewish, should be aware of this delicate balance. The discussions should touch on both aspects with the realization that for these clients, the preferred direction, the path the therapy should follow, is to first examine the client's perception of his or her commitment to Torah ideals and observance. This will directly influence the client's understanding of the depth of his or her belief and trust in God. The case material that I present in this chapter is designed to show various ways in which the relationship is expressed.

CASE HISTORIES ILLUSTRATING THE PRINCIPLES

The following two case histories exemplify the principles cited previously. One stresses the role of the unconscious, the other stresses the importance of interpersonal relations. Both reflect the client's perception of himself as deficient in Torah observance.

Danny

Danny is a 17-year-old rabbinical student whose presenting problem was that his progress in his studies was not commensurate with his capabilities. Although he smiled and spoke clearly and fluently, an underlying sadness was present. He is of above-average intelligence; his grasp of his environment and knowledge of events and people seemed fitting for someone 4 or 5 years older than he. Danny's father, with his permission, said he was convinced that his son was burdened with a problem, but he could not identify the exact nature of the problem. There was no indication of tension between Danny and his parents or siblings. In the third session, Danny spoke about his lustful feelings and occasional masturbation that perturbed him. The concept of the unconscious was helpful in that it enabled him to understand a recurring dream, which shall shortly be described. I presented the concept as described here, adding another example. I felt it appropriate and more meaningful to Danny, who is a member of a hassidic sect, to consider an example found in hassidic literature. Hassidim are an integral part of orthodox Jewry who observe certain customs rooted in kabbalistic doctrine. The "Sefat Emet" (a famous hassidic rabbi) writes of thoughts a person has of which he or she is unaware and uses this to explain Joshua's behavior. The sages criticize Joshua for waging what they consider unnecessarily prolonged wars. They attribute this to Joshua's realization that the liberation of Canaan and subsequent cessation of hostilities would signal his demise. The Sefat Emet explains that prolonging the war was not a conscious decision. Joshua, whom God calls His servant, would not consciously defer liberating Canaan for personal gain. However, unconsciously, this influenced him and led to postponement of the liberation, for which Joshua was punished (Sefat Emet, Book of Numbers, Matot). Danny reported dreaming several times that he observed the Sabbath law approximately 3 hours before sunset, which is the appointed hour to commence observing the Sabbath. He was baffled by this, especially because it kept recurring. I reminded him that we had discussed methods suggested in rabbinic and hassidic literature for alleviating the harshness of the sin of masturbation. One of the *tikunim* (procedures that can be followed to rectify the spiritual harm caused by sin) is intensified Sabbath observance. Danny was then able to understand the significance of his dream as an expression of his desire to be spiritually cleansed. This lowered his anxiety level facilitating further therapy.

David

David is a 22-year-old student in a prestigious yeshiva. His presenting complaint was that he could not fully concentrate on his studies. Because of this, he stopped attending lectures although he continued to study on his own, discussing difficult passages in Talmud with two senior lecturers. Although students pursue their studies in a large study hall in dyads, David preferred to study alone. He had previously attended other yeshivot, but they were not to his liking, thus prompting him to leave. He prayed in local synagogues rather than at the yeshiva, which is the accepted practice. The prayers in the synagogue are recited more quickly, granting him more time to devote to his studies. The Rosh Yeshiva (Dean) did not view this favorably. Family history revealed that his mother is anxious about possible harm caused by bacteria and this seems to have affected David as well, although to a lesser degree. There is also a separation problem. David enjoys being in the yeshiva, but if he cannot be there, he experiences an intense desire to be with his mother. David is aware of this problematic emotional attachment to his mother, but in other matters, for example, attitudes toward religion, he identifies with his father's position. It pains him to see his parents arguing on religious and other issues. Therapy centered on these problems and their effect on his behavior and his attitude toward father figures. His habit of distancing himself from his fellow students was also discussed.

Therapeutic Spiritual Counseling

Spiritual counseling focused on the importance of interpersonal relations and its role in forming a balanced healthy personality. Relevant material presented above was discussed. The ramifications of lack of friendship attachment were demonstrated by an analysis of Job's tribulations. Satan was granted permission to afflict Job with all manners of hardships with the exception of causing his death. Job's friends came to comfort and counsel him.

Satan could have prevented them from coming, which would have increased Job's pain to an even greater degree. Why, then, did Satan allow them to come? An explanation favored by commentators is that this would be tantamount to killing Job. This is based on the sages' statement, "either friends or death" (Talmud, Tractate Taanis 23A), which they attribute to "Chomi Hameagel," who slept for many years and awoke to find a new environment inhabited by strangers. This approach led David to view his actions from a spiritual religious perspective motivating him to seek change.

Further consideration of David's behavior leads me to ruminate whether his refusal to study with others is an emotional problem, a strength of character issue, or simple lack of humility. The line differentiating between them is not always clear or definite. Some psychotherapists claim that therapy, aside from alleviating emotional pain, influences patients to become better, kinder people. Others contend that some forms of therapy make people even more selfish and self-centered (Wallach & Wallach, 1983; Wicklund & Eckert, 1992). They argue that some therapies overemphasize the self to the exclusion of others, resulting in endowing the patient's feelings with the exclusive right to decide how he or she should behave. They marshal arguments that they believe show that this is diametrically opposed to the Judaic-Christian heritage that teaches, "Thou shalt love thy neighbor as thyself" (Leviticus, 9:18). The lack of unequivocal empirical evidence to decide this issue places therapists in a difficult position when confronted with situations such as that of David. It seems to me that such situations are those best suited for therapeutic spiritual counseling. Weaving spiritual counseling into the therapeutic process counteracts whatever deleterious influence (according to some theoreticians) therapy exerts. The process may be perceived as do Richards and Bergin (1997, p. 102) that getting in touch with one's spiritual core facilitates the dissolving of the "mortal overlay" leading to the dissolving of pathologies.

EXAMPLES ILLUSTRATING THE DILEMMA

The following two examples illustrate the dilemma and the unique problems it generates. They were similar in that their problems seemed to be closely related to the special niche their families occupied in the religious social hierarchy. One was a descendant of a prominent hassidic rabbi revered by many followers. The second client traced his lineage to many highly respected scholars of the past few centuries. The first was in his late 30s, the second in his 20s. Both were happily married and devoted fathers. They both felt that their distress was related to the families' social position.

The hassidic client told of his family being harassed by former friends. He maintained that this was a result of an erroneous notion that the client's immediate family was disrespectful to the tradition. The roots of the alleged disrespect were ideological, but with the passing of time turned personal and emotional. The client was not the instigator or chief protagonist and can be considered a victim of unfortunate circumstances. He did not know how to cope with the situation, became frustrated and slightly depressed on realizing that his heretofore rosy future now seemed out of reach. During the two sessions we met, he dwelled on his misfortune, leaving me with the impression that he expected me to pity and comfort him. He did not return for further sessions. My assessment was that he divined my intention to discuss the theological implications of not accepting the situation, of not gracefully acknowledging God's intent and will. My assumption was perhaps mistaken. He may have ceased coming because of factors in his psychological structure amenable to treatment by dynamic therapy. Furthermore, even if the assumption were correct, the intended therapeutic approach stressing theological–religious aspects may have unnerved and intimidated him. Being accosted with defects in that area may be more traumatic for him than facing personality psychological blemishes. This case exemplifies difficulties a therapist may encounter in such situations.

The second client, Jacob, felt that he was not true to his inner self, that his behavior reflected an exalted ideal to which he aspired but which at present was not authentic. This made him feel awkward and uncomfortable with friends. He longed to be freer with them, to achieve easy comradeship. These needs were stifled by a compulsion to live up to the very high standards of scholarship and moral standards for which his family was known. Here, too, I was faced with the dilemma. Was I to look for psychological factors, or was this "pride" that should be addressed as a moral problem? The issue was resolved when further sessions revealed unhealthy behavioral patterns and parental marital tensions. The therapeutic approach adopted integrated dynamic therapy with spiritual counseling—therapeutic spiritual counseling. Jacob was distressed and anxious, unsure whether to continue his present lifestyle; changing it would startle family and friends. His present behavior, in most respects, was above reproach, extreme in its suppression of anger even when warranted. From a dynamic viewpoint, it entailed siding with one of his parents who opposed the other parent's habit of denigrating others. The denigrator's behavior was rationalized as not being tolerant of sham and hypocrisy, which was true to some extent. It was, however, extreme and aggressive, conducing to consternation and a sense of shame, influencing Jacob to behave overly gentle. Jacob also followed a different course of study than that of other family members. His independence took its toll; the strain impaired his powers of concentration and led to minor sexual transgressions.

Therapeutic spiritual counseling included bolstering his self-image, easing the way for him to follow his inclinations, not to feel obligated to trod in the same paths of his forefathers. In addition to the material previously presented, I related a story told of a hassidic master. The rabbi was rebuked for not following in his father's ways regarding modes of prayer, study, and so forth. He retorted that he does not deviate from his father's customs; his father did not blindly follow in his father's footsteps and he as well does not imitate his father. It was also emphasized that the sages taught that each of the three patriarchs served the Almighty differently. Abraham is characterized as epitomizing the trait of *chesed*—loving-kindness; Isaac, the trait of *gevurah*—literally, strength. This is understood as strength of will, focusing only on achieving maximum closeness to God as befitting a sacrifice. Jacob combined both traits so as to reflect God's glory. The lesson derived is that within the Torah's parameters there is enough leeway for each person's spirituality to be expressed as he or she sees fit. This principle is vividly illustrated by the "Chofetz Chayim's" (the acknowledged leader of religious European Jewry prior to the Holocaust) interpretation of one of the sages' teachings. They portrayed the future metaphorically as God sitting in the center of a circle surrounded by the righteous. The center of a circle is equidistant from all points on its perimeter. This teaches that all methods of serving God that are grounded in justice and mercy are acceptable.

Jacob made slow but steady progress. He was fortunate in that his wife, although disappointed when he told her of his tumultuous inner conflicts and occasional sinful behavior, fully supported him. They are deeply attached to one another. It was not feasible to meet with her regularly, but I was able to counsel her from time to time. Her deep religious commitment provided her with inner strength to cope with recurring exigencies. Our discussions focused, in part, on the importance Judaism attaches to perceiving God as merciful and not willful or capricious.

AN IN-DEPTH EXAMPLE OF THERAPEUTIC SPIRITUAL COUNSELING

Norman is a 22-year-old yeshiva student. He enjoys studying and is considered an apt student and a pleasant person by his teachers. He has difficulty praying the thrice daily prayers required of every orthodox Jew. He is plagued by doubts as to whether he concentrates adequately when praying, especially when uttering God's name. Norman is bright, personable, and accepted by his peers. However, he seldom smiles during therapy; at times, he sits with his head bowed as if carrying all the burdens of the world. He says that he acts differently in school. Norman is the eldest of five children, is a respectful son, and has good relations with his siblings. He comes willingly to therapy, never missing a session or arriving late. However, he is not talkative and rarely volunteers information. Several sessions elapsed before he felt free to speak about his obsessive compulsions that revolve around religious ritual requirements. His mother is not a warm loving person. It took much gentle prodding to elicit this information. It took even longer for him to reveal that many years ago, his mother had suffered a mild stroke and had been hospitalized for a few months. Her speech was impaired, eventually improving, but on returning home she was even more distant from her children. At this point in therapy, he became distraught and cried. He broke out in tears a second time when a sibling, to whom he feels very close, told him that their father had verbally lashed out and humiliated him. Norman says that his father is concerned about his children, means well, and helps them, but does not show his love, is obstinate and insistent that his wishes be fulfilled. His memory of his mother's illness includes his recollection that she suffered her stroke after having argued with her husband. Norman feels greater attachment to his father, although he cannot carry on a normal conversation with him. They walk together in silence. When Norman is witness to a warm, loving relationship between other parents and children, he feels envious. It is difficult for Norman to talk about his relationships with friends or about his daily routine. He feels it is irrelevant to understanding his problem. Norman dismissed as meaningless the view that pathology is an integral part and not an isolated segment of personality.

Norman's religious beliefs did not bestow on him peace of mind; on the contrary, his laxity of observance (imagined or real) disturbed and caused him pain. I felt that an in-depth probe of his religious commitment was called for. This confirmed that his belief is authentic and important to him. I postulated that his problems were rooted in and stemmed from psychological factors and that therapy should concentrate on developmental and dynamic factors. However, the fact that his compulsions manifested themselves as difficulties in prayer and observance of other religious rituals indicated the need to include religious counseling.

This therapeutic plan was implemented by weaving into therapy the religious significance of the concepts of the unconscious and self-image, as explained earlier. There was slow progress and about 2 months later he realized that he was angry at God whom he held responsible for his predicament. Immediately he retracted and placed the onus on himself, declaring that his difficulties are justified because of his lax religious observance. This transformation is akin to what Pargament (1996) called "reframing the individual." However, the speed and immediacy are suspect. There was not any indication on Norman's part of profound reflection and, therefore, it seemed to be a compulsive reaction rather than a reasoned conclusion. This self-deprecation prevented him from connecting his love–hate relationship with his parents to his behavior, to what seems to be the displacement of his anger toward them, to God. I asked him how he perceives God, as warm and forgiving or stern and uncompromising. He indicated the latter, but again immediately retracted. He is aware that Judaism teaches that God is merciful, "And the Lord passed by before him (Moses) and proclaimed: The Lord, the Lord, God, merciful and gracious, long-suffering and abundant in goodness and truth" (Exodus 34:6, Hertz translation). I felt that, although there certainly is displacement of the anger at his parents onto the Almighty, this is not the full explanation. His total commitment to religion and his deeply held belief in God's mercy were genuine and, therefore, his contention that his psychological pain was warranted by his behavior could not be completely dismissed as being solely a function of displacement.

The new developments called for broadening the scope of the spiritual counseling dimension of the therapy and adjusting it to the specifics of the situation. Aside from his difficulty in prayer, Norman viewed himself as lax in religious observance in two areas: (a) lacking filial respect in that he allowed himself to argue with his father and (b) lustful thoughts and occasional masturbation. As to the latter, I refer the reader to the spiritual counseling method of dealing with this from a Judaic standpoint (Rabinowitz, 2000, pp. 254–255). As for the former, his negative perception of himself could not be divorced from what I suspected was his feeling that he does not love his parents as he should. Therapy intended to help him understand that this is a natural result of his parents' personality and behavior was not successful in mitigating his distress. Norman's resolve to abide by the fifth commandment to honor one's parents overwhelmed in its intensity any conceptual rationalization of his inner feelings. Norman would be able to accept himself only if his entire self-image could change, allowing him to assess his past from a more mature and balanced position. To bring about this hoped-for change, I initiated discussions of the following material. Tanya, a classic hassidic text, quotes the sages (Sayings of the Fathers, chap. 2) that one should not consider himself wicked. The significance of its being the opening passage of the book indicates its importance as being central to the author's thesis. The text is a guide on how to harness one's energies to serve God, how to forge a harmonious relationship between the divine and earthly attributes of human beings. The author stresses that a poor self-image, viewing oneself as a sinner, fosters sadness preventing serving God with joy, which is a biblical bidding (Deuteronomy, 28:47). Rabbi Zadok of Lublin, a later hassidic master, taught that believing in oneself is a necessary step to follow after establishing belief in the Creator. He explains this amazing statement as meaning that it is imperative to realize that humans are important to Him and that He is concerned even with individuals' mundane preoccupations. A useful method of differentiating between sadness that obstructs serving God and bittersweet sorrow (*merirut*) which, on the contrary, is a positive feeling leading to increased maturation to serve Him, was described in a previous publication (Rabinowitz, 2000, p. 254). Norman has improved, becoming more in touch with his inner feelings. His symptoms have decreased, but they have not at this point completely abated.

A COMPOSITE CASE REPORT OF SPIRITUAL COUNSELING

The following case report is a composite of therapy with three clients: two men and one woman. Their common feature is a pronounced reluctance

Ehud

Ehud had been under psychiatric care for 5 years following a psychotic episode. He was not hospitalized, drugs were prescribed, and he is still taking antipsychotic and antianxiety medication. The psychiatrist confined herself to the physiological medical aspects. She did not do psychotherapy. Ehud did not confide in or wish to be advised by her in religious or sexual issues. I suspect that she was not averse to this arrangement, a convenient one for a harassed psychiatrist. When I attempted to engage him in a therapeutic conversation, he was very reluctant. His advisors had cautioned him not to accept advice in matters pertaining to religion or sex from a nonrabbinic personage. I was certain that this did not apply to me and asked him to check with them. He did and they permitted and urged him to be frank and forthcoming with me.

Ehud's parents are simple, religious people not as devout as he. When in his early teenage years he decided to devote himself exclusively to studying the Talmud, his parents were not enthusiastic. Aside from preferring that he study secular subjects as well, Ehud's choice meant adopting a lifestyle different from that of his parents or his siblings, all of whom were older than he. It meant eschewing television, motion pictures, and so forth, and they assumed correctly that this would affect them as well. Ehud railed against having a TV at home. At first, his parents refused to comply with this request, but relented when he experienced the psychotic episode. Prior to the breakdown, he was an excellent student devoting many hours to study. His diligence, however, prevented him from forming friendships. Therapy revealed that his reluctance to forge friendships was also motivated by the fear that close relationships would lead to friends knowing that his parents had a TV in their home. He was anxiety ridden that this revelation would lead to expulsion from his yeshiva, a premise that had no basis in reality. It is reasonable to assume that the anxiety contributed to his breakdown. Viewed thusly, the psychotic episode is an example of secondary gain—removal of the TV set. Incidentally, it took some years for him to realize that many other students as well had TV sets in their homes. Ehud's devotion to study did not diminish after the breakdown, but his progress was arrested. His concentration was impaired, perhaps this was also a result of medication, and his level of understanding the depth and intricacies of talmudic analysis was reduced. His self-image was such that any deviation in conforming to the norms of his circle seemed catastrophic. Difficulty controlling his sexual urge aggravated his poor self-image.

Therapeutic spiritual counseling concentrated on the intrinsic importance of each individual in God's eyes. It was emphasized that each person is judged solely on his or her merits and actions. Numerous examples of biblical and talmudic figures were cited to support this contention—for example, the matriarch Rebecca who, according to the sages, was reared in a morally flawed household. Her brother Lavan is viewed as a conniving, immoral person, whereas Rebecca is a paragon of virtue and loving kindness (*chesed*). Rabbi Akiva, who is considered as one of the Talmudic giants, was also cited as an example who transcended a religiously flawed background to achieve unusual prominence. The examples bolstered and improved his self-image. This led to his becoming involved in meaningful social relationships that provided him the opportunity to display his positive attributes. For example, he was asked to speak publicly on festive occasions that afforded him great pleasure and initiated a healthier lifestyle.

Benjamin

Benjamin is a tall, fine-looking, bright young man. He is artistically inclined, which is unusual in his circle. This does not interfere with his commitment to Torah study. The presenting problem was his lack of being attracted to women. He insisted that his preference for the company of men was not sexual, but he was nevertheless concerned whether this meant that he had homosexual tendencies. He is the oldest of several brothers. His parents are observant orthodox Jews, his father having become more so in the past few years. This is one of several issues causing friction between the parents. Benjamin identifies with his father's religious level, but is closer emotionally to his mother whom he considers warmer and more sophisticated than his father. He enjoys his studies in the yeshiva, but savors the feeling of freedom he experiences when returning home at night. He prefers sleeping at home, although entitled to free dormitory lodgings. He explained that this enables him to enjoy his artistic pursuits. Therapy revealed that being at home gives him a measure of control, the opportunity to interfere and calm his parents when they argue. During the course of therapy, one of his parents left home. Benjamin suspected that the parent had entered into a romantic extramarital relationship. He was hurt and greatly distressed, triggering him to seek comfort and understanding from a male friend. This flowered into a partial sexual relationship not including full intimate contact. Spiritual counseling helped him confront the fact that his frustration led to behavior inconsistent with his beliefs. Benjamin is a totally committed religious person. Discussing his behavior did not elicit a defensive reaction, and consequently an elaborate "working through" period was not needed. The discussion was crucial in that it opened avenues of introspection relevant to his interpersonal relations, resulting in marked improvement in his reaching out to others. He began to plan and go on trips with friends.

The incident led me to wonder whether his reluctance to sleep in the dorm was not prompted by an amorphous fear that it might lead to undesirable sexual contacts. It should be noted that yeshivot, dedicated to talmudical study and research, are all-male schools. Students who attend this type of institution usually belong to a circle in which separation between the sexes is the norm until marriageable age. A positive development that can be viewed as a result of the incident was Benjamin's conclusion to begin dating women. He realized that confronting his problem required this move and indeed his attraction to men declined with a consequent heightened interest in women.

Deborah

Deborah is a young woman recently divorced from her husband of a few months. She did not initiate the divorce proceedings and could not specify why he wanted the divorce, merely saying without explaining that they were incompatible. She maintains that she did not want to marry him. Her father pressured her to do so, which is one of the many reasons she does not get along with him. Her mother died when Deborah was in her late teenage years and her father remarried. There are several siblings from her parents, and younger brothers and sisters from her father's second marriage. She was close to her mother; her relations with her siblings vary, with some better than with others. She says that she was a better student than her siblings and that this engendered jealousy. Her father did not want her to return to his home after her divorce. She boards with a family, paying with funds she receives as rental from an apartment she owns. She is a licensed teacher, but could not find employment. She has little support financially or emotionally from her father or extended family.

Deborah entered therapy as a result of her inability to establish good relations with the family with whom she lived. They were not ready to continue the arrangement if her behavior would not improve. She also neglected her relationships with former friends. Therapy helped in improving relationships with the family with whom she lived. Therapeutic spiritual counseling centered on the concept of accepting God's will. In principle, Deborah accepted this, but nevertheless wanted to know and understand its parameters. When is acceptance called for and when, on the contrary, should one strive to actively change the situation? I was able to elaborate on this point quoting relevant sources. This was then discussed touching on her personal, sensitive inner feelings. The therapy motivated her to study computer programming with the avowed purpose of acquiring a different profession. Her father offered to finance the cost of studying.

Elaboration and Summary of the Therapeutic Spiritual Counseling of the Three Cases

This section summarizes the spiritual counseling techniques implemented in the therapy. The importance of the feeling of belonging to a group was emphasized. It was made clear that this is not the same as cultivating friendships. The feeling of belonging is the sensation of having a place in the sun, of being a cog however small, and of being able to influence events in the stream of life. This fits in with a theistic approach and was not difficult for religious clients to apprehend. The concept of a community of people bound together by a common belief in a Divine Creator and committed to serving Him seemed natural to them. This was linked to "friendship" in that both belonging and friendship realize God's will that people live harmoniously in a community devoted to serving Him. The despondent feelings were addressed by quoting the material on joy discussed previously, as were the concepts of community and friendship. The approach was effective in that it provided a fresh perspective, releasing them from their heretofore restrictive perception of themselves and their environment.

Further reflection led me to consider that the spiritual counseling affected the men differently than it did the woman. The men's difficulties and resultant sadness were rooted in their self-perception as lacking in spirituality. Counseling reinforced the principle that God's love is nonconditional and present notwithstanding spiritual imperfections. The woman's belief in God's goodness did not need bolstering. She felt unloved by people, except by her deceased mother and this fostered a tarnished self-image. In her case, spiritual counseling helped in that it demonstrated that His love embraces all, regardless of their circumstances, misfortunes, or other people's assessments. I have found this gender distinction in some other instances as well. It is consistent with a principle enunciated by the Maharal of Prague (16th century): *Emunah*—faith or trust—is entrenched in women. Deborah found the verse (Psalms 27:10) especially meaningful: "Though my father and mother have forsaken me, God will gather me unto Him." Another verse that clients are touched by is from Psalms 34:19: "God is close to the broken-hearted, and those crushed in spirit He saves." Reciting Psalms at home, identifying with the yearning for the Almighty's closeness, has a salutary effect. Some of the material and concepts presented in the following section were also integrated in the therapy.

I trust that these cases have demonstrated the contribution and role of therapeutic spiritual counseling. Therapy that would not have included the spiritual elements would have been barred from relating to crucial issues relevant to the client's emotional pain. These issues were discussed utilizing concepts and language familiar and meaningful to the client. He or she felt understood, thereby reducing tension, and provided him or her with cognitive, conceptual and spiritual tools with which to confront the problem.

TESHUVA—REPENTANCE—AND THERAPEUTIC SPIRITUAL COUNSELING

The following sections expound on concepts vital to understanding and practicing therapeutic spiritual counseling with orthodox Jews. I believe that the core of the concepts are applicable to all clients, non-Jews as well as Jews. The cases that follow are not intended to be full accounts, but rather to briefly illustrate the ideas presented. They are presented to familiarize therapists, Jewish and non-Jewish, with the concepts so that they can be of use to them. Although it is not feasible to enumerate all the references or examples, the concepts can fruitfully be used by all therapists.

Teshuva—repentance—occupies an important niche in spiritual counseling. It signifies considerably more than erasure of sin. Teshuva's literal meaning is "return," returning to the Almighty. Teshuva was "created" before the creation of the cosmos, thereby endowing it with the importance and power of primacy. The sages teach that teshuva cannot be understood rationally; reason is not capable of explaining how an event can be eradicated. They teach that God, metaphorically, bore a hole under His throne to accommodate *baalei-teshuva*—penitents. Furthermore, the penitent is considered on a higher spiritual plane than one who has not sinned (Maimonides: The laws of Teshuva, chap. 7:4). Teshuva is a formal positive commandment (*mitzvah*); consequently its parameters are defined by Jewish law (*Halacha*). However, even when not all formal requirements are met, it is still acceptable (Mabit, Beit Elokim). This paradox and the seemingly irrational basis of teshuva prompted the exiled Jews of the prophet Ezekiel's generation to doubt its acceptability (Ezekiel, chap. 33). Scripture relates that only God's swearing that it is always acceptable allayed their doubts. Some clients, however, have to have the concept personalized, spelled out even more clearly. I do this by quoting the prayer for forgiveness, which is part of the *tefilat amidah*—the central prayer of the daily services. The prayer addresses God as one who continually forgives. The commentators (Tanya, Iggeret Hateshuva) explain that there is no limit to His forgiveness.

Jonathan, a young man in his late teenage years, was plagued by obsessive thoughts during prayer. He imagined that his bowing was directed to his genital area. Therapy was a prolonged affair, exploring many aspects of his development, including his reaction to not having complete physical control of one arm. He was beset by doubts, on the one hand questioning facets of his religious faith, and on the other hand agonizing over his occasionally lax religious observance. This was partly caused by conflicting parental messages regarding religious commitment. It was not surprising that he harbored anger toward God and his parents. Spiritual counseling focused on his intrinsic worth in God's eyes. Jonathan's lapses in his religious obligations were addressed by discussions of teshuva—repentance—as outlined previously. An intriguing aspect in his and other cases is that guilt feelings stem not only from perceived sinful behavior but also from insufficient time devoted to Torah study. Being knowledgeable and studying Torah are so important and central to living a full Jewish life that not complying with this mitzvah—commandment—causes anxiety and guilt feelings. Spiritual counseling lowered his anxiety level, easing his guilt feelings. He entered a prestigious university program that allowed him to devote a sizeable portion of his time to religious Torah studies. There was a marked improvement in his social life notwithstanding his physical deformity, attesting to his improved self-image.

Teshuva is a rich mosaic of ideas and concepts. Rabbi Dr. Soloveitchik (1983, p. 110) invests teshuva with the halo of creation, self-creation. Teshuva implies change; the sages advised the penitent, under certain circumstances, to move to a different location and adopt a new name. This signifies that he or she is a new, different person. Rabbi Kotler (1998, Mishnat Rebi Aharon, vol. 2, p. 193) elaborated on the concept of Rosh Hashana—New Year, as a new beginning. Rosh Hashana inaugurates the 10 days of repentance culminating on Yom Kippur—the Day of Atonement. The sages point out that the Torah phrases the obligation to offer sacrifices in the temple on Rosh Hashana using language in a different manner than it uses to describe other sacrifices. The language clearly indicates that the Torah perceives Rosh Hashana as a new beginning for all, even for sinners who have not as yet repented. The psychological value of this realization is that it facilitates the decision to change. Once this decision is reached, the person can devote himself or herself to cleansing oneself of the spiritual blemish of the transgression on Yom Kippur—the Day of Atonement.

The positive potential of these concepts was used in the therapy of three young singles, two men and one woman, who engaged in forbidden sexual relations: the men with prostitutes and the woman with a casual male acquaintance. This knowledge breathed new hope into them, restoring their sense of worth and rejuvenating their desire for future spiritual growth.

Analyzing teshuva's role in spiritual counseling is incomplete without discussing the concept of forgiveness. Only the Almighty can forgive sins committed against Him. This implies total reliance on Him; omitting God from our perception of reality is impossible. There are some who misinterpret one of the sages' teachings, reading into it the idea that it is acceptable to deny God providing one lives and acts according to His precepts (see, e.g., Blazer, 1998, p. 89). This misinterpretation seems to be based on a partial reading of the sages' teachings (Midrash, Lamentations). The full text is as follows: "I (God) prefer that people leave or ignore me, if (on condition) they continue to observe my Torah, for the light of Torah will influence them to return to goodness"; meaning that this is preferable to acknowledging God, but not His Torah. The misinterpretation is in stressing the first part and ignoring the latter part. The sages referred to a process, ways of behaving, for those who have strayed from the righteous path. Torah observance, they believed, will infuse them with spirituality that eventually will lead them to return to God—the giver of the Torah. Observing Torah and not affirming God who commanded its observance is foreign to Jewish doctrine. Torah minus God is an oxymoron. Not realizing this can seriously hamper the therapist's efforts to help the client. The client is apt to feel that his or her belief in the Almighty is questioned. This is a legitimate issue if the therapist feels that this may be. However, it is not, from the patient's view-point, proper to suggest that this is an acceptable Jewish view. Doing so may create a chasm between the therapist and the orthodox Jewish client.

OTHER RELEVANT ISSUES

Some clients question the principle that God is merciful. They cannot reconcile it with the magnitude of evil present in the world. It is perhaps superfluous to note that this is a highly charged emotional issue for Jews whose memory, personal or collective, of the Holocaust is still vivid. My response is that theodicy is a major theological issue addressed by thoughtful people throughout the ages and is the essence of the book of Job. I quote the Talmud (Berachot 7:A), which interprets Moses' request (Exodus 33:13) that God show him His ways, as referring to the enigma of the suffering of the righteous, whereas evildoers prosper. I do not engage them in a protracted theological debate, preferring, if need be, to refer them to rabbinic authorities.

Other clients are perturbed by a feeling of being unworthy of God's beneficence. This is characterized by a general sense of moral or ethical inadequacy, rather than a feeling engendered by specific instances of having sinned. Counseling the sinner is, as outlined previously, based on the concept of teshuva. The former seems less grave, but is much more convoluted, indicating a feeling of mediocrity. Therapeutic spiritual counseling is geared toward understanding how this developed. The spiritual religious dimension of the poor self-image is addressed by stressing the uniqueness and individuality of each person as presented here. I also discuss a basic principle taught by Rabbi Yisroel Meir of Radin (Chofetz Chayim). He commented on the dialogue between Joshua and Caleb on the one hand, and the Israelites who hesitated, out of fear, to go forth and conquer the Canaanites. Joshua and Caleb admonish the Israelites: "Only rebel not against the Lord" (Numbers, 14:9). This is interpreted by the Chofetz Chayim to mean that to benefit from God's benevolence, one does not necessarily have to be highly spiritual—not rebelling is sufficient. Clients are profoundly affected by the simplicity and empathic perception of human nature expressed by this concept.

I have also found the following concept useful with clients whose self-image is tarnished by a sense of spiritual failings. The basic theme is that evil or banality found in people is not to be viewed as reflecting the real or authentic person. The "evil inclination" (yetzer hara) is not the totality of the person. Judaism teaches (Tanya, chap. 9) that humans have two souls (neshamot), an earthly one and a spiritual one. They are inimical to one another and engage in continual conflict. The earthly and certainly the evil are not the entire "I." Rabbi Elijah of Vilna (Gra) teaches that the "person," the "I" is the ruach (spirit). This is a segment of the soul (neshama) that is entrusted with the power of choice and is influenced by one of the two inclinations, the good or the evil (Orot Hagra, p. 198). This approach helps the client see himself or herself as basically a worthy person.

Joseph, a man in his late 20s, was disheartened with his spiritual stature and accomplishments, castigating himself for his real or perceived failures. Therapy exploring the roots of his self-concept was not successful in getting him to figuratively step back and view himself objectively. He was then asked to define who the "I" is whom he is blaming. Joseph was familiar with the concept of good and evil inclinations. The question, which in effect challenged him to look closely at himself, led him to the realization that the inclinations are merely instigators of behavior; they do not define the person. He was then able to accept that they are in conflict, each of them vying for control over him, at times one gaining superiority and other times relinquishing control to the other. His self-perception changed from a simplistic one to a more sophisticated view allowing him to accept himself. For him, this meant understanding that his "I" is a spiritual entity and that his occasional lapses of proper religious observance are a function of the continual inner conflict common to all people.

REFERENCES

Blazer, D. (1998). *Freud vs. God*. Downers Grove, IL: InterVarsity Press.

Elijah of Vilma. (1986). *Mipayrushai hagra al hatorah*. Jerusalem: Asher Steinmetz. (Original work published 18th century)

Handelman, S. (1981). Interpretation as devotion: Freud's relation to rabbinic hermeneutics. *Psychoanalytic Review*, 68(21), 201–218.

Hertz, J. (Ed. & Trans.). (1941). *Pentateuch and Haftorahs*. New York: Metzudah.

Jennings, J., & Jennings, J. P. (1993). I knew the method: The unseen midrashic origins of Freud's psychoanalysis. *Journal of Psychology and Judaism, 17*(1), 51–75.

Kotler, A. (1998). *Mishnat rebi aharon*. Lakewood, NJ: Mochon Mishnat Rebi Aharon.

Miller, W. R. (Ed.). (1999). *Integrating spirituality into treatment*. Washington, DC: American Psychological Association.

Pargament, K. I. (1996). Religious methods of coping. In E. P. Shafranske (Ed.), *Religion and the clinical practice of psychology* (pp. 215–239). Washington, DC: American Psychological Association.

Rabinowitz, A. (1999). *Judaism and psychology: Meeting points*. Northvale, NJ: Jason Aronson.

Rabinowitz, A. (2000). Psychotherapy with orthodox Jews. In P. S. Richards & A. E. Bergin (Eds.), *Handbook of psychotherapy and religious diversity* (pp. 237–258). Washington, DC: American Psychological Association.

Rabinowitz, A. (2001). Halachic Judaism's influence on the practice of psychotherapy. *Journal of Psychology and Judaism, 24*(3), 193–204.

Richards, P. S., & Bergin, A. E. (1997). *A spiritual strategy for counseling and psychotherapy*. Washington, DC: American Psychological Association.

Soloveitchik, J. B. (1965, Spring). The lonely man of faith. *Tradition*, 5–67.

Soloveitchik, J. B. (1983). *Halakhic man*. Philadelphia: The Jewish Publication Society of America.

Wallach, M., & Wallach, L. (1983). *Psychology's sanction for selfishness*. San Francisco: Freeman.

Wicklund, R. A., & Eckert, M. (1992). *The self-knower: A hero under control*. New York: Plenum Press.

8

INTEGRATIVE SPIRITUALLY ORIENTED PSYCHOTHERAPY: A CASE STUDY OF SPIRITUAL AND PSYCHOLOGICAL TRANSFORMATION

LEN SPERRY

DESCRIPTION OF THERAPIST

Len Sperry is currently a clinical professor of psychiatry and behavioral medicine at the Medical College of Wisconsin and professor and coordinator of the doctoral program in counseling at Barry University. Sensitive to the spiritual dimension, he has practiced clinical psychology and psychiatry for more than 30 years. Dr. Sperry is 58 years old, White, married, and a lifelong, Roman Catholic layperson. He has earned doctorates in psychology, medicine, and theology.

Dr. Sperry is a diplomate of the American Board of Psychiatry and Neurology, the American Board of Preventive Medicine, as well as a diplomate in clinical psychology of the American Board of Professional Psychology. He has more than 300 professional publications, including 40 professional books. These include *Spirituality in Clinical Practice: Incorporating the Spiritual Dimension in Psychotherapy and Counseling, Ministry and Community: Recognizing,*

Healing and Preventing Ministry Impairment, and the *Handbook of Diagnosis and Treatment of the DSM–IV Personality Disorders*. He edited a special issue of the journal *Psychiatric Annals* on "Spirituality in Clinical Practice." A recent recipient of the Harry Levinson Award, a lifetime achievement award from the American Psychological Association, he is also a fellow of Division 36 (Psychology of Religion) of the American Psychological Association, a fellow of the American Psychiatric Association, and a member of the Committee on Psychiatry and Religion of the Group for the Advancement of Psychiatry.

SETTING

The client was seen in a private practice located in a southeastern metropolitan community. This is a practice that includes both psychotherapy sensitive to the spiritual domain with individuals and couples as well as psychiatric consultation to individuals and organizations.

CLIENT DEMOGRAPHIC CHARACTERISTICS

Gwen is a 45-year-old White woman who began treatment nearly 3 years ago. At the present time Gwen has been married to Jason for almost 23 years. They have a son, Alex, who is 22, and a daughter, Nancy, who is 21. Gwen is currently a guidance counselor in a local private high school, and Jason is a senior vice president at a local bank. Gwen indicated she had been a lifelong member of the Catholic Church. She attended a private elementary school and high school and after graduation immediately went on to the state university to major in English literature. She married Jason, whom she had met in her sophomore year at the university, soon after they graduated.

Gwen is the older of two siblings. Her younger sister is an insurance underwriter who has never married and has little, if any, "religious sentiment" according to Gwen. Both of Gwen's parents are alive and have lived in the same house for the past 39 years. Although they are relatively healthy, Gwen's father was recently diagnosed with early stage prostate cancer and has been treated for high blood pressure for more than 20 years. Her parents were reportedly active in their church for several years. Her father had served as the chair of the church's finance committee for nearly 30 years, and her mother was a religious education teacher in the church's Sunday school program for several years.

For 10 years prior to beginning treatment with me, Gwen indicated that she had not been active in her church congregation. She explained that she "didn't feel comfortable around those people anymore." When asked what she meant, she noted that after her son had grown and moved away her desire to serve on church committees with the friends of his parents had greatly diminished. Later, it would come to light that she felt "unworthy" around these same individuals "after I messed up my life" at the time of her inpatient hospitalization. This attitude toward her church congregation persisted until it was processed during the course of therapy.

PRESENTING PROBLEMS AND CONCERNS

Gwen was referred by her family physician for evaluation and treatment of "chronic depression" of approximately 5 years duration. She had been given a trial of an antidepressant by her family physician, which "had a lot of side effects but didn't work." Previous to beginning the antidepressant she had consulted with two psychotherapists for two and three sessions respectively, before terminating treatment. She claimed that neither had understood her and "probably couldn't help me anyway."

CLIENT HISTORY

Six years prior to onset of the treatment she had been hospitalized for an eating disorder, primarily involving bulimia. She had used exercise, self-induced vomiting, and laxatives as "control" measures. That short hospitalization—she left against medical advice—was apparently precipitated by marital conflict and increasing suspiciousness about Jason's motives. Hospital records also mentioned some initial suspiciousness about the motives of the treatment team. When I first evaluated her, she presented with prominent obsessive and perfectionistic traits as well as some narcissistic and paranoid features. She denied any family history of psychiatric or substance abuse treatment, although there may have been a distant aunt, her father's second cousin, whose early death was thought by some to have been by suicide following periods of up and down moods.

ASSESSMENT AND DIAGNOSIS

Records for the previous hospitalization were sent for and reviewed. Results of a Minnesota Multiphasic Personality Inventory (MMPI) administered to her during her inpatient hospitalization revealed a 9–4 pattern. On projective testing, consisting of Thematic Apperception Test (TAT) and Rorschach, considerable anger directed at her parents was elicited. TAT themes included fathers as demanding individuals whose expectations were impossible to meet as well as daughters not noticed by fathers. There were also themes of mothers who were ungiving, incompetent, and wanting to be taken care of by daughters. The report concludes that she "deals with her anger by being resisted in a child-like way rather than constructively by taking control of situations."

At the beginning of the treatment Millon Clinical Multiaxial Inventory–II (MCMI–II) and the Beck Depression Inventory (BDI) were administered. The MCMI–II suggested dysthymic disorder and somatoform disorder, NOS as well as obsessive–compulsive personality disorder with paranoid, narcissistic, and histrionic features. The BDI score was 17, suggestive of moderate degree of depression. She met criteria for the following *Diagnostic and Statistical Manual of Mental Disorders* (4th ed.; *DSM–IV*; American Psychiatric Association, 1994) diagnoses: Axis I diagnoses were mood disorder, NOS (296.50), and eating disorder NOS (307.50) by history. On Axis II, a diagnosis of obsessive–compulsive personality disorder (301.4) with narcissistic, histrionic, and paranoid features was given.

The formal practice of her religion had diminished considerably since her son Alex had graduated from a nearby Catholic high school. She indicated that she only kept up church attendance and traditional spiritual practice "to set a good example for my son." For the past several years her spiritual practices had included daily formula prayer, occasional scripture reading, and Sunday worship services. She had once tried to meditate but had given up after about a week or so, "because I was just too distracted and flooded with worrisome thoughts." At the outset of treatment, she described her image of God as "judge and taskmaster." On further inquiry, God was described as an elderly man who "made hard demands, who checked up on you and wasn't easily pleased." He was also emotionally withholding, unsupportive, and critical. Not surprisingly, but not recognized by Gwen at the outset of our therapy, her image of God was a composite description of both her own parents.

TREATMENT FOCUS AND MODALITIES

Gwen initially wanted medication and therapy with me but indicated that making a commitment to remain in treatment would be difficult for her. I agreed to meet with her weekly, more often if needed, and to carefully prescribe and monitor medications and involve her in all treatment decisions. It was mutually decided that the focus of the therapy would be on reducing the stressors related to her depression and eating disorder. I carefully avoided the kind of transference "traps" that were likely to result in her being sufficiently threatened to prematurely leave therapy. For nearly a year prior to our therapy she indicated only two instances of using laxatives or inducing vomiting, but she admitted to exercising vigorously every day. In time she agreed to refrain from any purging behaviors and to switch to a more moderate exercise plan, an agreement she would keep throughout the course of treatment.

Combined treatment consisting of psychotherapy and medication continued, but therapy became more directed toward the spiritual aspects of her drivenness and perfectionism as they related to her parents and her image of God. She described her father as strict, demanding, and verbally and emotionally abusive, and her mother as self-preoccupied and emotionally withholding. As noted earlier, her image of God was demanding, critical, and withholding. Her guidance and counseling practicum experience surfaced unfinished business with her estranged son, issues that were processed in her therapy and eventually led to a reconciliation.

TREATMENT PROCESS AND OUTCOMES

First Year of Treatment

After 6 months of weekly sessions she was sufficiently stable and confident to consider "going on with life" as she put it. For some time she had entertained the thought of going back to school to become a high school guidance counselor or possibly an addictions counselor working with eating disorder patients. Prior to her marriage she had taught for 2 years and had enjoyed the challenge of working with adolescents in a junior high school setting. She believed that staying at home alone only fostered her depressed thinking and ruminations and wanted to "get out and do something with my life." She had been accepted in a masters-level counseling program. Although she could attend full time, she opted for a part-time program of study because she feared that she could not be as good a student as she needed to be if she took more than two courses at a time. She also wanted to reduce session frequency from weekly to monthly sessions. Reluctantly, I agreed to this request.

Second Year of Treatment

Approximately one year later, when she was nearly halfway through her graduate program, she mentioned attending a weekend spirituality workshop at a Catholic retreat center. It was a retreat based on focusing, the experiential approach developed by Gendlin (1981). Something about this experience touched her deeply, but she had difficulty describing this experience and the feelings it triggered. She also indicated reading an article on spirituality that I had recently published and wondered if our sessions could include the religious and spiritual dimension. She said the prospects of starting a counseling practicum in a nearby high school was disconcerting to her and she was ready to resume weekly sessions. She entertained the thought of participating in additional spirituality retreats in the coming year.

Third Year of Treatment

Over the next year she became somewhat less self-critical and driven and more centered and at peace with herself. She attributed much of this centeredness and peacefulness to the regular practice of the focusing strategy she had learned during her various retreats. Her moodiness—now appearing more like a dysthymic disorder than major depression—seemed to have moderated considerably. As a result, we endeavored to wean her off the antidepressant and to monitor her without medications for the next few months. It appeared that she no longer needed the medication. Three years later she remains off medication.

She and her husband became more actively involved in their church community, with both involved in leading a youth group. With some trepidation, she took a job as a guidance counselor that fall. Just after Thanksgiving she experienced a brief relapse with her eating disorder. The next spring her husband opted for early retirement and announced that it was time for her "to be the breadwinner now." The prospect of taking such responsibility initially overwhelmed her as she feared somehow making a mistake and not being the perfect wife and guidance counselor. These concerns were processed from both a psychological and spiritual perspective. In time, sufficient progress was made and sessions were reduced to monthly and then quarterly.

Three years after beginning this process it was mutually agreed to terminate ongoing treatment. In the year since termination she has been stable and without depressive or eating disorder symptoms. She reports that her cravings for stimulating situations and substances are markedly reduced. And, when cravings do arise, Gwen quickly looks for internal and external stressors and attempts to address them directly and immediately. Gwen reports leading a more centered and paced life, continues to enjoy her work as a guidance counselor, and is now coordinating youth retreats for her church community. Interestingly, as she grew psychologically, her image of God gradually shifted to that of a smiling, caring grandmother.

THERAPIST COMMENTARY

What accounts for these therapeutic changes in Gwen? In this section I speculate on this change process and briefly describe my approach to spiritually oriented psychotherapy.

Integrative Spiritually Oriented Psychotherapy

One point of difference between a traditional psychotherapeutic perspective and the integrative spiritually oriented perspective that I practice involves different treatment goals, particularly with regard to individuals with personality disorders. Although the goal of traditional psychotherapy for individuals with personality disorders is typically symptom remission and return to baseline functioning, the goal of integrative spiritually oriented psychotherapy is personal and spiritual growth and well-being. More specifically, the goal is psychological and spiritual transformation.

I conceive of spiritually oriented psychotherapy as an integrative approach (i.e., a biopsychosocial approach that incorporates the spiritual dimension) that is developmentally focused (Sperry, 2001). This means that clients' needs and concerns are conceptualized on a continuum or developmental line from pathological states to growth states. Three distinct ranges on this developmental line can be specified: the disordered range, the adequate range, and the optimal range. Accordingly, the goal of traditional psychotherapy for individuals with personality disorders often focuses on moving the client from the disordered range to somewhere within the adequate range of functioning. When that point is reached, therapy is assumed to have been successful. However, from a spiritual perspective, such a goal for change or growth can be limiting. Instead, I would contend that the goal of spiritually oriented psychotherapy can extend as far into the optimal range of functioning as is possible.

With regard to the obsessive–compulsive personality style that characterized Gwen, three ranges of functioning have been noted. In the disordered range, the individual is characterized by perfectionism and feelings of avoidance that interfere with task completion and relationships. The individual's thinking and attitudes are overly rigid and they tend to be pessimistic and include feeling avoidant. In the adequate range of functioning, individuals are less perfectionistic and there is rigidity in tasks and relationships with some degree of emotional involvement and responsivity. In the optimal range, individuals are conscientious but not driven, and they are more spontaneous. They are individuals who display a balance of personal integrity with generosity, hopefulness, and kindness.

Goal of Therapy

The overall goal of therapy with Gwen was to modify her obsessive–compulsive style first from the disordered range to the adequate range, and then, by mutual agreement, from the adequate to the optimal range. Specifically, this meant attempting to transform her basic perfectionistic pattern so that she might become more comfortable with affects, less reliant on her thinking function, and thereby become more spontaneous and playful. Her core beliefs or schemas about being hardworking, good, and avoiding mistakes to feel accepted and worthwhile were examined and processed as well as her need to be in control and overly responsible. Interpretation and cognitive restructuring were the main therapeutic strategies used to modify the affective, cognitive, and relational aspects of her obsessive style. The specific goal was to increase her capacity for emotional involvement. This is represented as "average" level of functioning on the obsessive developmental line.

As treatment progressed and she was no longer symptomatic, was less driven, and felt much better about herself, we discussed the future. We agreed that she had achieved her stated treatment goals. We discussed two options: moving into a maintenance mode preparatory to termination or shifting the treatment focus to "growth" goals in therapy, that is, moving toward the optimal range of functioning. With little hesitation she chose to focus on growth goals. At the time, I recall making the predictive interpretation that she might find it difficult to discern the difference between true growth and more subtle perfectionistic strivings. Yet, I indicated that one of my roles on this journey would be to help her discern these differences.

Therapeutic Strategy

The general therapeutic strategy for fostering Gwen's movement from the adequate to the optimal range involved both reconstructive strategies and developmental strategies. With regard to reconstructive strategies, an initial treatment focus is to help the client specify those limited number of situations where it is reasonable or necessary to be especially goal-directed and conscientious. For Gwen this would mean 8:00 a.m. to 3:00 p.m. Monday to Friday, 9 months a year for her job, and perhaps another 10 hours a week on household duties and volunteer activities in her church. It would also mean that she would be prompted to practice becoming more spontaneous and less rigid in important and meaningful relationships in which she feels reasonably safe, such as with her husband, her boss, and her pastor.

Psychological Transformation

Several specific strategies were used in working toward this goal of psychological transformation. These included focusing on the theme of perfectionism in a fine-grained and focused manner. For example, Gwen's self-view or self-schema was, "I am responsible if something goes wrong," whereas her underlying view of the world was, "Life is always unpredictable and expects too much. So, I must always work hard, be in control, right, and not make mistakes." Characteristic of the disordered range is the absolute conviction that she must be responsible in all situations, that life is always unpredictable and demanding, and that she must do her best in all situations. At the average range, however, her schemas would be less absolute, which means that there are a limited number of circumstances and situations in which she could let down her guard with regard to conscientiousness, rigidity, and feeling avoidance. The rest of the time she was likely to be on her guard. In the optimal range, these convictions are still operative but are highly situation specific, meaning that Gwen could be more spontaneous and playful in many situations.

Another useful strategy was to help her master some of her subtle and persistent perfectionistic patterns, that is, those trigger events or thoughts that initiate a sequence of perfectionistic thinking—including self-righteousness—and behaviors and related responses. Three of Gwen's more subtle perfectionistic patterns involved safeguarding her money, being overly focused on time, and dealing with mild cravings.

With regard to money, her husband affectionately referred to her as "my little tightwad" because she shopped for bargains, used coupons, and looked for discounts. The transformation of this attitude of stinginess is generosity.

With regard to focus on time and deadlines, she set her watch and clocks in her home and car 20 minutes ahead so that she could be "on time," which was quite interesting because she would still be 5 to 10 minutes late for some of our sessions. Her packed schedule allowed no time for traffic delays— which were not supposed to happen in a perfect world. Needless to say, Gwen was extremely conscientious of time and resented others wasting her time. The transformation of this attitude of time conscientiousness is becoming more spontaneous and playful.

A third concern involved the way she dealt with cravings. When she felt stressed, tired, emotionally deprived, or queasy, she reached for caffeine— particularly chocolate, colas, and coffee—or sought out situations that were stimulating, such as high-adventure movies and TV programs. The resulting "adrenaline buzz," as she called it, temporarily appeased her cravings. She would immediately feel better but would soon feel like a worthless failure. While small doses of caffeine were preferable to full-scale binging and purging, the end result was the same—she felt she had failed and resolved to try harder to be perfect. Reframing her cravings as growth motivators and establishing a relapse prevention strategy allowed her to short circuit this vicious cycle.

Similarly, being fun loving and carefree was very difficult for Gwen. A common underlying maxim for her was "I must do it and do it exceedingly well." The transformation of this attitude of duty and conscientiousness would involve achieving a degree of balance in her life among conscientiousness, spontaneity, and integrity. In addition, she tended to live in the future rather than in the present. Accordingly, the transformation of this pattern involves the prescription to live in the present moment.

Not surprising, focusing exercises were initially quite difficult for Gwen given her ruminative cognitive style. She was constantly processing new and old concerns, so much so that she became overwhelmed by this mental chatter and background noise, which made it all but impossible to focus on the present. Because both centering meditation and focusing require a quieting or derailing of this ruminative style, she learned to use a simple prayer word—some would call it a mantra—"Jesus" to effectively derail this mental chatter.

Characteristically, Gwen was very demanding of herself as well as of others. She constantly monitored the actions of others against social norms as well as her own personal norms. Not surprising, few people matched up to her standards and she would judge others as being irresponsible. The actions of others triggered her moral indignation; hence others perceived her as judgmental and sometimes moralistic. For Gwen the transformation of this overall attitude would be hopefulness and kindness. Although these perfectionistic strivings are somewhat subtle and are not only acceptable but also reinforced in our culture of achievement and success, Gwen began to recognize that they were inhibiting her personal and spiritual development and that changing them would be challenging.

Such a therapeutic direction with Gwen was effective to the extent it focused on these fine-grained dimensions of perfectionism with the goal of becoming a conscientious but spontaneous person who could balance personal integrity with generosity, hopefulness, and kindness. In other words, instead of being compulsively perfectionistic in all matters, she might intentionally strive for a high level of excellence in a few selected areas of her life but not in other areas.

For Gwen, modifying the triggers for her perfectionistic pattern was essential in transforming this dynamic. On closer examination we found that self-righteous thoughts such as "That's not right" or "That's sloppy work" inevitably triggered her perfectionistic pattern. Subsequently, we worked together to find ways of neutralizing such triggers and replacing them with a nonrighteous thought: "This moment is as perfect as it can be." Such a neutralizing thought became like a mantra that Gwen repeated whenever she was in "high-risk" situations that might possibly trigger her perfectionistic pattern. With a little experimenting Gwen also found that if she hummed to herself while going into "high-risk" situations she could also derail the perfectionistic pattern.

Spiritual Transformation

As noted earlier, several spiritual disciplines were incorporated into the treatment process. These included prayer (particularly centering prayer and meditation), spiritual journaling, and participation in a healthy religious community. This participation provided her social support as well as a corrective emotional experience regarding some of her harsh and perfectionistic religious beliefs and attitudes. Spiritual discussion of her life situation and stressors in light of their spiritual meaning was a part of the therapeutic process. Furthermore, cognitive restructuring of dysfunctional religious beliefs appeared to influence a shift in her image of God.

Developing virtue and building on strengths was another focus of therapy. For Gwen efforts to further develop the virtues of patience and serenity facilitated movement to the optimal range of functioning. Gwen was quite receptive to focusing on these two virtues. Interestingly, Gwen came across a few research articles on "positive psychology" about the virtues of patience, which served to reinforce and validate her efforts in this area.

Interplay of Psychological and Spiritual Dynamics

It is interesting to speculate on the interplay between Gwen's perfectionistic pattern and her religious and spiritual beliefs and behaviors. There was little question that Gwen's religious upbringing confounded matters by unwittingly reinforcing certain obsessive–compulsive beliefs. For example, in the "faith" versus "works" view of salvation, her religious tradition seemed to emphasize "works," that is, the individual's own striving to make himself or herself worthy so that God would see fit to save him or her, over "faith," that is, wherein salvation comes from believing that God will save an individual despite his or her sins and failings. In our discussion of her compulsive work habits, she initially insisted that "God helps those who help themselves." Gwen could not conceive of leaving anything to chance, much less her prospects of eternal salvation.

For Gwen, faith had meant believing there was a God, and the rest was up to her. She had to work hard and be perfect or she would be viewed as worthless in the sight of God and in the sight of those in her parish. It is not surprising then that she felt "uncomfortable" in her church community when her world was falling apart before and after she was hospitalized.

Unfortunately, her perfectionistic beliefs that she was "never good enough" were ego-syntonic with her religious beliefs (i.e., "God helps those . . ." and "God is always watching and seeing your sins"). It should not be surprising that Gwen's image of God was that of judge and taskmaster. Fortunately, as treatment continued, these beliefs that supported her self-view began to moderate, and along with it, her image of God.

What Gwen brought to treatment were her brokenness and cravings as well as her intelligence, tenacity, and related strengths. Viewing therapy from the perspective of developmental lines, I focused treatment to reconfigure her basic obsessive–compulsive personality style and to build on her gifts and strengths. Not the least of these was her religious tradition. From the perspective of her religious tradition, her sense of brokenness and cravings served as the basis for spiritual transformation. My role was to support her efforts toward spiritual growth, particularly when she became discouraged. My role was also to refocus and reframe her cravings as motivators or prompters of spiritual and psychological growth. Because her religious tradition also holds that a community of believers (i.e., parishes, retreats, etc.) can be an instrument of healing and growth, it was important that I looked for ways of incorporating this community dimension, and particularly spiritual resources within the community, into the therapy process. Consequently, I supported her desire to participate in quarterly focusing retreats. Similarly, I encouraged her efforts to bring the focusing method and journaling "home" with her. Initially, she began practicing focusing with her husband on Sunday evenings. In time, they invited some friends to join them. Later, I supported her as she transitioned back to her parish community.

Influence of Theistic Beliefs on Treatment Process and Outcomes

It appears that theistic and spiritual beliefs—mine as well as Gwen's—did influence the therapeutic process and outcomes. It is likely that some of my own religious and spiritual beliefs influenced my work with Gwen. Presumably, my faith in God as well as my sensitivity to spiritual and religious issues positively predisposed me to accede to Gwen's request to include discussion of spiritual issues as a part of treatment. It also predisposed me to prescribe and encourage several spiritual interventions that were helpful to her treatment progress.

Gwen's faith in God led her to request that spiritual issues be included in her treatment. Her faith led her to engage in various spiritual practices such as prayer, focusing, and spiritual journaling. It seems that Gwen's faith and spiritual practices facilitated the process of transformation including overcoming her perfectionistic and obsessive–compulsive tendencies, as well as her bulimic behaviors.

Would the process and outcomes of Gwen's therapy have been different with a secular therapist who did not believe exploring spiritual issues was important? I assume that it very likely would have differed. For instance, in secular therapy it is unlikely that Gwen's religious beliefs and community would have been used as a resource during therapy. In fact, her initial negative attitude toward her religious community may have been reinforced. Furthermore, Gwen would not have experienced the benefits of praying, meditating, and participating in a healthy religious community.

In retrospect, it appears that a definite shift has occurred in Gwen's personal and spiritual world. Whereas, at one time Gwen's religious tradition only seemed to reinforce her personal pathology and her parish community appeared to be a source of suspicion and discomfort, now she perceives this tradition and community to actually be supportive of her journey of psychological and spiritual growth. This shift and journey is the basis of psychological and spiritual transformation.

REFERENCES

American Psychiatric Association. (1994). *Diagnostic and statistical manual of mental disorders* (4th ed.). Washington, DC: Author.

Gendlin, E. (1981). *Focusing.* New York: Bantam.

Sperry, L. (2001). *Spirituality in clinical practice: Incorporating the spiritual dimension in psychotherapy and counseling.* New York: Brunner/Routledge.

9

A PSYCHODYNAMIC CASE STUDY

EDWARD P. SHAFRANSKE

DESCRIPTION OF THERAPIST

Edward Shafranske is Professor of Psychology, Charles and Harriet Luckman Distinguished Teaching Fellow, and director of the doctoral program in clinical psychology at Pepperdine University. He is a member of the faculty of the Southern California Psychoanalytic Institute and is a training and supervising psychoanalyst at the Newport Psychoanalytic Institute.

Having received doctoral degrees in clinical psychology and in psychoanalysis, his clinical practice is informed by both disciplines as well as by contributions from neuroscience. Shafranske is a fellow of the American Psychological Association (APA), twice president of APA Division 36 (Psychology of Religion), former chair of the California Psychological Association Division of Education and Training, and served as editor of *Religion and the Clinical Practice of Psychology* (Shafranske, 1996), coeditor of *Spiritually Oriented Psychotherapy: A Contemporary Approach* (Sperry & Shafranske, in press), and coauthor of *The Practice of Clinical Supervision: A Competency-Based Approach* (Falender & Shafranske, in press). His research interests concern clinical and applied psychoanalysis, the psychotherapeutic process, clinical supervision, and the psychology of religion. He maintains a private practice in clinical psychology and psychoanalysis in Irvine, California. Shafranske, who is a Roman Catholic, has a long-standing interest in religion as a variable in mental health and psychological treatment. His personal faith, in addition to his scholarship, informs his appreciation of religious sources of meaning and the salience of spirituality in the orienting systems of many clients.

SETTING

The client was seen in a private practice setting in southern California. Shafranske was a member of a multidisciplinary and multitheoretical group practice of individual clinicians representing psychology, psychiatry, and social work.

CLIENT CHARACTERISTICS

The client, who I call Joan, was a 38-year-old Caucasian woman. She was married and the mother of three daughters whose ages ranged from 8 to 12 at the time of intake. She was a college graduate and had enjoyed a professional career in a business-related field before becoming a mother and choosing to focus her attention exclusively on her family as a homemaker. She appeared to be in good health, consistent with her self-report. She concluded that her marriage was generally satisfactory, although she commented that she had recently been feeling less interested in her husband, particularly in respect to their sexual relationship. She was very involved in her children's lives and supported their many school, club, and athletic activities.

Joan was raised as a Roman Catholic and, although she infrequently participated in her parish community, she described her worldview as "essentially Catholic." She moved with her husband, following their marriage 16 years ago, from a large city on the east coast of the United States to the suburbs of southern California. She felt isolated from her family and reported missing both the support of her extended family and the sense of community she had experienced as a child in her close-knit ethnic neighborhood.

CLIENT HISTORY

Joan was the third-born child and the first daughter in an intact Italian-American, Roman Catholic family; she had two older brothers, two younger sisters, and a brother. Her father worked at the shipyards, initially as a laborer and later as a dock supervisor employed by the port authority; he often took on additional part-time jobs to pay for the monthly expenses. She described her father as somewhat distant and "emotionally removed," yet at times he would be overcome by sentiment at weddings and funerals. Her father was an alcoholic who would periodically "fly into rages when drunk" and "terrorize" the family by breaking things or physically striking her brothers. He was often depressed and agitated and regularly complained about the pressures of supporting such a large family. Joan reported her mother to be a quiet, religious woman, who also could become emotionally upset when the pressures of the family situation became overwhelming. In such moments she would cry uncontrollably and then retire to bed, pray a novena to Mary the Blessed Mother, or leave the home and stay a few days with her sisters or mother who lived in the neighborhood. These situations of emotional dysregulation increased both in frequency and intensity over time. She recalled as a teenager being shuffled off with her younger siblings to one of her aunts' homes for weeks at a time when her father's drinking and outbursts escalated. Conflicts between the children would easily become out of control with aggressive outbursts because they lived in crowded quarters. The picture that Joan painted was of a chaotic, enmeshed family. She described herself as a child to be a quiet, shy, "little bookworm," who was easily frightened by her older brothers and the boys in the neighborhood. She recalled taking comfort in spending time with her maternal grandmother and staying at girlfriends' homes for dinner and sleepovers. She sought the peace of "normal" families. Although not particularly outgoing, Joan developed close relationships with her cousins and had a best girlfriend at school. She characterized herself as an average yet industrious student, who generally enjoyed school and found it to be a safe environment.

During adolescence, she became increasingly more confident in her relationships and occupied herself with activities outside of the home (e.g., school, work, and social involvement in the neighborhood Catholic parish). She maintained a small but close group of friends, and dated infrequently. She described high school as a time when it became more possible to live life outside of the family. She reported keeping her feelings generally to herself particularly in respect to the conflicts in her family and concerning her increasing disappointment and disengagement from her parents. She was an above average student in high school and was fortunate to be awarded a partial scholarship to attend a Catholic college in a neighboring city. She described college as a fulfilling time. She worked tirelessly in her academic studies and supported herself through part-time employment. She began dating a classmate whom she met while working at the Student Union. She described their relationship as a friendship that kind of "grew on her." When they became sexually intimate Joan experienced anxiety over the possibility of being discovered and guilty about her sexual impulses and behavior. She solved this conflict, in part, by vowing that she would marry her boyfriend. She completed college and shortly after her graduation they married. On later reflection, she remembered that, although she put on the appearance of confidence and optimism, she actually felt anxious about what life would bring and that she hoped that the security marriage would bring would assuage her worries. Marriage also allowed her to be sexual without guilt. She recalled that she felt both critical and envious of her girlfriends who "played around" sexually and seemed to not require a committed relationship. She was mostly satisfied with her marriage because she knew that her husband was a stable and caring man and that he would work hard to support his family. She particularly appreciated that he was unflappable; nothing ever upset him. She saw marriage as affording the opportunity of having her family different from her own. Shortly after their marriage, a career opportunity led to their move to California. Joan was excited about the move; however, she viewed this at the time as being temporary, almost like a vacation. She expected that they would return to the east coast, where she desired to raise their children in the company of many cousins, aunts, and uncles. However, once her husband's career became established, she acceded to his desire to stay in California. She marked the births of her children as the highlights of her life. She enjoyed her pregnancies and found pleasure in the "simple things" of raising her children, particularly when her daughters were babies and toddlers. She longed for the less complicated relationships she had experienced when her children were younger in contrast with the often-challenging moments of prepubescence and adolescence.

Religion played an essential role in Joan's intrapsychic life. Joan's identification with her mother included an internalization of her mother's piety and beliefs in God, particularly in respect to providence and autonomy. Many of her inhibitions and conflicts involved fears of judgment and retribution and were related to implicit religious beliefs and the dynamic construction of her primary God representation. Her Catholic upbringing, including moral proscriptions and prescriptions, was enhanced by the central position that the parish played in the ethnic borough in which she and her extended family lived. Although she was a nonpracticing Catholic when she entered treatment, a religious thread was woven throughout her psychological experiences and in many respects was central to both the conflicts she was facing and their ultimate resolution.

PRESENTING PROBLEMS AND CONCERNS

The precipitant for Joan's request for a consultation concerned recurrent headaches, which were evaluated by her primary care physician and a neurologist as including a psychological component. In the initial session, she was caught off guard by a spontaneous outpouring of sadness. She was surprised by her tears, apologized profusely for crying, and attempted to regain composure by directing her attention to conjecture about the causes of her headaches. When I gently commented that she seemed to move away from feeling her emotions, she burst out in tears, saying that she was sorry but that she could not help but cry. In the initial assessment phase, I came to understand that there were several difficulties that Joan was facing in her marriage and in her relationships with her children and others. These difficulties were characterized by an inability, or put more psychodynamically, a conflict in which she could not acknowledge or express feelings of frustration, disappointment, or anger in the face of situations in which others had let her down her in some fashion. Sadness was the emotion that she most readily experienced and expressed. She felt stuck in her situation and recalled with embarrassment that her mother had warned her before her marriage that "she had better be sure . . . that she would have to live the rest of her life in the bed she had made for herself." She described "feeling that she had been caught" when she expressed disappointment and could not tolerate the idea that she was not very happy.

ASSESSMENT AND DIAGNOSIS

The assessment process was conducted through clinical interviews and included consultation with her neurologist. Her ability to utilize an explorative psychotherapeutic approach and the early demonstration of the psychodynamics contributing to the development of symptoms were sufficient to arrive at an initial assessment and provisional diagnostic impression. It was noteworthy that in the initial consultations, she would report pressure building in her temple and following her talking about her emotional responses to a given situation and obtaining a measure of catharsis, she would report a cessation of pain. In addition to my ongoing assessment, her physicians conducted neurological and endocrinological workups and ruled out the nonpsychological conditions that would cause her symptoms. She was also prescribed a medication that was found to be effective in the treatment of migraine headaches. The preliminary *Diagnostic and Statistical Manual of Mental Disorders* (4th ed., *DSM–IV*; American Psychiatric Association, 1994) diagnosis was 316: Stress-Related Psychophysiological Response Affecting Migraine-Like Headaches. This was concluded in consideration of her neurologist's opinion that Joan had a biologically based susceptibility to migraine headaches and through my assessment of her history, which found that psychological factors involving external and internal stress exacerbated her symptoms. Although diagnoses were not obtained under the *DSM–IV* criteria, it was apparent that underlying and leading to psychic conflict, Joan experienced both depression and anxiety.

A psychodynamic diagnostic approach was also utilized in assessing her level of personality organization and character structure (Gabbard, 2000; see also McWilliams, 1994, 1999). A psychodynamic diagnosis builds on and goes beyond the descriptive approach of *DSM–IV* and aims to understand how the patient is ill, how ill, how she became ill, and how her illness serves her (cf. Menninger, Mayman, & Pruyser, 1963, cited in Gabbard, 2000, p. 79). In addition, an emphasis was placed on understanding the symptoms or psychological disturbance within the context of personality functioning.

Observations of her psychological functioning in session, together with her self-reported history, suggested that this client's personality organization would be classified within the neurotic spectrum (Kernberg, 1967). Reality testing was intact and it appeared that she primarily used higher order level defenses, including intellectualization, rationalization, undoing, and repression. Her personality structure was oriented toward repression and control of impulses and emotional expression. Cognitive processes were overvalued and were used in the service of repression and suppression. A psychoanalytic formulation (Perry, Cooper, & Michels, 1987) was developed, which considered her symptoms to be manifestations of a pervasive conflict between the expression and repression of thoughts, affects, and impulses that produced signal anxiety. From the perspective of ego psychology, I hypothesized that the headaches in part symbolized and expressed the intrapsychic conflict concerning the expression of dysphoric affective states and impulses as well as failures in her defensive operations to maintain repression. The headache reflected the intrapsychic strain in Joan's attempt to repress unacceptable thoughts and impulses. Similar to a clinical case study reported by Luborsky, Auerbach, and McLellan (1996), a review of the contexts in which Joan's headaches frequently occurred revealed a pattern of subjectively experienced pressure as feelings of anger surfaced. When frustrated or angered, Joan would defend against the conscious experience of anger, inhibit direct expressions of aggression, and assume a conflict avoidant interpersonal stance. In these contexts, Joan would often develop the symptoms of a headache and would retire to her bedroom, ostensibly removing herself from the situation of conflict. Her withdrawal from the family not only removed her from the scene of conflict but also could be seen as a passive expression of aggression in which her husband would bear the consequences of having offended or disappointed Joan. These response tendencies, although maladaptive in present circumstances, were in childhood effective maneuvers to manage aggression in the chaotic and emotionally dysregulated family system. Her responses also reflected a partial identification with her mother, in which Joan observed behaviors reflective of repression and isolation as her mother would retreat from situations of conflict. Her early religious training reinforced prohibitions against the expression of aggression, yet it also provided a template for the potential benefits of an expressive form of psychotherapy in which confessional aspects of disclosure might usefully support the treatment process. The therapist's familiarity with this religious tradition assisted in understanding of the potential religious influences on the treatment process, such as early confession experiences and attitudes toward the expression of aggression.

TREATMENT PROCESS AND OUTCOMES

The practice of psychoanalytic psychotherapy is informed by the scientific, clinical, and intellectual traditions within psychoanalysis. Although such treatment does not fully employ the techniques common to formal psychoanalysis, for example, frequency of sessions and the use of the couch, an authentic psychoanalytic experience can be obtained in psychotherapy. The following discussion presents an overview of the treatment approach, the psychoanalytic clinical orientation to religious content, an exemplar session, and a summary of process and treatment outcome.

Psychoanalytic Approach

Central to the psychoanalytic approach is the thesis that unconscious mental functioning, derived from critical developmental interpersonal events, organizes present experiences and shapes behaviors. Outside of awareness, meanings are constructed under the influence of unconscious invariant organizing principles (see Stolorow & Atwood, 1987, 1992) and internalized object relations, which produce response tendencies built into the neurobiology of the individual (see Ledoux, 1996; Schore, 1994; Siegel, 1999). Compromise formation occurs in which the motivations of expression and safety are conjoined; symptoms result from inadequate and conflicted attempts at achieving a synthesis of aims.

Contemporary psychoanalysis draws on multiple theoretical perspectives in explicating these processes, each of which orients the attention of the psychotherapist and guides the treatment process. Rather than considering such multiple perspectives to be a cacophony of voices, these theories contribute additively to a comprehensive psychoanalytic understanding (Rangell, 2000) and provide a common ground focusing on clinical practices that allow for the exploration of unconscious mental processes, particularly in respect to the transference (Wallerstein, 1990).

Although the conceptualization of Joan's symptoms was primarily based on ego psychology, perspectives drawn from self psychology and object relations theories were regularly applied. For example, self psychology contributed to the understanding that Joan's defenses were intended, in part, to prevent disintegration of her self and that "intensity" in and of itself posed a threat to her cohesiveness. Any experience of heightened sensation would provoke defensive withdrawal and attempts to isolate affect. She was not defending against the conscious experience of anger per se, but rather to the disintegrating effects that any intense experience of affect or impulse would provoke. This understanding allowed for a careful monitoring of her states of mind and the use of interventions to ensure that the intensity of her affect states would not lead to disintegration anxiety.

Psychodynamic psychotherapy was recommended with the intent of modifying her personality functioning to increase her ability to consciously experience and express more completely her thoughts, affects, and impulses. Such structural change would aim to eliminate maladaptive defensive operations, which were contributing in part to her presenting symptoms. Such modifications would bring about "a significant shift," according to Kernberg (1992), "in impulse/defense configurations, with a reduction of defenses that restrict the ego, a shift from repression to sublimation, and the incorporation of previously repressed drive derivatives into ego syntonic behavior" (p. 119). This would be accomplished through empathic understanding of her self-experience, the development of insight, further resolution of conflicts originating in childhood, and through the analysis of the organizing principles and defenses shaping her experience of the therapeutic and other relationships. Through understanding and corrective emotional experiences obtained in treatment, Joan would have the opportunity to address more effectively her psychological needs.

Religion played a central role in the orienting system in Joan's family and neighborhood, shaping and reinforcing beliefs, attitudes, and values. Lying outside of conscious awareness, internalizations of a religious nature conjured unconscious fantasy and contributed to the mental set against which Joan perceived, registered, interpreted, remembered, and responded to her affects and impulses (cf. Arlow, 1985). I turn now to the theoretical and technical considerations in addressing religious issues in psychodynamic psychotherapy.

Psychoanalytic Clinical Approach to Religious Experience

Psychodynamic psychotherapy involves the analysis of the conscious and unconscious meanings that individuals construct, and the dynamic forces and unconscious organizing principles that shape and delimit such constructions. For many people, if not most, religion plays a salient role in ascribing meaning to life events. Freud recognized the importance of religion particularly in respect to superego functioning and centered his critique of culture on its role in establishing moral order (Reiff, 1959; Van Herik, 1982). The psychoanalytic study of religion initiated by Freud (1927; see also Shafranske, 1995) has been more fully developed in recent scholarship by Rizzuto (1979, 1998), Meissner (1984, 1992), Jones (1991, 1996), Spero (1992), and others. These works built on and revised Freud's central thesis that the God concept is solely a projection originating in human need and religious beliefs are ultimately illusions.

Of particular interest to psychoanalysts has been the formation of personally held God representations. Contemporary theory posits that God representations are complex phenomena incorporating conscious and unconscious mental processes, which may include both symbolic and sensory representations. Through the sum of conscious and unconscious experience, internalizations of objects, learned concepts, and imagination, God representations are dynamically created as virtual objects for the believer and serve multiple psychological functions. Although drawing on the internalizations of primary maternal and paternal objects, "the God-representation," as Rizzuto

(1979, p. 46) states, "is more than the cornerstone upon which it was built. It is a *new* original representation which, because it is new, may have the varied components that serve to soothe and comfort, provide inspiration and courage—or terror and dread—far beyond that inspired by actual parents." In addition to God representations, other forms of religious association are pertinent to the psychotherapeutic process. Religious associations often articulate deeply held beliefs about the self in the world, causality, and purpose; reveal unconscious pathogenic beliefs; point to specific developmental events and epochs; or furnish a narrative to express ineffable states of mind.

Implicit assumptions about life, although not expressed by the patient in explicit religious language, may originate in early religious education and reflect internalizations of religious ideas and principles. For example, Joan's heightened anxiety and defenses against the conscious awareness and expression of anger and aggression and other impulses originated not only in prohibitions established by her parents but also were reinforced by religious instruction. Complementing her parents' injunctions against her expression of anger and aggressive impulses was the Catholic prescription to be pure in "thought, word, and deed." Early religious instruction contributed to Joan's implicit moral orientation, which considered murderous thoughts to be the moral equivalent of murderous deeds. Further, in the course of her treatment, it became clear that inhibition and self-restraint were consciously held virtues that were based in part on unconscious identifications to idealized religious objects. To suffer in silence was elevated to the meaning of suffering with Christ; the ability to suppress one's desires was equated with holiness and purity. Self-sacrifice and abstinence were not authentically chosen virtues but rather involved functions of undoing and performing penance to resolve intrapsychic conflict as well as behavioral expressions reflecting her ego ideals.

Culturally available religious leitmotifs provide for many people a source of identification and a means to construct and express meaning. Religious narrative may provide a means to bring subjective experience into conscious expression.

> Further, religious language provides in particular a mother tongue for the expression of affective experience in those familial and cultural settings in which religion has played a central role . . . although the richness of religious language is universally available, it holds particular significance for certain individuals in light of the unique function that religion served in their childhoods as well as in present life. That function concerns the expression of deeply felt states of mind and the articulation of psychic realities. (Shafranske, 2002, p. 246)

Associations of a religious nature in psychotherapy serve as avenues to deeply held beliefs and values and unconscious identifications, which shape meaning and ultimately influence behavior.

Religions provide rituals for the resolution of moral transgression or sin. For example, the Sacrament of Reconciliation, commonly referred to as confession, for many Catholics becomes internalized as the quintessential model of a psychological process for the resolution of guilt and conflict (Shafranske, 2000). Jackson (1999, pp. 143–162) in his comprehensive study of psychological healing, surveyed the anthropological literature and found the confessional act to be an aspect of modern psychotherapy common to all cultures and therapeutics throughout history. Joan's early experiences of confession were filled with anxiety and shame. She recalled as a child standing in the confessional line with mounting fear as she readied herself to recount her sins and to remember the proper verbal script to pray with the priest for forgiveness. At times in session she associated with anxiety that she would not find the right words and that she feared that I would be critical and that she "hadn't done it right." Although such a construction was undoubtedly multidetermined, her memories confirmed an associative link to these early religious experiences. She commented that something seemed to be missing following her disclosures of impulses she found troubling; she anticipated and in fact desired that I require her to do something (viz, penance). It was difficult initially for Joan to accept those affects and impulses that she had been brought up to consider as bad and to resist constructing a ritual of repentance to assuage the anxiety and guilt she felt. The therapeutic aim differed from her internalized model of resolution. Through the therapeutic process she came to accept the responsibility for determining her values and to establish what she believed was appropriate. With this came greater acceptance of her affects and impulse life and she established in her mind the distinction between spontaneously occurring ideas and deliberate actions. In sum, a patient's religious background contributes in like manner to that of other developmental features.

Technical Approaches to Religious Contents

Associations of a religious nature in psychoanalytic treatment serve the same functions as do other associations and are treated in a similar manner. Such associations are not a privileged class of psychological phenomena but rather are associations to be analyzed. Such content bears the same potential to articulate multiple levels of meaning, including references to past events, current object relations, present transferences, and so forth. Consistent with psychoanalytic practice, such associations are considered to be multidetermined and emphasis is placed on understanding the relevance to the therapeutic relationship and to transference rather than to any excursion into theology, religious counseling, or spiritual direction.

The appearance of God representations in dreams, memories, and associations is also taken up as content for analysis. A facile clinical approach allows for the presence of such objects within a transitional mode of experience in the reverie of free association. Although not assigned to the categories of reality or fantasy, God representations as objects within the patient's representational or internal world (Sandler & Rosenblatt, 1962) are considered in terms of their role in psychodynamics.

PSYCHOTHERAPEUTIC PROCESS

The course of treatment consisted of one session per week of psychodynamic psychotherapy with occasional increased frequency to two sessions. A psychodynamic form of expressive–supportive psychotherapy (Gabbard, 2000) was conducted in which interpretation was emphasized within the context of a supportive therapeutic relationship. Joan was encouraged to use free association, and the process was facilitated through a range of interventions including empathic validation, encouragement to elaborate, clarifications, confrontations, and interpretations. Essential to the psychoanalytic enterprise was the effort, through vicarious introspection, to empathically relate to Joan and to facilitate her ability to speak of her experience (Kohut, 1959). A therapeutic alliance was mutually created, which provided the foundation for the clinical work. This relationship served as a microcosm of her world in which the unconscious and conscious meanings she brought to life experience could be understood and new modes of relating initiated (cf. Stolorow, Atwood, & Ross, 1978, p. 250). The analytic relationship provided the opportunity for Joan to experience a new "object relationship" with her therapist (Loewald, 1957/1980) and in particular to be able to experience and to express her affects and impulses in the immediacy of the therapeutic relationship.

Resistance to the spontaneous expression of thoughts, affects, and impulses in the moment provided an avenue by means of transference interpretation to understand the origins of the conflicts she was experiencing. Such moments constituted a test of the therapist and the therapeutic relationship: Would the therapist react like past objects to her expressions of affect and impulse (Weiss, 1993)? Through the interpretive process, insight was obtained and subsequently used to initiate new behaviors. New experiences, supported within the therapeutic relationship, led to safety rather than anxiety over the course of treatment (Rangell, 1992). Joan gradually developed a new way of being with herself and with others. She was less often in a state of intrapsychic conflict, dominated by unconscious anxiety. Summoning defensive strategies to maintain repression and safety, she would be enabled to experience and express the totality of her affects and impulses and her head would no longer hurt.

Early Phase of Treatment: An Exemplar of the Therapeutic Process

An opportunity to explore the psychodynamics of her symptoms came early in treatment. While reporting the events of the week, she began to associate to an incident in which her husband had disappointed her by coming home late and had not called to inform her of his change in plans. As she began telling the story she noted that pressure was building in her temple and she immediately shifted focus to a more pleasant account regarding her children. I commented that she had abruptly changed topics. She returned to the matter involving her husband in response to my intervention and complained to me that she was coming down with a headache. She related that she had also gotten a headache at the time and had gone to bed early, which left him to put the children to bed. I commented that she had related her disappointment to me with little affect. I interpreted that rather than experience disappointment or other emotional reactions, it seemed that she was now in a state of intrapsychic conflict, the symptoms of which were experienced as a buildup of pressure in her mind as she struggled between expression and denial. This intervention drew attention to her defenses and reflected the ego psychology axiom of interpreting defense before content. She nodded and then began to cry uncontrollably. I quietly sat with her. Her mood shifted and she began an outpouring of emotional complaints; she related how angry she was at him for disregarding her feelings (and perhaps at me for disregarding her defenses). She associated to other like situations, of how miserable and dissatisfied she was in much of her life, and then she fell silent. She apologized for becoming upset, yet added that she felt better. We explored further the contents of her silence and her need to apologize. She said that she felt anxious and ashamed, and countered that she should be grateful for what she had in her life, that she had been foolish, and that she did not really have anything to complain about compared to others. In time, we would understand that this reaction constituted transference phenomena related to persistent experiences with her mother, who would tell her whenever she voiced a complaint that she had "nothing to cry about compared to living with Joan's father." We would later understand that her remarks were in part preemptive; she was trying to forestall what she anticipated would be my criticism or disinterest in her troubles, which in turn would then trigger aggression toward me inciting an even more dangerous situation. The dangers involved in expressing her aggressive feelings were reflected in a series of dreams early in treatment in which buildings were being burned down, huge waves destroyed villages, and all sorts of vicious dogs and menacing people would chase after her.

This session exemplified a psychological process that would be repeated numerous times in the early phase of treatment; little by little more of her psychological experience could be accepted into consciousness and gradually her guardedness and feelings of anxiety dissipated as a result of empathic understanding and interpretation. She gained confidence in the therapeutic alliance and became more aware of the unconscious fears and transference manifestations, which prompted her use of defenses. Focus was placed on the manifestations of transference shaping the content and process of our clinical work together (Gill, 1979). As the therapeutic work deepened, the multiple influences that shaped and constituted her unique psychic reality came clearer into focus.

Middle Phase of Treatment

After about 8 months of treatment, the therapeutic course took a decided turn to a deeper exploration of childhood experiences and her subjective responses within the transference. With increased trust, Joan entered into an "analytic space" in which memories, fantasies, affects, impulses, and physical sensations became more readily available in her conscious associations. She recounted situations of intense affect, of fear and shame, and began to discover memories and impulses previously isolated from awareness. Among her associations were memories of early religious experiences, which suggested important identifications with the Virgin Mary, idealized aspects of her mother, together with split aggressive and depreciating reactions to her father. She remembered trying to be perfect in her prayers, longing to be selected as the May Queen, and being fascinated with the lives of the saints. Her mother was pleased by her interest in religious devotions; she was so unlike her older brothers. She recalled that this period was interrupted by repeated bouts of her father's drinking binges and she remembered "shutting down" emotionally. The surfacing of these memories brought increased anxiety in the therapeutic relationship. At the end of a session in which she had expressed considerable hurt and anger in respect to her father and the turmoil in the home, she turned while leaving to ask if she could see me the following week. Her question was unusual in that we had a standing appointment; subsequent analysis revealed fears about expressing aggression as well as disappointment and hurt toward her father. Religious associations surfaced in which she recounted fears of being condemned to the "fires of hell" and memories of lying in bed, reciting prayers in the night on hearing fighting between her parents. She reported feeling unsettled during the day, somewhat disoriented, and felt increased concern about how I felt about her. She had a fear that something would happen to me; that I would be in an accident. This marked an intensification of focus on our relationship as she worked on the ambivalent feelings she experienced toward her father and consequently with other men, including me. She reported nightmares of catastrophe—earthquakes, tornados, hurricanes; images of Christ being crucified ran through her mind. She recalled being afraid of certain Catholic rituals in which incense was burned and made her nauseous. With the provision of increased sessions, she processed the intense feels of disorientation that were revisited from the past. Feelings of fear and anger were dysregulating as well as the trust, which she was now investing in me and in the analytic process. She was able to recount vivid details of anxiety as a child, fears she related particularly to the aggression and chaos in the family. She spoke of how she never let anyone see how she was feeling, that her mother had made it clear that she was not interested in hearing any more complaints. Throughout the middle phase of treatment, Joan processed the events from the past and became more willing to share her feelings and to confront areas of dissatisfaction in her marriage. She no longer experienced any headaches or other physical symptoms. She was able to work intensively in psychotherapy and simultaneously to make practical improvements in her lifestyle. She began to develop a genuine interest and investment in her sexual life with her husband; he was also responding positively to her needs and they began to enjoy their relationship and children in ways that they had not before. She described toward the end of the middle phase that she was feeling psychologically "lighter" and with less pressure. Toward the end of a session she casually mentioned that her family had begun to attend a local Christian church. She believed that it would be a good thing to join as her children were in the orbit of adolescence and there was an active youth group, which she believed might provide a place of values. She was reminded of the sense of community she obtained in her parish when she was a teenager. It seemed that the God she had once feared, with whom there was trepidation and anger, receded to be replaced with a more benign presence in her mind. She was becoming a more spontaneous, trusting person. She no longer felt the same degree of apprehension about her impulses and affects.

Termination Phase

As she became aware of how her life had substantially improved, she expressed gratitude to me and began to talk about her sadness that she would have to leave psychotherapy in the future. She wondered whether there would be anything wrong with just continuing forever. The focus of treatment shifted naturally to processing her feelings about our relationship and her experience of psychotherapy. She spoke of how I was in her mind and associated that perhaps death was not really a complete end of relationship. She recalled with great poignancy how she felt a loss when each of her children entered kindergarten that she would no longer have the young children whom she so loved and enjoyed. She spoke of the death of her father, years ago, as well as mourned more fully that she would not live her life in her childhood neighborhood. The problems of living did not evaporate; however, she no longer feared the contents of her mind and was better able to address conflicts. She realistically understood that psychotherapy could not erase the hurts of the past nor undo decisions she had made. She was now better able to live her life with greater awareness, acceptance, and gratitude. We ended psychotherapy after almost 4 years with an appreciation for each other and for the process, which honored the substance of her experience.

COMMENTARY

Every clinical case provides an opportunity to consider the theories and practices that inform psychological treatment. Although the findings of such inquiry do not allow for a formal evaluation of efficacy nor meet the standards of science to establish empirical support, case studies provide illustrations of selected aspects of the therapeutic process considered salient by the clinician and complement findings obtained through clinical-quantitative methods. Several factors contributed to the positive outcome in this case. Consistent with the research literature (Bergin & Garfield, 1994; Galatzer-Levy, Bachrach, Skolnikoff, & Waldron, 2000) the quality of the therapeutic relationship (Lambert & Barley, 2001), alliance (Horvath, 2001), and empathy (Greenberg, Elliott, Watson, & Bohart, 2001) were seen as crucial to both the process and outcome. In my view, the psychodynamic approach, with its emphasis on vicarious introspection and close attention to affect states and to the subjective experiences co-constructed within the relationship, was particularly well suited to establish a relationship that would produce the therapeutic results. Further, psychoanalytic theory offered explanatory models that described psychological mechanisms involved in the production of this patient's presenting symptoms. The systematic analysis of defenses and the identification of the interpersonal contexts in which early compromise formations developed enabled Joan to make sense of her response tendencies and with insight to more readily attempt alternative solutions. Joan's intelligence and motivation, as well as other psychological capacities, born in part out of a secure maternal attachment, prepared her to participate fully in an analytic experience. In keeping with psychoanalytic practice, the amelioration of symptoms was accomplished through interventions aimed at the level of personality functioning and included changes in her internalized objects and regulation of self-esteem.

This clinical discussion also provided an example of a clinical approach to religious material disclosed in psychotherapy. Although the presenting problem did not suggest religion to be the primary source of her difficulties, Joan's beliefs, experiences, and objects derived from religious experience were important features in her psychological life. Psychoanalytic theory allowed for consideration of the multiple sources that contributed to her creation of God representations as well as explication of the dynamic functions that God representations, religious beliefs, and moral instruction served. Through maintaining a clinical perspective, in which all mental contents were included in the analytic discourse, the religious dimension could be appreciated as important in psychological life.

REFERENCES

American Psychiatric Association. (1994). *Diagnostic and statistical manual of mental disorders* (4th ed.). Washington, DC: Author.

Arlow, J. (1985). The concept of psychic reality and related problems. *Journal of the American Psychoanalytic Association, 33*, 521–535.

Bergin, A. E., & Garfield, S. L. (1994). *Handbook of psychotherapy and behavior change* (4th ed.). New York: Wiley.

Falender, C. A., & Shafranske, E. P. (in press). *The practice of clinical supervision: A competency-based approach.* Washington, DC: American Psychological Association.

Freud, S. (1927). The future of an illusion. In *Standard edition of the complete psychological works of Sigmund Freud: Vol. 21* (pp. 5–56). London: Hogarth Press.

Gabbard, G. O. (2000). *Psychoanalytic psychiatry in clinical practice* (3rd ed.). Washington, DC: American Psychiatric Press.

Galatzer-Levy, R. M., Bachrach, H., Skolnikoff, A., & Waldron, W., Jr. (2000). *Does psychoanalysis work?* New Haven, CT: Yale University Press.

Gill, M. M. (1979). The analysis of the transference. *Journal of the American Psychoanalytic Association, 27*(Suppl.), 263–288.

Greenberg, L. S., Elliott, R., Watson, J. C., & Bohart, A. (2001). Empathy. *Psychotherapy: Theory/Research/Practice, 38*(4), 380–384.

Horvath, A. O. (2001). The alliance. *Psychotherapy: Theory/Research/Practice, 38*(4), 365–372.

Jackson, S. W. (1999). *Care of the psyche.* New Haven, CT: Yale University Press.

Jones, J. W. (1991). *Contemporary psychoanalysis and religion.* New Haven, CT: Yale University Press.

Jones, J. W. (1996). Religion and psychology in transition. New Haven, CT: Yale University Press.

Kernberg, O. (1967). Borderline personality organization. *Journal of the American Psychoanalytic Association, 15*, 641–685.

Kernberg, O. (1992). *Aggression in personality disorders and perversions.* New Haven, CT: Yale University Press.

Kohut, H. (1959). Introspection, empathy, and psychoanalysis. An examination of the relationship between mode of observation and theory. *Journal of the American Psychoanalytic Association, 7*(3), 459–482.

Lambert, M. J., & Barley, D. E. (2001). Research summary on the therapeutic relationship and psychotherapy outcome. *Psychotherapy: Theory/Research/Practice, 38*(4), 357–361.

Ledoux, J. (1996). *The emotional brain.* New York: Simon & Schuster.

Loewald, H. W. (1980). On the therapeutic action of psychoanalysis. In H. W. Loewald (Ed.), *Papers on psychoanalysis* (pp. 221–256). New Haven, CT: Yale University Press.(Original work published 1957)

Luborsky, L., Auerbach, A., & McLellan, A. T. (1996). The context for migraine-like headaches. In L. Luborsky (Ed.), *The symptom-context method* (pp. 201–215). Washington, DC: American Psychological Association.

McWilliams, N. (1994). *Psychoanalytic diagnosis.* New York: Guilford Press.

McWilliams, N. (1999). *Psychoanalytic case formulation.* New York: Guilford Press.

Meissner, W. W. (1984). *Psychoanalysis and religion*. New Haven, CT: Yale University Press.

Meissner, W. W. (1992). *Ignatius of Loyola. The psychology of a saint*. New Haven, CT: Yale University Press.

Menninger, K. A., Mayman, M., & Pruyser, P. W. (1963). *The vital balance: The life process in mental health and illness*. New York: Viking Press.

Perry, S., Cooper, A. M., & Michels, R. (1987). The psychodynamic formulation: Its purpose, structure, and clinical application. *American Journal of Psychiatry, 144*(5), 543–550.

Rangell, L. (1992). The psychoanalytic theory of change. *Psychoanalytic Psychology, 73*, 415–428.

Rangell, L. (2000). Psychoanalysis at the millennium: A unitary theory. *Psychoanalytic Psychology, 17*, 451–466.

Reiff, P. (1959). *Freud: The mind of the moralist*. New York: Viking Press.

Rizzuto, A.-M. (1979). *The birth of the living God*. Chicago: University of Chicago Press.

Rizzuto, A.-M. (1998). *Why did Freud reject God*. New Haven, CT: Yale University Press.

Sandler, J., & Rosenblatt, B. (1962). The concept of the representational world. *Psychoanalytic Study of the Child, 17*, 128–145.

Schore, A. N. (1994). *Affect regulation and the origin of the self*. Hillsdale, NJ: Erlbaum.

Shafranske, E. P. (1995). Freudian theory and religious experience. In R. W. Hood, Jr. (Ed.), *Handbook of religious experience* (pp. 200–230). Birmingham, AL: Religious Education Press.

Shafranske, E. P. (Ed.). (1996). *Religion and the clinical practice of psychology*. Washington, DC: American Psychological Association.

Shafranske, E. P. (2000). Psychotherapy with Roman Catholics. In P. S. Richards & A. E. Bergin (Eds.), *Handbook of psychotherapy and religious diversity* (pp. 59–88). Washington, DC: American Psychological Association.

Shafranske, E. P. (2002). The psychoanalytic meaning of religious experience. In M. Aletti & F. De Nardi (Eds.), *Psychoanalisi e religione* [Psychoanalysis and Religion]. Torino, Italy: Centro Scientifico Editore.

Siegel, D. J. (1999). *The developing mind*. New York: Guilford Press.

Spero, M. H. (1992). *Religious objects as psychological structures*. Chicago: University of Chicago Press.

Sperry, L., & Shafranske, E. P. (in press). *Spiritually oriented psychotherapy: Contemporary approaches*. Washington, DC: American Psychological Association.

Stolorow, R., & Atwood, G. (1987). *Psychoanalytic treatment: An intersubjective approach*. Hillsdale, NJ: Analytic Press.

Stolorow, R., & Atwood, G. (1992). *Contexts of being*. Hillsdale, NJ: Analytic Press.

Stolorow, R., Atwood, G., & Ross, J. (1978). The representational world in psychoanalytic therapy. *International review of psychoanalysis, 5*, 247–256.

Van Herik, J. (1982). *Freud on femininity and faith*. Berkeley: University of California Press.

Wallerstein, R. (1990). Psychoanalysis: The common ground. *International Journal of Psychoanalysis, 71*, 3–20.

Weiss, J. (1993). *How psychotherapy works*. New York: Guilford Press.

IV

INDIVIDUAL ECUMENICAL THERAPIES (ACROSS FAITHS)

10

CROSSING TRADITIONS: IGNATIAN PRAYER WITH A PROTESTANT AFRICAN AMERICAN COUNSELING DYAD

DONELDA A. COOK

This chapter presents a brief counseling case in which meditative prayer and spiritual imagery methods from a Catholic spiritual tradition, Ignatian spirituality, were used in a counseling dyad consisting of a Protestant African American counselor and client. Both the counselor and client were from worship traditions very expressive in their praise of God (i.e., singing, clapping, shouting, dancing) and relatively charismatic (i.e., invoking the power of the Holy Spirit through communal prayer). Interestingly enough, both also participated in spiritual retreat experiences of extended periods of silent meditative prayer, introduced to them through their employment (the counselor) and matriculation (the client) at a Jesuit college and university. Discussion of the brief counseling case will address how Ignatian prayer methods, though not a traditional aspect of either the counselor's or the client's religious backgrounds, was integrated into the counseling experience, and the impact on the process and outcome.

DESCRIPTION OF THERAPIST

Donelda A. Cook, an African American woman in her mid-40s, is currently assistant vice president for student development and director of the Counseling Center at Loyola College in Maryland. She is also an adjunct faculty member in Loyola's pastoral counseling department. Cook, a licensed psychologist, received her doctorate in counseling psychology and has been practicing in university settings for 20 years. She has published several journal articles and book chapters in multicultural counseling and psychotherapy, and supervision and training. Cook is coauthor of a book with Janet Helms entitled, *Using Race and Culture in Counseling and Psychotherapy: Theory and Process* (2nd ed., Helms & Cook, in press).

Since childhood, Cook has been affiliated with African American Baptist churches; however, she considers herself to be ecumenical in her religious faith and minimally orthodox. In 1998, she became affiliated with an African Methodist Episcopal church, Mt. Calvary A.M.E. Church, in Towson, MD. She serves on the church's ministerial staff under a nationally recognized pastor, Rev. Dr. Ann Lightner-Fuller, as a licensed preacher and director of the Ministry of Prayer and Spiritual Formation. Cook conducts meditative prayer retreats and workshops for clergy and laypeople, and on occasion, provides *pro bono* brief counseling for individuals as a follow-up to retreat experiences.

Cook's theoretical orientation is informed by multicultural psychology and spirituality. Her approach is person centered, engaging the whole person, including all aspects of one's social identities (i.e., race, age, gender, sexual orientation, and spiritual orientation) in the counseling process. She is also interpersonally oriented, addressing the interaction between the client's and the counselor's aforementioned social identities. Cook integrates family and societal dynamics in client conceptualization. She understands the negative influences of societal oppression and the positive influences of spirituality in the cultures of many African American, Asian, Latino, and Native American individuals. Consequently, Cook incorporates clients' racial identities and spiritual beliefs, traditions, and resources in the counseling and psychotherapy process.

As a therapist, Cook personally silently prays to invite God into all aspects of the therapeutic process, recognizing the power of the Spiritual Presence in the therapeutic process and outcome. She uses vocal prayer in therapy only when and if the assessment of the client's spiritual orientation calls for such.

Cook was introduced to the *Spiritual Exercises of St. Ignatius* (Fleming, 1978) in 1997 through the retreat programs sponsored by Campus Ministries at the Jesuit college where she is employed. Impressed by the spiritual growth potential of the retreats, she sought opportunities to learn more about Ignatian spirituality. Cook enrolled in seminary coursework, sought personal spiritual direction, engaged in independent study with Rev. Tim Brown, S.J., and continued personal retreat work based on the *Spiritual Exercises* (Fleming, 1978). She currently serves as a spiritual director for the college's 6-day Ignatian retreat.

SETTING

The setting for this counseling case was Cook's office at the college where she is employed as an administrator. Her office is housed in a beautifully stoned (comparable to the adjacent chapel), three-story building on the manicured quadrangle lawn of the Catholic campus. The building houses the offices of the college's senior administrators. The client was seen after regular business hours.

CLIENT DEMOGRAPHIC CHARACTERISTICS

The client, Grace, a 39-year-old, single African American woman, was affiliated with an African American Baptist church. She was assessed at a minimal level of religious orthodoxy. She obtained a master's degree in school counseling and was employed as head of a high school counseling department. Grace was a recently licensed minister in her church and in a ministry formation process toward ordination. She was also a part-time graduate student in a master's of theology program. The client was first introduced to the *Spiritual Exercises* (Fleming, 1978) through the Jesuit university where she conducted graduate studies.

PRESENTING PROBLEMS AND CONCERNS

Grace was a participant in a weekend Scripture-based meditative prayer retreat for persons entering ministry, which I conducted. The silent retreat included four meditative prayer periods each day and daily individual spiritual direction sessions with me. The client's presenting concerns emerged during the retreat and related to the demands of her life, including full-time employment, church ministry, and seminary. Grace had little time for herself. Because of her passion for ministry and her need for approval from her pastor, she put forth as much effort and energy in her part-time unpaid church ministry as in her full-time paid employment. Grace also had unresolved issues over having not yet married nor had children.

CLIENT HISTORY

Grace was the youngest of two children raised in an intact middle-class family. Both of her parents were still living, her mother a retired teacher and her father a retired postal service worker. Her older sister was a married teacher with two daughters. Grace was raised in an African American Methodist church, where she attended church regularly with her family and participated in Sunday school and the youth choir until she went away to college.

Grace became affiliated with her current church, an African American Baptist church, when she relocated after completing graduate school. Through her experiences with this church, she became more expressive in her worship, praising God through singing, clapping, shouting, dancing, and laying prostrate in prayer. She reported having developed more of a personal relationship with God, and experiencing joy in expressing her love to God. Grace became a Sunday school teacher for adolescents, and was later asked by the pastor to oversee the Christian education department. She accepted the formal call to ministry, to become an ordained preacher, 3 months before the spiritual formation retreat.

Socially, Grace has always maintained a small group of intimate friends, most of whom she met through work or church. She has been involved in a few long-term romantic relationships; however, she reported that they ended either because the men were not ready for marriage or they were not spiritually compatible. Grace reported that over the years, she has spent more of her free time involved in church activities and there are few single men in the church.

Grace has always excelled academically. She went to graduate school after teaching for a few years. As an adult seminarian student, Grace found school to be more of a challenge, which was due to other demands on her time.

ASSESSMENT AND DIAGNOSIS

Because of the time-limited counseling and the client's presenting concerns, empirical assessment instruments were not used. A "Level 1 multisystemic assessment," as described by Richards and Bergin (1997, p. 187), was conducted. During the initial session, the client's physical, social, behavioral, intellectual, educational–occupational, psychological–emotional, and religious–spiritual systems were assessed. The client reported a moderate to high level of functioning in each system. Lower levels of functioning were reported: (a) physically, in frequently feeling fatigued; (b) socially, in limited social outlets; and (c) spiritually, in a diminished prayer life. Grace was referred for a medical evaluation, which revealed no medical problems related to her fatigue. After assessing Grace's eating, sleeping, and work habits and schedule, it was assessed that her fatigue was related to poor habits in each of these areas. Similarly, her diminished social and spiritual capacities stemmed from lack of time devoted to these areas.

A clinical interview assessment of the client's religious–spiritual orientation and resources was conducted. Grace was actively involved in worship, service, and community fellowship in her church. She reported that each of these aspects of her church affiliation were emotionally uplifting. Grace typically engaged in spiritual disciplines such as meditative prayer with Scripture, Bible study, fasting, journaling, and listening to gospel and spiritually meditative music. In recent months, however, she had become too busy to devote time to most of these disciplines. Grace initiated counseling with me because the retreat reminded her of the spiritual power that she obtained from her spiritual disciplines, and she wanted help in recommitting to her spiritual life. She found the meditative prayer methods and journaling helpful during the retreat. Furthermore, unresolved issues emerged, which she wanted to continue to process after the retreat.

TREATMENT PROCESS AND OUTCOMES

Ignatian prayer methods were used during the spiritual formation retreat. As a result of Grace's response to this method during the retreat, Cook believed that the meditative prayer practices of Ignatian spirituality would be useful in integrating spiritual disciplines with Grace's psychological functioning.

Meditative prayer is a practice of physical and mental relaxation and surrender of control to a higher spiritual power. As Richards and Bergin (1997) explained, the practices of meditation, contemplation, and spiritual imagery "require a trusting, passive attitude of release and surrender of control, isolation from distracting environmental noise, active focusing or repetition of thoughts, task awareness, and muscle relaxation" (pp. 205–206). Meditative prayer has been associated with well-being and happiness (Richards & Bergin, 1997). Richards and Bergin (1997) have reported on research that shows psychotherapists use contemplation, meditation, and spiritual imagery infrequently with clients, perhaps because of the lack of training in spiritual, as opposed to secular, meditation practices. I did seek training in Ignatian meditative prayer practices. Although contemplation and meditation are often associated with Eastern spirituality, it is also a cornerstone of Catholic spirituality.

Ignatian spirituality, developed by St. Ignatius of Loyola, the founder of the Jesuit order of Catholic priests, uses spiritual imagery in meditative prayer to draw individuals into deep personal relationship with God. Through periods of meditative prayer with Scripture, particularly Gospel scenes, individuals use all of their senses to imagine seeing, hearing, smelling, and physically feeling or touching all that is going on in the Scriptural scene (Endean, 1990). St. Ignatius originally developed the *Spiritual Exercises of St. Ignatius* (Fleming, 1978) as a 30-day silent retreat experience for spiritual formation of novice priests. However, the *Spiritual Exercises* (Fleming, 1978) have been adapted to various formats for laypeople and for use ecumenically. Formats include 3-, 6-, or 8-day silent retreats, or daily prayer within the context of one's routine life. In the latter format, one meditates daily with Scripture, usually for an hour, and participates in weekly spiritual direction for approximately 6 months.

Using Ignatian prayer in this case, I instructed Grace to focus her attention on God through prayerful relationship with Jesus, cognitively, behaviorally, and affectively. Within the counseling process, Grace experienced (a) psychological practice of consciously attending to her thoughts, behavior, and feelings; (b) mystical experience of a personal and intimate relationship with Jesus; and (c) decreased physiological arousal through meditation. Prior to continued discussion of the case, further explanation of Ignatian spirituality and prayer methods is provided, as well as its potential use in counseling and psychotherapy.

Ignatian Prayer Methods

The Spiritual Exercises of St. Ignatius (Fleming, 1978) encourages individuals to recognize the presence of God in all things and to closely follow Jesus in seeking to live out the will of God. As theologian Monika Hellwigg (1991) explained, "Ignatian spirituality is grounded in intense gratitude and reverence. It begins with and continually reverts to the awareness of the presence and power and care of God everywhere, for everyone, and at all times" (p. 14). Thus, the core value of Ignatian spirituality is therapeutic in helping individuals to seek the loving presence of God in all things and in all aspects of an individual's life.

One of the basic premises of the *Spiritual Exercises* (Fleming, 1978) is that through the experience of meditative prayer one gains a sense of the here-and-now:

> Understanding of oneself as a created being and to bring appreciation of one's life as a gift . . . and cultivate a holy indifference toward things of the world to be free to respond to them appropriately. Retreat directors typically encourage one to realize all the things of the world as gifts of God, created in love, and also to recognize how much God has gifted the retreatant individually. These experiences establish a basis for valuing oneself sufficiently to be open to the tensions. . . . They can be considered analogous to establishing a relationship of reasonable comfort and trust with one's psychotherapist to feel safe enough to work on the issues that brought one to therapy. (Meadow, 1989, pp. 175–176)

Barry (cited in Meadow, 1989) reported another therapeutic occurrence in Ignatian prayer: "We find that many psychologically 'normal,' hard-working, faith-filled people have been staving off feelings . . . by overwork, alcohol, pills, the piling up of experiences . . . the continual seeking after companionship. . . . The first few days of prayer remove these 'defenses,' and the feelings come to the surface" (p. 177).

Empirically, Sacks (1979) conducted a study of the effect of a 30-day Ignatian retreat on the integration of self-systems or ego development of Jesuit retreatants. He hypothesized that the spiritual exercises would "result in increased cognitive integration for the individual, as measured by Loevinger and Wessler's test of ego development" (p. 47). Although results suggested the experience had an overall positive effect of increased self-systems for the Jesuit retreatants, it was impossible to identify which aspects of the retreat contributed to the positive results, due to lack of controls in the investigation (Sacks, 1979).

Meadow (1989) presented a conceptual comparison between Ignatian spirituality and Jungian psychotherapy. Regarding counseling and psychotherapy interventions, Ignatian spirituality uses various methods of prayer that may be helpful, including (a) imagery, (b) prayer of the senses, (c) colloquy or conversation, (d) rhythmic breathing, and (e) examen of consciousness. Through the use of imagery, one prays with one's imagination entering into Gospel scenes with Jesus. Through the spiritual power and grace of prayer, one may experience personal fellowship with Jesus (Bunker, 1986). Richards and Bergin (1997) cited research suggesting that the use of spiritual imagery and an individual's spiritual faith in a higher healing power may have more powerful healing effects than secular meditative practices.

To heighten the use of imagery, Ignatius recommended using prayer of the senses (Endean, 1990) in the Gospel scenes. In focusing all senses (e.g., seeing, hearing, smelling, and touching) and imagination in cognitive, behavioral, and affective interaction with Jesus, Lonsdale (1990) suggested:

> We are able to open our hearts and minds to hear the word of God as full as possible, to allow it to sink into our consciousness and to influence our feelings and our most important commitments and choices. . . . It can mould and change us . . . and can reach our innermost hearts, the most fundamental attitudes and dispositions which . . . give shape to our lives. (p. 88)

The imaginative prayer concludes with a conversation with Jesus or God, "a conversation in which the person praying expresses freely and with confidence the feelings that have been aroused by the contemplation, 'as one friend speaks to another' "(Lonsdale, 1990, p. 88). This can be therapeutic as Jesus becomes more accessible in His divinity and humanity. As clients begin to access the power and compassion of Jesus, therapists can encourage them to use prayerful imagery to invite Jesus into the scenes of their own lives. As they practice this method of prayer within and outside of therapy sessions, clients may engage in psychological mindfulness of Jesus accompanying them in their lives. Jesus might be perceived as a transitional object between therapy sessions or as a spiritual cotherapist. Furthermore, clients may invoke a spiritual manifestation of Jesus' divine power and grace.

The behavioral use of rhythmic breathing consists of alternating one's focus on a prayerful word and one's breathing, thereby giving full attention to breathing slowly with a spiritual image (Bunker, 1986). This can be particularly useful in reducing clients' anxiety, and helping clients to get centered and cognitively block irrational thoughts. As Bunker (1986) explained, "Ignatian meditation demands systematic, active concentration of one's entire mind, beginning with a period of preparation involving prayer and recollection of purpose" (p. 207).

Finally, the examen of consciousness helps integrate prayer and life. It is a ritual of looking back over the events of one's day and noting affective responses to the events, to "become more in tune with the presence and leading of God in all aspects of daily life" (Lonsdale, 1990, p. 98). Such conscious inventory of affective responses to the daily events in life can be very therapeutic, particularly for clients who tend to disconnect or disassociate from their feelings. The examen can help clients to discern how their inclinations toward and away from God, within the daily events of their lives, may be associated with healthy or unhealthy cognitive, affective, and behavioral reactions.

Ignatian Prayer Methods Integrated in Counseling Case

The aforementioned prayer methods were used in the case with Grace. The goals of counseling included (a) helping Grace to recommit to her spiritual disciplines to achieve balance in her ministry and personal life, (b) addressing her need for approval from her pastor as related to her tendency to overextend herself in service to the church, and (c) addressing her unresolved issues regarding her life as a single woman. Counseling was limited to eight weekly sessions with daily spiritual discipline assignments between sessions. Grace's previous experiences of daily Scripture meditations, focusing primarily on Gospel scenes, had been helpful in establishing a personal and intimate relationship with God through the person of Jesus. Thus, the counseling process began by inviting Grace to meditate on her current relationship with Jesus.

Through the use of rhythmic breathing, Grace was asked to choose a prayerful word, and alternate focusing on that word and her breathing, until she reached a relaxed state. Grace chose the word "Jesus." As Grace's breathing became slow and relaxed, I asked Grace to meditate on the Scripture, I Cor. 6:19 NIV, "Do you not know that your body is a temple of the Holy Spirit, who is in you, whom you have received from God?" Through this meditation, Grace was able to get in touch with the Spirit of God that lives within her. She became increasingly relaxed and less focused on distracting thoughts.

Next, I invited Grace to enter into a meditation in which she would converse with Jesus, as with an old friend, beginning by asking Jesus the question, "How is it with us?" Grace indicated that because of her diminished prayer discipline, she felt more personally distant from Jesus. Therefore, I wanted her to begin with a conversation with Jesus addressing her relationship with Jesus, how she felt, and how Jesus was feeling in the relationship. Grace silently meditated with this conversation for 20 minutes.

I asked Grace to share what happened during the meditation, and Grace reported that she initially asked Jesus why she was having such a difficult time being in His presence, and she wondered how she had been rejecting Him. Then Grace asked Jesus to forgive her for filling her mind, heart, and life with her ministry and her relationship with her pastor, more than with Jesus. She was able to articulate how she had become so preoccupied with seeking guidance, approval, and acceptance from her pastor. Grace ended by asking Jesus to lead her back to their relationship, to remind her of who Jesus had been to her, and of the intimacy that she used to experience with Jesus through prayer. I pointed out that the meditation was a monologue rather than a dialogue. Grace indicated that she was most aware of her own feelings of missing a personal relationship with Jesus, and she could not hear Jesus' response.

During the remainder of the session, Grace and I discussed her relationship with her pastor. This discussion included how the relationship evolved, the feelings that she had in the relationship, and her typical thoughts, feelings, and behaviors in the relationship. I recommended daily scriptural meditative prayer during the week before their next session.

When Grace returned for the next session, she was excited because she was led to pray with Scriptures from the Song of Solomon, which drew her into an intimate connection with Jesus. Grace reported that she "just ended up" reading the Song of Solomon and that she had never prayed with this Scripture before. She perceived this as Jesus answering her prayer. Grace stated, "the Holy Spirit inspired me to pray my mind free with this Scripture."

During this meditation Grace reported that "Jesus quieted my cluttered mind . . . kissed away the fears I speak . . . and deposited His Peace into me, far surpassing a drink of wine," all references to the Scripture text. Grace continued to report on the intimate connection that she experienced with Jesus. She described in detail how she experienced the presence of Jesus with all of her senses, including sight, sound, smell, and touch. She also described interactions that were initiated by Jesus. For example, at one point she became distracted with thoughts during the meditation, and Jesus "gently touched my eyes and closed them" and brought her attention back to Jesus' Presence with her. Grace also reported on a conversation that she had with Jesus, articulating how she tended to avoid Jesus during times of emotional pain. She reported that Jesus explained to her that He runs toward her and patiently waits for her to invite Him into her pain. This was also in reference to the Scripture text with which she meditated.

This degree of personal connection with Jesus remained with Grace beyond the prayer period. Consequently, she was able to call on Jesus' Spiritual Presence through the course of the routine events of her week. This was particularly important in interactions with her pastor, when she could prayerfully consult with Jesus rather than immediately agreeing to do all that the pastor asked of her. Grace found that the more time that she spent in prayer, the more she was able to discern what God was calling her to do. Thus, she was able to limit the additional responsibilities that her pastor was asking her to perform. She began to put forth more boundaries in her relationship with her pastor.

As Grace resumed her daily prayer discipline, Jesus became a transitional object that provided her with support between counseling sessions. As Jesus was invited into meditations on various situations in Grace's life, she received comfort, support, and at times challenge. Within a few weeks, Grace trusted Jesus enough to share her deeper vulnerable feelings, including her anger toward God and Jesus.

During the fourth counseling session, Grace shared with me the emptiness she felt in not having a significant romantic relationship, and having never married and had children. Grace reported that she had dealt with this loss in previous counseling, and functioned very well with her life, despite not having such significant relationships. However, there were times when she felt a deep emptiness and loss. Grace had accepted the possibility that she might never marry and have children, but during her prayer times with Jesus, she realized that she wanted more. She felt a sadness that she articulated as "dried up hope."

I invited Grace to enter into a meditative prayer with Jesus, to converse with Him regarding these issues. At the beginning of the meditation, Grace wrote down what she desired from the meditation. She wanted to open her deepest desire and longing to Jesus. Her prayer was "for openness, help me to invite Jesus into my deepest pain, into my barrenness, into my inner woman, help me to speak to Jesus from my womb and allow Jesus to speak back to me. Holy Spirit, I need You desperately to move in this prayer. I want the grace of God to come out of this prayer. I want to be healed of my feelings of barrenness, and want this prayer time to be Holy Spirit led. Amen."

This prayer speaks of how real Jesus had become to her, how she believed that she could interact with Jesus personally and intimately, and how she had developed the courage to name her deepest pain. It also revealed her faith in all parts of the Trinity, God, Jesus, and the Holy Spirit, and her faith in the healing power of the Holy Trinity. During the meditation, Grace interacted with God in all persons of the Holy Trinity. She found herself in the delivery room, lying on the birthing table, with Jesus at her head, holding her hand. She reported that "God, the Father" was at the foot of the table situated high against the wall, and the Holy Spirit was below God. She did not recognize any physical form for either of them, but she recognized each One's Presence.

A very intimate interaction proceeded, in which Grace spoke openly and frankly to God and Jesus about her longing and her anger that they had not provided for her, despite her faithfulness. She named her "dried up hope" and how she distanced herself from social situations because of it. She said that she wanted to be "open and life-giving" with others. As Grace shared her true feelings in the meditation, God and Jesus spoke back to her in very real and honest ways, both comforting and confronting. Grace reported that after conversing with them in the meditation, Jesus placed His hand on her womb and asked her to focus on the feeling of the "dried up hope" within her. Grace reported that after experiencing an internal physical sensation of "dried up hope," Jesus breathed the Holy Spirit into her and a radiant sparkling ball of life came from her womb. She reported that Jesus "held my hand and stroked my forehead and said, 'See what we can do together?'"

I witnessed visual signs of Grace's affect changing throughout the meditation. Periodically, I would gently ask Grace what was happening and Grace would speak about the experience and feelings she was having. Her feelings ranged from sadness, to anger, to joy over the course of the meditation. I asked Grace to journal about her experience of this meditation through the course of the week. The next week, Grace read from her journal entries, revealing an attitude of expectancy in the ways that she would be life giving in her interactions with others, and how she intended to embrace her life, to "stand tall and vibrant and walk in life." She articulated the difference in being a caregiver and being life giving, in that she would give from her heart rather than taking in other people's concerns and expectations; she would "project outwardly rather than absorbing inwardly." Grace wanted to remain mindful to "keep Jesus in the delivery room . . . together we can create new life!"

By the end of the 8 weeks, Grace felt confident that she would resume her disciplined prayer life. As she set more boundaries in her relationship with her pastor, she created more of a balance in her ministry and personal life. However, balancing a full-time job, part-time ministry, and seminary continued to overextend her. She committed to scheduling time with her family and friends as well as time alone for rest and relaxation. Grace had developed the discipline of performing the examen of consciousness, in looking back over the events of each day and noting her affective responses to the events to help her to assess when she was becoming overwhelmed.

Grace's previous experience with Ignatian spirituality through a 6-day silent retreat and continued daily prayer with Scripture made her an ideal candidate for using Ignatian prayer in brief counseling. She was familiar with the prayer methods and was motivated toward their use; consequently, Ignatian prayer methods were used immediately. My theoretical and practical understanding of Ignatian spirituality made her comfortable with the mystical experiences that Grace was having in her meditative prayer periods. Delusional thinking had been ruled out in the initial assessment phase. Both the client's and the counselor's faith in spiritual healing powers facilitated the use of nontraditional methods in the counseling process.

THERAPIST COMMENTARY

It is difficult to articulate, in psychological scholarship, the powerful imprint left from an encounter with God and the healing power of experiencing a deep sense of unity with God. It speaks to my personal spiritual development, that as a therapist I would so unashamedly speak of Jesus in such a personable and real manner. Furthermore, I would never have imagined myself sharing my faith life in public scholarship. However, it was through Ignatian spirituality that I personally came to experience Jesus' healing power. I know firsthand the mystical experiences that can occur in spiritual meditative prayer. Thus, I was neither skeptical nor intimidated by the mystical reports of the client.

I believe the psycho-spiritual nature of the counseling process would not have occurred without my spiritual faith and theoretical and practical knowledge of this spiritual meditative prayer form. I believe that Grace could have worked through the issues with which she presented with a purely secular approach to therapy. However, her presenting concerns were so intertwined with her faith and her vocation to ministry that my faith and knowledge of her religious tradition gave us common ground from which to work. Furthermore, my belief in the Spiritual Presence and power of Jesus encouraged me to take a back seat and allow the therapeutic interactions between Jesus and the client to evolve.

My personal recognition of the unconditional love of God frees me to take risks in incorporating spirituality in counseling and psychotherapy. The Spiritual Presence that is with me in therapy sessions is as nonjudgmental as the humanistic approach to therapy from which I practice. Regardless of presenting problems, social identities, or lifestyles, clients can engage with their own God images, seeking consolation or reconciliation. I openly state my own bias, that God created each of us in God's own image, and God loves each of us unconditionally.

The techniques of Ignatian prayer are not prescribed for secular use in psychotherapy but for working with the transforming God experience that a client may have obtained through an Ignatian retreat. A therapist with knowledge and experience in Ignatian spirituality, who has an understanding that clients have been changed by the retreat experience, could continue building on the growth that transpired from the retreat.

Lonsdale (1990) described the signs of growth from Ignatian prayer:

As people become increasingly contemplative in the midst of activity, what happens in prayer gives both impetus and shape to the rest of life, and particularly to the choices that they make. Their lives begin to change. . . . the changes appear most clearly in the quality of a person's responses to events and people who are already part of his or her daily life. (p. 90)

Ignatian prayer and psychotherapy are about healthy choices, life changes, and improved interpersonal relationships. As a retreat director and a retreat participant, as a therapist and a therapy client, I have experienced such life changing outcomes in both arenas.

In my limited experience directing Ignatian retreats, I have witnessed individuals with various forms of psychological disturbances and distress struggle with God during a retreat and make positive emotional shifts by the end of the retreat. However, I do not know how these individuals have fared in the aftermath of the retreat, as they returned to the circumstances of their lives. I do believe that some people, like Grace, could benefit from counseling and psychotherapy that continues spiritual and therapeutic work on the issues raised during the retreat. God initiates a spiritual and therapeutic work in the retreat, and through meditative prayer, God is invited to continue working in the counseling or psychotherapy process after the retreat.

The use of Ignatian prayer methods in psychotherapy can provide an integration of spirituality and psychotherapy. Psychiatrist Gerald May (1974) proposed such integration in his seminal works of the 1970s, arguing that psychotherapists "can begin more directly to help others enhance their spiritual lives as well as solve their psychological and interpersonal problems" (p. 90). As a therapist who integrates spirituality and psychotherapy, I have come to realize that the therapist's and the client's spiritual faith can be key factors in the therapeutic process.

REFERENCES

Bunker, D. (1986). Ignatian spirituality in the work of Morton Kelsey. *Journal of Psychology and Theology, 14,* 203–212.

Endean, P. (1990). The Ignatian Prayer of the Senses. *The Heythrop Journal, 31,* 391–418.

Fleming, D. (1978). *The spiritual exercises of St. Ignatius: A literal translation and a contemporary reading.* St. Louis, MO: Institute of Jesuit Sources.

Hellwigg, M. (1991). Finding God in all things: A spirituality for today. *Soujourner, 10,* 11–16.

Helms, J., & Cook, D. (in press). *Using race and culture in counseling and psychotherapy: Theory and process* (2nd ed.). Boston: Allyn & Bacon.

Lonsdale, D. (1990). *Eyes to see, ears to hear: An introduction to Ignatian spirituality.* Chicago: Loyola University Press.

May, G. (1974). The psychodynamics of spirituality. *The Journal of Pastoral Care, 28,* 84–91.

Meadow, M. J. (1989). Four stages of spiritual experiences: A comparison of the Ignatian exercises and Jungian psychotherapy. *Pastoral Psychology, 37,* 172–191.

Richards P. S., & Bergin, A. E. (1997). *A spiritual strategy for counseling and psychotherapy.* Washington, DC: American Psychological Association.

Sacks, H. (1979). The effect of spiritual exercises on the integration of self-system. *Journal of the Scientific Study of Religion, 18,* 46–50.

11

THE PERILOUS PRANKS OF PAUL:
A CASE OF SEXUAL ADDICTION

CAROLE A. RAYBURN

DESCRIPTION OF THERAPIST

Carole A. Rayburn is a clinical, consulting, and research psychologist. She has four degrees, including a doctorate in psychology and a Master of Divinity in ministry. She is a 65-year-old White woman and a third-generation American. A Seventh-day Adventist for the past 32 years, she was previously a United Methodist for more than 20 years. In terms of religious orthodoxy, she is fairly orthodox on biblical issues and moderate to liberal on traditional matters—particularly gender issues and equality of participation at all levels in the ecclesiastical hierarchy. She has been in private practice for 31 years, and besides serving as a consultant to various Montessori schools and professionals, she has been a staff psychologist for District of Columbia and Maryland facilities for adjudicated juvenile delinquents and emotionally disturbed populations. She also has been doing research for more than 22 years and has developed inventories on subjects such as religiousness, spirituality, morality, clergy stress, peacefulness, life choices, the relationship between work and the Supreme, body image and intimacy, and leadership, and has proposed the new field, *theobiology*. Her therapeutic orientation is cognitive and psychodynamic. Her theistic worldview—she considers herself to be a Christian feminist, a religious and spiritual person who practices being gender fair—influences her theoretical orientation and therapeutic approach in that all psychological theories must fit in or be in basic agreement with biblical teachings of a God-centered, Christ-centered, spiritual caring-for-others world. However, whenever those coming to her for psychotherapy hold a secular worldview or have not expressed a desire for a theistic psychological approach for help with their problem and resolution, she does not deal with their situations in a theistic framework. Rayburn does all humanly possible not to judge her patients or clients but to reflect to them what they are thinking and doing and what environmental and worldview influences may influence them and their decisions.

SETTING

The client was seen in a private practice office in the northeastern section of the United States. Primary services offered in this setting were individual and family psychotherapy, marital therapy, addiction treatment, personality assessment, and career counseling.

CLIENT DEMOGRAPHIC CHARACTERISTICS

The client was a 52-year-old White man. He was a Southern Baptist of moderate devoutness. He had a master's degree in computer science and taught at a junior college. The client was from the upper-middle socioeconomic status. The early years of his life were spent in the west coast of the United States, but his adolescent through adult years were spent in the eastern part of the country.

PRESENTING PROBLEMS AND CONCERNS

Paul presented an obsessive concern with why his family and friends had not accepted his extramarital lover of 3 years. Even his coworkers who knew of the relationship did not accept the woman. He indicated that he was still legally married to Cathy, age 51, to whom he had been married for 34 years. At the beginning of the extramarital affair, he spent most of his time and lived with his lover, Fritzi, age 48. Only recently had he moved out of the house that he purchased for a dwelling for himself and Fritzi and moved into a house with one of his three daughters. Fritzi remained in the house in which both of them had been living, claiming that she would not let him share a place with her until his friends, family, and coworkers accepted her as his significant other. She had been married three times before, and two of her husbands died while she was married to them. The third husband divorced her and died a short time later. Although Paul had been in marital therapy with Cathy before, claiming that she and definitely not he was at fault for any problems in the marriage, his one other excursion into therapy was with a male therapist whom family members had reported that Paul managed to tell only half-truths and so distorted realities that the therapist could be of little help to Paul. That therapist, however, had managed to see through Paul's convoluted relationships enough to advise him against staying with Fritzi. However, Paul completely ignored that advice. Nonetheless, he reported to Fritzi his therapist's advice about leaving her, then assuring her that he would never desert her—at the same time building up points for himself in courting Fritzi's loyalty to him. Paul became increasingly frustrated with the nonacceptance issue concerning Fritzi, and one of his friends suggested that he might find the answers of how to better understand women if he sought therapeutic help from a female therapist. This he decided to try.

CLIENT HISTORY

Paul, a fairly attractive man looking somewhat younger than 52 years old, was the youngest child in a family of two older sisters. Though he was pampered by his seductive and domineering mother and favored by his traditional and conservative father, Paul firmly believed that his parents favored his sisters. Before her marriage, his mother was a professional woman. His father was a blue-collar worker. The family finances allowed them to live quite comfortably. Although there did not seem to be evidence of physical sexual abuse by Paul's mother, her verbal seductiveness and possessiveness of him were a type of sexual abusiveness. She kept Paul as dependent on her for as long as she could, and she closely monitored his chances for dating.

At school, Paul believed that he lived in the shadow of his two academic-minded sisters. Teachers were always comparing him unfavorably to his sisters. He compensated for this somewhat by being very popular with his peers. Too, he had a strong desire to please others. Underneath this wanting to please others, however, was an equally strong sadistic sense of humor. For instance, he seemed to get great pleasure from distorting social situations in such a way that two girls or women would verbally or physically attack one another. Once, when he was about 14, his sisters overheard his telephone conversation in which he instructed another male adolescent on how to have sex with a female adolescent. He had managed to have this conversation within hearing of his sisters to irritate them, chuckling in great amusement at their indignation, embarrassment, and rage.

When he was 18, he met Cathy. She was from a different neighborhood and came from a broken home. She was quite different from the fragile, demure girls whom he attracted most often. Cathy was an aggressive and domineering person, but she wanted to hold onto Paul—the one really meaningful relationship in her life. Paul, perhaps seeing this relationship as his ticket to gaining his freedom from his dominant mother who was smothering him with her affection, got Cathy pregnant and was married by a justice of the peace. He lived at home for another year because he was afraid to tell his parents about the marriage until the baby was born, which gave him the final excuse for needing to be married and to live away from home. Occasionally he attended church with his wife, but he was not particularly devout. He was successful in his job, rarely drank or smoked, but he admitted to having many extramarital affairs during his marriage. He was quite determined to have his wife stay at home and not pursue her own vocation. He wanted a submissive, subservient mate, even though he had been fully aware that his wife's personality was very different from his image of what a wife should be.

His wife had pleaded with him to go into marital therapy throughout their troubled marriage. He would only enter into psychotherapeutic sessions, however, with the understanding that there was absolutely nothing wrong with him and that he was only going so that she might get herself corrected. In his mind, he could never do any wrong; he was the strong and perfect spouse. Yet, even when he was having his affairs, he managed for his wife to find out, such as charging gifts to other women on their credit card. After 31 years of marriage, Paul met Fritzi through his wife. Fritzi and her husband were their neighbors and Cathy had met Fritzi at several neighborhood children's parties and at church. Fritzi, claiming that her husband and she were having a lot of problems, came not to Cathy but to Paul for consolation. Very much wanting to rescue Fritzi and be a hero among men, he started taking Fritzi out to dinner and buying her gifts. Cathy and Fritzi almost came to blows in a public place, delighting Paul. He loved to have women fight over him. After 3 years of arguing over separation and divorce, Paul moved in with Fritzi but neither Fritzi nor Paul was divorced from their spouses. Finally, Fritzi got a divorce from her husband, but Paul did not go through with his divorce though everything was financially worked out and enforced. Fritzi and Paul continued to attend church, with both of them giving the appearance of being married to each other. Too, in the house that Paul had bought, Fritzi created the impression for the neighbors and for her coworkers on her job that she was married to Paul. That, however, was not enough to satisfy her: She forced herself on Paul's family, friends, coworkers and acquaintances, though they intensely disliked her repulsive, demanding ways and crude manners. She insulted Paul at every opportunity, criticizing his sexual prowess and appearance and anything else that she could. Paul, who had had diabetes and some heart problems and was taking medication for these conditions, had become impotent. Although Fritzi was cruel in her insults to him, he was still stinging from the affair that Cathy had with a younger man—mainly in retaliation for Paul's many affairs. That behavior just did not fit in with his scheme of things: Men, not women, were to be allowed to wander off the marital course and to sow wild oats. He only felt comfortable and in charge of his life when he had the women in his life fighting each other, preferably over him.

ASSESSMENT AND DIAGNOSIS

Assessment and diagnosis were made through a thorough interview and case history. Although Paul presented with what initially appeared to be an obsessive concern with his relationship with Fritzi and his intense fear that she would end their relationship if his family, friends, coworkers, and others did not accept her as his significant other, it soon became apparent that he had other and even more serious problems. From the clinical history that evolved during several sessions, it became clear that Paul was experiencing a sexual addiction involving intense feelings of inadequacy about his sexual performance—aggravated by his health problems—and his repeated sexual relationships with lovers whom Paul viewed primarily as objects to be used for his pleasure. The *Diagnostic and Statistical Manual of Mental Disorders* (DSM; 4th ed., American Psychiatric Association, 1994) states this as

> 302.9, Sexual Disorder Not Otherwise Specified. This category is included for coding a sexual disturbance that does not meet the criteria for any specific sexual disorder and is neither a sexual dysfunction nor a paraphilia. Examples include: (1) marked feelings of inadequacy concerning sexual performance or other traits related to self-imposed standards of masculinity or femininity, and (2) distress about a pattern of repeated sexual relationships involving a succession of lovers who are experienced by the individual only as things to be used. (p. 538)

When he was younger, Paul enjoyed using women as objects even more. However, as he grew older, his possibilities for manipulating women and not having them realize what he was doing were diminishing. He was also experiencing greater conflict in his wanting to please others and in his wanting to control women.

Paul's religious and spiritual background essentially involved a conservative and traditional stance on girls and women. Men were held to be the priests of the family and girls and women were to follow the lead of the male head of the family. In his childhood family, however, his mother and not his father was the dominant parent, and he thought that his sisters and not he were the family favorites. So he believed that his family was out of the path that should be religiously followed. He then could see himself as getting even with girls and women and righting wrongs whenever he manipulated and used them. He would be the man to reestablish the "male-order of things." Often he would maintain relationships with several women at the same time, never letting any one of them think that she was his one and only. Religiously and spiritually, he believed that girls and women were only second best in a man's world. That, he thought, was the God-given order of life. Within the branch of his religious denomination, Paul searched for a church in which he perceived the ministerial staff to take the most conservative patriarchal view toward the position of girls and women. He then would use his perception as justification to treat girls and women as inferior beings and boys and men as supremely superior persons.

As the therapist, my theistic worldview influenced my conceptualization of Paul and his outlook very intensely. Believing in the equality of men and women from the creation of life (Genesis 1:27, "in the image of God he created him, male and female he created them"; Galations 3:28, "there is neither male or female, for you are all one in Christ Jesus"; female images and identity of God, such as El Shaddai, "the breasted one"; Biale, 1982; Rayburn, 1995; Rayburn & Richmond, 1998, 2000, 2002), I sensed very strongly the severe theological and sociopsychological distortions that Paul was making to justify his misuse and abuse of women. To treat Paul most effectively, I as his therapist needed to contrast for him his goals in drawing close to the Christian community of believers and to God, and his unacceptable behavior in the eyes of God as detailed in scripture and of the religious community. He was seriously compartmentalizing his religious and spiritual aspirations, his very secular sexual misconduct and addiction, and his deceit toward himself and others. My worldview questions giving such importance to sexuality for the sake of sexuality per se and so little attention to the spiritual and the emotional side of sexuality and caring for others (Exodus 20:14; Deuteronomy 5:18; Galatians 5:19; 1 Thessalonians 4:30). Sexually using others as objects and in ways that would pain them would be antagonistic to caring for others and showing them loving kindness and spiritual concern. Such treatment would be degrading, because the woman would be seen as something less than human and less than a coequal in the creation of persons by God. The symbolism of the rib of Adam, in which the rib is one of a pair of cartilaginous or curved bony rods that stiffen the walls of the body and protect the viscera, is that man and woman are equal, partners in every sense, and both were created in the image of God (Rayburn, 1995). Jesus certainly taught Mary of Bethany in the same way that he taught his other disciples. Just because her sister Martha was a traditional homemaker did not mean that Jesus did not accept women disciples and give them the opportunity to benefit fully and directly from his teachings. Nowhere is there evidence that Jesus treated women as anything other than equal to men (Swidler, 1971, 1979). Certainly Jesus never encouraged or condoned abuse or misuse of women. Therefore, if Paul were using his own slant on conservative and traditional religious and spiritual beliefs to support his treating women as sexual objects, as toys for his amusement, he was missing the point of true Christian love. He was also allowing himself to be misguided in joining an unholy alliance with those who would battle in a gender war that would never really be won nor be pleasing to the Creator who made man and woman in the divine image of God. Consequently, Paul was not only deluding the women in his life, but as important he was deceiving himself—he was not really pleasing and loving others but was deceiving and hurting them. He would not be a hero to God for this deception but be one in need of repentance and humility before his Creator (Psalm 50:19, 101:7, 102:2; Proverbs 12:20, 14:8, 26:24–26). Paul's lack of loving kindness and the fallen angels were the true enemy, not women. As in Cervantes' *Don Quixote*, the therapist had to hold up a mirror before Paul, though with mercy, concern, and compassion, to allow him to see for himself how he had veered off the course to a more spiritual and sanctified life. He had to be helped to reflect on what he espoused to believe and what his actions were living out, and to then be better able to separate the "wheat from the tares" (Matthew 13:24–30) or the good from the bad. Initially, he had so separated his adultery, fornication, deception, and other lies from his church attendance and listening occasionally to conservative religious radio programs. As an assignment, he was asked to read through scripture to see if he could find any justification for his sexual behavior and deception, as well as reading what scripture taught about these matters. Midway in his therapy, he thought that maybe he was atoning for his addictive behavior and deception by church attendance and religious programs. Only later did he realize that he needed to change a lot in his behavior to grow spiritually and religiously and to get back on the track that he wanted to follow.

TREATMENT PROCESS AND OUTCOMES

After good rapport was established with Paul, the therapist was able to get a better picture of the real dynamics of Paul's personality. Paul not only freely admitted that he had had several affairs at the same time, but he seemed to derive pleasure in the shock value of revealing these liaisons to the therapist. In fact, shocking others with his manipulation and controlling of women and his response to their retaliating toward him were a large part of the games that Paul liked to play in a compulsive way.

Paul had a love–hate relationship with both his mother and father. For his mother, he felt admiration for her education, accomplishments, and ego strength. He admired his father for his sense of personal strength of character and his old-world traditionalism. Nonetheless, he had accepted his father's and society's biases against women and intensely disliked his mother's dominant role in the family and her control over his life. Just as strongly, he detested and disrespected his father's failure to place his mother in a subservient position within the family and to take over the reins of control. He did not sense his father's support for him and his rightful place of power as the only son in the family. Although his parents maintained a dysfunctional relationship much of the time, arguing over almost everything, Paul sought consolation from male peers who held his same male chauvinistic philosophy of life. Probably the single most determining event in Paul's life was his memory of walking in on a scene in which his mother was making love to a man who was a family friend. Paul was 6 years old at that time and, though shocked by this happening, never shared this with anyone except his wife Cathy and his latest lover, Fritzi. His mother had a far superior education to his father, and she attended church. The similarities to Paul and his situation, with the exception of his sexual behavior being addictive, were striking. Although his sisters tried to maintain a peaceful and even protective stance toward Paul, he saw them as competition for his parents' affection and for status and honors in the outside world. Most usually, however, he managed to just barely cover up his anger by a facade of charm and goodwill. Understandably hurt when his mother did not encourage his succeeding in school as she had his sisters, he made his own rules and successes by being the class clown, failing in an area in which his mother took pride in accomplishing much, and in carving out his own niche with charm, talent, and skill.

Along with Paul's tremendous need to please others, he longed for being truly appreciated—especially for his generosity. He often was very generous to those outside his family but stingy to his family. This puzzled others. He did not think that his family appreciated fully what he did for them but that they took him for granted. Therefore, he went to extremes and denied his family many things that he spontaneously did for others. Furthermore, if he were to befriend an especially needy person, one who had very few other friends—such as Fritzi—he could feel particularly secure in his rescuer position and even enjoy a sense of martyrdom if others thought him to be sacrificing himself for someone not worthy of his gifts and attention. The more that his relatives, friends, coworkers, and others were repelled by Fritzi, which was primarily due to her coldness, selfishness, and pushiness, the more Paul was convinced that he should protect and defend her. Then, because others could not at all understand Paul's attraction to such a woman, they grew to disrespect Paul and to seriously question his judgment. When Paul's health problems and the medications that he had to take brought on sexual impotence, Paul considered this the end of the world as he had known it. To him, sexual prowess was the *sine qua non* of masculine identity and male superiority and strength. Although he needed Fritzi to comfort and support now more than ever, she insulted him and threatened his masculine image by making fun of his sexual performance. Initially, she was more supportive and attentive to Paul, hoping to woo him away from his wife. But, when she realized that Paul had no intention of giving up even the remnants of his ailing marriage (only to find himself controlled by a mean-spirited and self-serving woman), she became even more ferocious in her dealings with and demands on Paul. Paul acted out his anger toward Fritzi by openly maintaining a connection with his wife Cathy and their children. There were other women to whom he related at that time also, especially women who had physical problems and for whom he could serve as a knight in shining armor. Using rational emotive behavior therapy (REBT) to tease out the irrationalities in Paul's thinking and feeling, as well as transactional analysis and scriptural teachings on what is really important in being a person in the eyes of God and the community of believers, the therapist drew out more realistic self-images from Paul and helped him to be more comfortable and at peace with himself.

Using psychodynamic and cognitive–behavioral therapy, the therapist encouraged Paul to look at his relationship with his mother. At first, he was highly resistive, denying that he had anything but love and respect for her. The therapist also analyzed the reaction that his mother had when she found out that Paul was dating and then married Cathy. He had a setback for 2 weeks, deciding to absent himself from therapy sessions. Encouraged by his daughters, who thought that he was improving, he came in the following week. He had an insight into feeling some satisfaction that his mother was angered by his marriage. To him, this established that he and not she was in control of his life. Achieving this "one-up" with his mother, he could now see this was a payoff for getting Cathy pregnant and getting married and thus out of the reach of his mother's control. With that insight, he began to change his thinking and feeling and to experience personal growth.

Considering himself to be a religious and spiritual person, Paul attended church services on a fairly regular basis and professed his belief in God and Christ. Although he justified his treating women as second-class citizens and as inferior to men by what he believed he was being taught in his Baptist church setting and from scripture, he isolated the fact that he was living with Fritzi while she was still married to Steve and while Paul was still married to Cathy. He did not want to talk about adultery and seemed in real pain to even consider that he was doing something wrong and not moral in the teachings of his church or scripture. In therapy, this inconsistency was pointed out to him, but he initially ignored it and would not seriously accept the discrepancy between religious teachings and his behavior. He was also helped to confront his penchant toward manipulation of women and his anger and annoyance at himself in wanting and needing to please others so much in order to gain their constant approval. Paul was asked to think how Christ would look at adultery, at controlling others by seeming to please them but being angered at them and holding them in disdain. He was also challenged to better understand his parents and sisters and to accept them more, seeing some ways in which they showed their love and respect for him, even though they may have had difficulty in showing these feelings more clearly and appropriately. Reflecting on his childhood, he could see more instances when his parents and sisters showed such love and concern for him, though his anger often got in the way of the more positive feelings directed his way. Furthermore, through REBT and transactional analysis, Paul was helped to build more confidence in himself and to realize that he was more than a penis and scrotum. In a gestalt exercise, he was asked to envision himself as a giant penis and scrotum and to experience how he would be feeling and thinking as these sexual organs. From this exercise, he could experience the sense of male strength and dominance but also of shame, fear, vulnerability, and threat of impotence. He could readily see the limits of restricting himself to thinking and feeling as these bodily parts alone.

Encouraged to pray about his problems, to really think about what he wanted from life and what he wanted to be and become as a creation of God, he began to see himself in a newer and more healthy light. As he gained self-confidence, really thought about what adultery and an excessively active sexual lifestyle meant, and realized that his parents and sisters saw some good in him, he saw that Fritzi was after all not good for him. He began to depend far less on superficial relationships and to substantially decrease his time spent with Fritzi and other women. He spent 50% more time with his family. Realizing that he is a child of God and that God never rejected him, he knew that he himself was blocking off several roads in his life to God and the Holy Spirit. He has much less need (less than 60%) to compartmentalize areas of his life. He is experiencing far more peace than he has had in a very long time. This has helped in lowering his anxiety, depression, and blood pressure. Paul spends most of his time staying with one of his daughters, going to see Fritzi only on one or two weekends a month and not being very enthused about seeing her but only responding to her severe demands. Growing increasingly aware of her self-interests and deleterious demands, he became more aware of what others had perceived about Fritzi from the beginning of their relationship. Paul began to talk more to his minister about what was happening in his life and to get yet another view of what he was doing. Initially, however, he was more prone to seeing blame in Cathy and in Fritzi but little or no responsibility for his own involvement in the convoluted relationships.

Because Paul gave much importance to his father's male chauvinism as well as the male biases of society at large, and because he had sought out a specific church that he perceived as upholding male superiority, he dismissed and discounted the caring that his mother and sisters had shown him throughout his life—protecting him from neighborhood bullies, helping him with his homework, buying him gifts, and giving him money when he really needed it. Because he believed that men should be in an undisputed superiority position in the family and in the community at large, anything less than full deference from the women in his life would be seen as insufficient. Thus, even when he was getting much love and attention from women, he felt insecure and neglected. Further, any wish on the part of women to establish a position of equality would be regarded by Paul as wrong, sinful, and outrageous. Yet, having lived with a strong mother and strong sisters, he admired such strength while thinking that he had a mission to reform these girls and women and to help them to become subservient to boys and men as he thought they were created to be. As long as he remained in that competitive position, he slowed any progress in personal growth.

In therapy, Paul was asked to look deeply into his real image of himself and how he thought God looked at him. Initially, he verbalized that he loved himself and accepted himself as a child of God. He thought that God had made him, as other men, superior to women, and that any attempt on the parts of girls or women to be equal to men was not only wrong but also evil. The therapist's worldview, however, stressed belief that men and women were created as equals by God. The therapist asked Paul if he thought that God would desire a superior creation to be linked meaningfully—as in marriage and procreation—to an inferior creation. He was not sure about this. Paul was asked if he would want his wife, daughters, or other women friends and acquaintances to restrain their skills and talents to appear less skilled and talented to the men in their lives. He related that, even if they did have certain abilities, they should not outshine men. He denied that he might have let his biases influence how he graded women in his classes. Paul was asked if he believed that God would be so cruel as to create women with capabilities equal to men and then ask the women to hide their skills and talents while requiring men to feign superiority over women and to live a lie throughout life. Most important, did Paul believe that God would not really love him if he were not superior to all women at all times? Could he not love and respect himself and could not God fully love and accept him if he were performing in superior ways with some but in inferior ways to some other women? Was his life to be a living hell, constantly comparing himself to women and having to distort reality in some instances? Was such imagined conditional love of himself and of God the path of contentment? Over several therapy sessions, he thought through these matters and decided that such perpetual competition was unnecessary and tormenting. Furthermore, Paul realized that he had been living a no-win situation. If he did his best to accomplish his goals in life, he could accept that others—women included—could also be worthy. He could establish a win-win situation. He saw that he had envisioned God as a very cruel patriarchal figure who demanded nothing but perfectionism in performance every moment of his life. This contradicted the picture of a loving Creator. Seeing God as more loving and accepting toward him, he was able to be more loving and accepting toward himself. He was not as obsessed with having to please others or having to manipulate and embarrass women. Paul now allowed himself to be less critical of others and of himself as well. In terms of his impotence, he was reexamining the need and the dosages of medications for his health in general, of medications to render him more potent, and getting information on penile implants. He was able to be more objective once his defensiveness about how masculine he was with his impotence was lessened.

THERAPIST COMMENTARY

In addition to having a sexual addiction in which he treated women as sexual objects or play toys, Paul was addicted to finding a religious and spiritual setting that would uphold his prejudice against women. Historically, the Southern Baptists have been divided on the inclusion of women in the pastorate and on high-level but nonclergy church positions. When men in such a setting interpret the teachings of the branch of their denomination as favoring men over women, this can hamper a more healthy and spiritual outlook of men in general. Using God and distortions of what God demands are not enabling for men to truly understand their relationship with God nor with their cocreatures. Such attitudes do not bode well for marital relationships, because to fulfill these beliefs of female inferiority necessitates that a man marry a woman whom he believes to be inferior to him in most ways or whom he can subjugate into being subservient and not resenting such treatment. Yet, such denial of a woman being able in many ways but having to hide this from her man will bring about open or hidden resentment. Such a "battle of the sexes" goes a long way to dooming any marriage and harming optimal growth and development of any children in the family. Any relationship that asks one of the significant persons to pretend to be inferior to the other significant person is asking the two people to live a terrible lie. To be in an "I'm okay, you're not okay" position is a loser position. There is nothing "okay" about feigning inferiority or in having to make another person less worthy to feel more worthy oneself.

Paul was psychologically caught in the middle of resenting while admiring superior, intelligent women—primarily due to living with his very capable mother and sisters—and seeing them as special challenges to be put down and made to accept positions of inferiority to men. Although he had not been to a woman therapist before and had been able or willing to tell the men therapists only what he wanted them to know, he took the current situation as an interesting challenge of manipulating a woman therapist into thinking that he was charming and quite emotionally healthy. In the latter pursuit, he quite certainly failed.

In Paul's case, his religious and spiritual involvement were highly relevant to his treatment, particularly for the contradictions that he was living: believing himself to be following all of the commandments of his faith and yet remaining in a doubly adulterous situation, admiring and resenting women's capabilities, seeing God's love and acceptance being highly conditional and based on successful performance as a superior man, and wanting to charm and protect women and at the same time manipulate and embarrass them.

Religious and spiritual interventions were useful in Paul's treatment because his belief system took the religious and spiritual into account and used them to justify his male chauvinism and his wanting to subjugate women.

Too, because he felt only conditional love from God and others, such intervention was helpful. One ethical concern and challenge associated with this case was the challenge to his perception of the traditional in his faith system. But was justifying a second-class citizenship of women a healthy situation for Paul, even though he might have thought that this was engendered by his church? The ethics of gender-fair psychotherapy—and the interpretation that many religious and spiritual people discern of scripture and inspiration—requires treatment of men and women as equals. To agree to support a prejudicial position of a client or patient would support an unhealthy lifestyle and belief system.

The theistic worldview of the therapist influenced the treatment processes and outcomes with this client in beneficial ways. The equality of the genders (supported by scripture as well as feminist tenets) is most usually seen as a healthier stance than an inferiority of men and women. In fact, it was this misbelief in the inferiority of women and the superiority of men that engendered and maintained Paul in his sexual addiction and even his obsessiveness in remaining with Fritzi for so long: He could martyr himself and vacillate between an "I'm okay, she's not okay" position and an "I'm not okay, she's not okay, and in fact, the whole world is not okay either." Thus he could make a self-fulfilling prediction—that women were evil and could bring men down to ruin, but that he—men—were heroic and would sacrifice themselves to right the wrongs and save the world from girls and women. It was essential that the religious and spiritual be brought into this case and used to deal with the underlying problems and beliefs. The positive treatment and outcome depended on such intervention.

The therapist's theistic beliefs influenced the therapy process and outcomes in that her belief in God, Christ, the Holy Spirit, and salvation were vital to both the process and the outcome in dealing compassionately and knowledgeably with a seeker of salvation who needed to get his religious/spiritual/psychosocial house in order. A nontheistic therapist might not have been sensitive enough to the nuances of what was happening to successfully deal with the problems presented by a sexual addict with religious ties. A theistic therapist also has a heavier burden, in dealing with religious and spiritual matters in psychotherapy, to avoid being judgmental or having the appearance of sitting in judgment.

The client's theistic beliefs influenced his problems in that his thinking and feelings were at times quite confused and convoluted and having to be unraveled sensitively and gently at times and firmly and decisively at other times. The onus on the therapist to be nonjudgmental is vital for the theistic client.

The process and outcomes potentially would have come out differently in the absence of a theistic spiritual perspective. If there were no reference to Christian admonitions against adultery, deceit, lies, and other maladaptive behavior, there would have been different and perhaps fewer motives for the client to change his behavior: He might have been encouraged to look meaningfully at his self-deceptions, compartmentalizing, and sexual addiction in terms of secular, healthy human development. However, to fully gain awareness of such problems and solutions regarding healthy and religious and spiritual behavior, the theistic spiritual perspective served as the *sine qua non*. Current feminist literature (Lerman & Porter, 1990), as well as much religious and spiritual commentary (Swidler, 1971, 1979; Rayburn & Richmond, 2000) would support working to change Paul's male chauvinism. As for getting him to examine more closely what his particular church and its ministers were teaching boys and men about girls and women, Paul was encouraged in his therapy to think more for himself and not to hide behind the clerical cloak of what he perceived his denominational branch and its staff members to be saying and teaching. Indeed, a most important element of working with one's addictive behavior is clearing away the cobwebs between impulsive acting-out behavior and rational thinking before acting. As his spiritual behavior and insights became more real and meaningful, so too did his relationships with others and his respect for and more realistic appreciation of himself and his place in the universe as a child of the Creator.

REFERENCES

American Psychiatric Association. (1994). *Diagnostic and statistical manual of mental disorders* (4th ed.). Washington, DC: Author.

Biale, D. (1982). The God with breasts: El Shaddai in the Bible. *History of Religions, 20*, 240–256.

Lerman, H., & Porter, N. (Eds.) (1990). *Feminist ethics in psychotherapy*. New York: Springer.

Rayburn, C. A. (1995). The body in religious experience. In R. W. Hood, Jr. (Ed.), *Handbook of religious experience* (pp. 476–494). Birmingham, AL: Religious Education Press.

Rayburn, C. A., & Richmond, L. J. (1998). "Theobiology": Attempting to understand God and ourselves. *Journal of Religion and Health, 37*, 345–356.

Rayburn, C. A., & Richmond, L. J. (2000). Women, whither goest thou? In L. H. Collins, M. R. Dunlap, & J. C. Chrisler (Eds.), *Charting a new course for feminist psychology* (pp. 167–189). Westport, CT: Praeger.

Rayburn, C. A., & Richmond, L. J. (2002). Theobiology: Interfacing theology and science. *American Behavioral Scientist, 45*(12), 1793–1811.

Swidler, L. (1971). Jesus was a feminist. *South East Asia Journal of Theology, 13*(1), 102–110.

Swidler, L. (1979). *Biblical affirmation of women*. Philadelphia: Westminster Press.

12

HUMANISTIC INTEGRATIVE SPIRITUAL PSYCHOTHERAPY WITH A SUFI CONVERT

WILLIAM WEST

DESCRIPTION OF THERAPIST

I am a White man, and I have been a member of the Religious Society of Friends (Quakers) since December 1992. Prior to that, I was a member of the Church of England, but I more or less gave up church membership when I enrolled in a university at the age of 18. However, I retained a keen interest in spirituality. I regard myself as fairly devout, attending Quaker Meetings for Worship every Sunday with my wife and child whenever possible, and I have served as an Elder of my previous Quaker meeting while living in Leeds, England.

Quakers are a religious group founded around 1652 by George Fox. There are currently about 20,000 Quakers in England and approximately 200,000 members worldwide. Quakers are a noncredal group; in England, many Friends

This case study would not have been possible without the active, ongoing, and informed consent of Matthew. My two supervisors, Anne Littlewood and Jim Davis, played an invaluable role in ensuring that my work with Matthew was as effective as possible.

would regard themselves as Christians but not all would do so. Quakers put great emphasis on what they call "the light within" their inner spiritual experience (Gillman, 1988). Their meetings take the form of sitting in silence and waiting on the Spirit. If anyone feels moved by the Spirit to speak, he or she may do so. This is referred to as *ministry*, and it should be spontaneous (Dandelion, 1996). In the United States, some Quaker meetings follow this British style of worship, which is called *unprogrammed*. Other meetings have a pastor and a more formal or *programmed* form of worship, although a period of silence is usually part of such meetings. Friends have a strong tradition of good works within both the therapeutic and other caring professions, as well as of peace-making.

At the time I began working with clients I was 29 years old. I have been in practice as a counselor or psychotherapist since 1979, and I am registered as a practitioner with the British Association for Counselling and Psychotherapy. After 10 years of full-time work as a practitioner, I pursued master's and doctoral studies in counseling from 1990 to1995. I have worked full time as an academic since 1995. I was made a Fellow of the British Association for Counselling and Psychotherapy in 2002.

I am currently senior lecturer in Counselling Studies at the University of Manchester (England), where I am director of Counselling Courses. I am also director of the Professional Doctorate in Counselling. I am a core member of the team for the Masters in Counselling Studies program and the Post Graduate Certificate in Counselling Supervision. In addition, I am Special Advisor on Research to the British Association for Counselling and Psychotherapy, and served from 1996 to 2001 on their Research and Evaluation Committee, with additional service as Chair. I am also an active member of the Society for Psychotherapy Research (International).

My therapeutic orientation is humanistic integrative (West, 2000a), and in the last 5 years I have sought for my small private practice clients who see spirituality as part of the solution to their problems. I felt it necessary to stipulate this as I wished to work in a more explicitly spiritual though not necessarily religious way. This gives me and my clients greater freedom in how we can work together therapeutically. Much of the therapy practiced in Britain is secular, and several therapists are antithetical to their clients exploring issues related to their spirituality (West, 2000b). It meant, for example, that insight that came to me from what I regarded as a spiritual source could be easily put to use; that my clients and I could talk explicitly in spiritual and religious terms when appropriate. It also meant that my clients were given explicit permission to include their spiritual lives in the therapeutic process, and that the therapeutic process itself could be understood in spiritual terms.

Nearly all schools of counseling and psychotherapy in England insist on regular, often individual, supervision of therapeutic practice throughout one's career as a practitioner. The spiritual aspect of my work was, and remains, a key element to be explored in supervision, as will become apparent later in this chapter. The inclusion of spirituality in therapy remains controversial within England and can be a contentious yet key focus of therapeutic supervision (West, 2000c). However, the supervisors for my therapy work during the past 5 years have all been accepting of, and experienced in, working with their clients' and supervisees' spirituality.

My clients welcome the spiritual approach, though I suspect those who do not value it will not have sought me out or been referred to me. However, one client who was keen to work with me, and who did not especially explicitly engage in his therapy work with me around spirituality, said at the end of his therapy with me that he valued the fact that I was spiritually and religiously orientated. This seemed to imply that my orientation nevertheless did have some influence on and meaning for him, despite my not making it explicit in therapy.

My clients mostly seem to be Buddhist or New Age in their orientation rather than Christian, which I find curious. I will not work with members of my own Quaker congregation but am willing to work with people from other Quaker meetings in my area. I often see people for spiritual direction and on occasion run retreats (West, 2001), though this is a separate matter from my therapeutic practice.

SETTING

I work alone in private practice seeing three or four clients a week in my home city of Manchester, a large city in the northwest of England. I invite my clients to set the fees involved according to their means, which has resulted in fees varying from £1 ($1.50) to £40 ($55) per hour. This seems spiritually appropriate, although I am aware that it does also have therapeutic significances, which are explored in supervision. Clients see me weekly or fortnightly for one hour, or occasionally twice weekly. My clients' therapy may last for a few sessions or for many months. Usually the therapy ends by mutual agreement when the therapeutic process appears complete.

CLIENT DEMOGRAPHIC DETAILS

The client, Matthew (his name and some personal details have been changed), was in his early 30s and of mixed race origins but was raised within a White working class family. Although raised within a fairly devout Christian (Church of England) family, Matthew had become a Sufi in his adult life and had regular contact with his Sufi teacher or master. His spiritual life was of great importance to him, and he would quote from Sufi poets, such as Rumi, during his therapy sessions. However, it was many months into his therapy with me when he chose to reveal his religious orientation. He was working as a psychiatric nurse at the time of his therapy with me.

Presenting Problems and Concerns

Matthew's immediate presenting issue was that of tension with a woman manager that was affecting his performance at work. He also reported that he was "out of touch with his feelings" and had some sense of "not taking his place in the world." He said that he did not feel grown up, and was not "coming into his power." He also expressed regret that he was not married or in a committed long-term sexual relationship.

CLIENT HISTORY

Matthew spent his first 6 weeks of life being looked after by Christian nuns in an orphanage until he was adopted. Matthew described himself as somewhat rebellious as an adolescent and in early adulthood, and as an underachiever at school. In his early 20s he had worked as a freelance journalist on a local paper developing a reputation for articles that had an angry and political edge to them. He resumed his studies in his mid-20s and chose nursing; he then realized that he had found his vocation.

However, it soon seemed very clear to me that although Matthew was making an apparent success of his working life, he felt that he was not realizing his full potential at work and in his life as a whole. He felt particularly aware of the fact that he was neither married nor in a committed relationship yet had a deep connection to his adopted Christian family in which being married and having children were expected. Matthew was living in Manchester on his own, but he made regular weekend visits to his parents' home some miles away, where a Sunday family meal usually occurred. Although such family life fit the Christian subculture in which he was raised and to which he felt he belonged, it also emphasized how young he still seemed. Questions often arose about whether or when he was going to meet a nice Christian girl and settle down.

ASSESSMENT AND DIAGNOSIS

My approach to assessment (West, 2000b) is to revisit it as an ongoing process rather than devoting an inordinate amount of time to it in the first session or two. Indeed, the assessment process begins with the telephone call, which is my usual way of contacting a prospective client. During the phone call I decide whether it is worthwhile for the prospective client and me to meet. Occasionally I will screen out a client over the phone, usually offering a more appropriate referral. If we both choose to meet to explore the possibility of working together therapeutically, then the key assessment question I pose to myself is whether I can work with this client. I also always make a screening diagnosis of whether there are mental health issues for the prospective client that mean that one-to-one sessions once or even twice a week will not be sufficient or effective treatment for their problems, or that their problems are beyond my skills to help. My work for a mental health charity in West London in the early 1970s gave me training in, and a deep understanding and experience of, the varieties of mental health problems that people have and how to recognize them.

The next question in this basic assessment is whether the client and I can establish an effective therapeutic alliance so that there is a good chance he or she can make progress through consulting me. Related to that question is whether the client recognizes that he or she has a problem that is treatable by psychotherapy. I have on occasion been consulted by prospective clients, at the instigation of their families or friends, who have not accepted that they have a problem, which makes therapeutic work impossible.

With Matthew there seemed a basic developmental issue of why he was not progressing into adulthood and starting a family, which seemed to form the basis of his therapy with me. This involved an exploration of his thoughts and feelings about his experience and understanding of his adoption, his early childhood, and also his difficult and sometimes rebellious adolescence. I felt at times like a mentor, older brother, or parent. At other times I felt more like a fellow traveler on the spiritual and therapeutic journey.

Matthew sometimes seemed to take up my suggestions too readily, something that I explored in supervision: Was I becoming too much of an expert for him? It seemed clear that, in fact, he was taking up that which was of use to him, making it his own, and developing it further for himself in his own unique way.

TREATMENT PROCESS AND OUTCOMES

Rather than cover Matthew's therapy with me in some detail, which, to do it justice, would take a whole book, I have decided to select some parts of the case narrative that especially reflect the spiritual interventions used. However, it must be recognized that much of the work could be seen and understood in fairly conventional therapeutic terms, but for Matthew and me this was a therapeutic encounter that was infused with spirituality and reflected the spiritual paths and spiritual journey we both saw ourselves as being on. From this perspective, the whole of life is both sacred and spiritual.

I have, after consultation with Matthew, chosen not to focus on most aspects of his family and his work life within this case study. It seemed especially and ethically important to gain Matthew's explicit permission to draw on his case material in a way that felt appropriate to him. Even when some of the details are changed, clients can still feel uncomfortable with publication of their experiences. (I have explored issues relating to ethics in therapy and therapy research elsewhere; West, 2002b.)

However, it does need to be acknowledged how important the therapeutic work was around Matthew's adoption. Previous therapeutic work with adopted clients had alerted me to how less firmly rooted or grounded they might feel. It felt as if the work around Matthew's adoption was a necessary prelude to him being able to move on developmentally in his life. It also raised profound spiritual questions, some of which were explored in the session I alluded to previously.

Inevitably the early sessions were spent in hearing something of his story, why he had come for counseling, and in an exploration of some immediate issues at work. To give a flavor of these early sessions, I include some extracts from my case notes at the time:

> *One session:* At work in the multidisciplinary team it had been easier for him this last week, but he felt that his spiritual side was still not fully acceptable, however he had challenged a woman who he felt was trying to shame him. He read me a poem he had written, which I was very moved by. Apparently I am the only person he can talk to about his spirituality outside of the weekly meditation group he belongs to. His work with me is getting more explicitly spiritual.
>
> *Next session:* He said that he feels he is now more authentic, more his true self, and he offered a powerful image of him spiritually climbing a ladder to heaven, but having other bits to his self that were maybe left behind.
>
> I feel that he is still telling me so little, but he is talking about things he tells no one else, and I value his sharing them with me, and I hope that I convey this to him. I praised him for the poem from our last session and said how it stayed with me all week, but it was very hard for him to accept this praise. He told me a moving Sufi story, which I compared to the death of Jesus.
>
> *One week later:* He said he was not ready to face the truth about his adoption and what it meant to him. Clearly, despite his feeling of not being ready, he is beginning the therapeutic and spiritual journey, but it feels painful and difficult.
>
> *Next session:* Perhaps this is a real turning point, he was angry with God in the session, and I feel that this could just help to begin to heal issues about his adoption.

There were also several key moments some months into his therapy. In one session, I was moved to share with him that his spirituality had a feeling or flavor of the Middle East or Istanbul, a sense of a place where East meets West. This reflected my feeling, which I had not expressed, that his spirituality was in some way different from Christianity. (In retrospect, it also could have reflected his mixed race origins.) He was pleased by what I said and shared the fact that he was a Sufi. Looking back on his therapy, there was a pattern of Matthew choosing when to share key aspects of himself with me. A similar withholding occurred later in relation to him telling me about a key sexual, possibly abusive, relationship from his past, which I am unable to discuss further here not having Matthew's permission to do so.

It is interesting to reflect that one way of understanding Quakers is to see them as essentially a mystical group (Jones, 1921); indeed the Quaker focus on experiencing God, on the value of silently waiting (Gillman, 1988), underlines this viewpoint. Likewise, Sufis are also considered as representing the mystical tradition within Islam. This I think made it more possible for Matthew and me to share the frequent silences that appeared to have a huge therapeutic value for him during our sessions. I think this shared mystical focus on experiencing the Divine and on waiting for Divine guidance gave us a common spiritual or theological base with which to work. I was consequently less challenged spiritually by Matthew than some of my other spiritually minded clients who held a religious outlook different than my own. It was as if with Matthew we simply shared the spiritual nature of our encounter rather than trying to make shared theological sense of it—the focus was on experiencing rather than on theorizing or theologizing.

One session soon after this Matthew said that he was afraid of the "spiritual intimacy" that was occurring between us. I was very struck by this phrase. By exploring what this meant, Matthew referred to the silences that arose in our sessions that had a healing effect on him, the synchronous way words and images that overlapped came to both of us, and the feelings of interconnectedness that arose especially in the silences. It seemed important to me to check out with him what role he was experiencing me in, as I was wary of in any way becoming his spiritual director and what that could mean. He replied that I was his counselor, that he had a spiritual teacher but that because his spirituality was important to him, he wanted to be able to explore it in his therapy with me. I was relieved to hear this.

A few sessions later I had an experience in the silence with him of dropping into a very deep place that I can, and do, reach on occasion in meditation or spiritual contemplation. I felt that I was on the edge of going so deep that I would lose all ordinary consciousness. I knew that it was not appropriate for me to go any deeper in the middle of a counseling session, but I was reluctant to bring myself out of being on the edge of this very deep and very spiritual space. I was thus able to relate to him from that deep space. It seemed very important. I assumed that my going there had meaning; it was not just an accident. It felt important to stay there in that deep space and not to break contact or consciousness. I did find a way of speaking to him from that deep space without losing it.

I felt that I was on an edge, I could either go deeper into the space or come back to a more ordinary way of relating. It was almost as if I was on the edge of falling or dropping down inside myself, which felt physically located. In that moment I did not quite know what this meant. It was, I think, part of that spiritual intimacy that he had referred to earlier, and part of that was not always knowing exactly what was going on but trusting in the spiritual process that was unfolding. Some of it, I think, was saying to him that this is OK, that it was OK for him to be in a similar deep and spiritual space. At some level it felt like a kind of mentoring, being in silence with him from a deep space, not having to come out of it, staying with that space and with him at the same time. There was something different about being there with him in that session and an extraordinary feeling of "holding" that deep space, not having to come out of it, and not going so deep that I lost that connection. It felt risky but very important.

Although Matthew had explored his difficulties at work throughout his therapy with me, especially working within a large multidisciplinary, multicultural team, the full story did not emerge for many months. He had been blamed and had subsequently felt both ashamed and angry for a mistake that had occurred at work. The mistake was for something that was not truly his fault. It seemed especially important that this whole area of his experience could be safely brought out into the light of day within his therapy with me. Clearly the whole incident had proven damaging to him and his relationships with colleagues. The challenge to him was to find a place from within which he could forgive and self-forgive. This all seemed part of a maturing process that also included him successfully applying for promotion to deputy in the nursing department he worked in.

THERAPIST COMMENTARY

Some of Matthew's therapy could be conceptualized in nonspiritual terms as being about a developmental need on his part, a need to heal the trauma of his adoption soon after birth, to deal with his difficulties at work, his need to find a sexual partner, and so on. However, this misses the truth that Matthew saw himself as being on a spiritual path, that he chose to have therapy with me because of my spiritual approach to therapy, and that there was for both of us some explicitly spiritual experiences and spiritual content in the therapeutic encounter.

It is hard to imagine the spiritual moments in Matthew's therapy with me occurring without our shared acceptance of the spiritual dimension to life. No doubt a skilled secular therapist would have benefited Matthew, but would such a therapist have welcomed Matthew's spiritual explorations? It is known that such acceptance is not always forthcoming (Richards & Bergin, 1997; Rowan, 1993; West, 2000b). A negative or nonwelcoming attitude to spirituality would have likely caused Matthew to withdraw. It is important to notice how long it took for him to make some key disclosures about his spirituality and sexual history to me. Without a positive attitude to spirituality, Matthew's therapy would have likely remained superficial and of a short duration.

It is apparent that Matthew changed in several key ways during his therapy with me—there were improvements in his self-esteem, his progress at work, and his ability to form intimate relationships (not covered in this case study). For a spiritually minded person like Matthew, these changes would be inseparable from his spirituality.

It could prove helpful to consider the spiritual aspects of my therapeutic work with Matthew in light of the list of possible spiritual intervention in therapy put forward by Richards and Bergin (1997). Their list is as follows:

> Praying for clients, encouraging clients to pray, discussing theological concepts, making references to scriptures, using spiritual relaxation and imagery techniques, encouraging forgiveness, helping clients live congruently with their spiritual values, self-disclosing spiritual beliefs or experiences, consulting with religious leaders, and using religious bibliotherapy. (p. 128)

I consider these items in turn:

1. Praying for clients. I did not specifically pray for Matthew, as I never felt that he was especially in need of prayer during or after his therapy sessions with me. I did on several occasions pray during a session that I would be of best use to him at moments when things seemed especially stuck or difficult.
2. Encouraging clients to pray. This did not seem at all appropriate. Matthew had his own active spiritual life that I knew included meditation and other spiritual practices that I was not fully aware of. I also have only somewhat limited knowledge of Islam and of Sufism.
3. Discussing theological concepts. This did occur on occasion, very often at Matthew's prompting.
4. Making references to scriptures. This occurred fairly often at Matthew's prompting and occasionally at mine.
5. Using spiritual relaxation and imagery techniques. In the occasions described previously, spiritual relaxation could be said to be implicitly happening.
6. Encouraging forgiveness. This occurred in the sense that Matthew needed to forgive members of his work team for their unwarranted attack on him over the alleged "mistake" discussed earlier and let go of his subsequent anger toward them. It also occurred, in a more defused sense, through my encouraging Matthew to self-forgive for not achieving and not becoming the full-fledged person that he was capable of being.

7. Helping clients live congruently with their spiritual values. This was implicitly and sometimes explicitly a key feature of Matthew's therapeutic work with me.
8. Self-disclosing spiritual beliefs or experiences. This was an important aspect of trust-building, especially in the early stages of our work together.
9. Consulting with religious leaders. This did not seem appropriate or necessary.
10. Using religious bibliotherapy. This did not arise in the course of therapy.

In my discussion elsewhere of Richards and Bergin's (1997) spiritual interventions (West, 2000b), I added one extra element—the rather broadly based "use of spiritual intuition or inspiration," which I felt was a key feature of Matthew's therapy with me. There is a growing body of literature and research that covers spiritual moments in psychotherapy (e.g., Mearns & Thorne, 1988; Richards & Bergin, 1997; Rogers, 1980; Rowan, 1993; Thorne, 1991; West, 2000b). Rogers (1980) in particular spoke of his experience of what he called *presence*:

> I find that when I am closer to my inner, intuitive self, when I am somehow in touch with the unknown in me, when perhaps I am in a slightly altered state of consciousness in the relationship, then whatever I do seems to be full of healing. Then simply my presence is releasing and helpful. . . . I may behave in strange and impulsive ways in the relationship, ways which I cannot justify rationally, which have nothing to do with my thought processes. . . . At these moments it seems that my inner spirit has reached out and touched the spirit of the other. . . . Profound growth and healing energies are present. (p. 129)

Was this experience described by Rogers a version of the "spiritual intimacy" that Matthew feared? Does it not also encompass the deep spiritual and meditative space that I found myself in with Matthew in the session described above? I think both are true.

Writing within the client-centered tradition, Thorne (1991) also spoke of special spiritual moments in therapy similar to Rogers's *presence*, which he called *tenderness*. Significantly, Thorne stated that he no longer had to "leave my eternal soul outside the door" of the counseling room and that he could now "capitalize on many hours spent in prayer and worship" (Mearns & Thorne, 1988, p. 37). It seems to me that my openness about wanting to work explicitly around spirituality with my clients had a similar healing effect on my own splitting off of some aspects of my spiritual nature from my therapist self.

To perhaps extend this further, one could consider the work of the Jewish philosopher Martin Buber (1923/1970), who has influenced many humanistic and transpersonal therapists, especially within modern gestalt therapy. Buber contrasted the potential to treat one another either as an object or It, and thus forming in an I–IT relationship, or to treat another as subject or Thou in an I–Thou relationship in which God or spirituality is to be found in the meeting, or between the people. It is a controversial question of how much the therapeutic encounter can be truly I–Thou, given the power imbalance in the relationship between client and therapist. This was discussed in a famous public dialogue between Rogers and Buber, and I have explored this issue in some depth elsewhere (West, 2000b). One could see the spiritual moments in Matthew's therapy with me as something akin to Buber's I–Thou relationship.

Through working with Matthew, I learned a lot about working with my clients' spirituality. I also learned a lot about my own spirituality. It was a challenging and rewarding experience to share his spiritual unfolding. As Rogers (1980) said about his idea of presence, "At these moments it seems that my inner spirit has reached out and touched the inner spirit of the other" (p. 129). It was, and is, a rare privilege to share that aspect of my nature so frequently in the human encounter that is the therapeutic relationship.

REFERENCES

Buber, M. (1970). *I and thou*. Edinburgh, England: Clark. (Original work published 1923)

Dandelion, B. P. (1996). *A sociological analysis of the theology of Quakers*. Lampeter, England: Edwin Mellen.

Gillman, H. (1988). *A light that is shining*. London: Quaker Home Service.

Jones, R. (1921). *The later periods of Quakerism*. London: MacMillan.

Mearns, D., & Thorne, B. (1988). *Person-centred counselling in action*. London: Sage.

Richards, P. S., & Bergin, A. (1997). *A spiritual strategy for counseling and psychotherapy*. Washington, DC: American Psychological Association.

Rogers, C. R. (1980). *A way of being*. Boston: Houghton Mifflin.

Rowan, J. (1993). *The transpersonal: Psychotherapy and counselling*. London: Routledge.

Thorne, B. (1991). *Person-centered, therapeutic and spiritual dimensions*. London: Whurr.

West, W. S. (2000a). Eclecticism and integration in humanistic therapy. In R. Woolfe & S. Palmer (Eds.), *Integrative and eclectic counselling and psychotherapy* (pp. 218–232). London: Sage.

West, W. S. (2000b). *Psychotherapy and spirituality: Crossing the line between therapy and religion*. London: Sage.

West, W. S. (2000c). Supervision difficulties and dilemmas for counsellors and psychotherapists around healing and spirituality. In C. Feltham & B. Lawton (Eds.), *Taking supervision forward: Dilemmas, insights and trends* (pp. 113–125). London: Sage.

West, W. S. (2001, August). Retreats. *Newsletter of the Association for Pastoral and Spiritual Care and Counselling*, 6–7.

West, W. S. (2002a). Being present to our clients' spirituality. *The Journal of Critical Psychology, Counselling and Psychotherapy*, 2(2), 86–93.

West, W. S. (2002b). Some ethical dilemmas in counselling and counselling research. *British Journal of Guidance and Counselling*, 30(3), 261–268.

13

A MORMON RATIONAL EMOTIVE BEHAVIOR THERAPIST ATTEMPTS QUR'ANIC RATIONAL EMOTIVE BEHAVIOR THERAPY

STEVAN LARS NIELSEN

DESCRIPTION OF THERAPIST

Professional and Religious Background

I received a doctorate in clinical psychology from the University of Washington (UW), practiced for 7 years in the U.S. Army, and have practiced for the last 14 years at the Counseling and Career Center at Brigham Young University (BYU), where I am a clinical professor. I teach and supervise for the counseling center's internship and BYU's clinical psychology program. I am an associate fellow of the Albert Ellis Institute for Rational Emotive Behavior Therapy (REBT) and a certified REBT supervisor. I have provided about 24,000 psychotherapy sessions to about 2,800 clients during my career.

I was born and raised in Salt Lake City, UT, headquarters of the Church of Jesus Christ of Latter-day Saints. My ancestors were among the Church's earliest members. One of my great-great-grandfathers was a friend of Joseph Smith, the first Mormon prophet. He joined the exodus from Illinois to escape the persecutions that cost Joseph Smith his life. With his family he helped explore and settle the Great Basin when it was a wilderness outside the United States. Despite this heritage, my father and two older brothers hated the Church and I grew up an agnostic hippie. Partly from curiosity and partly in rebellion against my family, I attended BYU where religion is an unabashed element of classroom instruction and Mormonism part of day-to-day university culture. At BYU my religious experiments led me to devout belief.

Religion, Psychology, and REBT

At BYU I took a personality course from and then worked as a research and teaching assistant for Allen Bergin. Allen's recounting of his religious conversion helped bring greater clarity to my thinking about religion and science. After working with Allen I decided to study clinical psychology. I worried initially that my beliefs would meet with hostility in graduate school, but my UW professors and most of the students were respectful of all kinds of diversity, including religious diversity. Clinical psychology at UW was overtly behavioral and aggressively scientific, but it was also encouraging of student investigation of various psychological topics and therapeutic orientations: My first supervisor, Leslie Rabkin, was a psychoanalytically oriented therapist. My dissertation chair, Irwin Sarason, encouraged, guided, and supported my curiosity about psychodynamic concepts, including experimental examination of selective attention as an analogue of unconscious processing (Nielsen & Sarason, 1981).

As an intern I experimented with and was won over by REBT's elegant goal of helping clients adopt more functional philosophies of life. With REBT organizing the psychotherapy I practice, I began to adopt a rational-emotive-religious philosophy of life. I remember feeling surprised that Ellis's atheism was irrelevant to my thinking about REBT, but I now see that his hostility toward religion was less severe and troubling than what I had experienced at home.

I Met Albert Ellis on a Dare

When I began practicing at the BYU counseling center, I saw that REBT worked well with my many devout clients. There was no contradiction between scripture and REBT—indeed, scripture facilitated REBT. Allen Bergin suggested I debate Ellis about this—he dared me, really. I wrote Ellis suggesting that we discuss integration of religion with REBT and he agreed (Ellis, 1994a; Nielsen, 1994; Nielsen & Ellis, 1994). We disagreed about religious verities—no surprise—but agreed that although he is an atheist, REBT is neutral toward religion. We also agreed that philosophical tenets in most major religions mix well with REBT and probably can facilitate treatment of religious clients. Subsequent collaborations (Ellis, 2000; Johnson & Nielsen, 1998; Johnson, Ridley, & Nielsen, 2000; Nielsen, Johnson, & Ridley, 2000; Robb, Schneiman, & Nielsen, 2001) led to development of an empirically supported (Johnson, DeVries, Ridley, Pettorini, & Peterson, 1994; Johnson & Ridley, 1992), religion-integrative version of REBT. A book-length treatment manual (Nielsen, Johnson, & Ellis, 2001) describes this approach. This chapter describes using the Qur'an with REBT to treat a Muslim woman.

SETTING FOR THE CASE

BYU's counseling center is one of the largest in the nation; we provided approximately 23,000 individual and group psychotherapy sessions to about 3,000 of BYU's 30,000 students in 2001. Most BYU students are devout Mormons who commit to attend worship services and religious instruction; to abstain from sexual intimacy outside marriage; and to abstain from coffee, tea, tobacco, alcohol, and drugs. Non-Mormon students commit to follow these rules as a condition of enrollment, but they are not required to attend worship services. Although most of the clients are devout, consistent with professional and ethical standards the counseling center requires neither religious belief nor adherence to university standards as conditions of treatment.

CLIENT DEMOGRAPHIC CHARACTERISTICS

Aisha, a 24-year-old single woman, had just begun her second semester of doctoral studies in biochemistry when she sought treatment. She was born in a New York City hospital while her father was assigned to the home country's United Nations mission. Two younger sisters were born in the home country, which, while officially secular, is predominantly Muslim. Aisha attended private schools in the home nation and in three international cities. She earned an undergraduate degree in organic chemistry at the home country's national university. She spoke four languages fluently, the predominant home country language, Arabic, French, and English.

Aisha and her family followed Sunna, the code of ethical and religious behavior derived from Muhammad's sayings and deeds; they heeded the five daily calls to prayer, attended worship at mosque, gave to the poor, abstained from pork and alcohol, and fasted daily during the monthlong celebration of Ramadan. Aisha, her sisters, and mother wore scarves to cover their hair during worship, but not in public. Her parents had completed the Hajj, the pilgrimage to Mecca required at least once in a lifetime of healthy, financially able Muslims. Aisha had, on arriving at BYU, ascertained the Qiblah, the direction of shortest distance to the Kaaba in Mecca toward which Muslims should pray. In Provo, UT, the Qiblah is 28.8°, North by Northeast.

Aisha prayed five times every day, though not always at prescribed times because of a lack of privacy.

PRESENTING PROBLEMS AND CONCERNS

At intake Aisha completed the Counseling Concerns Survey (Drum & Barón, 1998), an alphabetical list of 42 problems college students sometimes face, providing an index of her level of distress and focal topics for the intake interview. Aisha described "Extreme" or "Quite A Bit" of distress on 9 of the 42 problems: academics, depression, discrimination, homesickness, making friends, perfectionism, sexual assault, stress, and uncertainty about her future.

I asked first about sexual assault. Aisha wept and said, "That happened before I came here. I'm not ready to talk about it. Is that all right?" I assured her this was all right and asked whether she would prefer to meet with a woman. She said she preferred not to switch.

I next asked about discrimination. During her first semester, shortly after the attack on the USS Cole in Yemen, one of Aisha's professors—Professor Doe—had taken her aside and asked why Muslims want to kill Americans. She was shocked by the question and "froze up" briefly before replying that "fanatics do such things, not true believers." She received an "A–" grade in the course, though she believed she deserved an "A." Aisha's distress about academics, her perfectionism, and her uncertainty about the future were linked to fear that Doe's prejudices could ruin her grades.

Aisha tearfully explained that her other answers came from distress about finding a husband. She would not date non-Muslims and Muslim men at BYU were "too misogynistic." She had decided to assert her right to U.S. citizenship because of sexism at home. Her mother had encouraged this, but advised her not to tell her father or sisters. It might anger her father and make her sisters envious. There were growing numbers of professional women in the home nation and most women in the middle and upper classes rejected wearing scarves in public, but new fundamentalist movements had created tensions about this. Aisha believed women in the home country would face significant new difficulties in the future and she was sure that she would have more professional opportunities and find more like-minded Muslim men in the United States.

CLIENT HISTORY

Although not wealthy, Aisha's family enjoyed privileges because of her father's diplomatic work. Aisha had a close relationship with her mother, but she felt distant from her father, who was both austere and quite busy with his duties in the home country's diplomatic corps. The sisters attended private schools paid for by the government when posted outside the home country. Her parents had, with difficulty, paid for private schools in the home country. All three sisters had excelled academically, entitling them to free education at the national university.

A year earlier Aisha had failed in an attempt to gain admission to a U.S. medical school, probably because of a noncompetitive medical school admissions test score. Graduate study in biochemistry was a second choice, and BYU was a second tier biochemistry program by her estimation. Her parents had wanted her to attend BYU because of its conservative reputation. Aisha hoped that studying for the medical school admissions test and participating in scientific research could help her win admission to a U.S. medical school.

At the end of our sixth session Aisha was ready to discuss the sexual assault, but said she could only write, not talk about it. In an e-mail she wrote of coming to New York and moving in with two young women she knew from an international high school. She intended to work while managing her medical school applications. Her friends had sexual relationships with boyfriends, which appalled her, but she said nothing. One of the roommates had two Muslim friends, young men who were students, who visited the apartment. Aisha was uninterested in them, believing their home country more sexist than her own. One of these men called from the security door of the apartment building on a Friday evening when both roommates were away for the weekend. Aisha "buzzed" him in without stopping to think that she was alone. He asked about her roommates, struck up a conversation about being Muslim in the United States, then left. Aisha found him interesting, intelligent, and detected none of the sexism she had anticipated. She did not hesitate to let him in the following evening. He sat next to her as they spoke, and then suddenly kissed her. She had never kissed a man before and overt displays of affection are considered inappropriate in the home country. She also found the kiss exciting and kissed him back. He began to fondle her breasts. She tried to push him away, but he persisted. She tried again to stop him and he slapped her, restrained her, and raped her. As he left he told her she had, after all, let him in and kissed him back.

The next day, Sunday, Aisha called home, complained that she felt homesick, and asked for a plane ticket home. Monday morning she told her roommates, who had returned late Sunday night, that her father was seriously ill. She quit her job and flew home that evening. Aisha had no further contact with the roommates or with the man who had raped her. This was, a year later, the first time she had told anyone of the rape. She was uninterested in contacting police.

ASSESSMENT AND DIAGNOSIS

Psychiatric Diagnoses

Aisha described symptoms consistent with Posttraumatic Stress Disorder according to the *Diagnostic and Statistical Manual of Mental Disorders* (4th ed., text rev., *DSM–IV–TR*, American Psychiatric Association [APA], 2000) Axis I, code 309.31, including fear during the rape, later flashbacks, nightmares, and sudden physiological arousal. Women in the home country were considered responsible for rape if they had allowed themselves to be in "compromising circumstances." Subsequently, consistent with a major depressive episode of mild to moderate severity (Axis I, code 296.21; *DSM–IV–TR*, APA, 2000), she had lost interest in many formerly enjoyed activities, suffered at times from insomnia, from hypersomnia at other times, felt persistent guilt, and a sense of worthlessness. She often wanted to die, but had no intent to kill herself. Aisha was critical of herself and anticipated that others would also be critical of her. Fear of criticism led her to avoid most socializing. This was worse after the rape, suggesting that an avoidant personality style had been present before the rape and was now intensified. Her response to treatment suggested dependent tendencies. The attack on the USS Cole and professor Doe's comments had been moderately stressful (*DSM–IV–TR*, Axis IV). Despite these problems, Aisha performed well in rigorous course work, suggesting a Global Assessment of Functioning score of about 60 (*DSM–IV–TR*, Axis V).

Psychometric Assessment

Counseling center clients are encouraged to complete the 45-item Outcome Questionnaire (OQ 45; Lambert et al., 1996) before each session. The OQ 45 summarizes client report of near-term emotional, interpersonal, and role functioning; higher scores reveal report of worse functioning. I encouraged but did not insist that Aisha complete OQ 45s. Figure 13.1 depicts OQ 45s, annotated with session numbers and standardization indexes.

TREATMENT PROCESS AND OUTCOMES

The First Session

REBT's A-B-C model (Ellis, 1994b) proposes that it is not Activating events (A's) by themselves, but A's plus irrational *Beliefs* (B's) about A's which yield self-defeating emotional and behavioral Consequences (C's). REBT theory holds that three main kinds of irrationally evaluative beliefs (IEBs) cause self-defeating reactions: human rating, demanding, and catastrophizing. All three IEBs were obvious during the intake session: (a) Aisha downed herself about grades, (b) demanded near perfect grades, and (c) catastrophized about poor grades. The clarity with which Aisha expressed her IEBs allowed us to begin during the intake:

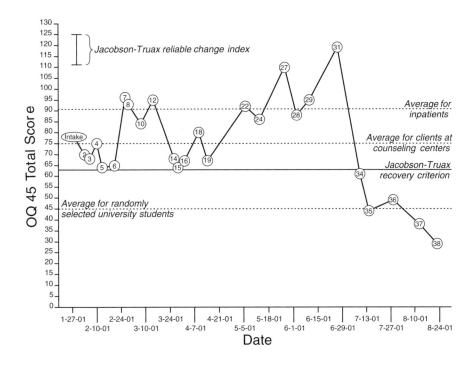

Figure 13.1. Aisha's scores on the 45-Item Outcome Questionnaire (OQ 45; Lambert et al., 1996) annotated with the session numbers when OQ 45s were completed. Dotted lines depict average scores among nonclient university students, clients at counseling centers, and psychiatric inpatients. A solid line depicts the statistical midpoint between mean scores in clinical and in nonclinical samples (63.4 points); this midpoint is suggested as a minimum criterion for judging a client's score to indicate clinically significant recovery (Jacobson & Truax, 1991). A bracketed vertical bar depicts the reliability boundary for a difference between any two OQ 45 scores (± 14 points) given the OQ 45's psychometric properties; Jacobson and Truax (1991) call this reliability range the reliable change index.

SLN: But you earned an A– in the class despite his discriminatory statement—I agree with you, by the way, that his statement was discriminatory. It's too bad other students didn't hear him, since he violated antidiscrimination policies. Was grading objective?

Aisha: Yes and no. If he had given me the credit I earned, I would have gotten an A. He said I left information out of a proof. When I look at that grade, I feel like a failure!

SLN: But failure is not a feeling. You're telling yourself that an A– makes you a failure and the emotion comes from *believing* that you are a failure. Let's try something: Close your eyes, look at your grade, now tell me again how your feel, but don't use the word failure.

Aisha: But I *feel* like a *failure!*

SLN: Okay. But what are some other feeling words that could describe how you feel?

Aisha: I feel like a *loser*, like I'm *bad*.

Aisha's self-rating and the shame it caused were fused. Her belief that she was a loser and the emotional consequence of that belief were one thing. I tried to help her analyze her experience:

SLN: Let's see if we can agree about something here: You believe that you are a failure and you feel ashamed. You believe that you are a failure if you fail a class or get an A–.

Aisha: I know that doesn't make much sense, but that's what I feel.

SLN: Oh, it makes *human rating* sense. If anyone believes—*really believes*—that they're worth *less*, they'll feel depressed. You are rating all of you based on your performance.

Aisha: What else would I do?

SLN: It may seem to make sense, but the implications don't hold up. For example, squeeze this handgrip dynamometer [for neuropsychological testing]. Now I'll squeeze it. My hand is more than twice as strong. So I'm twice as valuable as you?

Aisha: No [she laughed], only twice as strong.

SLN: The dynamometer *is* scientifically calibrated, but not for measuring *humanness*. If we can't make a valid instrument for measuring humanity, we can't evaluate human worth. It's not A, the *Adversity* of earning a lower grade than you want—go ahead and *want* what you *want*, by the way—but B, the *Belief* that you are less because of a lower grade creates C, the emotional *Consequence* of feeling ashamed or depressed.

Deepening and Generalizing

Aisha tentatively agreed with the A-B-C model and with trying to give up human rating. We discussed the university's discrimination complaint process, but decided the risks outweighed the possible slight benefits. As she worked on her self-rating she experienced gradual relief (see Sessions 2 through 6 in Figure 13.1). She e-mailed her account of the rape to me on the day before her seventh session. As she sat down in my office for Session 7 she hid her face, burst into tears, and said, "How can you stand to look at me? I feel so dirty! So guilty!"

Guilt is another important example of experiential fusion. REBT theory treats guilt not as an emotion, but as a complex blend of beliefs, emotions, and behavior (Nielsen et al., 2001). Aisha's Activating event was both recall of the rape and the inferential idea, "I am *guilty* of doing something dirty." Her A was both memory and inference that she was guilty. A was also blended with the evaluative Belief (B), "I, therefore, am dirty." B was then blended with the joint emotional and behavioral Consequence (the C) of shame.

B in the A-B-C model is more complex and deep than an internal declarative statement. REBT's goals are more holistic than changing internal self-talk. In both his first (1958) and in his most recent (2002) treatises about REBT, Ellis called experience inseparably holistic:

> Emotion, like thinking and sensori-motor processes, we may define as an exceptionally complex state of human reaction which is integrally related to all the other perception and response processes. It is not *one* thing, but a . . . holistic integration of several seemingly diverse, yet actually closely related, phenomena. (1958, p. 35, italics in original)

In 2002 he wrote:

> Instead, then, of saying, 'Jones thinks about his puzzle,' we may more accurately say, 'Jones perceives-moves-feels-thinks about his puzzle.' Because Jones' activity . . . may be *largely* focused upon solving it, and only *incidentally* on seeing, manipulating, and emoting about it, we may perhaps emphasize only his thinking. (p. 9, italics in original)

The discrete words *thought, perception, behavior,* and *feeling* can seem to separate facets of experience from one another. Disturbance is, more realistically, a holistic perception-inference-evaluative-belief-shame-avoidance experience like Aisha's "dirty," face-hiding, shame.

Language does, however, provide symbols useful in analyzing experience. The A-B-C model and the words REBTers cue in on as signs of irrational belief (*should, awful,* and so forth) are symbolic tools. Just as a musical score is not, itself, music, neither are words irrational beliefs. But just as music scores facilitate music theory, musical performance, practicing music, musical publication, pedagogy, and so on, symbolic representations of irrational beliefs can facilitate therapy. Human experience also mixes multiple, shifting levels of conscious and unconscious experience. Individuals are probably unconscious of most of our irrational believing (Ellis, 1994b). But again, just as reading music can raise our musical consciousness, so can highlighting the language of irrational beliefs raise our consciousness about the role and function of irrational beliefs in distress. Aisha's word "dirty" was a clear symbol of her shame. Understanding the symbols in her self-rating provided Aisha with useful tools for manipulating her beliefs.

Aisha had stopped rating herself about academics by Session 6, but her self-acceptance was insufficient when pitted against her self-damning about the rape. Her self-acceptance was conditional on viewing herself as clean or pure. More persuasive belief change was needed.

Qur'anic REBT

REBTers use a wide variety of cognitive, behavioral, and emotive interventions to dispute IEBs, and create deep and broad changes in believing. A variety of strategies and styles have been delineated (Beal, Kopec, & DiGiuseppe, 1996). The notion of a humanometer was a humorous attempt to point out the illogic of rating humans without a scientific rating system. I hoped the Qur'an could provide theologically authoritative material for disputing Aisha's human rating. If Aisha could stop damning herself about the rape, she would, I believed, move closer and closer to achieving unconditional acceptance of humans—but not unconditional acceptance of all human behavior—as a new philosophy of life.

God's view of humans increasingly seems benevolent to me. In the Mormon scripture called the Pearl of Great Price God is recorded telling Moses, "This is my work and my glory—to bring to pass the immortality and eternal life of man" (Moses 1:39). According to the Book of Mormon, only God may judge or rate humans: "The keeper of the gate [of judgment] is the Holy One of Israel; and he employeth no servant there" (2 Nephi 9:41). I thought I had read similar benevolent, fair-minded passages in the Qur'an, and hoped Aisha could find and use them:

SLN: Then Allah is the same God in whom I believe. But Muhammad was His only prophet?

Aisha: No. Abraham, Moses, Jesus, and others—all prophets. Muhammad was His last prophet.

SLN: Not you?

Aisha: Of course not! [She laughed.]

SLN: I just wanted to make sure. What did God tell Muhammad about who judges souls?

Aisha: He does.

SLN: Muhammad?

Aisha: No, no. God.

SLN: Not *you*?

Aisha: No! [She laughed.]

SLN: That's what you're doing. [She looked baffled.] Judging yourself, when it's God's job.

Aisha: I'm not sure what you mean.

SLN: Did you get a phone call from God telling you that He's busy, so please judge yourself? You tell me that not even Muhammad gets to judge people. But you call yourself dirty. I guess you have a special calling to stand in for God. Yes?

Aisha: No. [She laughed a bit.]

SLN: Let's try a little experiment. Try saying this: It's God's job to judge me. Not my job.

Aisha:	It's God's job to judge me. Not my job?
SLN:	Could you be *less* enthusiastic?
Aisha:	[She laughed.] God judges people, *no one else!*
SLN:	Did that feel any more believable?
Aisha:	Yes.
SLN:	Would you say it in [the home country language]? Say it as if you *really* believe it? [She did.] In French? [She did.] In Arabic? [She did.] Does that feel different?
Aisha:	I felt less upset when I kept saying it.
SLN:	Now I want you to shout it . . . [she shook her head] . . . in your head. Do you know what I mean by shouting in your head? [She nodded.] Did that feel any different?
Aisha:	I felt less upset.

These steps were attempts to add persuasiveness and pervasiveness to her disputations. It makes no sense for Aisha to judge herself when God commands otherwise, so I hoped pitting her against Muhammad would be humorously evocative and more persuasively contradictory of self-rating. I hoped that speaking more forcefully would be more evocative and persuasive. I hoped that speaking in different languages would make her self-talk more pervasively persuasive.

Believing that homework is the best way to create pervasive change, I asked if she prayed for guidance and she said yes. I asked her if a Muslim could, in good conscience, pray about self-rating and the other issues we had been discussing. Yes. Could she pray to see if we were on the right track? Yes. Could she look for verses in the Qur'an that discuss judgment? Yes. She returned to the next session with, "We [Allah] shall set up scales of justice for the day of Judgment, so that not a soul will be dealt with unjustly in the least" (Surat 3:47). This verse reassured her. Prayer had reassured her. Her OQ 45 scores at Session 10 suggested that her distress was declining (see Session 10 in Figure 13.1).

I asked Aisha if Muslims believe in repentance and forgiveness. She said they do. I asked about repentance rituals, like Christianity's baptism. She told me that repentance is a personal matter. I told her, "Even though I think you've done *nothing* wrong, let's take the strictest possible position and say it *was* a sin to be alone with that guy and that you are responsible. Remember, I *don't believe it!* But if it *is* true, what does the Qur'an say about forgiveness?" Aisha returned with this comforting verse, "If you love God, follow me, and God will love you, and forgive you all your sins; God is All-forgiving, All-compassionate" (Surat 3.31).

I attempted to challenge Aisha's self-rating in a more emotionally evocative manner by juxtaposing her situation with the fantasy of one of her sisters being in the same situation. I asked her to imagine that one of her sisters had been raped in New York by the same man. How would she evaluate them? "Kindly," she said. How would God evaluate them? "The same, I think." What would she, Aisha, think if someone, on learning that one of her sisters had been raped, considered that sister to be filthy? "I would think he is an idiot!" she said.

"Then why apply an idiotic standard to yourself?" I asked. This was risky, but fit the tenor of the moment and she laughed at the difference—the dissonance—between how she would judge her sister mildly, but judge herself harshly. She felt less upset as she reminded herself about this. I decided to try a still more forceful dissonance disputation: "Suppose you learned your mother and father had sex before they were married. Would you shun her?" No, she would still respect her. Her mother would be no less self-assured, assertive, or kind. By Session 15 her OQ 45 dropped to 64, just one point above the recovery criterion (see Figure 13.1).

Aisha found that she enjoyed basic biochemistry research, but this created new anxiety as she tried to decide between continuing in her doctoral program or again trying to get into medical school (Session 17). Which was right, she worried? She laughed when I asked which surat of the Qur'an commanded one to get a PhD or an MD. Then I asked, "Does the Qur'an declare that we *must* go to paradise?" She answered that God gives us agency. She laughed when I said, "If you don't *have to* go to paradise, you sure as *Hell* wouldn't *have to* get a PhD or an MD—either one!" As a homework assignment she wrote something like, "The Qur'an doesn't say I *must anything*," in Arabic on her hand and rehearsed this phrase to herself frequently. She returned to Session 18 with "O ye who believe! You have charge over your own souls" (Surat 5.105) and "No compulsion is there in religion" (Surat 2.256).

Aisha began to feel encouraged. She was delighted that she did not need to take any more classes from Professor Doe. Her advisor, Professor Jones, had adopted several of her suggestions for one of his projects and had also provided her with resources to conduct preliminary tests for a study she had suggested. Aisha had begun spending free time with a classmate named Maria and a postdoctoral fellow named Jan. Maria had converted to Mormonism while a graduate student in a South American country. Jan, an avowed atheist, was from Scandinavia.

Four interrelated events threw Aisha into turmoil that Spring: She had decided to apply to medical school, but feared this would upset Jones (Session 22); she discovered that Jan had placed his name ahead of hers on a technical report on which all three had worked, but which Aisha had designed and analyzed (Session 23); she discovered that Jan and Maria were having an affair (Session 26); finally, Jan invited, then pressured Aisha to have an affair with him (Session 30). Aisha was uninterested in Jan, but missed Maria, who was not working in the lab during that term. It was especially distressing when Jan began flirting with her (Session 29). He told Aisha that he and Maria were sexual partners and asked if she would like to join them (Session 30). She told Jan to leave her alone, but he kept asking. He had begun calling late at night trying to persuade her, which horrified her (Session 31, see Figure 13.1). I downloaded a copy of BYU's sexual harassment policy and assured her that BYU had no tolerance for such behavior. Aisha was paralyzed by fear of what Jan, Maria, and Jones might think and by fear about possible consequences for Maria if she made a formal complaint.

Before our next session I went to the Qur'an looking for something that might help her stand up for herself. I found an index heading which directed me to this verse, "And the believers, men and women, are protecting friends, one of another; they enjoin the right and forbid the wrong, and they establish worship and pay the poor-due, and they obey God and His messenger" (Surat 9.71). I read this to Aisha during Session 32 and asked if this spoke to her in any way. Aisha said it indicated that it would be best for everyone, Maria and Jan, if Jan stopped.

The next night Aisha tape-recorded a new harassing call from Jan—this is legal in Utah. She then wrote three letters: First a letter to the director of BYU's Equal Employment Opportunity office, which investigates and adjudicates harassment complaints, in which she identified herself and Jan and stated that Jan had made two unwanted romantic overtures to her. She wrote that she had declined the first overture and had asked Jan to desist, that after the second overture she had repeated her request that he desist, and that she had asked that he limit his contact with her to professional interactions at school. She delivered copies of this letter to Jones—he was also Jan's supervisor, to the chemistry chair, and to the physical sciences dean. She sent a copy of the letter to Jan by certified mail delivered at the laboratory. She included with the letter a note to Jan advising him that any further nonprofessional contacts or any retaliation would be met with an immediate complaint, plus full disclosure of all his previous statements, plus a transcript of the harassing call he had made the night before. The call had been filled with crude sexual references to Maria, which Jan thought might entice Aisha to meet him. Aisha also sent a copy of the letter to Maria with a note warning her that she could have disciplinary problems if she continued to spend time with Jan.

Aisha had worried most about how Jones would react. She felt quite anxious when he asked her to come to his office the afternoon after she had delivered her letters. To her surprise, Jones apologized for not having detected Jan's behavior. He informed her that he, the chair, and the dean had met with Jan, warning him that he was now in a probationary state and that termination would be immediate should any new complaints arise. Aisha felt encouraged by his reaction and exhilarated that she had been able to stand up for herself.

Her OQ 45 scores showed a remarkable degree of improvement over the next 2 weeks (Sessions 34 and 35). I wondered whether these changes might be something like a flight to health, but I felt optimistic when Aisha said she had come to believe she was no less deserving of respect than others. Her letter writing epitomized the kind of synergistic effects belief change mixed with behavior change can create: Self-acceptance had facilitated assertive behavior which then further strengthened Aisha's self-acceptance. We focused on assertiveness during Session 36, practicing specific maneuvers she might use when in situations where she would not have been assertive in the past. When she next saw Jan in the laboratory she was able to fight the impulse to look away by reminding herself that she was no more or less deserving of respect than anyone else and by looking between his eyes in order to appear to be making eye contact.

In a very interesting bit of philosophizing, Aisha told me that she was not angry with Jan. She made the interesting comment that his highly sexualized, atheistic background was more "out of culture" with BYU than her Muslim background.

Between Sessions 36 and 37 Aisha scheduled an appointment with Jones to tell him she wanted to apply to medical school. He surprised her, telling her she would be missed, but would make a fine physician if she chose that route. He knew of biochemists in joint MD/PhD programs where he might have some influence and offered to contact some of them.

We met one more time before the beginning of the next school year (Session 38), and Aisha said she would contact me if she felt she needed to meet again. Aisha told me she was not abandoning her romantic goals, though she was adopting a slow, cautious approach. Her research was enjoyable and time consuming, and she had become close friends with a group of women she had met playing tennis. With the little time she had left she was trying to get to know Muslim men at Internet chat sites; she said she had developed several lines of conversation that she used to detect misogyny.

Aisha called me on the afternoon of September 11, 2001 to express her outrage at the attacks on the World Trade Center and the Pentagon. I asked if she wanted to meet, but she did not think it necessary. Professor Jones and her tennis friends had asked her to spend time with them in case she became a target for retaliation. She announced to a class she was teaching that she was proud to be an American citizen and dismayed that vicious fanatics would subvert God's laws. She has phoned me seven more times over the past 15 months to tell me she is doing well. She is close to finishing her doctorate in biochemistry at BYU.

THERAPIST COMMENTARY

Rationality and Religious Neutrality in REBT

Although REBTers are alert to violations of consensually agreed-on reality—bizarre ideas, for example—this is not the problematic irrationality of primary interest in REBT. REBT focuses, rather, on absolutistic evaluations. Human rating, demanding, and catastrophizing can be conceptualized as absolute evaluations. In the case of human rating a human being's essential or absolute humanness is most often evaluated as unacceptable. During demanding and catastrophizing some event in the world is evaluated as being unacceptable. Aisha's shame epitomized this kind of arbitrary absolutism: She evaluated not just a few of her behaviors as flawed or possibly unwise, but because she let the man who eventually raped her into her apartment and because she kissed him, Aisha evaluated all of her, her essence, as dirty. *She* was unacceptable. Humans, their behavior, and the world in general are too complex for such global evaluations to be reasonable.

Cultural conceptions of morality in Aisha's home country led Aisha to see herself as culpable, whereas most Americans would see the man as culpable for rape—very different worldviews, to be sure. Religious doctrines may, similarly, dictate very different worldviews. But whether Aisha and I agreed about culpability for rape, whether we agreed about most religious doctrines, we could still reasonably work on helping her achieve self-acceptance. Without agreeing or disagreeing about her culpability, we could always work to show her that she was more than her behavior on the night she was raped.

It is possible, of course, that some religious traditions will rate humans, will make absolute demands, or will view some form of human adversity as catastrophic. This would complicate doing REBT with adherents of such religions and would likely preclude use of such religions' scriptures or theologies to support REBT. However, the Qur'an does not, the Bible does not, the Book of Mormon does not, the Baghavad-Gita does not, the fundamental scriptures and theologies of most religious traditions do not, at their core, seem to rate humans, impose demands counteracting human freedom of choice, or consider human adversity catastrophic. Quite the contrary, most scripture provides philosophical material for disputing human rating, demanding, and catastrophizing.

My Theistic Stance

Religious clients may fear that psychotherapists will disrespect their beliefs. It probably helped Aisha to see the Qur'an in my office, sitting next to copies of the Bible, Book of Mormon, Doctrine and Covenants, and Pearl of Great Price. She probably felt confidence that I would respect her beliefs when we opened my copy of the Qur'an and she saw that I had marked passages that interested me. I need not have been theistic to have read scripture, of course. I am what Richards and Bergin (1997) call a theistic therapist, but an atheistic therapist might have had a deeper, more expert understanding of Islam than I. Would the outcome have been different had I been an atheist? In the one controlled test comparing atheist and Christian therapists treating Christian clients, atheists who used religious material to supplement cognitive behavior therapy helped their clients at least as much as the Christian therapists (Propst, Ostrom, Watkins, Dean, & Mashburn, 1992).

Johnson, Ellis, and I contend in our book (Nielsen et al., 2001) that it is quite possible for an atheist therapist to accommodate a religious client's doctrinal beliefs during the practice of REBT, because most of the religious beliefs will be irrelevant to the evaluative beliefs needing disputation. There are no reasons except the limitations imposed by time that therapists who are atheists or who come from religious tradition differing from the religions of their clients cannot learn religious material at sufficient levels to allow integration of such information with REBT. Robb (1985), who is an atheist, is probably more familiar with the Bible than most Christians, and is quite adept at using verses from the Bible to demonstrate rational-emotive philosophies for living to his Christian clients. Part of Robb's skill is conveying respect for his clients' beliefs, even though he does not share their beliefs. Communicating respect for religious beliefs may be the most important feature of forming a working alliance with a religious client. Of course, clients have a powerful role in generating the trusting alliance, as well. I have had religious clients reject my treatment before they have met me because of preconceptions about how REBT would deal with their religious beliefs.

Would it have worked as well as it did had I been an atheist? There are subtleties in forming and maintaining the therapeutic alliance that I believe require all therapists to be artisans. For example, a therapist stating that there was nothing wrong with Aisha's roommates having sex before marriage, so long as it was safe sex, might have offended Aisha. Would an atheist be more likely to make such a statement than a theist? It would depend on the therapist. I think Aisha considered our two levels of religiosity identical in their degree and the forms and focus of our religious beliefs quite parallel. I think she trusted that we really believed in and prayed to the same God. She trusted my religiosity would work with hers.

REFERENCES

American Psychiatric Association. (2000). *Diagnostic and statistical manual of mental disorders* (4th ed., text rev.). Washington, DC: American Psychiatric Association.

Beal, D., Kopec, A. M., & DiGiuseppe, R. (1996). Disputing clients' irrational beliefs. *Journal of Rational Emotive and Cognitive Behavior Therapy, 14,* 215–229.

Drum, D. J., & Barón, A. (1998). *Highlights of the research consortium outcomes project.* Retrieved November 23, 2002, from University of Texas, Counseling and Mental Health Center Web site: http://www.utexas.edu/student/cmhc/research/rcpres98.pdf

Ellis, A. (1958). Rational psychotherapy. *Journal of General Psychology, 59*, 35–49.

Ellis, A. (1994a). My response to "Don't throw the therapeutic baby out with the holy water": Helpful and hurtful elements of religion. *Journal of Psychology and Christianity, 13*, 323–326.

Ellis, A. (1994b). *Reason and emotion in psychotherapy, revised and updated.* New York: Birch Lane Press.

Ellis, A. (2000). Can Rational Emotive Behavior Therapy (REBT) be effectively used with people who have devout beliefs in God and religion? *Professional Psychology: Research and Practice, 31*, 29–33.

Ellis, A. (2002). *Overcoming resistance: A rational emotive behavior therapy integrated approach* (2nd ed.). New York: Springer.

Jacobson, N. S., & Truax, P. (1991). Clinical significance: A statistical approach to defining meaningful change in psychotherapy research. *Journal of Consulting and Clinical Psychology, 59*, 12–19.

Johnson, W. B., DeVries, R., Ridley, C. R., Pettorini, D., & Peterson, D. (1994). The comparative efficacy of Christian and secular rational-emotive therapy with Christian clients. *Journal of Psychology and Theology, 22*, 130–140.

Johnson, W. B., & Nielsen, S. L. (1998). Rational emotive assessment with religious clients. *Journal of Rational Emotive and Cognitive Behavioral Therapy, 16*, 101–123.

Johnson, W. B., & Ridley, C. R. (1992). Brief Christian and non-Christian rational-emotive therapy with depressed Christian clients: An exploratory study. *Counseling and Values, 36*, 220–229.

Johnson, W. B., Ridley, C. R., & Nielsen, S. L. (2000). Religiously sensitive rational emotive behavior therapy: Elegant solutions and ethical risks. *Professional Psychology: Research and Practice, 31*, 14–20.

Lambert, M. J., Hansen, N. B., Umphress, V., Lunnen, K., Okiishi, J., Burlingame, G. M., et al. (1996). *Administration and scoring manual for the OQ 45.2.* Stevenson, MD: American Professional Credentialing Services.

Nielsen, S. L. (1994). Rational-emotive behavior therapy and religion: Don't throw the therapeutic baby out with the holy water. *Journal of Psychology and Christianity, 13*, 312–322.

Nielsen, S. L., & Ellis, A. (1994). A discussion with Albert Ellis: Reason, emotion and religion. *Journal of Psychology and Christianity, 13*, 327–341.

Nielsen, S. L., Johnson, W. B., & Ellis, A. (2001). *Counseling and psychotherapy with religious persons: A Rational Emotive Behavior Therapy approach.* Mahwah, NJ: Erlbaum.

Nielsen, S. L., Johnson, W. B., & Ridley, C. R. (2000). Religiously sensitive rational emotive behavior therapy: Theory, techniques, and brief excerpts from a case. *Professional Psychology: Research and Practice, 31*, 21–28.

Nielsen, S. L., & Sarason, I. G. (1981). Emotion, personality, and selective attention. *Journal of Personality and Social Psychology, 41*, 945–960.

Propst, L. R., Ostrom, R., Watkins, P., Dean, T., & Mashburn, D. (1992). Comparative efficacy of religious and nonreligious cognitive-behavioral therapy for the treatment of clinical depression in religious individuals. *Journal of Consulting and Clinical Psychology, 60,* 94–103.

Richards, P. S., & Bergin, A. E. (1997). *A spiritual strategy for counseling and psychotherapy.* Washington, DC: American Psychological Association.

Robb, H. (1985). *How to stop driving yourself crazy with help from the Bible.* New York: Albert Ellis Institute.

Robb, H., Schneiman, R., & Nielsen, S. L. (2001, June). *REBT and clients with religious, spiritual, or supernatural beliefs.* Skill-building workshop offered at the International Conference Celebrating the 45th Anniversary of REBT, Keystone, CO.

14

A PSYCHOBIOLOGICAL LINK TO SPIRITUAL HEALTH

ZARI HEDAYAT-DIBA

This chapter attempts to describe how my spiritual and religious background unconsciously guided me in the course of a therapeutic encounter with a patient who was particularly resistant to the language of psychology or what she called "psychobabble." To form a therapeutic alliance, I needed to rely on something more than what I had learned in graduate school. I had to have faith; faith in therapy as a spiritual process and faith in the wholeness of the mind, body, and spirit as a unit.

However, more important, I hope this chapter demonstrates that spirituality, like other aspects of personal growth, can best unfold in a relational context that is mutually influenced. This chapter does not describe a unidirectional relationship in which the therapist is the observer and the patient the observed, with the former guiding the latter toward "health," but rather as one in which both people are touched and in some ways changed.

DESCRIPTION OF THERAPIST

Personal Background

I am a woman of Persian descent, currently in my 40s, practicing as a marriage and family therapist in California since 1986. For my doctorate degree in clinical psychology, I wrote my dissertation on the "Selfobject Functions of the Koran," a portion of which was published in the *International Journal for the Psychology of Religion* (Hedayat-Diba, 1997).

My dissertation was inspired by a desire to connect with some of my Iranian/Muslim roots. I was raised in a non-practicing family, and spent most of my childhood in Europe where I attended catholic schools. I came to California to study psychology in 1978.

Although Islam was not a conscious part of my family life, it was nonetheless present through my nanny who was a devout Muslim, following all of the religious rituals, which led to intrigue and curiosity in me. It was not until I studied the topic of Islam for my dissertation that I realized how much of my life had actually been imbued by it, making me aware of the extent to which one's culture, and in this case, one's religious culture is incorporated in the unconscious and silently lives there as all other unconscious matters, until something stirs it to the surface.

Despite the lack of religious activities, the idea of God and a sense of spirituality had been present in me since childhood. Three dreams stand out in my mind, in which the idea of God was clearly present. The following is one such dream I had at age 17. In the dream, I am walking on a beautiful path, by a stream, in a beautiful green field blooming with colorful spring flowers. The feeling is one of peacefulness, along with a sense of awe for the overwhelming beauty and gratitude for being able to witness it. I then see an old man sitting under a big oak tree, crying. I go to him and say, "What is the matter. Why are you crying?" The old man looks up at me and says, "Why do you disturb me? I am talking to God." To this, I was left speechless and puzzled. The dream ends there.

This dream has never faded in clarity or vividness. As a therapist, it has served me well on the occasions when someone's tears felt so compelling that I would want to reach forth and intervene. Instead, I would hear the old man's words reminding me that God is listening and that I can, at best, just be present but unobtrusive.

Theoretical Orientation

My theoretical orientation is psychoanalytically informed. For the purpose of this chapter, I use and describe Kohut's theory of self psychology and Jung's theory of individuation, which have influenced my work with Mrs. A, both clinically and in a more spiritual realm. These theories bear resemblance with some of the Islamic ideas about the human condition; especially those described in Sufism, which is often known as the mystical Islam.

Carl G. Jung

Carl Jung's concepts of the individual and collective unconscious, along with his emphasis on dreams and their functions in the pattern of psychic growth have been of great interest and have inspired some of my spiritual attitudes toward therapy. Jung's description of the individuation process especially has been an invaluable signpost when a patient's growth seemed to be stalling or even appeared to be more destructive than constructive.

Jung (1921) described the individuation process as:

> The process by which individual beings are being formed and differentiated; in particular, it is the development of the psychological individual as a being distinct from the general, collective psychology. Individuation, therefore, is a process of differentiation having for its goal the development of the individual personality. (p. 757)

Jung's concept of individuation holds into account who the person really is, aside from what she wants to be and who society wants her to be. The individuation process is the psychological growth that is one's birthright, and which happens unconsciously and naturally without the necessity of willful effort. It is in essence an unconscious process propelling the true self toward wholeness. However, Western culture, social roles and responsibilities, along with many of life's necessities make it increasingly difficult for modern individuals to follow or even keep track of one's internal landscape. Neurosis and symptoms ensue when one's innermost need to find wholeness from within is thwarted by external forces, because as pointed out by Hollis (1993), "as long as we remain primarily identified with the outer, objective world, we will be estranged from our subjective reality" (p. 94). Thus, the symptoms can be viewed as blessings in disguise, a calling of attention back to the inner self, where one can find all the tools necessary toward spiritual growth, because "what we must know will come from within" (Hollis, 1993, p. 94). It is reminiscent of Jesus' utterance "if you bring forth what is within you, what you bring forth will save you. If you do not bring forth what is within you, what you do not bring forth will destroy you" (in Hollis, 1993, p. 96).

Such destruction or "such symptoms announce the need for substantive change in a person's life. Suffering quickens consciousness, and from new consciousness new life may follow" (Hollis, 1993, p. 95). This is the point that Jung made so well. That even in the midst of what may seem irrational, one can find symbols that are psychologically meaningful to that individual and guide them back to their innermost self, albeit through a lot of psychic pain.

The individuation process is not finite with a determined goal. It is an ongoing journey. Jung (1963) referred to it as "a religious capacity" and believed that nearly all religious systems on this planet contain images that represent various stages of the process.

Heinz Kohut

Post-Freudian psychoanalysts continued to build their theoretical constructs on the basis of the tripartite psychic structure originally proposed by

Freud, namely the id, ego, and superego, with little attention to the idea of the self. In the mid 1960s, Heinz Kohut, who was trained as a classical analyst, found a need to reframe the long-standing psychoanalytic paradigm of neurosis and symptom formation as arising from conflicts attributed to id impulses against which the ego erects defense mechanisms. Instead, Kohut (1971) proposed a new model, moving toward a theory of the self and its development throughout the life span. Pathology was now viewed not as arising from conflicts but rather from deficits in one's sense of self. His theory came to be known as self psychology. He defined the self as a "center of initiative and recipient of impressions" (Kohut, 1977, p. 99). The self is not synonymous with one's identity or self-image, an observable entity, but rather as an experience. The self is the center of one's psychological universe. It is not cognitively penetrable or observable from the outside; another can reach it only via introspection and empathy. For this reason, the notion of "intersubjectivity" and of "mutuality" hold crucial significance in the clinical work. Currently, intersubjectivity is defined as designating "the basic process of psychotherapy. The term emphasizes the idea that in the therapeutic situation two individuals co-create the relationship they live and talk about" (Natterson & Friedman, 1995, p. 1). In the case presented here, the two spiritualities of the patient and therapist came to have a reciprocal influence on each other.

From his clinical work, Kohut (1977) came to see that his patients' development had been most damaged in the area of the formation of self-esteem, often because of caretakers' lack of attunement to the child; and in therapy, it was the working through and resolution of their frustrated needs for understanding, appreciation, and empathy that led to maturation.

He believed that certain kinds of responses from the environment are essential to the development of a cohesive self, and that these reflect the existence of three kinds of underlying psychological needs. These are (a) the need to be mirrored (to feel validated, supported, and valued); (b) the need to belong and feel a part of something (to have a sense of sameness with someone, a group, or a community); and (c) the need to look up to an idealized other, in whose strength one can find either comfort or inspiration, or both.

Furthermore, one does not become independent from those basic human needs; rather those needs mature from archaic forms that are specific to early development to increasingly symbolic ones later in life. As Kohut (1984) explained:

> Throughout his life a person will experience himself as a cohesive harmonious firm unit in time and space, connected with his past and pointing meaningfully into a creative-productive future, only as long as, at each stage in his life, he experiences certain representatives of his human surroundings as joyfully responding to him, as available to him as

sources of idealized strength and calmness, as being silently present but in essence like him, and, at any rate, able to grasp his inner life more or less accurately so that their responses are attuned to his needs and allow him to grasp their inner life when his is in need of such sustenance. (p. 52)

Although Kohut's theoretical formulations and language were more "scientific" than Jung's, and were not imbued with the spiritual tone of the latter, he too, believed that the self has a central raison d'être, and that human growth was inevitably tied to the uncovering of one's destiny and the striving toward its fulfillment.

As with other psychoanalytic methods, the client/therapist relationship is viewed as central to healing, with the therapist often providing self-object experiences needed for the patient to resume their developmental growth. For Kohut, the establishment of empathic attunement is the main therapeutic tool. And empathy is achieved through a process of introspection, a turning inward to understand the patient's subjective experience.

Sufism

Sufism is a branch of Islam. Its doctrines are derived from the Koran and Islamic revelations. It is often referred to as the inner dimension of Islam; the mysticism or esoterism of Islam (Glasse, 1989, p. 375). The central issue in Sufism—similar to psychoanalysis—is the development of awareness to higher levels of consciousness, leading to a process of transformation towards the inner self, which is believed to have unlimited potential. The premise is that the individual is in search of his or her higher self; or as aptly put by Arasteh (1980) humans are a "psycho-religious being in search of our origin and in pursuit of our ultimate destiny" (p. 3). This destiny is to be found inward.

In Sufism, while on this spiritual self-realization journey, a teacher is necessary. The Sufi teacher is the transitional object between man and his true self. He is a guide in the individuation process. As explained by Dorst (1991), "In Sufism it is said: the teacher is without name. He or she doesn't work through teaching but through being. The teacher is an energetic current. The student, who submerges himself into it, is influenced by these energetic forces and his process is speeded up" (p. 21). Perhaps the main characteristic of the Sufi student is longing; a longing that has been translated as the search for God, for understanding, for love, or any other nameless yearnings. This longing is perhaps best represented and best known to the Westerner through the poetry of Rumi (1207–1273), one of the greatest mystics of Islam.

The Sufi tradition is also a group tradition. The group is organized around a teacher, but it is determined by commitment of group members to the same goals. In addition to the ritual prayers of Islam, meditation exercises are common practices for individuals and groups alike. These are God-centered meditations, such as repeating His name in remembrance, or using Him as the object of contemplation or even of active imagination (Spiegelman, 1991, p. 106). The purpose of meditation is to expand both consciousness of an inner spiritual self and consciousness of God. Finally, dreams are considered important vehicles of guidance and transformation along the spiritual path.

SETTING

The setting was a private practice office in Los Angeles, California. The patient was in weekly, individual psychotherapy.

CLIENT DEMOGRAPHIC CHARACTERISTICS

At the time of our first meeting, Mrs. A was a 32-year-old Caucasian woman from Australia, married to a French man of the same age. She holds two college degrees in education and psychology. She used to work as a schoolteacher in Europe, where she lived with her husband for several years before moving to Los Angeles, where both of them began to work for a film production company.

Her religious background is Anglican, but her family was not religious, did not go to church, nor encouraged theistic views. However, Mrs. A attended Catholic schools where she went to church on a daily basis. Her real sense of spirituality or of a higher power came from experiences with her grandmother who always admired nature and saw God in all of nature's beauty.

CLIENT HISTORY

Mrs. A was the third of four children. She has a sister 5 years older, a brother 4 years older, and another sister 4 years younger than herself. Following Mrs. A's birth, her mother nearly bled to death and was advised not to have another child, but her younger sister was nonetheless planned.

Her father was an engineer and her mother an artist who worked mostly from home. Mrs. A also had a nanny who helped look after the children.

They lived on a big property in Australia, with horses, tennis courts, a pool, and all the amenities of a luxurious lifestyle. She described her childhood as "charmed and privileged" and her parents as respectful and encouraging but also critical and very strict. She described herself as the "ugly duckling" because her two sisters were very pretty, whereas she was athletic and tomboyish. She was involved in many sports, with special interest in gymnastics and dance from an early age. She recalled with gratitude her mother driving her everywhere so Mrs. A could make it to her practices and sport events. In that sense her mother was encouraging and supportive, and Mrs. A probably was gratified with some degree of mirroring and appreciation through her athletic achievements. She was dedicated to her gymnastic training, as she was an Olympic hopeful, and for many years she endured sacrifices, including numerous separations from her home and family. In addition, she would frequently come home from gymnastics bruised or injured, but would brave through the pain for the love of the sport. Eventually, a serious back injury from a fall on the balance beam brought her Olympic dreams to a sudden end. She was on bed rest for almost a whole year.

In matters of parenting and discipline, the cultural norm in those days permitted the use of physical punishment. Thus, she and her siblings were spanked regularly, sometimes severely so. She claims her parents—especially her father—had calmed down considerably by the time they had her—the third child—and believes that her two older siblings got the worst of it. She realizes that according to current American standard, those experiences would today be considered child abuse, but she still downplays the emotional devastation that must have accompanied those physical punishments. One specific incident stands out in her memory. Her mother had been away for a few days. She returned in the evening, around bedtime. Mrs. A was excited to see her mother and wanted to stay up a bit longer to be with her. Father wanted her to go to bed. As then 6-year-old Mrs. A was not listening, he took her to her room and started "laying into her." That is the only time she remembers her mother actually stepping in, telling the father something like "darling, that's enough now." During her father's outbursts of rage, she would "separate her mind from her body," like she had learned to do in gymnastics and because of that she doesn't feel that her spirit has been damaged.

Mrs. A is a very grateful woman who does not easily complain. It took a while before she could comfortably speak of how critical her father was and how dismissing and unavailable her mother was. Her father especially was impossible to please. He was mercilessly critical and intolerant with the children as well as with his wife. He was very demanding, yet nothing anybody could do ever pleased him. When he would have an outburst of anger with its accompanying spanking, Mrs. A would typically go in her room and "break up inside." She would be devastated and cry alone until she felt better, or distracted herself with some athletic activity. She would not go to mother for comforting because "they wouldn't pamper us," she explained; the motto was "pull yourself together."

She remembered being loved, nurtured, and comforted by her maternal grandmother. Her family spent all their Christmas vacations at the grandmother's house by the sea, away from home. As a young child she cherished those times with her grandmother, to whom she had a strong connection. She described her as the "epitome of love and acceptance." If she felt sad or upset, being with her grandmother was comforting. To this day, Mrs.

A attributes her belief in God to her grandmother's capacity to love nature and to see God in it. She would always admire nature as a miracle—this reminded me of how in awe of nature I was in my dream. Mrs. A. thus learned from her that miracles are possible and can be found all around us. Therefore, since early childhood, she remembered having a "spiritual sense." Then, something happened to challenge her belief in God. Her sister who had suffered from scoliosis needed surgery, but a heart condition made surgery risky. She was taken to a healer who performed a ceremony after which the sister seemed "miraculously" better. "It's as though she had grown a couple of inches," recalled Mrs. A. This had a tremendous effect on her. She had witnessed God's healing power. She and a high school friend now began to read the Bible every night. She became eager to explore religion. But then, her sister ended up needing surgery nonetheless. This led to a spiritual crisis. She remembers thinking that God had not really healed her sister and was not really watching over her because she still needed an operation on her back. The sister survived the operation and the loss of faith was soon forgotten when Mrs. A. began college. She recalled feeling very good and happy during her first year of college. Studying came easily to her. She had a boyfriend for the first time and started exploring her sexuality.

Following college she decided to travel abroad. She first came to the United States and then traveled through Europe, where she met her husband. They came back to Los Angeles together before resuming traveling through Southeast Asia, where they were acquainted with several adventures including exploring monasteries, and discovering meditation and Buddhist practices.

On their return to the United States, they started working for a production company. Mrs. A was a dedicated and efficient project manager, working many hours and traveling a great deal. She was capable of handling much pressure. At times, it seemed like nothing was too much for her. All was seemingly going well when she unexpectedly found herself pregnant. This would be her first pregnancy. She was then 32 years old.

PRESENTING PROBLEM

When Mrs. A became aware of her pregnancy, she was on a very demanding schedule and because she was in good health, she postponed going to the doctor until she was about 3 months pregnant. At that time, she was told that the fetus was not growing and she needed to have a dilation and curettage procedure (D & C). The amniotic sac had grown in a normal fashion, but the fetus had not. She was devastated. She had the D & C performed in the following days. When she returned home from the hospital she found herself in a lot of pain and woke the next day in a pool of blood. She called the hospital and was told to come in right away. She had developed a blood clot between the uterus and cervix area. The doctor said they needed to perform a quick and simple vaginal intervention. Presumably they were going to puncture the blood clot, but in the process, apparently punctured her uterus by mistake, which led to hemorrhaging. She was losing so much blood they thought she might die and were considering performing a hysterectomy when one of the surgeons successfully cauterized the uterus to stop the bleeding. She was told she probably would not be able to get pregnant for quite some time—this was reminiscent of her mother's experiences following her pregnancy with Mrs. A.

Three months later, Mrs. A. was pregnant again. This time, she went to the doctor very early on and was followed very carefully because her pregnancy was considered high risk. She was still so grieved by the previous loss that she was not letting herself get emotionally attached to the new fetus, for fear she might lose this one as well. She remained detached, continuing to work and live as if she was not pregnant so as to avoid feeling the grief of the previous loss and protecting herself from having to experience that grief again.

Because pregnancy and the postpartum period is an area of special interest to me, Mrs. A was referred to me by her gynecologist. Mrs. A presented with a mix of anxiety and optimism. The anxiety was that she might again lose a fetus, and thus she feared getting attached to it. There was also anxiety about medical procedures and interventions as well as the physicians themselves. She had been traumatized by medical errors and mishaps and did not feel safe at all in the hands of doctors—and that, I thought included me, although I am not a physician. In spite of her anxiety, she was optimistic that things would turn out for the better. I could not quite tell if her optimism was a form of denial or if it was a spiritual attitude of having faith.

ASSESSMENT AND DIAGNOSIS

Mrs. A was suffering from post-traumatic stress disorder due to the catastrophic medical experiences during which she risked losing her life. I also felt that the current trauma was compounded by numerous smaller, but nonetheless significant childhood traumas that had not been resolved. As pointed out by Shapiro (2001), when trauma occurs, the brain's capacity to process the information it is receiving becomes ineffective and the perceptions that were there at the time of the event become locked in the nervous system. In other words, the events of the trauma are remembered by the body, are felt in the body, but remain inaccessible to the mind and to language—the medium of psychotherapy. It was as though her body was trying to say something, to tell a story, or to remember something and to free itself.

I felt that she had much to grieve for, but had not yet given herself permission to do so. It was imperative that she be able to experience the fullness of her emotions and grieve for not having felt seen in the gleam of her parents' eyes, not having been heard, not having been known for her true self. She had to undo the pseudoautonomy, imposed in the name of self-reliance at too young an age, which made her circumvent her overwhelming needs for the mother's nurturing. Her denial was self-preservative as it was also protective of her parents. To acknowledge what she had missed would be betraying her parents as well as the image she maintained of a "charmed and privileged childhood." To do so also probably meant, "creating undue drama."

She also needed to forgive: Forgive herself for not making the Olympic team. Forgive herself for all that in her child's mind she had internalized as "her fault." Forgive the father whose criticisms of her were no doubt transformed in self-reproach and self-blame that was perpetuating the initial insult. Finally, I thought she needed to forgive herself for her mother nearly bleeding to death following her birth. Did she have to almost bleed to death herself after the D & C as a way to do that? Had she been punished enough yet?

TREATMENT PROCESS

Initially, Mrs. A gave the impression that she came to see me on the basis of her physician's recommendations. She was doing the "right thing" by following the doctor's orders. Yet, there was more to it than that, as she was aware that she was not bonding with the fetus and was concerned about that.

She was ambivalent about psychotherapy because she feared I would define her in terms of a diagnostic category that would be dehumanizing. This in fact was her experience with the doctor who had told her that she would not be able to get pregnant again in a while, confining her to the difficult-to-get-pregnant category. In fact she became pregnant readily. The doctor had said the blood clot would be taken care of with a 5-minute vaginal intervention, and she ended up with an incision in her belly, a near-miss hysterectomy, and hemorrhaging to the point of needing a blood transfusion. How could she trust me when the doctors had been wrong all along? In the transference I was just an extension of those doctors.

In addition, she felt that relying on someone else would be more "drama than necessary. It would complicate the issue more than necessary." This, I would realize later, resonated with the experience of the little girl who would "just go in her room and break up inside" to come back out only when she had pulled herself together. To do otherwise would be "dramatic." Pseudoautonomy was valued, respected, and in fact, demanded. To go to someone for comfort or reassurance, to rely on another person, to trust the restorative function of a relationship was not a familiar experience.

I was a little intimidated by her lack of trust, yet I felt a desire to work with her. I did not argue with her doubts, nor try to convince her otherwise.

Now, I was the one feeling confined and limited, pinned to my chair unable to be much of a therapist. This feeling—confined and limited—matched her description of therapy as she imagined it would feel to her. In feeling it myself, I could now have an appreciation for that experience. It was uncomfortable, yet I felt a connection to her and knew that we could work well together. I just let her know that I understood and remained mostly silent. I also encouraged her, as I often do with all patients, to remember her dreams.

My main clinical concern was for her to be able to let herself feel and get attached to the baby inside her womb so that eventually she could explore her fantasies about the baby inside her mind. The "motherhood constellation" (Stern, 1995), that is her psychological birth as a mother, was what I was hoping to address. But her physical body had been so traumatized by the previous pregnancy experience that I was not sure if she would be available to explore motherhood yet. And because she had been told to prepare herself for not becoming a mother for a long time, she was naturally unprepared to face the impending reality of motherhood now. I feared that if I proceeded as I would with most patients, I would run the risk of "confining" her into a clinical model of intervention that would confirm her anxiety about therapy and send her running away. I realized how much I wanted to protect her from that disappointment and betrayal; how much I wanted to protect her the way her mother had not.

During our weekly sessions, I continued to feel pinned to my chair, unable to say much of anything at all. I took that as my clue to just sit back and let the process unfold. For some reason, I had faith in this woman. There was something very powerful about her—which I did not think of as pathological. I had faith in her process. I had faith she needed to be here and I had a strong sense that I should let go of all expectation, just let myself be as empty of intellectual content as possible, and let the student/client teach me—a Sufi stance.

Because my countertransference reactions often led me to think about Jung and Sufism, I decided to inquire more about her spiritual beliefs. She revealed that her childhood disappointment in God that she had experienced around her sister's health problems had now resurfaced with the loss of the pregnancy and the physical traumas that ensued. I felt strongly that for her physical well-being as well as her psychological well-being, Mrs. A needed to find a way to reconcile with God. I thus did an informal "spiritual assessment" (Richards & Bergin, 1997). I asked her whether prior to the pregnancy, she actually believed in a Creator or God. She confirmed "absolutely." I asked how she imagined this Creator, what was her image of Him? She said that to her "God is energy. It's a God force that is eternal and all encompassing, embracing everything in every realm of life." The depth of her response and the clarity with which she spoke these words struck me. I asked her if this God was punishing or loving, or had any such qualities commonly attributed to Him? She did not think God was punishing. "I think we punish ourselves.

And our purpose in life is to discover the God within us: to discover through Him the source of power, inspiration and healing that is in us," she said. I was once more reminded of Sufism and its eternal quest for the Divine within.

This line of inquiry seemed to free us both from the therapeutic confines that her fears had imposed on us. I no longer felt pinned to my chair, and she seemed very at ease talking about her beliefs. Then, she asked me if I believed in God. I told her a little bit about Sufism and the similarity of its tenets with the ones she had described. Then, I said I thought there were two kinds of Gods. The God that in our child's mind we see in our all-powerful parents—who often end up disappointing us—and the God that she experienced through her grandmother, best made visible in the miracles of nature. I told her I believed in both. She was able to take that in and I took that as my clue that she was ready for a more detailed interpretation. I wondered out loud if maybe it was not her parents she was really mad at. I suggested that maybe God became confused with the all-powerful parents who abused their authority. Just like God became confused with the all-powerful doctors who made so many mistakes. But the God of her grandmother, I suggested, was still with her and their relationship intact.

It is in this way that slowly she opened up and began to trust me. One day, she revealed that I had become like a "security blanket," her weekly connection to the baby, and she looked forward to coming in. By the fourth month of pregnancy, she felt attached to the baby, experiencing its reality both in her belly and in her mind, with fantasies of how life will be with a baby. She was now contemplating stopping work and nesting. This was a major shift for her because her identity and self-esteem was so far largely tied to her productiveness and success at work.

Mrs. A did slow down considerably and gave birth to a healthy baby girl. To her surprise she was very happy to stay home with the baby. She would go to the beach every day and take long walks. She continued therapy. This was a happy and healthy time.

One day, I asked her if she had forgiven God. She confessed it was impossible to have a baby and be angry with God. Nowhere is His creation more manifest than in the miracle of babies. She revealed that in fact, her spiritual sense was still with her, and probably had never really left her, but had been overshadowed by disappointment, fear, and anger. Unbeknownst to either one of us, she would need that spiritual sense very soon, when a new series of medical mishaps led to a near-death experience.

When her baby was one year old, Mrs. A started experiencing sharp pains in the lower abdominal area. One night, the pain became so severe she was taken to the hospital where she had an ultrasound, which revealed what the doctors suspected was a tumor, the size of an orange, in the large intestine area. They had to operate immediately. They removed 3 inches of her large intestine, her appendix, and 10 inches of her small intestine and the illiosacral valve, which is responsible for removing the moisture from the stool.

She was in the hospital for 10 days. The tumor was not malignant. It was a growth created by an overactive immune system. The doctors diagnosed the condition as Crohn's disease. Three weeks after her surgery she had to go in for a colonoscopy. She was watching on the TV monitor and could see blood gushing out with every biopsy pinch. It did not seem right to her. After the procedure she drove herself home. Hours later, she started feeling a lot of pain. She was taken to the hospital again, where they discovered her colon had been punctured during the procedure—reminiscent of her uterus having been punctured earlier. They had to operate to try to find the hole and seal it. They could not find the hole. They tried to give her intravenous antibiotics but her veins would collapse with every attempt. She would look at a picture of her baby every time they tried, because the thought of her kept her going. But still, the IV never got in. By the third day, the doctors said there was nothing more they could do and told her husband to bring the baby in to say goodbye. He did bring the baby and then had someone take the baby away while he stayed with Mrs. A. He held her hand, leaned his head on their joined hands and they fell asleep. According to the nurses, neither one of them could be roused for 45 minutes. She woke up first and knew at that moment that she would live. When she later asked him what had happened, he said he was trying "to pour all of his life energy into her." It seemed he succeeded, because 10 minutes later, her veins opened up and the IV was successfully inserted. Two days later, she decided to discharge herself from the hospital against the doctors' advice. She felt she needed to save herself from the hospital and the doctors. The next day, a celebrity friend of hers sent a limousine to pick her up and take her directly to a Chi Gong master who would perform bodywork. She had never heard of Chi Gong before. This Chinese man put her on a bed and started a healing session, where he would chant or pray over her. She did not feel anything or any change. However that night she had the following dream:

> I see a Black man and a friend of mine from college. My friend used to have a very bad knee. I watch this man do something energetically, without ever touching my friend. Then she started walking without any pain at all. Then he said, "come with me" and took me behind a glass door. There was a swimming pool, and a boy—I thought his son—was swimming in it. He pointed to the boy and said, "Do what he's doing." I protested: "But I'm not in water." He said, "Move like if you were in water." Then the little boy got out of the pool and said to his dad, "I know what is wrong with her." The dad took the boy inside, had a talk with him, then said to me, "You can go now." The next part of the dream was that I was at a place in Santa Monica that I could recognize. In my dream, it was called the BUS.

The next morning, she was compelled to go to that place in Santa Monica. She drove herself to the place she knew from the dream. She arrived at the studio where the man in her dream was teaching a Tai Chi class. People were doing "strange" movements. She joined them as best she could. During a move called "Golden eagle spreads wings to embrace child," she started sobbing uncontrollably.

After class, the teacher said to her, "I know you are very ill. If you work with virtue, I will teach you how to heal yourself." He was on his way to another class at another location. She went with him. From then on, they worked together on a daily and continuous basis. She started getting stronger and stronger until she was well again.

THERAPIST COMMENTARY

Both religion and psychology are guilty of a common mistake: They have excluded the body from spiritual and psychological growth and development. In religion, it is abstinence from physical desires that leads to spiritual purity and the attainment of a higher self; in psychology, therapists simply have continued Descartes's error of placing the mind outside the body (Damasio, 1994), well despite the fact that Freud (1923/1961) had initially suggested that "the ego is first and foremost a body ego" (p. 26). Cognition and affect are interrelated and both have a physical corollary.

As pointed out by Lillas (2000), "psychoanalytic work has focused on interpreting bodily processes as metaphors for psychic processes that need to be made conscious, with the primary emphasis on the mental domain . . . but some types of information can be accessed only through the body because words provide inaccurate representations" (p. 21). Children are a testimony to this: When their feelings are hurt, they will describe a physical pain.

My experience with Mrs. A made me realize this fully and my work has changed because of it. I no longer accuse the body of doing the mind's work or suspect the patient of displacing their feelings into their physical symptoms. I now in fact ask patients where they feel their pain, depression, anxiety, craving, or joy in their body, because we can fully know an emotion, including a spiritual one, only after we sense it in the body. Because as beautifully said by Moore (1998), after all, the body is the soul perceived by the senses.

That is how Mrs. A came to be so flooded with emotion during some of the Tai Chi movements. She could feel the feelings of grief as sensations in her body. The movements in Tai Chi became the words she did not have. Once she could be the recipient of the feelings, she could in turn talk about them too.

As Mrs. A learned a new language by putting words to the feelings in her body, I learned through my work with her that the body is a central pathway in the individuation process, in the journey toward wholeness and in some cases even toward God.

Tai Chi is known as a martial art; but it really is a spiritual discipline, one that emphasizes breathing, relaxation, and meditation. It is a movement-based meditation technique, during which "the whole body must be relaxed, loose and open, so that the *ch'i*, the vital energy, can pass through without blockage. This is the principle of Tai Chi as a health exercise, as well as a system of self-defense" (Lowenthal, 1991, p. 6). The movement of "Golden eagle spreads wings to embrace child" is one in which one stretches the whole body slightly arched back with arms extended toward the heavens; then one gathers oneself moving straight down toward the earth, bending the knees, head bowed forward, chin tucked into the chest, crossing arms across the heart, as if embracing a child. It is a movement that feels like a "letting go" and then a "coming back to self." In Mrs. A's words, "while you gather unto-ward your own heart, there is a feeling of unconditional love and tenderness as if nurturing the child within or a loved one. Then you slowly come back to standing, exhaling and releasing the breath, allowing a feeling of loss or sad-ness for a moment, but with the next inhale, you gather that love once again, opening the heart."

It was in doing that movement that Mrs. A's feelings of grief and for-giveness finally emerged and were freed from her body so she could now embrace the child that had never been truly embraced in the way she had needed; and in doing so, she could embrace her inner self.

The Tai Chi master became the teacher and father she could look up to, in whose strength and calmness she could find refuge, and in whose eyes she could finally see a reflection of her true self: vulnerable yet capable of virtue and in possession of a creative inner healing capacity.

One may ask why that did not happen in therapy? I believe the therapy was a stepping stone, and in the transference, I was the grandmother in whose safety she could bond with her fetus as well as reconnect with her own spiri-tuality. I was the grandmother who had known the beauty of God through nature—as manifested by my own dream. In addition, I think I provided some of the "twinship selfobject functions" she longed for. We both had children, both were athletic, and we both studied psychology. But perhaps most important, we both shared a similar spiritual proclivity that helped cre-ate a sense of sameness that was comforting and reassuring to her, despite our actual cultural and religious differences.

My theistic views—unconscious as they may have been—guided me toward a spiritual approach, making it possible for Mrs. A to access her own internal faith. In her words, "both the therapy and the body work helped restore my connection to my life force and eternal energy, finding my way back to the God within and to my own buried true self, not judged or dam-aged by people or forces outside of myself."

REFERENCES

Arasteh, A. R. (1980). *Growth to selfhood: The Sufi contribution.* London: Routledge & Kegan Paul.

Damasio, A. R. (1994). *Descarte's error: Emotion, reason, and the human brain.* New York: Grosset/Putnam.

Dorst, B. (1991). The master, the student and the Sufi-group: Sufi-relationships today. In M. Spiegelman, P. V. Inayat Khan, & T. Fernandez (Eds.), *Sufism, Islam and Jungian psychology* (pp. 19–28). Scottsdale, AZ: New Falcon Publications.

Freud, S. (1961). The ego and the id. In J. Strachey (Ed. & Trans.), *The standard edition of the complete psychological works of Sigmund Freud* (Vol. 19, pp. 3–66). London: Hogarth Press. (Original work published 1923)

Glasse, C. (1989). *The concise encyclopedia of Islam.* San Francisco: Harper & Row.

Hedayat-Diba, Z. (1997). The selfobject functions of the Koran. *International Journal for the Psychology of Religion, 7*(4), 211–236.

Hollis, J. (1993). *The middle passage: From misery to meaning,* Toronto, Ontario, Canada: Inner City Books.

Jung, C. G. (1921). Psychological types. In R. F. C. Hull, H. Read, M. Fordham, & G. Adler (Trans. & Eds.), *The collected works* (Vol. 8). London: Routledge & Kegan Paul.

Jung, C. G. (1963). Psychology and religion: West and East. In R. F. C. Hull, H. Read, M. Fordham, & G. Adler (Trans. & Eds.), *The collected works* (Vol. 11). London: Routledge & Kegan Paul.

Kohut, H. (1971). *The analysis of the self.* New York: International University Press.

Kohut, H. (1977). *The restoration of the self.* New York: International University Press.

Kohut, H. (1984). *How does analysis cure?* Chicago: University of Chicago Press.

Lillas, C. (2000). Applying neurobiological principles to psychoanalysis. *Psychologist-Psychoanalyst: Official Publication of Division 39 of the American Psychological Association, 20*(3), pp. 21–28.

Lowenthal, W. (1991). *There are no secrets: Professor Cheng Man-ch'ing and his Tai Chi Chuan.* Berkeley, CA: North Atlantic Books.

Moore, T. (1998). *The soul of sex* (audiocassette). New York: Harpor Audio.

Richards, P. S., & Bergin, A. E. (1997). *A spiritual strategy for counseling and psychotherapy.* Washington, DC: American Psychological Association.

Shapiro, F. (2001, March). *Healing trauma: Attachment, trauma, the brain, and the mind.* Paper presented at the Lifespan Learning Institute Conference, San Diego, CA.

Spiegelman, M. (1991). Active imagination in Ibn' Arabi and C. G. Jung. In M. Spiegelman, P. V. Inayat Khan, & T. Fernandez (Eds.), *Sufism, Islam and Jungian psychology* (pp. 104–118). Scottsdale, AZ: New Falcon Publications.

Stern, D., (1995). *The motherhood constellation.* New York: Basic Books.

15

RATIONAL EMOTIVE BEHAVIOR THERAPY FOR DISTURBANCE ABOUT SEXUAL ORIENTATION

W. BRAD JOHNSON

DESCRIPTION OF THERAPIST

I am a 39-year-old White man. A licensed clinical psychologist, I received my doctorate from the Graduate School of Psychology and my master's degree from the School of Theology at Fuller Theological Seminary. I practiced full time for 4 years as a U.S. Navy psychologist, then continued my clinical career while serving as a faculty member in a doctoral training program—first in part-time private practice and then as a consulting psychologist in a clinic for low-income children and adolescents. For the past couple of years, my responsibilities have been exclusively academic and supervisory.

I consider myself Christian in a broad and ecumenical sense and no longer identify with any single protestant denomination, though my background is conservative and evangelical. I do not endorse some of the tenets or doctrinal views common of most evangelical denominations. I have no interest in literalism, dogma, or religious performance, but I have a great deal of interest in the person of Jesus and modeling Christlike humanity for those I engage professionally.

During my second year in graduate school, I became intrigued with the writings of Albert Ellis and his unique psychotherapeutic approach—rational emotive behavior therapy (REBT). I was immediately impressed by two aspects of Ellis's work. First, I was impressed with his willingness to boldly dispense with all but the most essential truths and elegant solutions when helping clients. Second, I was impressed by the strongly negative views about Ellis among my peers and teachers—most were offended by Ellis's Epicurean personal behavior, his atheistic philosophy, and his overt rejection of most religious belief as largely pathogenic.

During the remainder of graduate school and my early career as a psychologist, I explored the application of REBT to religious clients and their unique concerns (Johnson & Nielsen, 1998; Johnson, Ridley, & Nielsen, 2000; Nielsen, Johnson, & Ridley, 2000; Nielsen, Johnson, & Ellis, 2001). Contrary to prevailing opinion among religious psychologists, I found that REBT had much to offer religious clients; like other human beings, religious clients often make themselves miserable by rating themselves and others or making irrational (and mostly unbiblical) demands of themselves and various situations. In fact, I found that religious persons sometimes create irrational disturbances with help from their religion or their own idiosyncratic rendering of doctrine and scripture. Research applying REBT to depressed religious clients has clearly supported its efficacy as a treatment approach for religious persons.

Although I have undergone formal training in REBT at the Institute for REBT in New York, and although I largely use REBT as my treatment paradigm when helping clients, religious or not, I am not much like Albert Ellis in the counseling session. Whereas Ellis can come across to clients as brash, highly vocal, and given to a range of confrontational and humorous techniques early on in treatment, I am more interested in establishing rapport and engaging the client relationally before moving to dispute irrational beliefs. Although Ellis downplays the significance of warmth on the part of the therapist (Ellis & Dryden, 1997), I see it as markedly important—if not essential—to maximal outcome. So, I might practice a kinder, gentler approach to REBT, but it is REBT nonetheless.

In my clinical work, integration of faith and practice occurs in several ways. Most broadly, I work at being Christlike in my relationships with clients. This means offering clients care and positive regard without condition. It means avoiding judgment, disdain, or collusion in the client's self-damnation or the damnation of others. Although always imperfect, I hope to offer depressed, anxious, or angry clients a glimpse of what dwelling in the presence of the tolerant and loving Christ might be. More specifically, I sometimes augment traditional REBT techniques with religious content (e.g., a scripture verse or biblical parable) to reinforce the point or make an intervention more meaningful to a client. In some cases, I may use religiously sensitive REBT disputation techniques to counter irrationally demanding or evaluative client beliefs. When client religious beliefs are directly linked to emotional disturbance—clinically salient religion—I am willing to point out inconsistent or incongruent aspects of their religious framework (e.g., "you say you are forgiven for your sins, yet you rate yourself as worthless because of things you have done. How can that be?"), and to challenge and debate the demanding and evaluative quality in their religious beliefs.

SETTING

The setting was a midsized county community mental center in the Pacific Northwest. The center offered services specifically to children, adolescents, and families. Adult services were offered elsewhere in the county system. The range of services provided in this mental health center included individual counseling sessions, psychological assessments, group therapy for children and adolescents with both general and specialized clinical concerns (e.g., sexual abuse issues, eating disorders, and postdivorce concerns), family therapy, and various programs for addictions.

CLIENT DEMOGRAPHIC CHARACTERISTICS

Gary was a 17-year-old White male student in a private Christian school. Gary hailed from an upper-middle class family. His father was a successful attorney and his mother a homemaker. The family was devoutly religious and identified with a charismatic nondenominational Christian church. The church was on the fundamental end of the evangelical Christian church spectrum. Gary espoused very conservative religious beliefs and would be considered quite devout in his own Christian commitments and practices. At the beginning of his senior year, Gary was an excellent student and quite active in both school and community fine arts programs. Choir, band, and art courses occupied much of Gary's extracurricular time.

PRESENTING PROBLEMS AND CONCERNS

Gary was referred for counseling by his psychiatrist. The psychiatrist had been treating Gary for depression for approximately 6 months and had placed Gary on a selective serotonin reuptake inhibitor (SSRI) antidepressant, which had resulted in moderate reduction in Gary's depressive symptoms. The primary reason for referral was depression with a duration of at least one year prior to referral to me. Gary's symptoms included dysphoric mood, sleep disruption, fatigue, hopeless ideation, episodic thoughts of suicide (although he had never formulated a plan for suicide or made any suicide gesture), feelings of shame, thoughts of worthlessness, and episodic withdrawal from family and friends. Although all of these symptoms had lessened in severity by the time Gary was referred, his psychiatrist and family noted that Gary continued to evidence milder symptoms of low mood, social withdrawal, and a cognitive tendency toward self-deprecation. Gary's father brought him to the community mental health center, rather than to a psychologist in private practice specifically because the psychiatrist had included me among a list of psychologists who were Christian.

CLIENT HISTORY

Gary was the second of three children born to loving and committed Christian parents. He had achieved normal developmental milestones, scored above average on standardized achievement tests, and performed extremely well in school. Although he was not particularly athletic, Gary's interests were primarily musical and artistic. His brother James had been both an academic and athletic standout in the same Christian school and, to the pleasure of his parents, had gone off to a competitive Christian college. His younger sister Amy was 2 years behind Gary, and by all accounts, Gary had solid relationships with both siblings. The family was quite involved in the church and Gary's father was an elder. Gary was active in choir and youth group and nearly all of the family's friends were also members of their church. Gary had a few friends both in church and in school, and nearly all shared his conservative and charismatic religious views.

There was a family genetic diathesis for depression. Several members of Gary's extended family had mood disorder symptoms, including his maternal grandmother who had been treated long-term with antidepressant medication. When Gary first evidenced signs of depression at age 16, his parents had initially taken him to their pastor, who saw Gary for several sessions of pastoral counseling. When Gary's symptoms worsened and he acknowledged some suicidal ideation, he had been taken to a psychiatrist who had initiated a trial of SSRI medication. Although antidepressants helped diminish many of Gary's more severe depressive symptoms, his parents noted that he continued to seem "down" and "withdrawn" from the family at times. Gary's psychiatrist recommended a period of cognitive–behavioral psychotherapy as a supplement to psychotropic intervention.

ASSESSMENT AND DIAGNOSIS

Mood Disorder

Prior to Gary's first appointment, I was able to review copies of his psychiatrist's case notes. The only clinical diagnosis was major depression, moderate, single episode. When he had begun treatment 6 months prior at age 16, Gary had been markedly depressed with episodic thoughts of suicide, and daily symptoms of sleep disruption, hopelessness, decreased appetite, feelings of shame and guilt, and general mood dysphoria. At that time, Gary's intake score on the Beck Depression Inventory (BDI) was 34, indicating rather severe clinical depression. Almost immediately, Gary was started on a trial of Paxil and the dose had been modified twice until maximally therapeutic for Gary. In the months following this intake, case notes documented a significant decline in depressive symptoms. By Gary's report, sessions with his psychiatrist consisted mainly of a brief discussion of his depressive symptoms, medication side effects, and encouragement for Gary to become increasingly involved in school and social activities. Gary's most recent BDI scores had fluctuated between 12 and 18.

During my own assessment with Gary, I saw him as mildly to moderately depressed, and felt that the existing clinical diagnosis was quite accurate. In addition to a rather detailed client history form, Gary completed the BDI and scored 16—indicating mild depression. The only other clinical tool utilized at intake with Gary was a simple Sentence Completion Questionnaire. Responses to this measure were notable for themes of pessimism—if not hopelessness—and ambivalence in relationships.

Gary was a medium-sized soft-spoken White adolescent with some facial acne. During the intake session he indicated an understanding of why his psychiatrist had recommended therapy, and how talking therapy would differ from his appointments with his physician. Gary showed good insight and his intellectual level was clinically assessed to be well above average. He also showed glimmers of humor—a particularly good prognostic sign for response to cognitive psychotherapy. When asked about his own understanding of his depression, Gary said, "well, I'm afraid I have bad genes for depression. My grandmother had it, and I guess other people in my family too." Gary attributed most of his treatment gain to the SSRI medication, yet also seemed to understand the potential efficacy of exploring his thoughts and behaviors.

Sexual Orientation

During our fourth session together, Gary disclosed considerable distress about his sexual orientation—an orientation that I would eventually come to understand as primarily homosexual. Although homosexuality is not a disorder (Haldeman, 2002), and although it is certainly not an issue for clinical diagnosis, I include a discussion of sexual orientation in this section on assessment because Gary's concerns about sexual orientation were deeply connected to his emotional tumult and depressed mood. Because homosexuality was so central to this case, I include a very brief description of my own understanding of sexual orientation, as well as a brief synopsis of Gary's very conservative and religiously orthodox views about homosexuality. It is important to note that although our assumptions about sexual orientation were disparate, both were rooted in a Christian worldview.

Serra (2001) defined sexual orientation as "an innate predisposition to respond with enduring emotional, erotic, affectionate, or romantic attraction to individuals of a particular sex" (p. 170). Research on the development of sexual orientation shows that most homosexuals experience homosexual feelings by early adolescence and that many report same-sex attraction well before puberty (Hershberger & D'Augelli, 2000; Money, 1987). Most models of sexual identity development posit a period of identity confusion or crisis in which the experience of same-sex attraction can be confusing and distressing (Yarhouse, 2001). Self-labeling of same-sex sexual orientation generally occurs around the age of 15 and is often described as "coming out to oneself" (Hershberger & D'Augelli, 2000, p. 227). Still, the nature of one's sexual expression and other factors such as attribution of same-sex attraction and religious beliefs can significantly affect the rate of sexual-orientation consolidation. Although I see sexual orientation as remarkably complex in origin—typically involving an unknowable mix of genetic, biological, relational, and contextual factors—I see sexual orientation as largely determined by early adulthood, and most often, by late adolescence.

Lewis Smedes, a professor of mine in seminary, helped me to conceptualize a Christian framework for sexual orientation. He taught me that Jesus was a savior, not a moralist (Smedes, 1983). In his own life and ministry, Jesus showed that traditional rules surrounding the divine commandments were invalid if they kept people from the humanizing intent of the law. Smedes suggested that there are really only two fundamental commandments of the moral life—love and justice. Smedes frequently cites the Old Testament passage from Micah 6:8 "and what does the Lord require of you but to do justice, and to love kindness, and to walk humbly with your God?" In my work, I am most concerned with how to best love lesbian, gay, or bisexual (LGB) persons and actively incorporate them in the Christian community.

Gary's view of sexual orientation, and homosexuality in particular, was largely congruent with very conservative Christian theological tradition on the topic. Many organized religions (particularly the three monotheistic religions) view same-sex identification as incompatible with normative or prescriptive dimensions of religion and many are relatively intolerant of openly LGB individuals (Davidson, 2000; Swidler, 1993). From a conservative religious perspective, people who experience homosexual desires and attractions are not morally bad, unworthy, or sinful; however, people who act on their homosexual desires and engage in homosexual behavior are committing sin because homosexual behavior is morally wrong. From this viewpoint, the most moral way to respond to homosexual desires and attractions is to seek control, minimize, and when possible, overcome them. Quaker theologian Richard Foster offers an example of this perspective: "The practice of homosexuality is sin, to be sure. . . . The Christian fellowship cannot give permission to practice homosexuality to those who feel unable to change their orientation or to embrace celibacy" (Foster, 1985, p. 112).

From the moment in psychotherapy when Gary first began describing his struggle with sexuality and the possibility of being gay, it was apparent that Gary held very orthodox and anti-LGB religious beliefs. Gary's primary fear was that he was gay and therefore exposed to the danger (in terms of committing a mortal sin) of homosexual behavior. Although it was clear that Gary and I operated from significantly disparate understandings of both sexual orientation and how sexual orientation can be understood and accepted within a religious faith, Gary's specific sexual orientation was never the focus of our brief period of psychotherapy; we did not work at determining whether Gary was primarily heterosexual, bisexual, or homosexual. Instead, the focus of treatment became Gary's catastrophic and depressogenic response to the feelings of same-sex attraction and the possibility of being gay in sexual orientation.

TREATMENT PROCESS AND OUTCOMES

REBT in the Dark: ABCs Without the A

After my intake session with Gary and a brief session with Gary's parents to outline my treatment plan and highlight the importance of Gary's right to confidentiality, I was eager to commence a trial of REBT for Gary's clinical depression. I have found that REBT is often a particularly elegant approach to therapy with religious clients because it focuses specifically on foundational beliefs, emphasizes client responsibility for working hard at change, and is quite existential and philosophical at the core (Johnson, 2001; Nielsen, Johnson, & Ellis, 2001). The primary difference between REBT and other psychotherapies is REBT's emphasis on evaluative beliefs (Ellis & Dryden, 1997), or the "B" in the ABC model in which "A" is the Activating event, and "C" is the negative emotional consequence (depression, anxiety, anger, and shame). In REBT, the therapist quickly works with the client to discern irrational evaluative beliefs related to emotional upset, help them clearly understand the connection between these irrational beliefs and their current disturbance, and then help the client move from irrational, absolutistic, evaluative beliefs toward more rational preferences. Beliefs are considered irrational if they are logically inconsistent, inconsistent with empirical reality, absolutistic and dogmatic, prone to elicit disturbed emotions, and likely to block the client's goal attainment. Finally, the primary therapeutic approach in REBT (although there are many) is disputation or the persistent, forceful, and concise challenging of the client's primary irrational beliefs while simultaneously showing the client how more rational alternatives will likely lead to less disturbed emotional and behavioral outcomes. (I offer clearer examples of various REBT cognitive interventions later in this chapter.)

Because Gary was intelligent, insightful, and blessed with a sense of humor, I believed that his lingering depressive symptoms might be quite treatable with REBT. To this end, I quickly began a process of rational emotive assessment with Gary—searching for examples of activating events (As), irrational beliefs (Bs), and depressive emotional consequences (Cs). Gary had great difficulty articulating specific events or situations that tended to foreshadow depressed mood. In fact, Gary could only describe some "problems with friends" (these problems were described only in the vaguest of terms) as precipitating some of his depressive episodes. When pressed, he described feeling like he did not "fit in" with many peers and wishing that he had a few close friends versus numerous "acquaintances."

It is often the case in REBT that primary emotional problems (depression) cannot be effectively addressed until secondary emotional disturbances (shame about depression) are handled (Ellis & Dryden, 1997). In light of Gary's very conservative religious views, I wondered if he felt guilt or shame or additional depression related to his diagnosis and treatment for a mood disorder. Gary appeared initially quite animated by this suggestion and agreed that he was often self-condemnatory in response to his mood problems and his inability to "get over it." I proceeded to teach him to dispute this irrational belief (demanding) with both standard ("where is it written that you must be perfect?") and religiously oriented ("can you remember that biblical passage where Jesus says that depressed people are less worthy?") disputations.

Although Gary began to understand the REBT process, and perhaps to benefit slightly from our work on his secondary emotional disturbance (shame), it became clear by our fourth session together that we had yet to identify a particularly "hot" irrational belief for Gary. That is, it did not appear that Gary really believed firmly that being depressed was awful, or that not fitting in socially led directly to depression-causing irrational beliefs. Although our rapport appeared to be growing, and although Gary was clearly present in the sessions, he continued to report substantial depression. With approximately 20 minutes remaining in the fourth session, I made these observations to Gary. He concurred with our apparent "stuckness." As I sometimes do when stuck with a client, I returned to the ABC model and asked Gary if we could talk in more detail about a recent example of an activating event in which he felt alienated socially (only because he had noted that most of these events involved friends).

Understanding Gary's Primary Activating Event

At this point, with tremendous trepidation and a look of sober pain, Gary nearly blurted out "one thing I worry about is what my friends would think if they thought I was attracted to men." Surprised but quite relieved to better understand my client, I thanked Gary for sharing this concern and endorsed it as quite important. In our remaining moments of that session, I used no specific technique save for the essential elements of unconditional regard, warmth, and sincere affirmation of Gary's concern as well as his willingness to entrust this to me. Gary appeared simultaneously shaken (perhaps at his own boldness) and relieved to be discussing this crucial component of his life and depression.

In three subsequent sessions with Gary, I adopted a client-centered therapeutic stance; I attempted to surround him with warmth and acceptance while he shared some of his long-standing concern about sexual orientation—including several homoerotic experiences. Hershberger and D'Augelli (2000) noted that the first disclosure of homoerotic orientation is often the most difficult and fraught with perceived risk for the client. I could see that Gary was simultaneously anxious and deeply relieved about these disclosures.

Gary recalled feeling sexually aroused around other boys, his brother, and when looking at pictures or artwork of men's bodies from about age 13 onward. At the age of 15 he had been humiliated when apprehended by a department store clerk for stealing small cardboard pictures of young men in briefs from packages of men's underwear. The clerk did not summon his parents or the police. Gary had "stashes" of bodybuilding and sports magazines depicting attractive men and frequently masturbated with these. He appeared forlorn when acknowledging almost no sexual attraction to women that he could recall. He noted that most of his good friends over the years had been girls. He had had two homoerotic sexual encounters with other boys, once when 15 during a weeklong church camp, and once just before turning 17 with a friend from school. Both experiences were single episode and involved mutual masturbation, and in the second case, oral sex.

SEXUAL ORIENTATION CONCERNS IN PSYCHOTHERAPY: A SYNOPSIS OF THE CONTROVERSY

Although I have mentioned that my focus in treating Gary was not to change or affirm a particular sexual orientation, I am aware that Gary will eventually have to address this issue—either alone or in the context of a subsequent helping relationship. Unfortunately, few topics have generated such acrimonious controversy both within the mental health establishment and between mainstream mental health practitioners and conservatively religious groups. In this section, I briefly summarize the primary perspectives on treating persons with concern about sexual orientation with emphasis on both gay-affirmative and conservative religious points of view. For those with additional interest in this issue, I recommend an excellent series of recent articles in *Professional Psychology: Research and Practice* (Benedict, VandenBos, & Kenkel, 2002).

A gay-affirmative approach to sexual orientation rests on several assumptions including the following: (a) homosexual orientation is largely genetic and biological in origin, (b) a homosexual or bisexual orientation represents an enduring or lifelong sexual orientation, (c) homosexual attractions and preferences are largely unchangeable, (d) ethical and appropriate psychotherapy for these LGB persons involves affirmation of an LGB identity, reduction in internalized homophobia, and eventual integration into an LGB lifestyle and community, and (e) attempts to change or "convert" sexual orientation are ethically dubious and often harmful to LGB clients.

In contrast, a conservatively religious view of psychotherapy and sexual orientation assumes that (a) people have a right to choose their own values and lifestyle, including those relevant to sexual orientation, (b) many religious clients may find homosexual behavior to be morally wrong and these religious views should be respected and affirmed, (c) clients who decide they do not wish to pursue the gay lifestyle, but would prefer to seek, reduce, minimize, or overcome their homosexual attractions and desires may benefit from working with a therapist who has training in sexual reorientation therapy.

Research bearing on sexual reorientation or "reparative" therapy for LGB men and women who wish to change their sexual orientation or reduce their same-sex attraction is preliminary (Haldeman, 2002; Throckmorton, 2002). A review of the scanty empirical literature indicates that although some who define themselves as "ex-gay" feel reorientation therapy was useful, others report the opposite and a minority feel significantly harmed by such treatment approaches (Throckmorton, 2002). Perhaps not surprisingly, studies emanating from both conservative religious (Nicolosi, Byrd, & Potts, 2000) and gay-affirmative (Shidlo & Schroeder, 2002) camps tend to show that clients are either largely satisfied with reorientation therapy or deeply wounded by such services, depending on the study's design and who is surveyed.

To their credit, professionals from both sides of the debate now seem to agree that respect for client diversity (sexual and religious) and autonomy should be a preeminent clinical concern:

> Neither gay-affirmative nor ex-gay interventions should be assumed to be the preferred approach to recommend to clients presenting with concerns over sexual identity. Generally, gay-affirmative therapy or referral should be offered to those clients who want to adjust to and affirm a same-sex sexual orientation. Clients who decide they want to modify same-sex patterns of sexual arousal could consider ex-gay or reorientation therapy or should seek referral to ex-gay ministries. (Throckmorton, 2002, p. 246)

My View of Psychotherapy With LGB Persons

I am supportive of the American Psychological Association's (1998) resolution on appropriate therapeutic responses to sexual orientation concerns in therapy which affirms, among other things, that (a) homosexuality is not a mental illness, (b) mental health services to this client population should be free of bias, prejudice, and discrimination, and (c) such services should be provided by mental health professionals who are trained in this area.

My fundamental approach to counseling LGB youth (or young adults) who are questioning and exploring their sexual identity is one of acceptance first and foremost (Hershberger & D'Augelli, 2000). To this, I would add affirmation and admiration. By this I mean conveying that the client has unconditional value and worth regardless of sexual orientation, and that their courage—evidenced in disclosing—is admirable. Of course, decisions about sexual orientation—or more accurately acknowledging sexual orientation—are often more weighty and often perceived as danger-laden for the client.

I personally do not practice reorientation therapy and would be quite hesitant to refer an LGB client for such services unless it was quite clear that they were seeking such services after careful informed consent regarding potentially negative outcomes (Schneider, Brown, & Glassgold, 2002; Shidlo & Schroeder, 2002). Although my own approach to addressing issues of sexual orientation issues in psychotherapy is most congruent with a gay-affirmative model, I agree heartily that gay-affirmative therapists need to take seriously the experiences of their religious clients, refraining from encouraging an abandonment of their spiritual traditions in favor of a more gay-affirmative doctrine (Haldeman, 2002).

I am particularly concerned about the experience of gay youth and recognize that they face a number of substantial stressors not shared by their heterosexual peers. These include the experience of invisibility or open rejection (sometimes including violence), development of a negative self-concept, lack of information and resources to assist them in self-understanding, potential conflict with and rejection by family and friends, and higher rates of various emotional difficulties including mood disorders and active suicidality (Davidson, 2000; Hershberger & D'Augelli, 2000).

In some religious subcultures, these hurdles are exacerbated by both subtle and overt messages that a homosexual orientation implies spiritual weakness, moral depravity, or intentional sinfulness. Young LGB parishioners may feel compelled to choose between their religious community (perhaps their only link to the divine) and the LGB community or lifestyle (Davidson, 2000). Research suggests that adolescents from traditional families perceive greater disapproval and rejection when revealing their LGB orientation (Newman & Muzzonigro, 1993). Paradoxically, a religious community may be a religious youth's primary source of social support and corporate identity—making it considerably more difficult for him or her to successfully blend religious and sexual identities (Davidson, 2000; Yarhouse, 2001).

In Gary's case, these complex stressors were clearly in play. Gary initially avoided use of the terms *gay* or *homosexual*, and although he spoke matter-of-factly about being "attracted to men," he preferred to speak in terms of the hypothetical with respect to his sexual orientation. He also made it very clear that "if I end up being gay, I would never tell my parents." Gary also insisted he would never disclose his sexual orientation to members of the church or even his siblings. In fact, I was somewhat surprised that he had already formulated a clear plan for heterosexual marriage. Though he worried such a marriage may be "not very fair" to his wife, he thought he could manage this with help from God. He also believed that having children was very important both personally and religiously. Throughout these three to four sessions of exploration and disclosure, it became clear to me that although Gary's sexual orientation was almost certainly homosexual, he viewed such an orientation as repellant and immoral. He felt simultaneously eroticized and guilty about his daily homosexual fantasies and masturbation as well as firm in his resolve to keep his sexuality silent as he lived an overtly heterosexual life in the community and the church. Gary admitted that concerns about his sexuality had often caused him to feel depressed.

REBT for Gary's Disturbance About Sexual Orientation: Seeking the Elegant Solution

I believe that efforts to disabuse clients of foundational religious beliefs are both ethically and clinically inappropriate (Johnson, 2001; Richards & Bergin, 1997). At the same time, it is not uncommon for clients to present with clinically salient religious beliefs and behaviors that are discordant or incongruent with other elements of the client's religious worldview. When religion has become clinically salient and the therapist has both familiarity with and respect for the client's theistic beliefs and practices, it is both possible and preferable for the therapist to engage in REBT disputation aimed at both the evaluative and demanding nature of the client's beliefs, as well as at problematic or discordant beliefs themselves. I have elsewhere referred to this as *specialized* disputation with religious clients (Johnson, 2001).

In Gary's case, it was possible for me to approach the client with an overarching assumption of theistic realism or the notion that God is real and sustaining humankind's existence (Richards & Bergin, 1997) and to communicate some shared Christian commitments. I was also interested in helping Gary to examine the effect his religious beliefs had on his presenting problem (depression) while being careful to consider Gary's religiousness a potential asset in treatment. In terms of clinically significant dimensions of religiosity discussed by Richards and Bergin (1997), it was apparent that Gary was suffering from clinical distress related to both belief orthodoxy and value–lifestyle incongruence. Belief orthodoxy involves acceptance of the doctrinal beliefs of one's religion even when these are incongruent or produce destructive outcomes. Value–lifestyle incongruence typically refers to value- or belief-discordant behaviors. In Gary's case this included largely covert behavior such as homoerotic fantasy and masturbation.

It is essential to point out here that during my treatment of Gary, I made no attempt to help him clarify or label his sexual orientation, nor did I make an effort to move him in the direction of either accepting a gay identity or working to ameliorate his same-sex attraction and sexual behavior. Rather, because Gary's depression appeared to be most clearly driven by his strong demanding and evaluative beliefs about the possibility of being gay, it was most important to begin helping him change these cognitions. In REBT, the elegant solution (Ellis & Dryden, 1997; Walen, DiGiuseppe, & Dryden, 1992) involves helping a client make a profound philosophic change or fundamental attitudinal shift in the way he or she thinks about a problem or an inference about a problem. The elegant solution assumes that the activating event is true and will remain so or could easily occur (assuming the worst) and then encourages the client to change his or her evaluation of this given reality. In Gary's case, the elegant solution was epitomized by helping him to make a profound shift from evaluative and demanding beliefs (e.g., "If I am gay, that would be awful and catastrophic. I must not be gay! I could not stand or tolerate being gay. If I were gay, it would prove I am worthless and evil.") to preferential and functional beliefs (e.g., "It would be too bad and a real problem for me in many ways if I were gay, but with God's love and assistance, I could bear it and find some way to cope with that reality. I would be merely gay, not unworthy or unlovable."). So, the elegant REBT solution is aimed at helping the client to make a profound shift from extreme demanding and evaluating (which was clearly depressogenic in Gary's case) to preferring and observing. It is worth noting that the elegant solution in REBT is also elegant from a spiritual and religious perspective. For example, Christian spirituality will rarely support catastrophic or demanding beliefs and there are numerous scriptural challenges and contradictions to such disturbed thinking.

During our eighth session, I asked Gary if we could explore how his worries about sexuality may be related to his mood problems. Having vented and disclosed importantly about his struggles with sexual orientation and the very negative implications of possibly being gay, Gary appeared ready to return to some focus on the presenting problem. He agreed that the two were probably connected and we again began to formulate an REBT assessment of Gary's depression—this time considering various activating events (As) related to his sexuality.

In our subsequent REBT treatment sessions, Gary quickly identified several important activating events that typically preceded bouts of more severe depression. These included interactions with other young men he found interesting or attractive; questions from peers, siblings, or parents about why he did not date or show particular romantic interest in some of the girls who had pursued him; and imagining a lifetime of hiding his sexual orientation or sharing his orientation with family. Gary was quick to pick up the REBT model of disturbance and showed some obvious amusement at the suggestion that these events (As) alone were not enough to "cause" his depression, but that he was indoctrinating himself with certain "crazy" beliefs about these events to really get depressed.

Although Gary was able to articulate several irrational beliefs (Bs), in the interest of space I will highlight just three of these—each representative of the main types of irrational belief (Ellis & Dryden, 1997): (a) awfulizing (e.g., if I am a gay man, it is awful, terrible, and catastrophic); (b) demanding (e.g., I absolutely must not disappoint God and my parents by acting on my sexual desires); and (c) global human rating (e.g., feeling attracted to men and masturbating while fantasizing about men shows that I am not worthy in God's eyes).

As we moved to disputation in the next several sessions I began with a general approach to disputation—focusing primarily on the evaluative and demanding nature of Gary's beliefs without questioning or creating dissonance regarding specific religious beliefs. In REBT disputation, there are several strategies available to the therapist. In my work with Gary, I used logical, empirical, and functional disputations—both because I am comfortable with these strategies and because Gary seemed to respond favorably. Regarding style of disputation, I tend to use Socratic, self-disclosing, and humorous approaches when possible. Examples of some of the disputes I used with Gary follow.

Logical disputes were designed to help Gary see the unreasonable and arbitrary nature of his irrational beliefs ("help me understand how being gay, if that ends up being true for you, qualifies as a catastrophe," "How does it follow that because you wish you wouldn't disappoint your parents, then you absolutely must not do so under any circumstances?"). Empirical disputations helped Gary see that the facts of the world did not support his irrational beliefs ("Where is it written that feeling sexual pleasure around men is one of life's greatest calamities?" "Everyday I make lots of mistakes as a father, husband, and teacher. This proves that I am worthless. Right?"). Finally, functional disputations were used to help Gary see how his irrational beliefs both created and sustained self-defeating emotions and behaviors, in other words, one function of adopting more rational beliefs is suffering less ("I wonder if insisting that your sexuality is awful is helping you to feel less depressed?" "Help me understand how rating yourself as worthless is making you feel").

Because Gary was bright, somewhat philosophically oriented, and engaged in treatment, these general REBT disputations helped Gary to better understand how his demanding and harshly evaluative thoughts were naturally intensifying his experience of depression. Because Gary did not speak of himself as gay or homosexual in certain terms, I felt it important to present these disputations in the hypothetical (e.g., "if it is true that," or "if you end up discovering that you are gay"). I believe this allowed Gary to experiment with new ways of believing without feeling so threatened.

Navigating a Minefield: Disputing Religious Beliefs

Although Gary was experiencing some relief, it also became clear that several of his most salient and depressogenic irrational beliefs were deeply intertwined with long-held religious doctrine regarding homosexuality. For instance, Gary frequently engaged in selective abstraction (DiGiuseppe, Robin, & Dryden, 1990)—becoming disturbed by selectively focusing one aspect of his religion to the exclusion of the bigger picture or larger meaning of his faith. Specifically, Gary was prone to see himself as damned and worthless for his homosexual urges—often entirely ignoring the grace-filled purpose of the life of Jesus. In addition, Gary tended to (unbiblically) rate his own perceived sin as measurably worse or more severe than other forms. For this reason, I also began to incorporate more specialized (Johnson, 2001; Nielsen, Johnson, & Ellis, 2001) disputations to create dissonance between discordant beliefs and instill doubt about dubious (often unbiblical) doctrine.

Although I generally contend that practitioners should avoid disputing religious beliefs, there are times when strong religious views are contrary to the entire body of a religion and clearly linked to emotional and behavioral dysfunction and pain. In Gary's case, I felt it imperative to question his strongly dogmatic and depressing beliefs about the possibility of being gay. I explained to Gary that although I shared his general Christian view of the world, I thought it might be useful to explore some of his specific beliefs surrounding this issue (e.g., "God will reject me if I am gay. If I am gay, it just proves I am sinful and unworthy"). Some examples of these more specialized disputations for Gary's main irrational beliefs follow.

For Gary's pervasive awfulizing about homoerotic impulses and the possibility of being gay (both of which he identified as forms of sin), I used the following disputations ("The Bible says that all of us sin and fall short of the glory of God [Romans 3:23], that is we all sin all the time. Where is it written that feeling attracted to men is one of the worst sins? I'm confused; the Bible says that for those who believe and ask for grace, all sins are forgiven. That must only apply to everyone EXCEPT you? You know Gary, Jesus didn't seem to say much about homosexuality. It didn't seem very upsetting to him. What did seem important were kindness, mercy, and love. I'd like you to read through the gospel as homework and next week, show me that scripture where Jesus says homosexual feelings are terrible, awful, or the worst possible sort of sin").

For Gary's self-rating, the following appeared helpful ("If your best friend had the same kinds of gay feelings that you have, would you tell him he was a worthless sinner in God's eyes? Something's wrong here, Gary. You're telling me you believe God created you [as the Bible says], but that the way God created you [your sexual feelings] is wrong. This just doesn't make sense does it?"). Finally, for Gary's demand that he not be homosexual, and that he live a heterosexual existence, the following functional dispute seemed particularly helpful for Gary ("I agree that your life might seem a bit easier and less confusing right now if you were exclusively heterosexual. But, from what you've told me, that is simply not the case. So, it seems that you can either keep demanding that you be someone you are not and stay depressed or accept all facets of who you are today and get busy living").

I moved to Maryland after only 16 sessions with Gary. Although he was by no means free of depressive symptoms at termination, his two final BDI scores (I administered the BDI monthly) were 8 and 10. I believe that our 4 months together helped Gary understand how to apply REBT himself, and how to be kinder and gentler to himself as a Christian man struggling with reconciliation of sexual orientation and religious beliefs regarding sexuality. There has been no follow-up and I am uncertain regarding Gary's status today. During our final session, I gave Gary referrals to two other psychologists—both of whom I felt certain would help Gary to continue exploring these issues, and both of whom were competent providers of service to LGB persons, and persons with strong religious commitments.

THERAPIST COMMENTARY

Although I believe I helped Gary with several REBT disputations, both general and religiously oriented, and although I believe our REBT work helped him to become less catastrophic, demanding, and self-downing in his thinking (and thereby less vulnerable to depression in the long run), it is quite possible that the most therapeutic thing I did for Gary was listen and accept him when he first disclosed his homosexuality. On that day, and those immediately after, I witnessed a leviathan lift from Gary's shoulders. Offering authentic admiration, empathy, and unconditional acceptance felt both maximally therapeutic and clearly Christian. I believe that Gary expected me to affirm his damning self-view as vile, morally flawed, and chuck full of the worst sort of sin. I also believe that in his selective brand of Christianity, he expected the same of God.

I believe this case highlights the ethical and professional challenges inherent in treating a religious client when the therapist does not share salient elements of the client's worldview, and in fact, may see some aspects of the client's religiousness as connected to his or her disturbance. To fully address Gary's suffering, it was necessary to carefully challenge elements of Gary's religious dogma without questioning the veracity of his more fundamental faith commitments. Therefore, instead of saying "What makes you think any supernatural being gives a damn about you?" as my teacher Albert Ellis might, I prefer to work gently from within the client's own faith surround using more subtle disputes of those aspects of a client's religion that appear clinically harmful. At the same time, I believe it imperative to honor the client's religious commitments and preferences. Had my work with Gary continued, we would certainly have reached a crossroads at which Gary may have benefited from a referral to a therapist with more competence than I in helping young LGB persons adapt and adjust fully to a gay lifestyle. Alternatively, had Gary ultimately requested assistance with sexual "reorientation," I believe I would have been obligated to provide him with such referrals (although this would have pained me professionally and I would have done so only after careful informed consent regarding the potential drawbacks of these techniques).

In closing, I want to acknowledge that some of my conservatively religious colleagues will feel that I am far too religiously liberal on the topic of sexual orientation, and may believe that I should have confirmed Gary's view of homosexuality as sin while perhaps helping him accept an asexual life ("love the sinner but hate the sin"). I understand that others more strongly committed to gay-affirmative services in all circumstances in which a person explores sexual orientation in therapy might criticize me for not pushing Gary to "come out" further, self-identify as exclusively gay, and perhaps begin exploring homosexual relationships more actively. The first option is simply incongruent with my own therapeutic and faith perspective. The second option would have been disrespectful of Gary's strong religious views and his tentative stage of sexual identity consolidation (Haldeman, 2002; Yarhouse, 2001). In the end, I hope that seeking the elegant solution helped to reduce Gary's depression in such a way that he will be better prepared to address these difficult and meaningful questions when the time comes.

REFERENCES

American Psychological Association. (1998). Resolution on the appropriate therapeutic responses to sexual orientation. Proceedings of the American Psychological Association, Incorporated, for the Legislative year 1997. *American Psychologist, 53,* 882–935.

Benedict, J. G., VandenBos, G. R., & Kenkel, M. B. (Eds.). (2002). *Professional Psychology: Research and Practice, 33*(3).

Davidson, M. G. (2000). Religion and spirituality. In R. M. Perez, K. A. DeBord, & K. J. Bieschke (Eds.), *Handbook of counseling and psychotherapy with lesbian, gay, and bisexual clients* (pp. 409–433). Washington, DC: American Psychological Association.

DiGiuseppe, R. A., Robin, M. W., & Dryden, W. (1990). On the compatibility of rational emotive therapy and Judeo-Christian philosophy: A focus on clinical strategies. *Journal of Cognitive Psychotherapy: An International Quarterly, 4,* 355–368.

Ellis, A., & Dryden, W. (1997). *The practice of rational emotive behavior therapy* (rev. ed.). New York: Springer.

Foster, R. (1985). *The challenge of the disciplined life: Christian reflections on money, sex, and power.* San Francisco: Harper.

Greene, B., & Herek, G. (Eds.) (1994). *Lesbian and gay psychology: Theory, research and clinical applications.* Thousand Oaks, CA: Sage.

Haldeman, D. C. (2002). Gay rights, patient rights: The implications of sexual orientation conversion therapy. *Professional Psychology: Research and Practice, 33,* 260–264.

Hershberger, S. L., & D'Augelli, A. R. (2000). Issues in counseling lesbian, gay, and bisexual adolescents. In R. M. Perez, K. A. DeBord, & K. J. Bieschke (Eds.), *Handbook of counseling and psychotherapy with lesbian, gay, and bisexual clients* (pp. 225–247). Washington, DC: American Psychological Association.

Johnson, W. B. (2001). To dispute or not to dispute: Ethical REBT with religious clients. *Cognitive and Behavioral Practice, 8,* 39–47.

Johnson, W. B., & Nielsen, S. L. (1998). Rational emotive assessment with religious clients. *Journal of Rational Emotive and Cognitive Behavioral Therapy, 16,* 101–123.

Johnson, W. B., Ridley, C. R., & Nielsen, S. L. (2000). Religiously sensitive rational emotive behavior therapy: Elegant solutions and ethical risks. *Professional Psychology: Research and Practice, 31,* 14–20.

Money, J. (1987). Sin, sickness, or status? Homosexual gender identity and psychoneuroendocrinology. *American Psychologist, 42,* 384–399.

Newman, B. S., & Muzzonigro, P. G. (1993). The effects of traditional family values on the coming-out process of gay male adolescents. *Adolescence, 28,* 213–234.

Nicolosi, J., Byrd, A. D., & Potts, R. W. (2000). Retrospective self-reports of changes in homosexual orientation: A consumer survey of conversion therapy clients. *Psychological Reports, 86,* 1071–1088.

Nielsen, S. L., Johnson, W. B., & Ellis, A. (2001). *Counseling and psychotherapy with religious persons: A rational emotive behavior therapy approach.* Mahwah, NJ: Lawrence Erlbaum.

Nielsen, S. L., Johnson, W. B., & Ridley, C. R. (2000). Religiously sensitive rational emotive behavior therapy: Theory, techniques, and brief excerpts from a case. *Professional Psychology: Research and Practice, 31,* 21–28.

Richards, P. S., & Bergin, A. E. (1997). *A spiritual strategy for counseling and psychotherapy.* Washington, DC: American Psychological Association.

Schneider, M. S., Brown, L. S., & Glassgold, J. M. (2002). Implementing the resolution on therapeutic responses to sexual orientation: A guide for the perplexed. *Professional Psychology: Research and Practice, 33,* 265–276.

Serra, R. (2001). The continuing struggle for civil rights in the gay community. *Journal of Psychology and Christianity, 20,* 168–175.

Shidlo, A., & Schroeder, M. (2002). Changing sexual orientation: A consumer's report. *Professional Psychology: Research and Practice, 33,* 249–259.

Smedes, L. B. (1983). *Mere morality*. Grand Rapids, MI: Eerdmans.

Swidler, A. (Ed.) (1993). *Homosexuality and world religions*. Valley Forge, PA: Trinity Press International.

Throckmorton, W. (2002). Initial empirical and clinical findings concerning the change process for ex-gays. *Professional Psychology: Research and Practice, 33,* 242–248.

Walen, S. R., DiGiuseppe, R., & Dryden, W. (1992). *A practitioner's guide to rational-emotive therapy* (2nd ed.). New York: Oxford University Press.

Yarhouse, M. A. (2001). Sexual identity development: The influence of valuative frameworks on identity synthesis. *Psychotherapy, 38,* 331–341.

16

RELIGIOUS CROSS-MATCHES BETWEEN THERAPISTS AND CLIENTS

ROBERT J. LOVINGER AND SOPHIE L. LOVINGER

More than 80% of the American population is either Protestant or Catholic (Hoge, 1996), and although Jews comprise perhaps 2% of the general population, it seems that a considerably higher percentage are represented in the population of psychotherapists, at least in major metropolitan areas. Because some 85% of Americans have at least a conventional connection with religion in some form, much of which falls under the general umbrella of Christianity, there is a significant likelihood of a cross-match between the therapist and client on this broad religious variable of affiliation/ background. With the growing realization of the complexities of the therapist–client interaction, it can no longer be assumed that thorough training, careful supervision, and long experience will prevent the therapist's personal qualities from slowly permeating the therapy in subtle and perhaps overt ways.

The therapeutic relationship, especially when conducted in a psychodynamic framework, has no real parallel to any other type of relationship in adult life. This induces some sense of mystery in the client who may wonder what the therapist is about and where they are going together. More than one client has said to us that if she or he knew where we were going they might not have started, but at the conclusion of therapy, she or he was glad we journeyed together. When a Jewish therapist works with a Christian client, there is likely to be even more of a sense of mystery about the therapist. Unsophisticated clients and children may fall back on what they have heard, or absent that, may fill in the information gap with a variety of fantasies. Even knowledgeable and sophisticated adults will blend information and fantasy to develop a composite portrait of their therapists. If the therapist works outside of a large metropolitan area where anonymity is less easily maintained, the situation becomes still more complex. The intertwining issues of mystery and familiarity, often in the background of the therapies we describe, nevertheless surfaced occasionally and influenced these treatments in sometimes surprising ways.

Although Judaism and Christianity share a great deal of features, the differences embedded in their respective cultures are quite significant, the more so because they are largely implicit (Lovinger, 1984). Some of the more important ones are as follows:

1. Although obedience to God's will is a familiar theme in both Christianity and Judaism, Jews have a more disputatious relationship with God and with each other because their goal is to determine what is the right thing to do rather than the right thing to believe. Study and debate lead to the right path in Jewish thought, so tolerance for minority opinions is much greater.
2. Justice for the less fortunate and for strangers is a powerful imperative in Judaism, so Jews in general, and Jewish therapists in particular, are likely to be on the liberal end of the political spectrum. For Jews, charity is not the beneficent bestowing of gracious alms by the giver, but an obligation on the giver and a right of the receiver whose dignity should not be impaired by the act of giving.
3. Although there is an ascetic strain in Christianity and Judaism, it is not as emphasized in Jewish practice. Because the world created by God was good, it is proper that it be enjoyed in a permissible manner. It is a Talmudic dictum that one who neglects a legitimate pleasure in this world will be punished for ingratitude to God in the world next to come.
4. Sin and forgiveness are somewhat differently construed. In Jewish thought, sin (whether through error or deliberate action) is a choice, rather than a choice that overlays an inherent condition as in Christianity. Forgiveness is more of an imperative in Christian thought and more available, whereas in Judaism only the injured party can forgive, after an apology and reparation (if appropriate).

We present three cases: Alfred, a mature, sophisticated adult man nearing 50 when he initiated therapy; Danny, an adolescent boy who began therapy while still in grade school; and Jody, a child just beginning school. In these cases, religious themes surfaced from time to time, coloring some sessions and serving as a counterpoint to whatever issues were present at that point in treatment.

DESCRIPTION OF THERAPISTS

When these three therapies began, we held full-time faculty appointments in the psychology department of a regional, midwestern university located in a small town and taught classes in the graduate program in clinical psychology as well as some undergraduate classes. We were known in both "town" and "gown" settings. Growing up in New York City, where we received our public school, college, and graduate educations, left us marked by accent and attitude as outsiders in our midwestern town even though relationships with "townies" were always amicable. Still, the faster pace and obscurity that characterized New York life, coupled with the expectation of psychoanalytic anonymity in our work, indirectly jarred our sensibilities at times. We came to accept the occasional encounters with clients in local stores with relative equanimity, but we always experienced ourselves as "strangers in a strange land," locking doors and cars when it was not necessary and being perpetually but pleasantly surprised when a proffered check was accepted in a store without identification.

In our thinking, we were broadly psychoanalytic, evolving at the time of these therapies from a mainly ego psychology stance toward an object relations perspective, further flavored by concepts from self psychology. We were also influenced by the work of Harry Stack Sullivan, but we did not regard ourselves as eclectic. Rather, it might be better to say we saw ourselves as adaptive, modifying our methods and conceptualizations over time and in accord with our perceptions of the needs of the client. Robert Lovinger attended to the adult case and Sophie Lovinger attended to the two child cases.

SETTING

At work there were the usual political abrasions in a university department. We had also served the university outside the department and we were fairly well known. Our department had several married couples, a relatively unusual policy when so-called antinepotism rules were common in many universities. Our differences and our capacity to say what we thought, sometimes more bluntly than was absolutely necessary, gave us some further prominence that eventually affected the work with Alfred in indirect fashion. The sometimes-irrepressible humor in the form of puns that Alfred's therapist expressed also probably influenced that therapy.

When we moved to this midwestern town, we joined the local synagogue and became involved in the Sunday school as a way to ensure that our young children (boys ages 5 years and 9 years) would realize that we took our Judaism and their Jewish education seriously. We went to services quite regularly, observed many of the Sabbath rituals, and observed Passover and other holidays. The boys helped their mother (Sophie Lovinger) with much of the preparation for Passover because sometimes more than 30 people attended the Passover Seders we held in our home. Their father (Robert Lovinger) studied with a man who led Sabbath services to help prepare both boys for their bar mitzvahs. Although not Orthodox in practice, we were moderately observant and fully committed Jews in a synagogue affiliated with the conservative movement (Miller & Lovinger, 2000).

THE CASE OF ALFRED

Client Demographic Characteristics

Alfred was near 50 years old when he first consulted me (Robert Lovinger), deeply unhappy in his marriage, and emotionally and sexually frustrated. He held a tenured faculty position in philosophy specializing in the philosophical and theological underpinnings of religions, and also a mid-level administrative position in the university. Handsome, quiet, and with a gentle but earnest demeanor, I had known him slightly when I had presented an early draft of a couple of chapters in a book I was writing to a colloquium that included his faculty colleagues. His wife, Rachel, also knew me slightly from mutual service on the board of a local community agency.

Presenting Problems

Although sexual frustration was presented as an initial issue and remained present for a considerable period of time, Alfred's anger related to deeper feelings of insecurity, inadequacy, and an angry, hurt response to slights, disparagement, or rejection. In the first session, his initial uncertainty of whether his problem was important enough to need therapy yielded to my assurance that I had never had a request for therapy from someone who did not have ample reason to start. Because the question of continuance of his marriage was an implicit issue in the first session, and he was perturbed by sexual responses he felt to attractive women he met, his deeply felt religious background (mainline Protestant) aggravated an already sensitive conscience. Values were a larger issue. In my notes I wrote that he "feels I have a clear cut set of moral values and fears being told to go do whatever he wants. I acknowledged having values but also said I didn't put them on people and he felt he didn't want that either." The wish in this obvious contradiction between recognizing my moral values and his fear of being told to do whatever he wants did not register with me at the time. Perhaps mindful of Jesus' statement about lusting in his heart, he felt that he had already committed nearly a mortal sin. Although Alfred was aware that I was Jewish, that issue did not emerge openly again for many sessions.

Assessment and Diagnosis

We agreed to meet once a week on a face-to-face basis. My initial diagnostic impression of Alfred, reinforced as therapy continued, was of a classical neurotic structure marked by good self-control, an overactive conscience, strong ego functions, effective work habits, and substantial accomplishments. His investment in his children and his marriage was what would be expected in this personality constellation, as was his ability to see others as people whose existence was beyond that to serve his needs. Although powerful pre-Oedipal issues dating to his first year of life eventually emerged in therapy, my view of his basic personality organization remained essentially unchanged. Early in therapy, his education, academic specialization in philosophy, and overall sophistication allowed him to dismiss some of my interpretations as coming from a textbook, although he eventually came to see that they did indeed fit him well. Because the importance of very early issues was not immediately apparent, I was probably premature in some of my Oedipal interpretations.

Client History

As we explored Alfred's current situation, he soon told Rachel of his entrance into therapy and she expressed her own thought of going into therapy to deal with her long-standing depression. This depression and her emotional and sexual withdrawal were coincident with the birth of their first child. This discussion opened several themes. They perceived their respective parents as critical and demanding, people who neither Alfred nor Rachel felt they could quite please. This apparently made each of them very susceptible to real or apparent slights or rejections, followed by a tendency toward withdrawal, depressive affect, and self-blame. Whenever I made inquiries in therapy, Alfred quite readily heard this as criticism. Before we reached the 20th session, we agreed to meet twice a week, and sometime afterward he agreed to try the couch. I suggested that this would help because he could not see my face and be overly influenced by my perceived or actual facial expressions.

The complex nature of his early experiences of closeness to his mother, interrupted by his father's return from service overseas, became a dominant theme. Over the course of therapy the early image of his mother's warmth gave way to a greater realization of her emotional coolness compounded by a classical Oedipal struggle with his father to whom he also turned for support and affection. His father seemed present but not emotionally expressive, even at times of severe grief. Raised with a typical midwestern stance of "boys don't cry," asking for help was a matter of shame and embarrassment for Alfred. Similarly, making clear his needs and wishes to Rachel (and eventually to me) was difficult. His religious upbringing was Calvinist, which seems to have reinforced his self-critical tendencies, although at the time of his therapy he had a more Lutheran stance that he summarized as "everyone sins, so do your best."

Treatment Process

We directly explored conflicting loyalties between several pairs of people and I directly raised my being Jewish. Admitting to being exposed to the usual prejudices that he probably absorbed to some degree, he also confessed to a quiet admiration and respect. Criticism cut him deeply yet he admired my presenting an early draft of some book chapters (eventually, Lovinger, 1984) to a faculty colloquium and my listening openly and nondefensively to the frank criticism I received. Of course, in a subsequent session typical stereotypes of Jews emerged, and ambivalent feelings and perceptions emerged in subsequent sessions as well.

Alfred's relationship with his wife showed some improvement rather quickly and then he had to face his own reluctance to respond fully to this change, motivated by unacceptable desires for revenge and even deeper difficulties in emotional responsiveness. About 100 sessions into the more than 250 that comprised Alfred's therapy, we came to his "secret," that he could not love the other person enough to be what he or she needed and this was his core defect. This was eventually understood to derive from a little boy's inability to "cure" his mother's depression over her husband's missing-in-action status. This emotional equation of his failure was likely reinforced by the Calvinistic nature of his early religious indoctrination.

Religious themes emerged over the course of therapy. In an early session, he reported having read a selection in church about David's replacement of Saul. David was described as handsome and ruddy, which also fit his son. A group of associations referred to killing Goliath, the murder of Uriah, and his being his mother and grandmother's favorite when his father was missing in action. I made the obvious Oedipal link. Anger, defiance, and submission to male authority issues developed and were recurrent issues through much of Alfred's therapy. A couple of months later, a dream about a work associate somewhat his senior named Joseph was connected to Joseph and his brothers. Paralleling the biblical story, I interpreted this as expressing his desire to be assertive as well as his fear of displacement.

Around the 40th session, his reluctance to disclose in therapy came into focus, as he feared humiliation related to an experience of conversion in graduate school, where he accepted Jesus as his personal savior. Acceptance of conversion would lead to some unnamed terrifying recognition. In the following session, he related his dream of being in the army and dealing with a rebellion. Cornered in a building, all his ammunition was exhausted, and he was hiding in a room. He heard noises outside that he feared were rebels trying to break in, but instead a tall, super-powerful savior entered. He appreciated the rescue but resented the implication that he was inadequate. By this point, Alfred was beginning to do his own interpretive work in therapy, and he identified the "savior" as both his father and me. Conversion would make him "a new man," but he did not deserve it. The concept of the savior originated in the Old Testament as the *mashiach* or "anointed one" and was carried forward into the New Testament, and the "new man" appeared in the letters of St. Paul, with which he was well acquainted. Alfred's conflict between wanting help and fearing the loss of independence, wanting to identify with his father (and me) but fearing something terrible, became more sharply delineated. The conflict between his loyalty to his family and his Protestant background and his attraction to me as a Jew who heard and accepted him surfaced several times. Late in November of that year when I announced a plan to raise my per session fee, he agreed willingly. Later in the session, he disclosed stereotypes of Jews as pushy and aggressive and reported a dream of being in New York City in which a cab driver takes financial advantage of a friend.

As he became more experienced and sophisticated about a dynamic approach to psychotherapy, his expression of some difficult issues became more subtle. After about one year of therapy, he was better able to communicate not only with his wife but also with his parents. Nevertheless, in one session he reported that the improvement with his parents was moving at a "galatial" (sic) pace. I inquired about Galatians, and he recalled that in Jesus all are free: men and women, Greek and Jew, bond and free. Although I interpreted this in terms of other themes that seemed more significant, in retrospect this may have expressed a wish for a closer affiliation with me that would have been easier had I converted to Christianity.

The complex nature of Alfred's difficulties with relationships was opened to deeper scrutiny after the first year of therapy had passed. The first year of his marriage to Rachel was felt to be very satisfactory, as was the first year with a previous girlfriend. Suspecting this pattern hid the imprint of an earlier life experience, I found that there was a year between his birth and the report of his father's MIA status. When I delineated this pattern, it had a considerable effect on Alfred's view of himself and left him feeling like a puppet. I suggested that he has the pieces now and we were working to understand them. He left feeling more hopeful about his relationship to Rachel.

Some degree of humor began to appear. Alfred teased me about my macho, four-wheel off-road vehicle and then talked about wanting to change some troublesome behaviors. I replied that I thought Christians emphasized changes in the heart and we both laughed. At another time when the campus was plagued by serious electrical outages, he asked me if I was out of power in the Psychology Center, where I was director. I replied, "No . . . but we don't have any electricity." Again, we both laughed. As we continued to work, there were steady improvements in his relationships, especially with his wife. The embedded criticisms he carried with him decreased but did not end. Religious concerns, as a vehicle for his self-disparagement, waned, and the important figures and experiences behind those feelings came into sharper focus.

Alfred's self-critical attitudes were a recurrent theme. Nearly halfway through our therapy he challenged me, asking if there was anything that I criticized him for, in my mind. I thought that clients' perceptions of their therapists are a complex mixture of their projections and accurate perceptions and that mystifying clients is rarely if ever useful, especially when a solid therapeutic alliance has been established. I affirmed that the way he had handled an administrative matter in his job that he reported about some time previously felt shoddy to me. He felt relieved and four sessions later he reported the unbidden thought "You're really a pretty good person after all." It seemed there was an increased sense of self-worth after hearing a legitimate criticism from me, which dispelled a vague sense of dread, especially about being exposed.

One of the most explicit instances of the appearance and use of religious materials occurred about 10 sessions later. Alfred reported, with some discomfort, a Bible study session at church. The pastor discussed chapter 7 from Acts, which involved the stoning of Stephen. Stephen was a Hellenized Jew who talked to a Jewish mob about freedom from the law and he is stoned. Alfred expressed a poignant sense of the beginning divergence of two valid traditions and commented that the pastor's position was the standard Christian one of freedom from the Law. Alfred had the uncomfortable thought that he might have this idea to please me. As we explored this further, I thought that the actual content of this chapter in Acts might be important to know and I took the Anchor Bible edition of Acts (Fitzmyer, 1982) from a shelf and scanned the chapter. My clinical notes show

> Stephen reviews Jewish history from Abraham to Moses to the prophets and accuses Jews of murdering the Righteous One. He is stoned and Saul approved (Paul). He felt he identified with Stephen but I suggested that I was Stephen saying unpleasant truths and he [Alfred] did not want to change. He agreed that was also true.

A further theme, not interpreted, may be Alfred's sense of the essential gap between us as a function of Jewish–Christian history, of which he was cognizant.

Subsequent sessions were emotionally flat, and in retrospect, I think I missed an important theme. It would be an error to characterize his lack of productivity as resistance although it had that character; rather it represented my failure to be adequately attuned to his mood and implicit message. Just a few sessions later, I had an opportunity to repair this breach. The session began with the flat tone that had recently developed. He began with some dreams that led to his conflict in which he wished for something from me but to take it would change him. "Like grace?" I inquired and that fit. Alfred talked about how grace is given freely yet (citing a theologian) people want grace without accepting the obligations of living a grace-filled life. I contrasted the contradiction of freely given grace, contingent on obligation, which surprised Alfred. Although I had not directly dealt with the rupture in empathic understanding of a few sessions before, this seemed to have repaired it as at the end of the session he remarked that he could not believe that I could listen to him for so long and patiently. In the session after the Christmas holiday, he was more upbeat as his relationship with Rachel continued to improve but he felt that change was something he had to do himself. In view of the repetitive religious themes being expressed, I asked about his theology and he described three views of God: as a benign helper that does not take away his initiative; a distant, barely available or helpful God; or a Calvinistic God making demands one cannot meet. Drawing the parallel between the second view and therapy, I noted there was no view of God—or me as a collaborative partner, and this surprised Alfred.

Two sessions later, Alfred focused more intensely on not getting his needs met in therapy but he did not allow himself to get these needs met. As we explored his fear of shame and ridicule, plus his anger at the expected deprivation, he was able to sense the child within that he had to protect or he would dissolve, as if without a skeleton. I replied that he had to develop a too-early maturity to compensate for his mother's deficits and called this a brilliant solution. Alfred felt this was devastatingly accurate, but I remarked on his lack of compassion for himself. This appeared to delineate a major characterological dimension.

Outcomes

Religiously related themes continued to appear in session, sometimes in dreams, sometimes in church-related activities, and sometimes in professional activities. About 6 months after the sessions just described, Alfred's efforts to find a higher level administrative position finally paid off and he was offered a deanship at a small but prestigious college in Oregon. This had many advantages, including being somewhat closer to both their families. Both he and Rachel were very pleased, although it meant they would sever many of the good relationships they had developed while at the university. Two sessions later he reported the wish, with Rachel's approval, to help financially someone at their church take a course but he did not want anyone to know because he would feel mortified. He did not want to disclose this to me nor did he have many associations. I now think that, at one time, his philosophical training put him in contact with the teachings of Maimonides, the preeminent medieval Jewish philosopher. It was Maimonides who described the concept of the ladder of charity and one of the higher levels is to help someone without being asked and without identifying the giver. Although this was never established, given the paucity of his associations, it seemed plausible and suggested that he may have made a considerable unconscious identification with my values.

The differences in background, upbringing, and religious affiliation surfaced from time to time. I think that the Jewish roots of my attitude that life is to be lived and enjoyed in the here-and-now, indirectly influenced therapy as I attempted to modify Alfred's negative self-image but also to get him to own his personal contributions to the issues that beset his life. Having the dean's position offered to him represented a way to start over and to draw closer to his wife, as their mutual support in a new environment would be very helpful to each other.

DANNY

Client Characteristics

I began seeing Danny when he was 9 years old. He had been in treatment for about 2 years before he was transferred to me.

Presenting Problems

Danny was an angry youngster with serious learning problems and difficulties with impulsivity. For about 2 years in once-a-week treatment we worked on the anxiety he chronically experienced. Any mention of his internal states made him quite angry with me, for as is typical with middle childhood children, they experience interpretations and explanations as accusations of being a less than adequate child. As a result, Danny kept away from discussing anything he considered a secret. I did not even know that he struggled with the issues of having a Catholic mother and Protestant father with whom he went to church, each to their own, but not as a family. During a session with his mother and myself he lashed out at me with a swinging punch as he was leaving the room. His mother was mortified but we continued to discuss this event and other issues. She wanted him to continue in treatment with me and he wanted to leave. I supported this child's need to leave. She finally accepted this. I did not hear from the family for about a year. I received a call form Danny's mother telling me that Danny asked to come back to talk to me. Once I had ascertained that this request came from the child, I agreed to see him for one session. I took Danny to my office, which surprised him as he expected to go back into the playroom. For the session we talked about how angry he was the last time I had seen him and what had made him so angry. He mentioned that I had talked about all those wiggly feelings he had inside which made him very upset, not only because he had those feelings but also because I had not labeled them as anxiety and because I was right about them. He also felt I had been saying that he was not a good kid and that he was very different from everyone else I knew. Some things were clarified during this session, and he reiterated his wish to come back.

Assessment and Diagnosis

Danny's having hit me at the end of our last session a year previously was a repetitive, emotional, and moral theme for him for a long time. He began to address the anger that was part and parcel of most areas of functioning for him. The anger was not the problem as he felt he could come in and see me and talk about his angry feelings and punch on the punching bag to get rid of the feelings. Rather it was the fantasies he generated, which were about doing away with the person involved. This was very difficult for him because he thought it was morally wrong to think such things. My theistic views came into play around this issue, because for me thinking is not the same as doing as it was in his religious views from his mother. We worked on sorting out the difference between the two concepts. As he slowly understood that his fantasies were the result of his confusing the thought with the deed, he could allow himself the pleasure of his fantasies without the fear he would express the content of them. At about the same time he began playing his father's drums, and using the drum I had in the playroom as well. This further aided the resolution of his dilemma as he could express his feelings through the rhythms he played out on the drum.

For both of us, diagnosis means an understanding of what are the major factors operating in the dynamics and character structure of the child or adult we are working with. This understanding changes over time as the patient changes. Danny seemed to have a basically neurotic structure. Although in the first phase of therapy his anxiety led to some aggressive acting out, he was able to recognize this was wrong, that he responded to internal pressures, and that he needed help in dealing with his problems rather than just blaming others.

Client History and Treatment Process

During this period in treatment, Danny began to periodically raise moral and ethical issues. For example, he came into session, and told me about his biracial friend who had asked a girl to go to the movies with him. The mother said she could not go with this youngster, but Danny knew she had gone to the movies with other boys. Danny wondered whether the girl's mother refused permission because his friend came from those people who were "slaves once?" Danny and I got into a long discussion about prejudice and the morality of it and how angry it made him for his friend and then what he could do about it. He also moved to talking about his sense of difference from others—mostly in negative terms. Danny also expressed much anger toward his parents, especially his mother whom he experienced as not hearing him or even understanding him. Weeks of sessions followed as he struggled with his difference from others and his parents seeming insensitivity to him. School was an added factor, given his hearing loss in one ear and his difficulties with the learning process. Slowly he sorted out his feelings about what he could and could not say in response to the assault he experiences from others. He also began to process how he is like and different from others and where he belongs. The flow of the sessions enabled him to look at these issues more directly than he had previously, but in the process his anxiety was aroused. As a result he moved toward me and then distanced himself in the relationship, almost as though he were looking for a comfortable place for himself in relation to me. Shortly thereafter, Danny began raising the issue of our religious differences and what being Jewish meant.

Starting with issues of celebrating holidays—which ones he celebrated and which ones I celebrated—he began to look at the differences between us. Although this was not a week-by-week discussion, he would raise the religious issue as he struggled with both of his parents. At one point he came into a session and told me about having watched all the presidential debates. He had come to the conclusion that Clinton was correct in all his positions, and that if he could vote, he would vote for Clinton, in spite of the fact that both parents were staunch Republicans. In a sense then, he was using our religious differences to work through issues of separation and differentiation. I also think that my religious difference underscored how differently I responded to him: different from his parents and teachers. Danny began to wonder about what made for the differences.

One of the first religious differences he questioned was why Jews did not believe in Jesus and did it mean they did not believe in God. I could find no easy way to deal with these questions in a more traditionally therapeutic manner and so I dealt with it in a straightforward cognitive manner. Although I explained that Jews certainly believed in God, they just did not believe in Jesus, this was a very hard concept for him to process. We came back to these questions repeatedly during the remaining course of treatment. Although he could verbally express my response to him on this issue, it was clear he could not understand it fully. At other times, when he was angry with me, or needed more distance in our relationship he would angrily attack through statements regarding the lack of belief in God by the Jews. At other points during sessions he would present me with scenarios questioning how I would respond if the Nazis would come back and do a variety of atrocious things to the Jews. He would become outraged if I did not immediately fight back. He did not tolerate processing a response or trying to figure out the best way of handling the situation.

Outcomes

Danny used the religious differences between us in the service of understanding and working through his sense of difference from family, friends, and peers. Although this was the predominant issue in later stages of treatment, he was also curious as to how someone so different from himself could understand him better than his family with whom he lived. This was a real existential issue for this young man. The use of religious differences, at this point in Danny's life, was in the service of resolving personal issues, and not for religious reasons. In contrast, I briefly present the case of a 7-year-old who also expressed religious themes in the service of emotional issues.

JODY

Client Characteristics

Jody, a 7-year-old, the second of two children, was adopted at birth. She had a naturally born sister some 8 years older who was reported to be functioning well.

Presenting Problem

The parents reported noncompliance with parental requests and demands. Maternal requests were either ignored or done at a very slow pace. Jody was reported to be functioning satisfactorily at school.

Assessment and Diagnosis

For reasons that will become clear, Jody was understood to have an attachment disorder. She and her mother seemed to have very different temperamental styles, expressed in their mutual pace of activity and response. Jody appeared very angry with her mother, who was experienced as unresponsive to Jody's needs for a slower pace and greater patience.

Client History and Treatment Process

Some months after therapy had begun she came into the playroom, took all the furniture and people out of the dollhouse and jumbled everything together in front of the dollhouse. She then rummaged through the mess she had created and found an adult female doll, a cradle, and a baby. She then rummaged through my collection of animals and chose a ferocious-looking tiger. She placed this entire collection in front of the mess in front of the dollhouse. She had trouble deciding where to place the female doll that she labeled as the mother and finally decided on placing her around the corner of the house at the left side, out of sight. The baby was placed in the cradle at the front of the house toward the right side. The tiger was placed off in the distance but visible from the front of the house. She was then ready to play out her theme. Mother was around the corner hanging up the wash, the baby Jesus was in his cradle and the tiger was slowly coming toward the house to get the baby Jesus. As the tiger neared the house, it began to slink along so it could not be seen or captured. It reached the cradle, snatched the baby Jesus, ate him up, and ran away. Feeling remorse, the tiger came back to the house, threw the baby Jesus up, left him on the ground, and ran away. Mother then came from around the house to take care of the baby Jesus. This theme was repeated many times in the ensuing weeks.

When I discussed this scenario with the parents in a parent conference, Jody's father commented that Jody's theology left a lot to be desired. He clearly saw it as a problem with understanding the religious significance of the birth of Jesus. I, on the other hand, saw an emotional conundrum the child was expressing through the use of the religious issues. We will return to the meaning of this vignette shortly.

After the Christmas holidays, this theme was not repeated. Instead, Jody began playing with a set of anatomically correct baby dolls. She mothered them throughout the sessions. Some time later during a session, she played out getting a babysitter to take care of these twins she had as she and her husband wanted to go out. The sitter came; mother gave her instructions about the care of the baby and mother left. The sitter did some of the mothering Jody had enacted, but then the sitter took the clothes off the baby, put the babies in a roasting pan and roasted them in the oven. When the parents returned, the sitter told the parents the babies were good and were now asleep. The sitter served the parents dinner . . . roasted baby.

These two play enactments carry a similar theme although one is couched in religious terms and the other is not. They both express this youngster's issues with adoption and her relationship with her mother. The play enactment begins with this youngster creating a mess in front of the dollhouse. It seems plausible to hypothesize that the mess represents the internal mess and confusion Jody experiences both within her home and within her head when she thinks about this. There is an assumption here that the play of a child is a reflection of the thought processes within a child's head. As they cannot deal with thinking processes internally, playing them out where children can visualize their thoughts is the next best thing. Eventually children do learn to think in their heads, but they need to have achieved concrete thinking, in Piagetian terms, before they can do this. One must remember that the acquisition of this skill is a slowly developing achievement. Jody started her play with a sense of confusion that she slowly works through as the play develops. She does have a mother in the sequence, but the mother is placed outside the action.

At a psychoanalytic conference in Michigan, Umberto Nagera, chief of the adolescent service at the University of Michigan Hospital, discussed the complex issues adoptive children deal with regarding their adoption. They have two mothers to contend with, the reality of the adoptive mother and the fantasy of the birth mother.

It is never clear which mother is being described either verbally or in play. They may even be confused in the child's own thoughts about them. More likely, the birth mother becomes the idealized mother while the adoptive mother can become the less than adequate mother of reality. This is one of the dilemmas in understanding Jody's depiction of her mother. In any case, both mothers in this play were unavailable. Not only was mother not around but the baby was left all alone; no one was caring for it. I would hypothesize that the story of there being no room at the inn, and the birth of Jesus in the stable was translated by this child as being alone. This also fits with her feelings that there was no room in her family, in her relationship with her mother for her or her slower style of functioning.

With no one to care for the baby Jesus, he was vulnerable to all kinds of "bad" things happening. At first the baby Jesus was stolen. Being stolen is one of the explanations young adoptive children develop to explain why their birth mother gave them up for adoption. Unable to grasp or understand how a mommy could give them away, they assume that they were stolen from their "good, birth mommies" by their "bad" adoptive mothers. For Jody this conceptualization did some important things: (a) it preserved herself as a "good baby" through her identification with the baby Jesus; (b) it established her adoptive mother as the "bad" one; (c) it affirmed her lack of identification with her adoptive family; and (d) it allowed herself to be identified with the fantasized "good/perfect" family.

In spite of the identification with the perfect baby Jesus, this approach did not save her from being devoured. No matter how many times this child played out the original scenario, she could neither alter the ending nor benefit from her identification with goodness. Thus, when the holiday season ended and some months had passed, she came back to the same theme and expressed her feelings in a very brutal, uncaring, unsympathetic manner. I do think her brutal expression of the theme represents her experience of her mother's treatment of her as well as her increasing loss of sense of self. In her original play, the tiger first ate, but then threw up the baby Jesus unharmed. In the second play sequence the babies were roasted and served up to the parents. There was no saving of the babies. Interpretively one could suggest that this child is sending a message to her birth mother, such as, look what you have done while at the same time expressing how hopeless things seem to her and that because things can be no different for her, she is paying everybody back.

Outcomes

Attachment disorders are quite difficult to treat and Jody's parents did not wait for therapy to take effect, removing her at the end of the school year. Although here too, there was a difference between the therapist and the patient in religious affiliation, Jody was developmentally much younger than Danny and thus this factor did not emerge in therapy in any detectable fashion. In Judaism, although the Bible records stories of the childhood of major figures, these childhood narratives do not have the same place in the religious education or imagination of Jewish children. I think I found Jody's graphic use of the baby dolls startling and off-putting. Whether this countertransference reaction had any effect on therapy I do not know, although I could not detect any.

THERAPISTS' COMMENTS

When children have a usable religious base to express their internal conflicts, these religious ideas as well as other learnings become drawn into the unconscious workings of their dilemmas. For both of these youngsters religion was brought into the session as an aid in the resolution of individual conflicts each was dealing with. However, when religion, or any other experience does not help in the resolution of the issue, the child will go on to try out other means of solution. This was obvious in the material presented on Jody. For Jody, the Jesus story was a convenient vehicle to express an issue that was deeply important to her—adoption and what that meant.

Jody's use of religious stories could have been used in treatment with anyone. It was not specific to the therapeutic relationship she developed with me. In fact, these religious overtones quickly disappeared from our dialogue when the problems she was struggling with did not readily resolve. She then went on to other ways of struggling with her concerns about being adopted.

Danny's use of religious differences between us was a vehicle to explore his sense of difference from others, but also his sameness, which would allow for further differentiation. Danny struggled with differentiation of himself from his family throughout the therapy. My representing a different "other" from all the "others" he came in contact with was very important to the treatment. One must remember that his questioning of the religious differences between the two of us did not occur until later in therapy when a solid relationship had been developed, and he could trust me to maintain the relationship with him even though he was challenging and testing me. Thus, my difference gave him the needed courage to face and accept his own differences, not only from me but also from his peers, his teachers, and his family.

I do think that the older the child is, the nearer she or he is likely to be to formal operations, hence the ability to think about experience not yet encountered is an important underpinning for the use of religious experience and understanding in the resolution of difficulties. The adolescent is only just beginning to be able to do this, whereas the younger child does not yet have this capacity.

Although many adults have at least some capacity to think symbolically, this is not always maintained when the person regresses deeply in the course of intense therapy, or suffers from a developmental arrest (Stolorow & Lachman, 1980) at the point they enter therapy. However, this was not the case with Danny or Alfred, both of whom had neurotic personality structures that could tolerate considerable emotional stress. By virtue of his intelligence, sophistication, educational background, therapeutic issues, and personal religious orientation, Alfred would have brought religious issues into any therapy where it was not actively discouraged. Because we lived in a relatively small community where we as therapists were relatively well known, and in particular where Alfred knew of his therapist's background and professional interests, religious issues were likely to be prominent in therapy—and so they were. The religious component of his personality organization allowed for a fuller engagement and resolution of his personal issues in therapy, and his experience of another person who respected and defended his integrity, even on religious issues, contributed to Alfred's recovery. Even when vulnerable in therapy, the therapist made no effort to "convert" him as Alfred might have expected from a Christian therapist (whether realistic or not).

It is plausible to assume that if the therapist and patient have similar backgrounds and similar values, therapy is likely to proceed more smoothly and produce a better outcome. At least with regard to religious issues, there is some evidence that such similarities may not necessarily lead to better outcomes (Propst et al, 1992). In the cases presented in this chapter, the differences were larger than would be typical with a patient–therapist dyad drawn from two different Christian denominations. For Danny and Alfred these differences, attended to by the therapists and responded to in therapy, may have helped resolve more fully certain of the issues both of them had and rather than be an obstacle to the therapy, these differences had a facilitating effect.

REFERENCES

Fitzmyer, J. A. (Ed.). (1982). *The Acts of the Apostles: A new translation with introduction and commentary*. Garden City, NY: Doubleday.

Hoge, D. R. (1996). Religion in America: The demographics of belief and affiliation. In E. P. Shafranske (Ed.), *Religion and the clinical practice of psychology*. Washington, DC: American Psychological Association.

Lovinger, R. J. (1984). *Working with religious issues in therapy*. New York: Jason Aronson.

Miller, L., & Lovinger, R. J. (2000). Psychotherapy with conservative and reform Jews. In P. S. Richards & A. E. Bergin (Eds.), *Handbook of psychotherapy and religious diversity* (pp. 259–286). Washington, DC: American Psychological Association.

Propst, L. R., Ostrom, R., Watkins, P., Dean, T., & Mashburn, D. (1992). Comparative efficacy of religious and nonreligious cognitive-behavioral therapy for the treatment of clinical depression in religious individuals. *Journal of Consulting and Clinical Psychology, 60,* 94–103.

Stolorow, R., & Lachman, F. (1980) *The psychoanalysis of developmental arrests*. New York: International Universities Press.

V

CONCLUSION

17

THEISTIC PERSPECTIVES IN PSYCHOTHERAPY: CONCLUSIONS AND RECOMMENDATIONS

P. SCOTT RICHARDS AND ALLEN E. BERGIN

We hope that you have found the diversity of case reports described in this book fascinating and helpful. We were impressed by the many similarities among the cases, as well as the differences. We hope they have given you additional ideas about how you might apply theistic spiritual perspectives in your own work.

In this chapter we briefly consider how we think theistic spiritual perspectives and interventions uniquely influenced the processes and outcomes of these cases. We then discuss some objections and concerns that have been raised about integrating theistic perspectives into mainstream psychotherapy. We conclude by offering some recommendations for those who wish to incorporate theistic perspectives into their work.

INFLUENCE OF THEISTIC PERSPECTIVES ON THEORETICAL FRAMEWORKS

There was considerable diversity in the theoretical frameworks and treatment approaches described in the case reports. In Table 17.1 one can see

TABLE 17.1
Incorporation of Theistic Perspectives Into Therapists' Theoretical
Orientations and Approaches

Therapist (Case)	Integrative combinations	Theistic theoretical assumptions	Spiritual interventions used
Slife, Mitchell, & Whoolery (Laura)	Community-theistic traditions	God exists. Moral framework for therapy. Spiritual inspiration for client. Faith and spirituality important for healing. Altruism, agency, and holism important guiding assumptions.	Encouraged client to pray. Encouraged client to read spiritual readings. Spiritual journaling. Spiritual discussions. Spiritual exploration in group setting occurred. Client participated in acts of altruistic service as part of treatment program. Client was taught to listen to the "Source" (God, the Spirit) to help guide her life decisions.
Hardman, Berrett, & Richards (Jan)	Cognitive-psychodynamic-theistic traditions	God exists. Moral framework for therapy. Spiritual inspiration for client. Faith and spiritual experiences important for healing.	Encouraged client to pray. Encouraged client to read scriptures and other spiritual readings. Spiritual journaling. Spiritual discussions. Spiritual exploration group. Therapist privately prayed for client.
Miller (Renee & Ilana)	Interpersonal-theistic traditions	God exists. Moral framework for therapy (Spirit of Truth). Spiritual inspiration for client. Faith and spiritual experiences important for healing.	Spiritual discussions in group. Discussed and affirmed spiritual and moral truths (universals).
Krejci (Mary & John)	Humanistic-cognitive-theistic traditions	God exists. Moral framework for therapy (virtues such as forgiveness, love, tolerance). Faith important for healing.	Encouraged clients to forgive. Encouraged client to read scriptures for religious stories and images about forgiveness. Clients prayed for their spouse and with each other. Altruistic service to each other.

continues

TABLE 17.1 *(Continued)*

Therapist (Case)	Integrative combinations	Theistic theoretical assumptions	Spiritual interventions used
			Participated in Bible study with each other. Spiritual discussions during therapy.
Dobbins (Kathy)	Cognitive-psychodynamic-theistic traditions	God exists. Moral framework for therapy. Spiritual inspiration for client. Faith and spiritual experiences important for healing.	Encouraged client to pray for new interpretations of past painful experiences. Encouraged client to read scriptures. Spiritual discussions. "Putting off the old man" technique to control drinking. "Praying through" technique to emotionally work through pain from childhood. Encouraging self-forgiveness.
Rabinowitz (multiple cases)	Psychodynamic-cognitive-theistic traditions	God exists. Moral framework for therapy. Faith important for healing.	Encouraged clients to read scriptures and other spiritual readings. Spiritual discussions. Cognitive restructuring of dysfunctional religious beliefs. Interpreted religious themes in a psychodynamic framework. Encouraged involvement in religious community.
Sperry (Gwen)	Biopsychosocial: medication-psychodynamic-cognitive-psychoeducational-social-theistic traditions	God exists. Moral framework for therapy. Faith and spiritual experiences important for healing.	Encouraged client to pray, focus, and meditate. Spiritual journaling. Spiritual discussions. Cognitive restructuring of dysfunctional religious beliefs. Encouraged client to participate in religious community.
Shafranske (Joan)	Psychodynamic-theistic traditions	God exists. Moral framework for therapy.	Spiritual discussions. Interpreted religious themes in a psychodynamic framework.

continues

TABLE 17.1 *(Continued)*

Therapist (Case)	Integrative combinations	Theistic theoretical assumptions	Spiritual interventions used
Cook (Grace)	Multicultural-person centered-theistic traditions	God exists. Spiritual inspiration for client. Faith and spiritual experiences important for healing.	Encouraged client to pray, meditate, and engage in spiritual imagery alone and during therapy sessions. Encouraged client to read scriptures and other spiritual readings. Spiritual journaling. Spiritual discussions. Therapist privately prayed for client.
Rayburn (Paul)	Cognitive-psychodynamic-theistic traditions	God exists. Moral framework for therapy (e.g., equality of men and women). Spiritual inspiration for client. Faith and spiritual experiences important for healing.	Encouraged client to pray. Spiritual discussions. Challenged unhealthy religious beliefs with cognitive therapy techniques.
West (Matthew)	Humanistic-theistic traditions	God exists. Moral framework for therapy. Spiritual inspiration for client. Faith and spiritual experiences important for healing.	Discussed theological concepts. Made references to scripture. Spiritual "silences;" feeling connected spirituality with each other. Encouraged forgiveness. Helped clients live congruently with their spiritual values. Self-disclosed spiritual beliefs or experiences.
Nielsen (Aisha)	REBT-theistic	God exists. Moral framework for therapy. Faith and scriptural rationales important for healing.	Rational disputations of irrational religious beliefs. Used scriptures to challenge irrational beliefs.

continues

TABLE 17.1 (Continued)

Therapist (Case)	Integrative combinations	Theistic theoretical assumptions	Spiritual interventions used
Hedayat-Diba (Mrs. A)	Psychodynamic-theistic traditions	God exists. Moral framework for therapy. Spiritual inspiration for client. Faith and spiritual experiences important for healing.	Discussed spiritual experiences and concepts. Self-disclosed spiritual beliefs or experiences.
Johnson (Gary)	REBT-theistic traditions	God exists. Moral framework for therapy that emphasizes tolerance and love and downplays specific behavioral prescriptions about morality or sexual behavior.	Religious and spiritual assessment. Engaged in REBT disputations of client's depressogenic religious beliefs about what it means if he is "gay."
Lovinger & Lovinger (Alfred, Danny, Jody)	Psychodynamic-theistic traditions	God exists. Moral framework for therapy.	Spiritual discussions. Interpreted religious themes in a psychodynamic framework.

Note. REBT = Rational emotive behavior therapy.

that the theoretical traditions that the therapists combined in their integrative approaches are (a) psychodynamic-theistic ($N = 4$), (b) psychodynamic-cognitive-theistic ($N = 4$), (c) rational emotive behavior therapy (REBT) - theistic ($N = 2$), (d) cognitive-theistic ($N = 1$), (e) interpersonal-theistic ($N = 1$), (f) multicultural-person-centered-theistic ($N = 1$), biopsychosocial-theistic ($N = 1$), and (g) community-theistic ($N = 1$).

The therapists also differed in the manner and degree to which they have incorporated theistic perspectives into their work. Some of them used theistic perspectives in an implicit, minimal fashion and seemed to rely quite heavily on traditional mainstream perspectives and interventions (e.g., Shafranske and Lovinger and Lovinger). Other therapists integrated theistic perspectives and interventions into their approach in a much more explicit and encompassing manner (e.g., Dobbins, Cook, Slife and colleagues, and Rabinowitz), and others adopted more of a middle-ground approach (e.g., Rayburn; Miller; Sperry; and Hardman, Berrett, and Johnson).

We think it is problematic to attempt to pass judgment about which approach is best because we think that the manner and degree to which theistic perspectives and interventions may appropriately come to the forefront during therapy depends on a variety of things. These include clients' presenting problems and issues, religious backgrounds, and current spiritual orientations. In addition, therapists must feel free to integrate theistic perspectives and interventions in the manner and degree to which they feel comfortable. Therapists' theoretical orientations, religious backgrounds and beliefs, and level of training and expertise in religious and spiritual issues may all influence their decision about how fully they wish to integrate theistic perspectives.

Although we have described our own theistic psychotherapy orientation and approach in considerable detail in chapter 1, and in *A Spiritual Strategy for Counseling and Psychotherapy* (Richards & Bergin, 1997), we wish to emphasize here that we do not think therapists must incorporate all of our approach to be regarded as theistic psychotherapists. In our view, counselors and psychotherapists who believe in God in a manner that is generally consistent with the theistic world religions, and whose theistic beliefs influence their theoretical perspective and therapeutic approach in an appreciable way, are theistic psychotherapists. If a therapist responds "yes" to all or most of the following questions, then by our definition it would be appropriate to refer to her or him as a theistic psychotherapist:

1. Do you believe in God or a Supreme Being?
2. Do you believe that human beings are creations of God?
3. Does your theistic worldview influence your view of human nature and personality theory?
4. Do your theistic beliefs influence your ideas about human dysfunction and therapeutic change?
5. Do your theistic beliefs have any impact on the manner in which you relate, assess, or intervene with your clients?

Most psychotherapists are not accustomed to using the term *theistic* in descriptions of their therapeutic orientation, perhaps in part because this has not previously been offered as an option for mainstream professionals. We would like to offer it as one now. Although many contemporary psychotherapists profess to reject philosophical assumptions such as atheistic-naturalism, determinism, reductionism, atomism, mechanism, materialism, ethical hedonism, and ethical relativism, they still often profess theoretical allegiance to mainstream traditions that are grounded in these assumptions (Jensen & Bergin, 1988; Richards & Bergin, 1997; Slife, 2003; Slife & Williams, 1995). On the basis of surveys that have shown that sizable percentages of psychotherapists are members of one of the theistic world religions, believe in God, and use spiritual interventions in their professional practices

(Ball & Goodyear, 1991; Bergin & Jensen, 1990; Richards & Potts, 1995; Shafranske, 2000; Shafranske & Malony, 1990), we hypothesize that many therapists might appropriately be called theistic psychotherapists. At the least, perhaps they may wish to include the term *theistic* in describing their approach (e.g., I am a theistic-psychodynamic psychotherapist).

Table 17.1 reveals that for many of the therapists who contributed to this book, the label theistic psychotherapist may be appropriate, for all of them to one degree or another accept at least some theistic theoretical assumptions and interventions. For example, virtually all of the therapists believe that God exists and that human beings are the creations of God. These assumptions sometimes explicitly, but most often implicitly, influence how they conceptualize and relate to their clients. Most, if not all of them, reject ethical relativism and to one degree or another use a moral framework to guide their therapeutic work. Although the therapists undoubtedly differ with regard to the specific moral values they endorse, all of them seem to generally adhere to moral values and principles that are grounded in and consistent with those of the theistic religious traditions.

Many of the therapists also either explicitly or implicitly affirmed their belief that faith and spirituality are important resources for healing. Several therapists also discussed the role of inspiration and other spiritual experiences in therapy. Some of them personally sought and/or encouraged their clients to seek spiritual guidance and inspiration in the healing and recovery process. Table 17.1 also reveals that almost all of the therapists used spiritual interventions that assume that God exists and intervenes to assist human beings.

Although counselors and psychotherapists who do not personally believe in God will undoubtedly not wish to refer to themselves as theistic psychotherapists, we think that it is possible for therapists from diverse perspectives, including those with Eastern, transpersonal, and humanistic spiritual beliefs—and even those who regard themselves as agnostic or atheistic—to accept many aspects of our theistic spiritual strategy. In our view, therapists are practicing consistent with our theistic psychotherapy approach if they seek to accept, affirm, and use the healing potential of their clients' faith in God, personal spirituality, and religious community. As we expressed elsewhere:

> We hope that professionals who find such perspectives [theistic ones] and recommendations [using various spiritual interventions] objectionable will not 'throw the baby out with the bath water' and conclude that there is nothing of value for them in this book. Those who feel negatively about a specific perspective or intervention can certainly disregard it. They may still find considerable value in the overall strategy we describe, and it should assist them in working more sensitively and effectively with their theistic clients. (Richards & Bergin, 1997, p. 16)

INFLUENCE OF THEISTIC PERSPECTIVES ON THERAPY PROCESSES AND OUTCOMES

Table 17.2 summarizes the variety of ways that the theistic perspectives of the clients and therapists influenced the processes and outcomes of psychotherapy in these cases. It was clear in the case reports that theistic perspectives had some influence, and sometimes a major influence, on virtually every aspect of therapy, including presenting problems, therapeutic relationships, therapeutic goals, assessment and diagnosis, therapeutic interventions, and evaluation of therapy outcomes.

The therapists' theistic beliefs influenced the ways they viewed and related to their clients. Most of the therapists viewed their clients as creations of God who were of great spiritual worth and potential. These views were not usually explicitly discussed in the case reports, but they were communicated implicitly and subtly in the accepting, caring, and affirming manner in which the therapists described and related to their clients.

Because of their theistic beliefs, the therapists sought to create a spiritually safe and open relationship with their clients. There were several ways therapists did this. First, many of the therapists informed their clients that it was appropriate and even desirable to discuss spiritual issues during therapy by explicitly mentioning this. Second, all of the therapists showed respect and interest when their clients brought up spiritual topics during therapy. Third, some of the therapists inquired about spiritual issues during the assessment phase of therapy and thereby implicitly communicated to their clients that such topics were open to discussion.

All of the therapists sought to respond respectfully and sensitively to their clients' religious and spiritual beliefs rather than discounting or pathologizing them. In some cases, the therapists felt it was necessary to interpret or even raise questions regarding the doctrinal soundness, or mental health consequences, of clients' religious beliefs, but they always respectfully affirmed their clinical relevance. In many cases, the therapists recognized and honored the healing potential of their clients' spiritual beliefs and practices by using them as a resource during therapy.

The majority of therapists adopted an ecumenical therapeutic stance with their clients. This was appropriate because most of the therapists worked with clients whose religious affiliation differed from their own (e.g., Jewish therapists working with Christian clients, a Roman Catholic therapist working with a Protestant client, and a Quaker therapist working with a Muslim [Sufi] client). Several therapists did adopt a denominational therapeutic stance with clients from their own faith (e.g., Dobbins; Hardman et al.; and Shafranske). Without exception, the therapists avoided proselyting and did not seek to convert clients to their own religious tradition.

The therapists' theistic beliefs also influenced them to include consideration of religious and spiritual dimensions of functioning as they assessed

TABLE 17.2
Influence of Theistic Perspectives on Therapy Processes and Outcomes

Therapist (Case)	Influence of client's faith	Influence of therapist's faith	Differences in case without theistic perspectives
Slife, Mitchell, & Whoolery (Laura)	The client's growing faith and trust in "the Source" as a guide in her life, as well as her acceptance and internalization of theistically based values such as honesty, altruism, responsibility, community, and service, played a central role in her recovery and change.	The treatment team's faith in the Source (God) as a valid source of guidance in adolescents' lives, as well as their belief in theistically based moral values, totally shaped the treatment philosophy and approach. Their faith helped the client believe in and internalize these beliefs and values, which helped her change her life in a positive manner.	Values such as honesty, community, and responsibility could still have been taught, but they would not have been anchored in a spiritual perspective that such values are universal and emanate from God. Also, the client would not have learned that "the Source" could be a reliable guide.
Hardman, Berrett, & Richards (Jan)	The client's faith and spiritual experiences reassured her of God's love and strengthened her eternal spiritual sense of identity and worth. These assurances served as an anchor during the challenging recovery process—gave her the courage to take risks in therapy and to face her pain from the past (e.g., abuse).	The therapist's faith in God led him to encourage client to read scriptures, and to pray and meditate. When the client reported her spiritual experiences, the therapist's faith led him to validate the truth of what she had learned about her worth and identity. The therapist's faith led him to tap into the resources of the client's faith and spirituality during treatment.	Spiritual interventions of prayer and scripture reading would not have been used. The client would probably not have received spiritual assurances of her worth and of God's love. It is questionable whether her sense of identity and worth would have healed so quickly and deeply.
Miller (Renee & Ilana)	The clients' faith in God influenced their choice to have baby rather than to have an abortion. Their	The therapist's faith in God influenced the way she conceptualized her client's problems and issues—as	In secular therapy it is unlikely that moral universals would have been discussed and affirmed. It is

continues

TABLE 17.2 (Continued)

Therapist (Case)	Influence of client's faith	Influence of therapist's faith	Differences in case without theistic perspectives
	faith influenced their desire to love and protect their babies and be good mothers. Their faith in spiritual truths influenced them to take courageous stands on behalf of their babies' welfare.	quest to find spiritual love and to live in harmony with the Spirit of Truth and moral universals regarding motherhood. The therapist's faith also influenced her decision to affirm moral universals during therapy.	unlikely that the young mothers' decision to have their babies would have been conceptualized and framed in such a positive manner (as a quest for spirituality and spiritual love).
Krejci (Mary & John)	The couple's faith in God motivated them to work on their marriage and to overcome and forgive each other of their differences, even their religious differences. It also led them to pray with and for each other. Ultimately, their faith and spirituality helped heal the conflicts in their marriage and brought them greater marital happiness.	The therapist's faith in God led him to view spirituality as highly relevant to the couple's progress. Rather than viewing the couple's religious differences solely as a cause of problems, he viewed their faith commitments as a resource. He encouraged the couple to use their shared interest in spirituality to strengthen their relationship.	A secular therapist may have failed to tap into the healing power of the couple's shared spiritual beliefs. The couple's motivation and ability to forgive may not have been as great without their Christian belief that forgiveness is desirable and possible. Also, without faith in prayer, the couple would not have enjoyed the benefits that came from praying with and for each other.
Dobbins (Kathy)	The client's faith in God motivated her to pray, read scriptures, and seek spiritual help in healing her pain. Her faith also gave her added strength to help her overcome her alcohol problem. The client's faith in the atonement of Jesus Christ	The therapist's faith in God had a major impact on his view of the client, goals for therapy, and the spiritual interventions he prescribed. The therapist's faith led him to encourage client to include God in the healing process.	In secular therapy the client would not have been encouraged to pray, read scriptures, or ask God for assistance in changing her unhealthy interpretations of her childhood experiences. The therapist would not have appealed to

continues

TABLE 17.2 *(Continued)*

Therapist (Case)	Influence of client's faith	Influence of therapist's faith	Differences in case without theistic perspectives
	helped her forgive herself for "hating her father" and "betraying her mother."		Christ's atonement to help client forgive herself.
Rabinowitz (multiple cases)	The clients' faith made them willing to examine religious issues and to engage in discussions and readings about their religious issues and problems.	The therapist's faith in God caused him to view religion and spirituality as important in the treatment process. He recognized that religion can be understood and used in dysfunctional ways, but he also viewed the client's religious beliefs as a potential resource. Because of the therapist's faith he engaged in religious discussions with clients and recommends spiritual interventions.	A secular therapist may have viewed client's religious beliefs in a pathological manner. The client's faith and beliefs may not have been used as potential resources in therapy. The clients' orthodox religious values may not have been so readily understood and accepted.
Sperry (Gwen)	The client's faith in God led her to request that spiritual issues be included in her treatment. Her faith led her to engage in spiritual practices (e.g., prayer). Her faith and spiritual practices helped her overcome her perfectionistic and obsessive–compulsive tendencies, including her bulimic behaviors.	The therapist's faith in God led him to accept client's request to include discussion of spiritual issues as a part of treatment. It also led him to encourage and recommend several spiritual interventions that were helpful to client's treatment progress.	In secular therapy it is unlikely that the client's religious beliefs and community would have been used as a resource during therapy. In fact, the client's initial negative attitude toward her religious community may have been reinforced. The client would not have experienced the benefits of praying, meditating, and participating in her religious community.

continues

TABLE 17.2 *(Continued)*

Therapist (Case)	Influence of client's faith	Influence of therapist's faith	Differences in case without theistic perspectives
Shafranske (Joan)	The client's faith was central both to the conflicts she was facing and to their ultimate resolution. The client's faith made her willing to examine her religious issues during treatment.	The therapist's faith led him to view religion as an important variable in mental health and psychological treatment. As a result, the therapist was alert to religious themes during treatment and interpreted them when appropriate. The therapist viewed client's religious beliefs as a potential resource in treatment.	Secular therapist may have viewed client's religious beliefs in a pathological manner. The client's faith and beliefs may not have been viewed as potential resources in therapy. The client's religious values may not have been so readily understood and interpreted.
Cook (Grace)	The client's faith in God influenced her goals for therapy and the interventions she was willing to participate in (e.g., prayer, meditation). Because of the client's faith in God and Jesus Christ, and her willingness to reach out to them in prayer, she had spiritual experiences during therapy where she felt their love and guidance. This helped her establish more appropriate boundaries and feel less lonely.	The therapist's faith in God had a major impact on her conceptualization of the client, treatment goals, and interventions she used. The therapist's faith that spiritual resources are available to help people heal influenced her to tap into these resources. Her faith influenced her to encourage the client to seek God's assistance through prayer and meditation.	The spiritual interventions and practices the client engaged in would not have been used. The client would not have had spiritual experiences with God that affirmed her worth and lovability. Spiritual healing would not have occurred and so other avenues to helping the client heal socially and psychologically would have been necessary.
Rayburn (Paul)	The client's faith in God helped motivate him to examine the incongruences	The therapist's theistic worldview, which included a belief in the worth and equality of men and	A secular therapist may have challenged the client's sexist attitudes and behaviors but may

continues

TABLE 17.2 *(Continued)*

Therapist (Case)	Influence of client's faith	Influence of therapist's faith	Differences in case without theistic perspectives
	between his beliefs and behavior. Prayer helped him begin to see himself as a creation of God and increased his self-confidence. His desire to live more in harmony with God and the Holy Spirit led him to spend more time with his family and less time with his extramarital lover.	women, influenced her treatment goals. She sought to help the client live more congruently with Christian teachings about sexuality and in his attitudes toward women. The therapist's belief in God also led her to encourage Paul to pray about his problems.	have lacked the religious credibility to challenge the religious justifications of the client's sexism. The therapist's Christian faith and knowledge allowed her to use religious rationales to challenge some of Paul's distorted religious understandings about women. Also, in secular therapy, the client would probably not have been encouraged to pray or benefited from doing so.
West (Matthew)	The client's faith in God led him to discuss spiritual issues during treatment. His faith also allowed him to experience moments of spiritual presence during therapy, which helped him trust his therapist and contributed to healing and growth concerning his family issues and conflicts at work.	The therapist's faith influenced him to view the client's issues, in part, as a spiritual journey and quest. The therapist's faith also led to his use of spiritual interventions in therapy. It also led him to be open to moments of spiritual experiencing during therapy sessions where he and the client felt spiritually connected.	In secular therapy, spiritual interventions would not been used. The moments of spiritual presence and experiencing during therapy sessions would probably also not have happened.
Nielsen (Aisha)	The client's faith made her willing to examine the effects of her religious understandings on her emotions. The client's belief in scriptural writings	The therapist's faith in God caused him to view religion and spirituality as important in the treatment process. His belief in the value of scriptural teachings led him to	A secular therapist may have viewed the client's religious beliefs as irrelevant or as a barrier to effective treatment. Scriptural teachings and rationales would not have been used

continues

TABLE 17.2 *(Continued)*

Therapist (Case)	Influence of client's faith	Influence of therapist's faith	Differences in case without theistic perspectives
	made her willing to discuss scriptural teachings in therapy.	use scriptural rationales to dispute client's irrational beliefs.	to help dispute irrational beliefs. The religious roots to the client's irrational beliefs may have gone unexamined.
Hedayat-Diba (Mrs. A)	Client's faith in God made her willing to discuss spiritual issues during therapy. Her therapy became a spiritual quest and journey, as well as a psychological healing process.	The therapist's spiritual proclivity led her to be open to discussions with client about spiritual matters. This also led the therapist to encourage the client in her spiritual journey. The therapist's implicit spiritual beliefs and faith helped her to affirm her client's faith.	A secular therapist would probably not have provided such a spiritually safe relationship. Therapy probably would not have become both a psychological and spiritual healing journey—only psychological healing.
Johnson (Gary)	Influenced client's views about homosexuality— made him depressed and anxious about it.	Therapist's faith led him to treat the client as worthwhile and good—he adopted a nonjudgmental affirming attitude. Therapist's faith also led him to challenge client's catastrophic beliefs about homosexuality and to encourage the client to be more self-accepting.	A secular gay affirmative therapist may have been more aggressive in challenging the client's religious beliefs about homosexuality— perhaps even to the extent of seeking to challenge or undermine core aspects of the client's faith.
Lovinger & Lovinger (Alfred, Danny, & Jody)	Clients' religious issues were intertwined with their psychological issues and emerged as themes during therapy. It is not clear whether their belief or faith promoted healing,	Therapists' faith in God and their loving, tolerant view of humanity contributed to their humorous and tolerant manner with their clients, including their complete acceptance of the	Secular therapists may not have been as effective at accepting their clients' religious beliefs and differences. Also, they may have been more inclined to view the religious themes that

continues

TABLE 17.2 *(Continued)*

Therapist (Case)	Influence of client's faith	Influence of therapist's faith	Differences in case without theistic perspectives
	but the religious themes did provide therapist with insight at times into their psychological dynamics.	religious differences that existed.	surfaced in therapy as indicators of neurosis, rather than treating these themes as valuable (but nonpathological) interpretive material.

and diagnosed their clients. Their theistic beliefs also helped them avoid ascribing pathology to normative religious beliefs and practices. Most often, they recognized the healing potentialities of their clients' faith and spirituality, and they sought to tap into these resources during therapy.

Because of their theistic beliefs, both clients and therapists often identified spiritual issues and concerns as an important focus for treatment. Therapists were willing to recommend spiritual interventions during treatment and clients were willing to participate in them. Many of the therapists regarded the spiritual interventions and faith of their clients as essential aspects of the therapeutic process. For the clients, their faith in God and personal spirituality seemed to enhance their motivation, courage, and willingness to risk and work in therapy—and ultimately, for many of them, were central to their healing and recovery.

CHALLENGES OF INTEGRATING THEISTIC PERSPECTIVES INTO MAINSTREAM PSYCHOTHERAPY

In this book we have emphasized the positive aspects and potential benefits of integrating theistic perspectives into mainstream psychotherapy, but we would be negligent if we did not acknowledge some of the objections or concerns that have been raised about doing so. One objection that has been raised about integrating theistic perspectives into mainstream psychotherapy is that leaders and members of some theistic religions have been responsible for much harm and discrimination in the world. We agree that this is so. In advocating for theistic psychotherapy, we wish to reaffirm that we do not endorse all theistic beliefs or practices. As we have written elsewhere:

> We recognize that there has been, and still is, much harm done in the name of religion. For example, the oppression of minority groups and women, acts of violence, and war have been waged in the name of religion. . . . We deplore the use of religion for such destructive purposes.

We endorse in the theistic world religions only that which is healthy and beneficial to all of humankind. (Richards & Bergin, 1997, p. 12)

We think psychotherapists need to be discriminating about religion and recognize that there are healthy and unhealthy, constructive and destructive, ways of being religious (Bergin, 1980a, 1991). We hope that theistic psychotherapists will be careful not to endorse all theistic beliefs and practices. Fortunately, there is a growing body of literature about religion and mental health that not only provides empirical evidence concerning the positive aspects of theistic religion but also helps identify some of the unhealthy and destructive forms of it (e.g., Galanter, 1996; Lovinger, 1984; Pruyser, 1971; Meadow & Kahoe, 1984; Meissner, 1996; Richards & Bergin, 1997, 2000). Conversely, we hope that the negative possibilities in the theistic religions will not cause professionals to close their minds to the therapeutic potential that also exists (e.g., Benson, 1996; Koenig, McCullough, & Larson, 2001; Plante & Sherman, 2001; Richard & Bergin, 1997). We encourage theistic psychotherapists to carefully consider what theistic beliefs and practices they will accept and recommend, and help their clients learn to do this for themselves. The case reports in this book provide numerous examples of therapists doing this.

Another objection that has been raised about integrating theistic perspectives into mainstream psychotherapy is the concern that theistic psychotherapists may be more likely to impose their religious beliefs and values on clients (e.g., Seligman, 1988). We have written about this complex ethical issue in some detail elsewhere (Bergin, 1980a, 1980b, 1980c, 1985, 1991; Bergin, Payne, & Richards, 1996; Richards & Bergin, 1997; Richards, Rector, & Tjeltveit, 1999), and will not revisit it fully here. But we will comment on a few points that we think are especially pertinent to this book of case reports.

First, we do not believe that theistic psychotherapists are more likely to violate their clients' value autonomy than other therapists. Although it is true that we advocate that therapists use a moral framework to guide and evaluate psychotherapy, we also strongly oppose attempts to coerce or implicitly influence or change clients' core values and doctrinally correct religious beliefs. We recommend that therapists adopt an explicit minimizing valuing approach, which simply means that therapists are open and explicit with clients about their values and beliefs when appropriate, but at the same time are strongly affirming of their clients' rights to disagree with them about value and doctrinal issues (Richards & Bergin, 1997; Richards et al., 1999).

We think that therapists who honestly acknowledge the moral and worldview framework that guides their therapeutic approach, and who adopt an explicit minimizing valuing approach during therapy, are actually much less likely to impose or coerce their clients into alien value and worldview frameworks than are therapists who claim to be "value-free." We have written elsewhere about the problems of ethical relativism (Bergin, 1980a; Bergin et al., 1996; Richards et al., 1999). All we wish to say about it here is that we think therapists who attempt to adopt a relativistic therapeutic stance—often with the claim that they are doing so out of tolerance for diversity—are actually at greater risk of implicitly and covertly manipulating or coercing clients with alien value or doctrinal perspectives (Bergin, 1980a, 1980b, 1980c; Bergin et al., 1996).

Having said this, what do we think therapists should do when they encounter clients who have religious beliefs that seem to be contributing to their emotional distress or relationship problems? We think that if clients' religious beliefs are intertwined with or contributing to their presenting symptoms and problems, these beliefs in all likelihood will need to be examined during therapy in order for therapeutic change to occur. Perhaps the first step in doing so is to explore the belief so that both the therapist and client accurately understand it and how it affects the client emotionally, behaviorally, and spiritually.

The next step may be to ascertain whether the client's belief is doctrinally correct. That is, is it in harmony with the official teachings of the client's religious tradition? If the therapist is a member of the client's religious tradition, or an expert in its doctrines, this may immediately be apparent. If not, the therapist may wish to invite the client to do some doctrinal study or research (through study or by visiting with church leaders) to find out if his or her understanding of the doctrine is in harmony with official church teachings. Once the doctrinal accuracy or inaccuracy of the client's religious belief is ascertained, the therapist will have a better idea about how to proceed. If a client's problematic religious belief is found to be doctrinally incorrect, this can give the therapist and client leverage to modify it, hopefully into an understanding that is less dysfunctional for the client. If the client's religious belief is doctrinally correct, we think the therapist needs to help the client examine why it is a problem in her or his life, and then defer to the client about how she or he wishes to handle it.

We think that to avoid imposing their religious views on clients, therapists need to show deference and respect toward official doctrines of their clients' religious traditions. We do not think therapists should challenge or dispute official church teachings, nor should they recommend that clients do so. Of course, if clients choose to do this of their own accord, then we think therapists are obligated to listen and help clients explore their reasons for doing so. But therapists should not actively align themselves against church teachings or attempt to challenge and displace religious authority and teachings (Richards & Bergin, 1997).

In conclusion, although integrating theistic psychotherapy into mainstream practice can raise the specter of values imposition in the minds of some professionals, we do not think that theistic psychotherapists are any more likely to do this than are other therapists. Nevertheless, theistic psychotherapists must be aware of this issue and do their best to handle it appropriately.

Another concern that has been raised about integrating theistic perspectives into mainstream psychotherapy regards the question of whether psychotherapists can do this in a philosophically and theoretically defensible manner. Most psychotherapists seek to integrate theistic perspectives and interventions with mainstream secular therapy traditions. As discussed in chapter 1 and elsewhere (e.g., Richards & Bergin, 1997; Slife, 2003), the mainstream secular traditions are grounded in the naturalistic-atheistic worldview, and in philosophies and theories that rather dramatically conflict with theistic perspectives. How will theistic psychotherapists resolve these conflicting philosophical and theoretical notions so that their conceptual frameworks and therapeutic approaches are not riddled with inconsistencies?

We think that the first step for therapists in developing a sound theistic conceptual framework consists of carefully examining the philosophical and theoretical assumptions that underlie their approach—both the theistic and secular ones (Slife, 2003; Slife & Williams, 1995). Psychotherapists may find that to be conceptually consistent, they have to abandon, revise, or reframe some of the secular perspectives they accepted earlier in their careers. The process of developing a conceptually consistent and sound theistic framework will probably not be an easy task for most psychotherapists.

We did not ask the therapists who contributed to this book to make it clear how they have resolved the conflicts between their theistic and secular perspectives—and few of them chose to do so. In the future we plan to give this issue more attention. We invite psychotherapists who wish to integrate their theistic beliefs with mainstream secular traditions to make efforts to resolve the conceptual conflicts. We hope that many of them will share how they have done this through publications and presentations. We think this is necessary if the theory and practice of theistic psychotherapy is to advance in a respected and influential manner.

RECOMMENDATIONS

The ethical guidelines of most mental health professions prohibit their members from practicing outside the boundaries of their professional competence. In light of such guidelines, we encourage therapists who wish to incorporate theistic perspectives and interventions into their work to seek adequate training before doing so. Unfortunately, it is still the case that most mental health training programs are inadequate at preparing therapists to intervene in the spiritual dimensions of their clients' lives. Few mainstream mental health programs provide course work or supervision on religious and spiritual issues in mental health and psychotherapy (Kelly, 1993; Shafranske & Malony, 1996). Thus, most psychotherapists will need additional education and training beyond graduate school to ethically and effectively use a theistic spiritual strategy.

Fortunately, many resources are now available to help therapists acquire training and competency in the religious and spiritual domains. There is a large body of professional literature that provides insight into the relations among religion, spirituality, mental health, and psychotherapy. Some universities now offer specialized courses on the psychology and sociology of religion and on religious and spiritual issues in counseling and psychotherapy. Continuing education workshops on these topics have become more widely available. We recommend that psychotherapists do the following as they seek to obtain and enhance their competency in this domain (Richards & Bergin, 1997, p. 166):

1. Obtain training in multicultural counseling.
2. Read good books on the psychology of religion and spiritual issues in psychotherapy.
3. Read scholarly literature about religion and spirituality in mainstream mental health journals and in specialty journals devoted to these topics.
4. Take workshops or classes on the psychology of religion and spiritual issues in psychotherapy.
5. Read good books or take a class on the theistic world religions.
6. Seek in-depth knowledge about religious traditions that you frequently encounter in therapy.
7. Consult with colleagues when you first work with clients from a particular religious tradition, when clients present challenging spiritual issues, and when you first use spiritual interventions.

We also encourage leaders of graduate training programs to include religious and spiritual content in graduate curriculum and clinical training experiences. Shafranske and Malony (1996) proposed that the ideal curriculum would include four components: "a 'values in psychological treatment' component, a 'psychology of religion' component, a 'comparative-religion' component, and a 'working with religious issues' component" (Shafranske & Malony, 1996, p. 576). We wish that every graduate training program in the mental health professions would incorporate these recommendations fully. At the least, we hope that program administrators will find a way to offer at least one course that explores spiritual issues in mental health and psychotherapy, as well as provide supervisors who have competency in this domain.

We also encourage scholars and researchers to join with our colleagues and us in doing research about a theistic spiritual strategy for psychotherapy. More philosophical, theoretical, and research work is needed if this approach is to advance and mature. Philosophical and empirical work is needed about the following topics (Richards & Bergin, 1997, p. 335):

1. implications of a theistic view of human nature and personality;
2. effectiveness of theistic integrative psychotherapy;
3. nature of spirit, spirituality, and spiritual well-being;
4. religious and spiritual development across the life span;
5. spiritual needs and issues of human beings;
6. prevalence and role of intuition and inspiration in therapeutic change and scientific discovery;
7. nature, prevalence, effects, and meaning of spiritual experiences (e.g., near-death experiences, afterlife visions, inspirational and revelatory experiences, conversion experiences, healings);
8. implications and usefulness of epistemological and methodological pluralism; and
9. assessment and outcome measurement of religious and spiritual functioning.

As can be seen, there is no shortage of fascinating and challenging projects for the future in this domain. We invite those with interest to join us in investigating these and other philosophical and research questions. We are pleased that financial and political support for research on spirituality, mental health, and healing has increased dramatically during the past decade. We hope that such support continues to grow.

CONCLUSION

Jones (1994) argued that religious worldviews could contribute to the progress of psychological science and practice "by suggesting new modes of thought . . . and new theories" (p. 194). We agree with this. We think that the theistic worldview, in particular, contributes important insights into previously neglected aspects of human nature, personality, therapeutic change, and the practice of psychotherapy.

The most serious deficiency in modern mainstream theories of personality and psychotherapy is their neglect of God and the human spirit. This needs to be rectified. As we have expressed elsewhere:

> The human spirit, under God, is vital to understanding personality and therapeutic change. If we omit such spiritual realities from our account of human behavior, it won't matter much what else we keep in, because we will have omitted the most fundamental aspect of human nature. With this dimension included, our ability to advance psychological sci-

ence, professional practice, and human welfare can truly soar. (Richards & Bergin, 1997, p. xi)

We believe that theistic psychotherapy will help psychological practice soar. It will enhance the ability of mental health professionals to understand and work more sensitively and effectively with their theistic clients. The case reports presented in this book provide support for our optimism.

REFERENCES

Ball, R. A., & Goodyear, R. K. (1991). Self-reported professional practices of Christian psychologists. *Journal of Psychology and Christianity, 10,* 144–153.

Benson, H. (1996). *Timeless healing: The power and biology of belief.* New York: Scribner.

Bergin, A. E. (1980a). Behavior therapy and ethical relativism: Time for clarity. *Journal of Consulting and Clinical Psychology, 48,* 11–13.

Bergin, A. E. (1980b). Psychotherapy and religious values. *Journal of Consulting and Clinical Psychology, 48,* 75–105.

Bergin, A. E. (1980c). Religious and humanistic values: A reply to Ellis and Walls. *Journal of Consulting and Clinical Psychology, 48,* 642–645.

Bergin, A. E. (1985). Proposed values for guiding and evaluating counseling and psychotherapy. *Counseling and Values, 29,* 99–116.

Bergin, A. E. (1991). Values and religious issues in psychotherapy and mental health. *American Psychologist, 46,* 394–403.

Bergin, A. E., & Jensen, J. P. (1990). Religiosity of psychotherapists: A national survey. *Psychotherapy, 27*(1), 3–7.

Bergin, A. E., Payne, I. R., & Richards, P. S. (1996). Values in psychotherapy. In E. Shafranske (Ed.), *Religion and the clinical practice of psychology* (pp. 297–325). Washington, DC: American Psychological Association.

Galanter, M. (1996). Cults and charismatic groups. In E. Shafranske (Ed.), *Religion and the clinical practice of psychology* (pp. 269–296). Washington, DC: American Psychological Association.

Jensen, J. P., & Bergin, A. E. (1988). Mental health values of professional therapists: A national interdisciplinary survey. *Professional Psychology: Research and Practice, 19,* 290–297.

Jones, S. L. (1994). A constructive relationship for religion with the science and profession of psychology: Perhaps the boldest model yet. *American Psychologist, 49,* 184–199.

Kelly, E. W. (1993, March). *The status of religious and spiritual issues in counselor education.* Paper presented at the annual convention of the American Counseling Association, Atlanta, GA.

Koenig, H. G., McCullough, M. E., & Larson, D. B. (Eds.). (2001). *Handbook of religion and health.* New York: Oxford University Press.

Lovinger, R. J. (1984). *Working with religious issues in therapy.* Northwale, NJ: Jason Aronson.

Meadow, M. J., & Kahoe, R. D. (1984). *Psychology of religion: Religion in individual lives.* New York: Harper & Row.

Meissner, M. W. (1996). The pathology of beliefs and the beliefs of pathology. In E. Shafranske (Ed.), *Religion and the clinical practice of psychology* (pp. 241–267). Washington, DC: American Psychological Association.

Plante, T. G., & Sherman, A. C. (Eds.). (2001). *Faith and health: Psychological perspectives.* New York: Guilford Press.

Pruyser, P. (1971). Assessment of the patient's religious attitudes in the psychiatric case study. *Bulletin of the Menninger Clinic, 35,* 272–291.

Richards, P. S., & Bergin, A. E. (1997). *A spiritual strategy for counseling and psychotherapy.* Washington, DC: American Psychological Association.

Richards, P. S., & Bergin, A. E. (Eds.). (2000). *Handbook of psychotherapy and religious diversity.* Washington, DC: American Psychological Association.

Richards, P. S., & Potts, R. W. (1995). Using spiritual interventions in psychotherapy: Practices, successes, failures, and ethical concerns of Mormon psychotherapists. *Professional Psychology: Research and Practice, 26,* 163–170.

Richards, P. S., & Rector, J. R., & Tjeltveit, A. C. (1999). Values, spirituality, and psychotherapy (pp. 133–160). In W. R. Miller (Ed.), *Integrating spirituality in treatment: Resources for practitioners.* Washington, DC: American Psychological Association.

Seligman, L. (1988). Invited commentary: Three contributions of a spiritual perspective to counseling, psychotherapy, and behavior change. *Counseling and Values, 33,* 55–56.

Shafranske, E. P. (2000). Religious involvement and professional practices of psychiatrists and other mental health professionals. *Psychiatric Annals, 30,* 525–532.

Shafranske, E. P., & Malony, H. N. (1990). Clinical psychologists' religious and spiritual orientations and their practice of psychotherapy. *Psychotherapy, 27,* 72–78.

Shafranske, E. P., & Malony, H. N. (1996). Religion and the clinical practice of psychology: A case for inclusion. In E. P. Shafranske (Ed.), *Religion and the clinical practice of psychology* (pp. 561–586). Washington, DC: American Psychological Association.

Slife, B. D. (2003). Theoretical challenges to therapy practice and research: The constraint of naturalism. In M. J. Lambert (Ed.), *Bergin and Garfield's handbook of psychotherapy and behavior change* (5th ed., pp. 44–83). New York: Wiley.

Slife, B. D., & Williams, R. N. (1995). What's behind the research? Discovering hidden assumptions in the behavioral sciences. Thousand Oaks, CA: Sage.

AUTHOR INDEX

Numbers in italics refer to listings in the references.

Elliott, R., 167, *168*
Ellis, A., 4, *30*, 214, 215, 218, 221, *229*, 248, 253, 254, 259, 260, 261, *264*
Ellison, C. W., 63, *72*
Emmons, R. A., 17, *29*
Endean, P., 177, 179, 184
Enright, R. D., 96, *102*
Epstein, M., 3, *29*
Epstein, S., 63, *72*
Erlander, Rev. M., 55, *72*

Fairburn, C. G., 63, *71*
Faiver, C., 4, *29*
Falender, C. A., 153, *168*
Feltham, C., *211*
Fernandez, T., *246*
Fischer, L., 55, *72*
Fisher, A. M., 40, *53*
Fisher-Smith, A. M., 39, *52*
Fitzmyer, J. A., 274, *283*
Fleming, D., 174, 175, 177, 178, 184
Fletcher, L. A., 55, *72*
Fordham, M., *246*
Foster, R., 253, *264*
Fowers, B. J., 38, *53*
Freedman, S., 96, *102*
Freud, S., 160, *168*, 244, *246*
Friedman, 234
Frost, H. A., 55, 58, *72*
Fullerton, J. T., 92, *102*

Gabbard, G. O., 157, 163, *168*
Galanter, M., 302, *307*
Galatzer-Levy, R. M., 167, *168*
Garfield, S. L., *31*, 167, *168*
Garfinkel, P. E., 63, *71*
Garner, D. M., 63, *71*
Gaskin, T. A., *29*
Gendlin, E., 145, *152*
Gill, M. M., 165, *168*
Gillman, H., 202, 207, *211*
Glasse, C., 235, *246*
Glassgold, J. M., 257, *264*
Goodyear, R. K., 16, *28*, 293, *307*
Gorman, 50
Greenberg, L. S., 167, *168*
Greene, B., *264*
Griffin, D. R., 8, 12, *29*, 36, 37, *52*
Griffith, J. L., 4, *29*
Griffith, M. E., 4, *29*
Guignon, C. B., 38, *53*
Gunton, C. E., 36, 40, *52*

Haftorahs, *139*
Haldeman, D. C., 251, 256, 257, 263, *264*
Hall, L., 55, *71*
Hall, T. W., 69, *71*
Hamilton, A., 79, *86*
Handelman, S., 122, *139*
Hansen, N. B., 229
Hardman, R. K., 55, 58, 59, *72*
Heatherton, T., *30*
Hedayat-Diba, Z., 3, *29*, 232, *246*
Hellwigg, M., 178, *185*
Helminiak, D. A., 4, *30*
Helms, J., 174, *185*
Henning, L. H., 21, *30*
Herek, G., *264*
Hermann, R. L., 8, *31*
Hershberger, S. L., 252, 255, 257, *264*
Hertz, J., 130, *139*
Higgins, E. T., 49, *52*
Hill, C. H., 24, *30*
Hill, D. B., *53*
Hoge, D. R., 267, *284*
Hollis, J., 233, *246*
Honer, S. M., 36, *52*
Hood, R. W., 24, *30*, 169, *200*
Hope, C., 8, *31*, 36, *53*
Horvath, A. O., 167, *168*
Howard, G. S., 40, *52*
Hsu, L. K., 55, *72*
Hull, R. F. C., *246*
Hunsberger, B., 92, *102*
Hunt, T. C., 36, *52*

Inayat Khan, P. V., *246*
Ingersoll, R. E., 4, *29*

Jackson, S. W., 162, *168*
Jacobson, N. S., 219, *229*
Jennings, J., 122, *139*
Jennings, J. P., 122, *139*
Jensen, J. P., 16, *30*, 292, 293, *307*
Johnson, T. M., 4, *28*
Johnson, W. B., 4, *30*, 215, *229*, 248, 253, 258, 261, *264*
Jones, J. W., 160, *168*
Jones, R., 207, *211*
Jones, S. L., 8, 15, *30*, 306, *307*
Jung, C. G., 233, *246*

Kahoe, R. D., 302, *308*
Keller, R. R., 4, *30*
Kelly, E. W., 4, 16, *30*, 304, *307*

Kenkel, M. B., *263*
Kernberg, O., 158, 160, *168*
King, D. B., 36, 37, *53*
Klerman, G. L., 75, 86
Koenig, H. G., 302, *307*
Kohut, H., 163, *168*, 234, *246*
Kopec, A. M., *222*, *228*
Kotler, A., 137, *139*
Kral, M. J., *53*

Lachman, F., 283, *284*
Lambert, M. J., *31, 53, 63, 72*, 167, *168*, 218, *229*
Larson, D. B., 3, *30*, 302, *307*
Larson, S., 3, *30*
Lawton, B., *211*
Leahey, T. H., 36, *52*
Ledoux, J., 159, *168*
Lerman, H., 200, *200*
Lillas, C., 244, *246*
Loewald, H. W., 163, *168*
Lohfink, G., 35, *52*
Lonsdale, D., 179, 180, 184, *185*
Lovinger, R. J., 4, *30*, 268, 270, 272, *284*, 302, *308*
Lowenthal, W., 245, *246*
Luborsky, L., 158, *168*
Lunnen, K., *229*

Malony, H. N., 15, *30*, 293, 304, 305, *308*
Mashburn, D., 228, *229*, *284*
Masters, K. S., *29*
May, G., 185, *186*
Mayman, 157
McCullough, M. E., 96, *102*, 302, *307*
McLellen, A. T., 158, *168*
McNally, C., 4, *29*
McWilliams, N., 157, *168*
Meadow, M. J., 178, 179, *186*, 302, *308*
Mearns, D., 210, *211*
Meissner, W. W., 160, *169*, 302, *308*
Melton, J. G., 26, *30*
Menninger, K. A., 157, *169*
Michels, R., 158, *169*
Miller, L., 270, *284*
Miller, W. R., 3, 17, *30, 31*, 122, *139*, *308*
Mitchell, J. E., 55, *72*
Mitchell, L. J., 36, *54*
Money, J., 252, *264*
Moore, T., 244, *246*
Muzzonigro, P. G., 257, *264*

Nathan, 50
Natterson, 234
Nebeker, R. S., 8, *31*, 36, *53*
Newman, B. S., 257, *264*
Nicolosi, J., 256, *264*
Nielsen, S. L., 4, *30*, 214, 215, 220, 228, *229*, *230*, 248, 253, 261, *264*
North, J., *102*

O'Brien, E., 4, *29*
O'Brien, E. J., 63, *72*
Okiishi, J., *229*
Ostrom, R., 228, *229*, *284*

Paloutzian, R. F., 63, *72*
Pargament, K. I., 130, *139*
Payne, I. R., 22, *29*, 302, *307*
Peck, M. S., 3, *30*
Pentateuch, *139*
Perez, R. M., *263*, *264*
Perry, S., 158, *169*
Peterson, D., 215, *229*
Pettorini, D., 215, *229*
Plante, T. G., 302, *308*
Porter, N., 200, *200*
Potts, R. W., 16, 22, *31*, 59, *72*, 256, *264*, 293, *308*
Propst, L. R., 228, *229*, 283, *284*
Provine, W., 12, *30*
Pruyser, 157
Pruyser, P., 302, *308*
Pyle, R. L., 55, *72*

Rabinowitz, A., 3, *30*, 120, 121, 131, *139*
Rachal, K. C., 96, *102*
Rangell, L., 159, 163, *169*
Rayburn, C. A., 192, 200, *200*
Read, H., *246*
Rector, J. R., 15, *31*, 302, *308*
Reiff, P., 160, *169*
Reynolds, E. M., *29*
Richards, P. S., xiii, xiiin, 3, 4, 6, 7, 8, 10, 12, 12n, 13, 15, 16, 17, 19n, 20, 22, *29, 30, 31*, 36, 37, 39, *53*, 55, 56, 58, 59, 60, 63, 70, *72*, 73, 76, 86, 119, 121, 127, *139*, 140, *169*, 176, 177, 179, *186*, 208, 209, 210, *211*, 227, *230*, 241, *246*, 258, *264*, *284*, 292, 293, 302, 303, 304, 305, 306, *307, 307, 308*
Richardson, F. C., 38, 40, 41, *52, 53*

Richmond, L. J., 192, 200, *200*
Ridley, C. R., 215, *229*, 248, *264*
Rique, J., 96, *102*
Rizzuto, A.-M., 160, 160–161, *169*
Robb, H., 215, 228, *230*
Robin, M. W., *263*
Robinson, D. N., 8, *29*, 261
Rogers, C. R., 210, 211, *211*
Rorty, M., 55, *72*
Rosenblatt, B., 163, *169*
Ross, J., 163, *169*
Ross, J. M., 63, *71*
Rossotto, E., 55, *72*
Rounsaville, B. J., 75, *86*
Rowan, J., 208, 210, *211*
Rubin, J. B., 3, *31*
Rychlak, J. F., 37, 40, *53*

Sacks, H., 179, *186*
Sandler, J., 163, *169*
Sarason, I. G., 214, *229*
Scharman, J. S., 17, *29*
Schneider, M. S., 257, *264*
Schneiman, C. R., 215, *230*
Schore, A. N., 159, *169*
Schroeder, G. L., 8, *31*, *264*
Schroeder, M., 256, 257
Seligman, L., 302, *308*
Serra, R., 252, *264*
Shafranske, E. P., 3, *29*, *31*, *32*, 59, *72*, *102*,
        139, 153, 160, 161, 162, *168*, *169*,
        284, 293, 304, 305, *307*, *308*
Shapiro, F., 239, *246*
Sharma, A. R., 3, *31*
Shaver, R., 40, *53*
Sherman, A. C., 302, *308*
Shidlo, A., 256, 257, *264*
Siegel, D. J., 159, *169*
Skolnikoff, A., 167, *168*
Slife, B. D., 8, 12, *31*, 36, 37, 38, 39, 40, 41,
        50, *52*, *53*, *54*, 292, 304, *308*
Smart, N., 7, 16, *31*
Smedes, L. B., 252, *265*
Smith, A. M., 39, *53*
Smith, F. T., 55, 59, *72*
Smith, H., 36, 40, *53*
Smith, T. B., 63, *72*
Snyder, D. K., 92, *102*
Soloveitchik, J. B., 121, 123, 137, *140*
Spero, M. H., 3, *31*, 160, *169*
Sperry, L., 4, *31*, 147, *152*, 153, *169*

Spiegelman, M., 236, *246*
Stern, D., 241, *246*
Stern, E. M., *30*
Stinchfield, R. D., *29*
Stolorow, R., 159, 163, *169*, 283, *284*
Strachey, J., *246*
Sue, D., 20, *31*
Sue, D. W., 20, *31*
Sue, S., 20, *31*
Sullivan, C. E., *29*
Swidler, A., 252, *265*
Swidler, L., 192, 200, *200*
Swinton, J., 4, *31*

Tan, S. T., 94, *102*
Taylor, M., 63, *71*
Templeton, J. M., 8, *31*
Thorne, B., 210, *211*
Throckmorton, W., 256, *265*
Tirrell, F. J., 21, *30*
Tisdale, T. C., 69, *71*
Tjeltveit, A. C., 15, 22, *31*, *32*, 302,
        308
Truax, P., 219, *229*

Ulrich, W. L., 60, *73*
Umphress, V., *229*

Valentine, E. R., 37, *53*
Van Herik, J., 170, *169*
Vandenbos, G. R., *263*
Vaughan, F., 4, *32*
Viney, W., 36, 37, *53*

Waldron, W., Jr., 167, *168*
Walen, S. R., 259, *265*
Wallach, L., 127, *140*
Wallach, M., 127, *140*
Wallerstein, R., 159, *170*
Walsh, R., 4, *32*
Watkins, P., 228, *229*, *284*
Watson, J. C., 167, *168*
Watzlawick, P., *54*
Webster, 39
Weinberger, J., *30*
Weiss, J., 163, *170*
Weissman, M. M., 75, *86*
West, W. S., 4, *32*, 202, 203, 204, 206, 208,
        210, 211, *211*, *212*
Whoolery, M., 36, *54*
Wicklund, R. A., 127, *140*

SUBJECT INDEX

as naturalistic assumption, 11, 38, 40–41
Attachment disorder, of Jody, 279
Attention deficit/hyperactivity disorder (ADHD), of Laura, 42

"Battle of the sexes," 198
Beck Depression Inventory (BDI), 144, 251, 262
Beliefs
    irrationally evaluative (IEBs), 218, 253–254, 260
    See also Religious beliefs
Benjamin (case report), 133–134
Bergin, Allen, 214
Berrett, Michael E., 56–57, 67, 288, 291, 295
Bias-free research, and Alldredge Academy, 50
Biopsychosocial traditions, 147, 289
Body, need to recognize, 244
Body Shape Questionnaire (BSQ), for Jan (case report), 63, 64, 65, 68
Brigham Young University (BYU)
    counseling center of, 215
    and culture of Aisha vs. sexual harasser (case report), 226
Brown, Rev. Tim, S.J., 174
Buber, Martin, 210–211
Buddhists
    and Mrs. A, 238
    as clients, 203
    religion as positive force in therapy with, 102
Bulimia, of Gwen (case report), 143
BYU. *See* Brigham Young University

Case reports, 27–28, 167
    Mrs. A, 236–245, 291, 300
    Aisha, 215–228, 290, 299–300
    Alfred, 269–270, 270–276, 283, 291, 300–301
    Benjamin, 133–134
    Danny (9-year-old), 276–279, 282–283, 283, 291, 300
    Danny (17-year-old rabbinical student), 125–126
    David, 126–127
    Deborah, 134, 135
    Ehud, 132–133
    Gary, 249–255, 258–63, 291, 300
    Grace, 5, 173, 175–178, 180–184, 185, 290, 298

Gwen, 142–152, 289, 297
hassidic client, 127–128
Ilana, 82–85, 288, 295–296
Jacob, 128–129
Jan, 60–71, 288, 295
Joan, 154–167, 289, 298
Jody, 279–282, 291, 300
Jonathan, 136–137
Joseph, 139
Kathy, 106–117, 289, 296–297
Laura, 4–5, 42–52, 288, 295
Mary and John, 88–102, 288, 296
Matthew, 203–211, 290, 299
Norman, 129–131
Paul, 5, 188–200, 290, 298–299
Renee, 5–6, 79–82, 288, 295–296
Center for Change (CFC), 55–56
    and Jan (case report), 60–66, 70–71
        postdischarge functioning of, 69–70
        psychological and spiritual outcome measures, 68–69
        role of faith and spirituality for, 66–68
    theistic convictions of, 70
    therapists in, 56–57
    spiritual component of treatment program at, 59–60
    treatment setting and program at, 57–59
Chi Gong, and Mrs. A. (case report), 243
Children's play, 280
Chofetz Chayim, 129, 138
Christianity, 7
    and freedom from law, 273, 274
    vs. Judaism, 268
    of Danny (9-year-old), 277
    See also Jesus
Christian life, Blazer on, 121
Christian love
    of Mary and John, 100
    vs. Paul's treatment of women (case report), 192
Christian Orthodoxy Scale, 92
Christian principles in marriage, 94
    forgiveness as, 100 (*see also* Forgiveness)
Christian therapists, vs. atheist therapists, 227–228
Client's faith, influence of, 295–301
Client's role in therapy (theistic psychotherapy), 18–19
Cognitive–behavioral therapy, in case of Paul, 195

Eating disorder, of Gwen (case report), 143
Eating disorder treatment programs, 55
    at Center for Change, 55–59, 70
        and case report (Jan), 60–71
        spiritual component of, 59–60
Ecumenical therapeutic stance, 20, 294
Ehud (case report), 132–133
Elijah of Vilna (Gra), Rabbi, 138
Ellis, Albert, 214–215, 221, 248, 262
EMERGE Ministries, 105
    and Kathy (case report), 106–107, 117
        assessment and diagnosis of, 107–108
        treatment process and outcome for, 108–117
Emotion, Ellis on, 221
Empiricism, as naturalistic-atheistic assumption, 11–12
Epistemological pluralism, in theistic vs. naturalistic-atheistic worldview, 11–12
Ethical concerns, 7
    in theistic psychotherapy, 21–22
    See also Morality
Ethical hedonism, in theistic vs. naturalistic-atheistic worldview, 11
Ethical relativism, 302–303
    rejection of, 293
    in theistic vs. naturalistic-atheistic worldview, 11
Evaluations, absolutistic, 227
Expressive-supportive psychotherapy, 163

Faith, in case of Jan, 66–68
"Faith factor," 17
Family therapy
    at Center for Change (Jan), 66
    See also Marital therapy case
Forgiveness
    and Mrs. A, 240
    and Aisha (case report), 223
    and Judaism vs. Christianity, 268
    and Laura at Alldredge Academy, 48–49
    in marital therapy, 94, 95–96, 98–100, 100, 101
    and Matthew (case report), 209
    and teshuva, 137
Foster, Richard, 252–253
Free will, as theistic assumption, 11
Freud, Sigmund
    on body ego, 244

psychic structure proposed by, 233–234
on religion, 160

Gary (case report), 249–250, 262–263, 291, 300
    assessment and diagnosis of, 250–253
    rational emotive behavioral therapy with, 254–255, 258–261, 262
        disputing of religious beliefs in, 261–262
    treatment process and outcomes for, 253–255
Gender-fair psychotherapy, 199
Gender relations
    in case of Paul, 191–192, 193
    harm from inequality in, 198
Gestalt exercise, in case of Paul, 196
Global Assessment of Functioning, 218
Goals of therapy, in theistic psychotherapy, 18–19, 24–25
God, 7–8
    affirmation of required, 137
    believers in, 13
    in case reports
        Mrs. A., 237–238, 241, 245
        Aisha, 222, 228
        Alfred, 275
        Deborah, 134, 135
        Gary, 261–262, 262
        Grace, 182–183
        Gwen, 144, 145, 150, 151
        and Jacob, 129
        Jan, 65, 67, 68, 70–71
        Joan, 166
        Kathy, 115, 116
        Mary and John, 93, 98
        Matthew, 206
        Norman, 130–131
        Paul, 196, 197, 198, 199
    in Center for Change, 70
    in Christianity vs. Judaism, 268
    distorted views of, 198
    and dream of crying man, 232
    female images and identity of, 192
    in Ignatian prayer and spirituality, 179, 184
    and I-Thou relationship, 211
    Jews' belief in, 278
    Judaic tradition on, 124, 129, 268
    love from, 184
    mainstream neglect of, 306
    and naturalism, 36, 37

and naturalistic assumptions, 49–51
in school phase, 47–49
in village phase, 45–47
Lesbian, gay or bisexual (LGB) persons, 252, 256
psychotherapy with, 256–257
See also Sexual orientation
Life after death, in spiritual vs. naturalistic-atheistic worldview, 9–10, 12
Life transitions, 76
Lipkin, Rabbi Israel (Yisroel Salanter), 122
Log of Interactions, in marital therapy, 95
Lovinger, Robert J., 267, 269–270, 291, 300–301
Lovinger, Sophie L., 267, 269–270, 291, 300–301

Maharal of Prague, 135
Maimonides, 136, 276
Mantra, of Gwen (case report), 149, 150
Marital Satisfaction Inventory, 92
Marital therapy case, 88–92, 100–102
assessment and diagnosis in, 92–94
treatment process and outcome in, 94–100
Mary and John (case report), 88–92, 100–102, 288, 296
assessment and diagnosis of, 92–94
treatment process and outcome in, 94–100
Materialism/mechanism, as naturalistic-atheistic assumption, 11
Matthew (case report), 203–204, 208–211, 290, 299
assessment and diagnosis of, 204–205
and spiritual intimacy, 207, 208, 210
treatment process and outcomes for, 205–208
May, Gerald, 185
Meaning, in case of Jan, 69, 70
Measures. *See* Tests and other measures
Meditation
and Catholic spirituality, 177
and Gwen (case report), 144
Ignatian, 180
by Grace (case report), 180–182
and psychotherapy, 177
in Sufism, 235–236
Meditative prayer, 177, 184
and Grace (case report), 173, 175, 177, 178, 182–183, 184, 185
and *Spiritual Exercises*, 178

Meditative or prayerful moments, 17
Meir of Radin, Rabbi Yisroel (Chofetz Chayim), 138
Metaphysical assumptions, of spiritual vs. naturalistic-atheistic worldview, 8
Midrash, 120, 122, 124, 137
Miller, Lisa, 6, 75–76, 288, 291, 295
Millon Clinical Multiaxial Inventory–II (MCMI–II), 144
Mind-body relationship, 244
Minnesota Multiphasic Personality Inventory–2 (MMPI–2)
for Jan (case report), 63, 64
for Kathy (case report), 107
Minors, spiritual intervention contraindicated for, 25
Mitchell, L. J., 41–42, 288, 295
Modernistic naturalistic-atheistic worldview, 8–13
Mood disorder
in case of Gary, 250–251
See also Depression
Morality
as framework for psychotherapy, 15
on spiritual vs. naturalistic-atheistic worldview, 9–10
and theistic view of psychotherapy, 16
See also Ethical
"Mortal overlay," 127
Motherhood
and Mrs. A, 241, 242
for pregnant girls with depression, 76, 77–78, 85–86
Ilana, 84, 85
Renee, 80, 81
Mountain search and rescue phase at Alldredge Academy, 42–45
Mrs. A. (case report), 236–239, 244–245, 291, 300
assessment and diagnosis of, 239–240
treatment process for, 240–244
Multicultural-person centered-theistic traditions, 290
Multicultural psychotherapy approaches, 4
Multicultural spiritual sensitivity, 7, 20
Multidimensional Self-Esteem Inventory (MSEI), for Jan (case report), 63, 64, 65, 68
Mystical experiences, of Grace, 183–184
Mystical focus, in case of Matthew, 207

Nachmanides, 123

Nagera, Umberto, 281
Native Americans, religion as positive force in therapy with, 102
Naturalism, 36
    assumptions of (vs. non-naturalistic), 37–38
        atomism vs. holism, 11, 38, 40–41
        determinism vs. agency, 38, 39–40
        hedonism vs. altruism, 38, 39
        and Laura's therapeutic journey, 49–51
        objectivity (vs. value-laden methodology), 38–39
        rational vs. dialectical approach, 38, 40
    and theism, 36–37
    in therapeutic communities, 35–37
Naturalistic-atheistic worldview, 8–13, 304
Naturalistic therapeutic communities, 35–37, 51, 51–52
Natural laws, in theistic vs. naturalistic-atheistic worldview, 11
Needs, Kohut on, 234–235
New Age clients, 203
Nielsen, Stevan Lars, 213–215, 290, 299–300
Norman (case report), 129–131

Objectivity
    and Laura's therapeutic journey, 50
    as naturalistic assumption, 38–39
Obsessive–compulsive personality
    of Gwen (case report), 144, 147, 151
    See also Perfectionism
Obsessive thoughts, of Jonathan (case report), 136
Oedipal issues, in case of Alfred, 271, 272
Outcome Questionnaire (OQ 45), 63, 64, 65, 68, 218, 219, 223, 224, 225

Pain, psychological, and religion or spirituality, 119
Pathology. See Dysfunction; Psychopathology
Paul (case report), 5, 188–191, 198–200, 290, 298–299
    assessment and diagnosis of, 191–193
    treatment process and outcomes for, 193–198
Paul, Apostle
    on "dark glass," 114
    and "putting off the old self . . .," 108
Perfectionism

of Aisha (case report), 216
of Gwen (case report), 143, 148, 149, 150, 151
in obsessive-compulsive personality, 147
Person, uniqueness of, in Judaic tradition, 124
Personality, theistic view of, 13–15
Philosophical foundations, for theistic psychotherapy, 7–13
Play of child, 280
Posttraumatic stress disorder
    of Mrs. A. (case report), 239
    of Aisha (case report), 217–218
Potential ethical concerns, in theistic psychotherapy, 21–22
Prayer
    in case reports
        Aisha, 223
        Gwen, 150
        Jan, 67
        John, 97
        Laura (at Alldredge Academy), 47
        Matthew, 209
    in Cook's practice, 174
    Ignatian prayer methods, 177–180, 184–185
        and Grace (case report), 173, 177, 178, 180–184
    in marital therapy, 99, 101
    "praying through" (in case of Kathy), 113–116, 117
    of the senses (Ignatius), 179
Prayerful moments, 17
Pregnant girls, treatment for depression of (Interpersonal Psychotherapy), 76–78, 85–86
    and Ilana (case report), 82–85
    and Renee (case report), 79–82
Presence, Rogers on, 210, 211
Professional Psychology: Research and Practice, sexual orientation articles in, 255
Provine, William, 12
Psalms
    and Deborah (case report), 135
    and Kathy (case report), 114
Pseudoautonomy, of Mrs. A. (case report), 240
Psychiatry, and religion, 121
Psychoanalytic approach
    to case of Joan, 159–160

and Sufism, 235

Psychoanalytic clinical approach, to religious experience (case of Joan), 160–163

Psychodynamic case report (Joan), 154–157, 167

assessment and diagnosis in, 157–158

treatment process and outcomes for, 158–163

psychotherapeutic process in, 163–166

Psychodynamic-cognitive-theistic traditions, 289

Psychodynamic-theistic traditions, 289

Psychodynamic theory, in case of Paul, 195

Psychological pain, and religion or spirituality, 119

Psychological and spiritual outcome measures, in case of Jan at CFC, 68–69

Psychological transformation, for Gwen (case report), 148–150

Psychology

body excluded by, 244

and religion, 3, 121

Psychology of Religion Newsletter, 87

Psychopathology

as integral to personality (case of Norman), 130

theistic view on, 14

See also Dysfunction

Psychotherapeutic process, in case of Joan, 163–166

Psychotherapists

theistic, 292–293

See also Therapist(s)

Psychotherapy

gender-fair, 199

Ignatian prayer methods in, 184–185 (*see also* Ignatian prayer methods)

integration of theistic perspectives into, 301–304

self-centered vs. other-centered results of, 127

and sexual orientation, 255–257

theistic, 307

and traumatic memories, 239

Psychotherapy, theistic, 6–7, 307

conceptual framework for

theological and philosophical foundations, 7–13

view of personality, 13–15

view of psychotherapy, 15–17, 18–19

discriminating view of religion in, 301–302

and imposition of religious beliefs, 302–304

influence of theistic perspective on, 294–301

process guidelines for, 17

implementing interventions, 25–26

multicultural spiritual sensitivity, 20

potential ethical concerns, 21–22

religious and spiritual assessment, 22–24

setting appropriate goals, 24–25

spiritually open and safe relationship, 20–21

Psychotic patients, spiritual intervention contraindicated for, 25

Public tax-supported setting, spiritual intervention contraindicated for, 25

Purpose of life

in case of Jan, 69, 70

in spiritual vs. naturalistic-atheistic worldview, 9–10

"Putting off the old self and putting on the new self," and Kathy (case report), 108, 110–111, 112, 117

Quakers, 201–202, 207

Questionnaires. *See* Tests and other measures

Questions

for assessment, 23–24

about case reports, 27–28

Qur'an, in case of Aisha, 215, 227

Qur'anic REBT, 221–226

Rabinowitz, Aaron, 119–120, 289, 291, 297

Rabkin, Leslie, 214

Rape, of Aisha (case report), 216, 217, 220, 227

Rashi, 123

Rating, human, 218, 220, 222, 227

Rational approach

as naturalistic assumption, 38, 40

and Laura's therapeutic journey, 51

Rational emotive behavior therapy (REBT), 195, 213, 214, 228, 248, 253–254

A-B-C model of, 218, 220, 221, 253

elegant solution in, 259

and Gary (case report), 254–255, 258–261, 262

and disputing of religious beliefs, 261–262

on guilt, 220–221
Qur'anic, 221–226
rational and religious neutrality in, 226–227
and religion, 214–215
See also REBT-theistic traditions
Rayburn, Carole A, 5, 187–188, 290, 298–299
RCIA (Rite of Christian Initiation for Adults), 90
Realism, theistic, 11, 258
Griffin on, 13
Realism/positivism, in theistic vs. naturalistic-atheistic worldview, 11
Rebecca (Biblical figure), 133
REBT. See Rational emotive behavior therapy
REBT-theistic traditions, 290, 291
Reconciliation, RC sacrament of, 97, 162
Reductionism/atomism, as naturalistic-atheistic assumption, 11
Reductive naturalism. See Naturalism
"Reframing the individual," 130
Relativism, ethical, 11, 293, 302–303
Relaxation response, and spiritual convictions, 17
Religion
    body excluded by, 244
    and children in therapy, 282, 283
    conservative viewpoint in (on sexual orientation), 255, 256, 257, 263
    harm done in name of, 301
    North American traditions and groups, 26
    and U.S. population, 267
    and popular ideology (Soloveitchik), 121
    and psychiatry or psychology, 3, 121
    and REBT, 214–215
Religious authority and teaching, therapists' respect for, 303
Religious beliefs
    communicating respect for, 228
    disputing of, 261–262
    distress-producing, 303
    therapists' imposition of, 302–304
"Religious capacity," Jung on, 233
Religious differences between therapist and client, 283, 294
    Jewish-Christian, 268
        with Alfred, 276, 283 (see also Alfred)

with Danny, 278, 279, 282–283 (see also Danny, 9-year old)
Religious experience, psychoanalytic clinical approach to (case of Joan), 160–163
Religious Orientation Scale (ROS), for Jan (case report), 63, 64, 65
Religious and spiritual assessment, 22–24
Religious worldviews, insights from, 306
Renee (case report), 5–6, 79–82, 288, 295–296
Repentance (teshuva)
    and case report of Aisha, 223
    and therapeutic spiritual counseling, 135–138, 138
Research, on theistic spiritual strategy for psychologists, 305
Retreats
    for Gwen (case report), 145, 151
    Ignatian, 179, 183, 185
Richards, P. Scott, 288, 295
Rite of Christian Initiation for Adults (RCIA), 90
Rogers, Carl, on presence, 210, 211
Rorschach test, 143
Rosh Hashana, 137
Rumi, 203, 235

Salanter, Yisroel, 122
Sarason, Irwin, 214
Satan
    and Job, 126–127
    and Kathy (case report), 113
Scales. See Tests and other measures
Schedule for Affective Disorders and Schizophrenia for Children (K-SADS), 83
School phase of Alldredge Academy, 47–49
Science, and naturalism, 36
"Sefat Emet," 125–126
Self, Kohut on, 234, 235
Self-acceptance, by Aisha (case report), 221, 222–224, 226, 227
Self-image
    and religious philosophy, 122
    and therapeutic spiritual counseling, 123–124, 138
    of Norman (case report), 131
Self-psychology, in case of Joan, 159
Seligman, Martin, 75
Sentence Completion Blank (SCB), for Kathy (case report), 107
Sentence Completion Questionnaire, 251
Sexual abuse

Global Assessment of Functioning, 218
Hamilton Rating Scale for Depression, 79, 82, 83, 85
Marital Satisfaction Inventory, 92
Millon Clinical Multiaxial Inventory–II (MCMI–II), 144
Minnesota Multiphasic Personality Inventory–2 (MMPI–2), 63, 64, 107
Multidimensional Self-Esteem Inventory (MSEI), 63, 64, 65, 68
Outcome Questionnaire (OQ45), 63, 64, 65, 68, 218, 219, 224, 225
Religious Orientation Scale (ROS), 63, 64, 65
Rorschach test, 143
Schedule for Affective Disorders and Schizophrenia for Children (K-SADS), 83
Sentence Completion Blank (SCB), 107
Sentence Completion Questionnaire, 251
Spiritual outcome measures, 68–69
Spiritual Outcome Scale (SOS), 63, 64, 65, 68, 69
Spiritual Well-Being Scale (SWBS), 63, 64, 65, 68–69
Thematic Apperception Test (TAT), 143
Theism
    and community, 35
    and naturalism, 36–37
Theistic interventions, 52
    See also Interventions
Theistic perspective
    in case of Paul, 199–200
    and case reports, 4–6
    insights from, 306
    integration of into psychotherapy, 301–304
    in marital therapy, 101
    and theoretical frameworks, 287–293, 304
    and therapy processes or outcomes, 294–301
    training in, 304–305
    See also Spiritually oriented psychotherapy
Theistic therapists or psychotherapists, 227, 292–293
Theistic psychotherapy. See Psychotherapy, theistic

Theistic realism, 11, 258
    Griffin on, 13
Theistic spiritual strategy, 4, 6–7
    conceptual framework for theistic psychotherapy
        theological and philosophical foundations, 7–13
        view of personality, 13–15
        view of psychotherapy, 15–17, 18–19
    process guidelines for, 17
        implementing interventions, 25–26
        multicultural spiritual sensitivity, 20
        potential ethical concerns, 21–22
        religious and spiritual assessment, 22–24
        setting appropriate goals, 24–25
        spiritually open and safe relationship, 20–21
Theistic theoretical assumptions, 288–291
Theistic therapist, 227
Thematic Apperception Test (TAT), 143
Theobiology, 187
Theodicy, 138
Theological foundations, for theistic psychotherapy, 7–13
Theoretical frameworks
    conceptual framework for theistic psychotherapy, 7–13
    and theistic perspectives, 287–293, 304
Therapeutic change, theistic psychotherapy on, 14, 15, 292
Therapeutic community(ies), 51–52
    Alldredge Academy, 41–42 (see also Alldredge Academy)
    naturalistic, 35–37, 51, 51–52
    and naturalistic vs. non-naturalistic assumptions, 37–41, 50–51
Therapeutic relationship (alliance)
    in assessment (case of Matthew), 205
    in case of Joan, 163
    clients' perceptions of therapists in, 274
    Kohut on, 234
    spiritually safe and open, 20–21
    theistic vs. atheistic therapists in, 227–228
    in theistic psychotherapy, 18–19
    in therapeutic spiritual counseling, 124
    and therapist's personal qualities, 267–268
Therapeutic spiritual counseling, 120
    and complexity of religious consciousness, 121–122

ABOUT THE EDITORS

P. Scott Richards received his PhD in counseling psychology in 1988 from the University of Minnesota. He has been a faculty member at Brigham Young University since 1990 and is a professor in the Department of Counseling Psychology and Special Education. He is coauthor of *A Spiritual Strategy for Counseling and Psychotherapy* (American Psychological Association [APA], 1997) and coeditor of the *Handbook of Psychotherapy and Religious Diversity* (APA, 2000). He was given the Dissertation of the Year Award in 1990 from Division 5 (Evaluation, Measurement, and Statistics) of APA for his psychometric investigation of religious bias in moral development research. In 1999, he was awarded the William C. Bier Award from APA Division 36 (Psychology of Religion). He is a fellow of Division 36, served as secretary of the division from 2000 to 2003, and is currently president-elect of the division. Dr. Richards is a licensed psychologist and maintains a small private psychotherapy practice at the Center for Change in Orem, Utah.

Allen E. Bergin received his PhD in clinical psychology in 1960 from Stanford University. He was a faculty member at Teachers College, Columbia University, from 1961 to 1972. He was a professor of psychology at Brigham Young University from 1972 until his retirement in 2001. Dr. Bergin is past president of the Society for Psychotherapy Research and coeditor of the classic *Handbook of Psychotherapy and Behavior Change*. He is coauthor of *A Spiritual Strategy for Counseling and Psychotherapy* (APA, 1997) and coeditor of the *Handbook of Psychotherapy and Religious Diversity* (APA, 2000). In 1989, he received the Distinguished Professional Contributions to Knowledge Award from the APA. In 1990, Division 36 (Psychology of Religion) of APA presented him with the William James Award for Psychology of Religion Research. He has also received the Society for Psychotherapy Research's Distinguished Career Award (1998) and the American Psychiatric Association's Oskar Pfister Award in Psychiatry and Religion (1998).